Javier E. Díaz-Vera (Ed.)
Metaphor and Metonymy across Time and Cultures

Cognitive Linguistics Research

Editors
Dirk Geeraerts
John R. Taylor

Honorary editors
René Dirven
Ronald W. Langacker

Volume 52

Metaphor and Metonymy across Time and Cultures

―

Perspectives on the Sociohistorical Linguistics
of Figurative Language

Edited by
Javier E. Díaz-Vera

DE GRUYTER
MOUTON

ISBN 978-3-11-055509-7
e-ISBN (PDF) 978-3-11-033545-3
e-ISBN (EPUB) 978-3-11-039539-6
ISSN 1861-4132

Library of Congress Cataloging-in-Publication Data
A CIP catalog record for this book has been applied for at the Library of Congress

Bibliographic information published by the Deutsche Nationalbibliothek
The Deutsche Nationalbibliothek lists this publication in the Deutsche Nationalbibliografie;
detailed bibliographic data are available on the Internet at http://dnb.dnb.de.

© 2017 Walter de Gruyter GmbH, Berlin/Munich/Boston
This volume is text- and page-identical with the hardback published in 2015.
Typesetting: Meta Systems Publishing & Printservices GmbH, Wustermark
Printing and binding: CPI books GmbH, Leck

♾ Printed on acid-free paper
Printed in Germany

www.degruyter.com

Contents

Introductory chapter

Javier E. Díaz-Vera
Figuration and language history: Universality and variation — 3

Diachronic metaphor research

Dirk Geeraerts
Four guidelines for diachronic metaphor research — 15

Conceptual variation and change

Kathryn Allan
Lost in transmission? The sense development of borrowed metaphor — 31

Xavier Dekeyser
Loss of the prototypical meaning and lexical borrowing: A case of semantic redeployment — 51

Roslyn M. Frank
A complex adaptive systems approach to language, cultural schemas and serial metonymy: Charting the cognitive innovations of 'fingers' and 'claws' in Basque — 65

Richard Trim
The interface between synchronic and diachronic conceptual metaphor: The role of embodiment, culture and semantic field — 95

Figuration and grammaticalization

Andrew D. M. Smith and Stefan H. Höfler
The pivotal role of metaphor in the evolution of human language — 123

Miao-Hsia Chang
Two counter-expectation markers in Chinese — 141

Wolfgang Schulze
The emergence of diathesis markers from MOTION concepts — 171

Figurative language in culture variation

Javier E. Díaz-Vera and Teodoro Manrique-Antón
'Better shamed before one than shamed before all': Shaping shame in Old English and Old Norse texts — 225

Dylan Glynn
The conceptual profile of the lexeme home: A multifactorial diachronic analysis — 265

Cristóbal Pagán Cánovas
Cognitive patterns in Greek poetic metaphors of emotion: A diachronic approach — 295

Juan Gabriel Vázquez González
'Thou com'st in such a questionable shape': Embodying the cultural model for GHOST across the history of English — 319

Index — 349

Introductory chapter

Javier E. Díaz-Vera
Figuration and language history: Universality and variation

> And make time's spoils despised everywhere
> Give my love fame faster than time wastes life;
> So, thou prevene'st his scythe and crooked knife.
> Shakespeare, Sonnet 100 (11–14)

1 Figuration and lexico-semantic change

These verses by Shakespeare illustrate one instance of what literary theorists have traditionally referred to as figurative language: the attribution of typically human features to an abstract entity. Such figures of speech as personification, simile, irony, hyperbole, metaphor and metonymy have been traditionally described as poetic devices used by writers for specific aesthetic purposes. Only after the late-twentieth century development of Conceptual Metaphor Theory (henceforth CMT; Lakoff and Johnson 1980, Ortony 1993, Goatly 2007), figurative language started to attract the attention of a growing number of linguists interested in the study of these figures of speech within the realm of everyday language and, much more importantly, of our ordinary conceptual system. CMT has since developed and elaborated, although not always in complete agreement.

Figuration refers to a meaning that is dependent on a figurative extension from another meaning. Figurative language has got an inherently second-order nature. Figurative expressions (such as *it made my blood boil*) can only be recognized as such because of their contrast with more literal expressions (as in *it made me angry*). From a diachronic perspective, figurative expressions are historically later than the corresponding conventional ones. As Croft and Cruse (2004) put it, metaphors have their own life-cycle that normally runs from a first coinage as an instance of semantic innovation (a novel metaphor requiring an interpretative strategy on the side of language user) to a more commonplace metaphor (a conventional metaphor whose meaning has become well-established in the speakers' mental lexicon). Eventually, the literal meaning of an expression may fall out of use, interrupting its dependency relationship with the corresponding figurative meaning (a dead metaphor).

Javier E. Díaz-Vera: Universidad de Castilla-La Mancha

Cognitive semantics regards polysemy as involving family resemblances, stressing the systematic relationship between the different meanings (both literal and figurative) of a word and including polysemy as a result of conceptual organisation such as categorisation. This view has given rise to a variety of models for lexical networks (Lakoff 1987; Langacker 1990) based on the notion that the different meanings of a lexeme "form a radially structured category, with a central member and links defined by image-schema transformation and metaphors" (Lakoff 1987: 460). In other words, each instantiation of a word always retains its whole range of senses regardless of the context in which it appears, senses which are related to one another by various means. Thus, a given word belongs to a complex semantic network determined by different domains and cognitive processes, where there may be senses more representative than others. Things being so, it can be argued that these polysemic networks are shaped by the course of a series of diachronic processes of semantic extension, through which new figurative expressions emerge and evolve. As Nerlich and Clarke (2001: 252) put it,

> metaphor is a pragmatic strategy used by speakers to convey to hearers something new that cannot easily be said or understood otherwise or to give an old concept a novel, witty or amusing package, whereas metonymy is a pragmatic strategy used by speakers to convey to hearers something new about something already well known. Using metaphors speakers tell you more than what they actually say, using metonyms they tell you more while saying less. From the point of view of the hearer, metaphor is a strategy used to extract new information from old words, whereas metonymy is a strategy used to extract more information from fewer words.

For example, the progressive rise in the frequency of embodied expressions showing the ANGER IS THE HEAT OF A FLUID IN A CONTAINER emotion metaphor in a corpus of 11th to 15th century English texts has been connected to the popularization of humoural doctrine in later medieval England, according to which anger is an effect of the overproduction of yellow bile (or choler), considered a warm and dry substance (Gevaert 2002: 202). As Gevaert convincingly shows, the use of words and expressions directly taken from the humoural theory, such as the verbs ME *distemperen* and *boilen*, indicates a completely different conceptualization of anger by speakers of Middle English. As this new cultural model advanced, people started to use the original heat-related items as anger expressions, which clearly differ from the old anger expressions in terms of their capacity to add new information (as encoded in the metaphor ANGER IS THE HEAT OF A FLUID IN A CONTAINER, which implies not only that ANGER IS A HOT FLUID, but also that THE BODY IS A CONTAINER) to the already existing one. Furthermore, through the expansion of the new anger words over the language community, this metaphor became a dominant expression of anger in Middle

English, producing the progressive neglect of other expressions based on the Anglo-Saxon ANGER IS SWELLING metonymy (i.e. EMOTION IS ONE OF THE PHYSIOLOGICAL EFFECTS OF THAT EMOTION). As Geeraerts (2010) puts it, "words die out because speakers refuse to choose them, and words are added to the lexical inventory of a language because some speakers introduce them and some others imitate these speakers" (p. 265). These lexical choices show a strong sociolinguistic facet, characterized by a pragmatic and a cognitive side (Blank 1999: 62): when speakers of a language decide to adopt a new expression because it is convincing to any extent, this is a pragmatic decision based on the good cognitive performance of the innovation.

Similarly, metonymy has been traditionally described as a cognitive abbreviation mechanism (Esnault 1925), and the metonymical stretching of a word has been considered an indicator of cost-effective communication. Rather than adding new information to our knowledge of a given emotional experience, emotion metonymies exploit a wide range of metonymic relations based on image-schemata (as in the case of EMOTION IS AN EFFECT OF THAT EMOTION) in order to let us shorten conceptual distances and ultimately say things quicker (Nerlich and Clarke 2001: 256). For example, the list of Old English expressions of fear (Díaz-Vera 2011; Díaz-Vera 2013) includes a wide variety of metonymic extensions, such as FEAR IS MOTION BACKWARDS (as in OE *wandian* 'to turn away from something' hence 'to turn away from a source of fear'), FEAR IS MOTION DOWNWARDS (as in OE *creopan* 'to creep' hence 'to creep with fear') and FEAR IS PARALYSIS (as in OE *bīdan* 'to wait' hence 'to await with fear'). In these three cases, the Old English predicates that illustrate these metonymies are able to express with one single word both (i) the emotion that the experiencer is feeling and (ii) his/her physiological reaction to that emotion. The mechanism followed by these semantic changes is quite evident and straightforward: from a historically earlier meaning (i.e. the prototypical or central meaning of a word, such as 'to turn away', 'to creep' or 'to wait') speakers derive one (or more, as in the case of serial metonymy) meaning extensions towards the domain of fear, taking advantage of the widely-known proximity relation between the emotion and its various effects on the experiencer.

As in the case of metaphor, the cumulative effect of the multiple individual choices on the side of the speakers will eventually result into a general acceptance of the new metonymic expression over the language community. Furthermore, entire polysemic networks will be developed as a consequence of the actuation of diachronic metaphor and metonymy over long periods of time through the progressive addition of new senses to the historically earlier ones. The detailed reconstruction and analysis of these conceptual networks are indicative not only of the different ways a given domain was conceptualized by speakers in the different historical stages of a language but, perhaps more importantly, of some of the possible ways the mind works in conjunction with language.

2 Figuration and lexico-grammatical change

The impact of figuration on grammatical structure has been demonstrated by a number of researchers, including Barcelona (2003, 2004, 2005, 2008), Ruiz de Mendoza Ibanez and Mairal (2007), Ziegeler (2007), Brdar (2007) and Panther, Thornburg and Barcelona (2009). Broadly speaking, these studies show that there is no clear-cut distinction between the lexicon and grammar. Within this view, individual lexical items and function words and morphemes are considered meaning-bearing units and, and such, their properties can be motivated by figurative thought.

In the same way as lexemes, grammatical categories frequently convey figurative extended uses, forming networks of related meanings. Grammatical constructions can be used figuratively and, as in the case of lexical metaphor and metonymy, they can cue figurative cognitive structures. In fact, the same general types of conceptual metonymies operate at different linguistic levels. Diachronic processes of grammatical recategorization illustrate the central role of metonymy in grammatical change. For example, the Old English noun *angul* 'angle' started to be used as a verb meaning 'to use an angle' by the end of the 15th century (INSTRUMENT FOR ACTION metonymy). Similarly, the grammatical recategorization of place names (such as *champagne*, *porto* and *chianti*, all of which illustrate the metonymic mapping PLACE FOR PRODUCT MADE THERE) and personal names (as in *a jack*, *a peter* or *a magdalen*; IDEAL MEMBER FOR CLASS) as common nouns can be frequently attributed to metonymic processes.

The relationship between metonymy and metaphor, on the one hand, and syntactic processes, on the other, has been amply dealt with in recent research.

Tab. 1: Metonymy and metaphor in grammaticalization (Hopper and Traugott 2003)

Metonymy	Metaphor
– Syntagmatic level	– Paradigmatic level
– Reanalysis (abduction)	– Analogy
– Conversational implicature	– Conventional implicature
– Operates through interdependent syntactic constituents	– Operates through conceptual domains

Hopper and Traugott (2003) propose a grammaticalization model based on both metonymy and metaphor, which are seen as pragmatic processes. Whereas metonymy is the result of conversational implicature and is linked to reanalysis, metaphor is the result of conventional inferencing and is linked to analogy.

According to Hilpert (2007), figuration also plays an important role in the process of grammaticalization of body part names into prepositions, postpositions or adverbs in a wide variety of languages. For example, the noun *head* develops the metaphorical meaning 'top part' (metaphor OBJECTS ARE HUMAN BEINGS), from where the grammatical meaning 'over' is developed in a number of languages through the PART FOR ORIENTATION metonymy. Also, Barcelona (2008) shows that metonymy is a conceptual mechanism that operates not only at the lexical level, but also under the lexicon (phonology, morphemics) and above the lexicon (phrase, clause, sentence, utterance and discourse).

3 Figuration and conceptual change

One major area of debate is the pretended universality of conceptual patterns. Cognitive linguists assume that non-literal conceptualizations are grounded in embodied experience. Things being so, figurative linguistic expressions should be considered mostly universal and, as such, without a cultural basis. However, cross-cultural studies of figurative expressions clearly show that mental conceptualizations can differ not only between languages but also between dialectal and diachronic varieties of the same language. Every single human language uses non-literal expressions, some of which seem highly stable across time and space. For example, the conceptual metaphor of JOURNEY, according to which we conceptualize such experiences as life or love as a journey, is recorded in a wide variety of cultures since ancient times. However, different languages have got different specific-level elaborations of this metaphoric conceptualization, grounded in cultural salience. For example, whereas English speakers conceptualize love as a JOURNEY ON A VEHICLE (either on water or land), Akan speakers will normally refer to love as a JOURNEY ON FOOT, indicating the cultural relevance of walking in their culture (Ansah 2011). In a similar fashion, multimodal evidence demonstrates that the same concept can be expressed in very different ways: this is the case, for example, of the recurrent use of 'loss of hands' in Japanese mangas with reference to loss of emotional control (Abbott and Forceville 2011), or the frequent representation of characters with their upper arms attached to the body to indicate fear in the Bayeux Tapestry (Díaz-Vera 2013).

Based on these differences, some authors (see especially Kövecses 2000) have argued the existence of two different levels of conceptualization: a generic level of human embodied cognition and a more specific level of elaboration of these universal schemas. Conceptual variation, according to these researchers, would be limited to the second level. However, as Gevaert's (2007) historical data described above shows, cultural variation can also affect general level conceptualizations. This is the case of the PRESSURIZED CONTAINER metaphor for emotions, traditionally described as an instance of physiological embodiment. According to her Old English data, Anglo-Saxon speakers show a strong preference for non-embodied conceptualizations of anger. It is only after the rise of humoral theory in Western Europe that English (and, probably, other European vernaculars) will develop new metaphorical expressions based on the EMOTION IS A HOT FLUID IN A CONTAINER mapping. The spread and popularization of this medical doctrine produced, to start with, a new physiological association between emotions (i.e. anger) and bodily temperature (i.e. heat). As a consequence, speakers of Middle English started to substitute some of their old literal and figurative emotional expressions by a brand-new set of metaphors based on the new mapping EMOTION IS A HOT FLUID IN A CONTAINER.

As demonstrated by Gevaert, cultural change can lead to some forms of cognitive change which, on the long run, will contribute to the development and spread of new figurative expressions. More importantly, her study of diachronic variation in figurative language illustrates some of the possible ways in which cultural practice and knowledge can shape bodily experience by changing the way we conceptualize and, very probably, feel emotions.

4 Contributions to this volume

The papers included in this volume examine and expand on some of the questions discussed above. The main aim of this book is to provide an interdisciplinary view of diachronic conceptual variation and its linguistic and cultural manifestations. The volume is arranged in three different sections, ranging from papers on the analysis of semantic extension through metaphorization, to the role of figurative language in processes of grammaticalization, and the interplay between cultural change and figurative language. A foreword by Dirk Geeraerts introduces a list of frequent shortcomings to avoid by diachronic metaphor researchers, the so-called four fallacies: 'the dominant reading only' fallacy, the 'semasiology only' fallacy, the 'natural experience only' fallacy and the 'metaphorization only' fallacy. A common denominator behind these principles is the recognition that language is culturally transmitted and, as such, it should be considered a predominantly historical phenomenon.

The first section in this volume focuses on some of the manifold relationships between polysemy, semantic change and figurative language. Kathryn Allan ("Lost in transmission? The sense development of borrowed metaphor") presents a discussion of the significance of borrowing in the histories of metaphors. Through the detailed analysis of the literal and figurative uses of three different lexical items borrowed by Middle English speakers (the noun *muscle*, the verb *inculcate* and the adjective *ardent*), the author describes the later evolution of all the senses of these words in the target language. According to her analysis, while the figurative meanings of these loanwords were retained, their original, literal meanings were lost in the process of transmission into English. Similarly, Xavier Dekeyser ("Loss of prototypical meaning and lexical borrowing: A case of semantic redeployment") describes the process of semantic restructuring undergone by two English lexical sets: the noun and adverb *deal* and the verb *starve*. The study of the meanings expressed by these words throughout the long period of time between the Old English and the early Modern English period indicates how the original, ancestral meanings of a lexical item can become peripheral or even get lost in favour of newer, figurative senses of the same word. Roslyn M. Frank ("A complex adaptive systems approach to language, cultural schemas and serial metonymy: Charting the cognitive innovations of 'fingers' and 'claws' in Basque") proposes a study of the Basque lexeme *hatz* and the different meanings developed by it through serial metonymy. Her analysis shows that the lexicon acts both as a memory bank and a fluid vehicle for the transmission of cultural cognition across time and space. Finally, Richard Trim ("The interface between synchronic and diachronic conceptual metaphor: The role of embodiment, culture and semantic field") compares figurative language data from English and Oriental language in order to analyse variation in synchronic and diachronic metaphor.

The second section focuses on the role of metaphor and metonymy in processes of grammaticalization. The three papers included in this section take the view that all grammatical elements in language are meaningful and that they impose and symbolize particular ways of construing conceptual content. In the opening chapter ("The pivotal role of metaphor in the evolution of human language"), Andrew D. M. Smith and Stefan H. Höfler claim that the cognitive mechanisms underlying metaphor can provide a unified explanation of the evolution of two different aspects of language: symbols and grammar. Based on this model, the authors propose suggest a reconstruction of how human language could have initially emerged from 'no language' to complex grammatical structures. Miao-Hsia Chang ("Two counter-expectation markers in Chinese") studies the origins and the diachronic development of Chinese of *sha4* 煞 and *jieguo* 結果, two markers of counter-expectation grammatizalized through a series of intricate processes of metaphorization, metonymization and metaphtonymy. As the author shows here, the changes undergone by these two lexemes in the history of Chinese are indicative of the pervasive effect of metaphor and metonymy on the semanticization and adverbialization of a verbal morpheme from a content word to a highly grammaticalized sentential. Similarly, Wolfgang Schulze ("The emergence of diathesis markers from MOTION concepts") analyses the grammaticalization background behind the development of East Caucasian passive constructions. As the data presented here shows, verbal forms expressing MOTION underwent a process of semantic change into CHANGE-OF-STATE and, from there, they grammaticalized into passive auxiliaries.

Conceptual change provides evidence of the link between between linguistic change and sociocultural change. The chapters in the last section explore some of the relationships between cultural, linguistic and cognitive change. Javier E. Díaz-Vera and Teodoro Manrique-Antón ("'Better shamed before one than shamed before all': Shaping shame in Old English and Old Norse texts") propose an analysis of shame-expressions in Old English and in Old Norse. According to their research, the Christianization of these two Germanic societies implied the introduction and spread of new shame-related values through the use of a brand-new set of expressions that illustrate the progressive individualization of this social emotion. Similarly, Dylan Glynn ("The conceptual profile of the lexeme *home*: A multifactorial diachronic analysis") proposes a diachronic study of the American concept of HOME over the course of two centuries. Through the fine-grained analysis of a series of sample texts by three 19th century American writers, the author demonstrates the feasibility of the multivariate usage-feature method for the description of conceptual structures. Cristóbal Pagán Cánovas ("Cognitive patterns in Greek poetic metaphors of emotion: A diachronic approach") uses Bending Theory's dynamic model to analyze love expressions in ancient Greek poetry. Finally, Juan Gabriel Vázquez González ("'Thou com'st in such a questionable shape': Embodying the cultural model for GHOST across the history of English") proposes a contrastive reconstruction of the cultural model for GHOST in Old English and in Present-Day British English. The type of cultural variation envisaged by the author incorporates a diachronic and a within-culture perspective.

In short, the papers in this volume show that metaphor and metonymy are not just linguistic phenomena but, rather, they reflect dynamic cognitive patterns of thought and emotion. Through the fine-grained examination of diachronic data from a variety of languages and linguistic families, this volume contributes to our understanding of the dominant conceptual mechanisms of linguistic change and their interaction with sociocultural factors.

References

Abbott, Michael & Charles Forceville. 2011. Visual representations of emotion in manga: LOSS OF CONTROL IS LOSS OF HANDS in Azumanga Daioh volume 4. *Language and Literature* 20(2). 1–22.

Ansah, Gladys Nyarko. 2011. The cultural basis of conceptual metaphors: The case of emotions in Akan and English. In Kathrin Kaufhold, Sharon McCulloch & Ana Tominc (eds.), *Papers from the Lancaster University Postgraduate Conference in Linguistics & Language Teaching 5*, 2–24. Lancaster: Department of Linguistics and English Language.

Barcelona, Antonio. 2003. Names: A metonymic 'return ticket' in five languages. *Jezikoslovlje* 4: 11–41.

Barcelona, Antonio. 2004. Metonymy behind grammar: The motivation of the seemingly "irregular" grammatical behavior of English paragon names. In Günter Radden & Klaus-Uwe Panther (eds.), *Studies in linguistic motivation*, 357–374. Berlin & New York: Mouton de Gruyter.

Barcelona, Antonio. 2005. The multilevel operation of metonymy in grammar and discourse, with particular attention to metonymic chain. In Francisco José Ruiz de Mendoza Ibáñez & M. Sandra Peña Cerbel (eds.), *Cognitive linguistics: Internal dynamics and interdisciplinary interaction*, 313–352. Berlin & New York: Mouton de Gruyter.

Barcelona, Antonio. 2008. Metonymy is not just a lexical phenomenon: On the operation of metonymy in grammar and discourse. In Christina Alm-Arvius, Nils-Lennart Johannesson & David C. Minuch (eds.), *Selected papers from the Stockholm 2008 Metaphor Festival*, 3–41. Stockholm: Stockholm University Press.

Brdar, Mario. 2007. *Metonymy in grammar: Towards motivating extensions of grammatical categories and constructions*. Osijek: Faculty of Philosophy, Josip Juraj Strossmayer University.

Croft, William & D. Alan Cruse. 2004. *Cognitive linguistics*. Cambridge: Cambridge University Press.

Díaz-Vera, J. E. 2011. Reconstructing the Old English cultural model for 'fear'. *Atlantis: Journal of the Spanish Association of Anglo-American Studies*, 33(1). 85–103.

Díaz-Vera, Javier E. 2013. Embodied emotions in medieval English language and visual arts. In Rosario Caballero & Javier E. Díaz-Vera (eds.), *Sensuous cognition – Explorations into human sentience: Imagination, (e)motion and perception*, 195–220. Berlin & New York: Mouton de Gruyter.

Esnault, Gaston. 1925. *L'Imagination populaire – Métaphores occidentales*. Paris: Les Presses Universitaires de France.

Geeraerts, Dirk. 2010. Prospects for the past: Perspectives for diachronic cognitive semantics. In Margaret E. Winters, Heli Tissari & Kathryn Allan (eds.), *Historical cognitive linguistics*, 333–356. Berlin & New York: Mouton de Gruyter.

Gevaert, Caroline. 2002. The evolution of the lexical and conceptual field of ANGER in Old and Middle English. In Javier Enrique Díaz-Vera (ed.), *A changing world of words: Studies in English historical lexicology, lexicography and semantics*, 275–299. Amsterdam: Rodopi.
Gevaert, Caroline. 2007. *The history of ANGER: The lexical field of anger from Old to Early Modern English*. Leuven: Katholieke Universiteit Leuven dissertation.
Goatly, Andrew. 2007. *Washing the brain: Metaphor and hidden ideology*. Amsterdam & Philadelphia: John Benjamins.
Hilpert, Martin. 2007. Chained metonymies in lexicon and grammar. In Günter Radden, Klaus-Michael Köpcke, Thomas Berg & Peter Siemund (eds.), *Aspects of meaning construction*, 77–98. Amsterdam & Philadelphia: John Benjamins.
Hopper, Paul J., & Elizabeth Closs Traugott. 2003. *Grammaticalization*, 2nd edn. Cambridge: Cambridge University Press.
Kövecses, Zoltan. 2000. *Metaphor and emotion: Language, culture, and body in human feeling*. Cambridge: Cambridge University Press.
Lakoff, George. 1987. *Women, fire and dangerous things. What categories reveal about the mind*. Chicago: University of Chicago Press.
Lakoff, George & Mark Johnson. 1980. *Metaphors we live by*. Chicago: University of Chicago Press.
Langacker, Ronald. 1990. *Concept, image and symbol*. Berlin & New York: Mouton de Gruyter.
Nerlich, Brigitte & David D. Clarke. 2001. Serial metonymy: A study of reference-based polysemisation. *Journal of Historical Pragmatics* 2(2). 245–272.
Ortony, Andrew. 1993. *Metaphor and thought*, 2nd edn. Cambridge: Cambridge University Press.
Panther, Klaus-Uwe & Linda L. Thorburg. 2009. Introduction: On figuration in grammar. In Antonio Barcelona, Klaus-Uwe Panther, Günter Radden & Linda L. Thorburg (eds.), *Metonymy and metaphor in grammar*, 1–44. Amsterdam & Philadelphia: John Benjamins.
Ruiz de Mendoza, Francisco & Ricardo Mairal. 2007. High-level metaphor and metonymy in meaning construction. In Günter Radden, Klaus-Michael Köpcke, Thomas Berg & Peter Siemund (eds.), *Aspects of meaning construction in lexicon and grammar*, 33–49. Amsterdam & Philadelphia: John Benjamins.
Ziegeler, Debra. 2007. Arguing the case against coercion. In Günter Radden, Klaus-Michael Köpcke, Thomas Berg & Peter Siemund (eds.), *Aspects of meaning construction in lexicon and grammar*, 99–123. Amsterdam & Philadelphia: John Benjamins.

Diachronic metaphor research

Dirk Geeraerts
Four guidelines for diachronic metaphor research

Abstract: Drawing on earlier (and fairly scattered) work that I have been doing on diachronic metaphor theory, I would like to point out a number of difficulties that such studies are faced with. In particular, I will draw the attention to the following methodological mistakes. The 'dominant reading only' fallacy takes the historically original meaning of an item to be the source of any metaphorical meaning arising in the course of its history. This approach is ironically a-historical, because it denies the importance of the intermediate steps in a word's history. The 'semasiology only' fallacy measures the importance of a metaphorical pattern by counting the relative frequency of semasiological source-target mappings in the lexical field of the source, rather than the relative (onomasiological) frequency of the source within the field of the target. The 'natural experience only' fallacy substitutes the motivational ground of a metaphor by the vehicle expressing that ground. While a focus on vehicles at the expense of grounds is perhaps the most conspicuous danger besetting Conceptual Metaphor Theory, its consequences for diachronic studies need to be spelled out. The 'metaphorization only' fallacy biases universalist interpretations of metaphorical patterns at the expense of culture-specific analyses. Methodologically, the universalist attitude neglects the transmitted nature of language by favouring interpretations that assume direct access to the original motivation of an expression. The latter assumption also triggers the neglect of a phenomenon that illustrates that transmitted nature very well, viz. the emergence of metaphor through deliteralization, i.e. the construction of a metaphorical interpretation for an item whose literal motivation has waned.

1 Introduction

The modest purpose of this short paper is to formulate a gentle reminder about a few features that Cognitive Linguistics attributes to meaning, and that have important (but perhaps slightly underestimated) consequences for diachronic metaphor research. The points whose consequences I would like to explore

---

Dirk Geeraerts: University of Leuven

are the following: first, that meaning is prototypically structured; second, that meaning is structured both semasiologically and onomasiologically; third, that meaning is embodied in both natural and cultural experience, and fourth, that meaning is transmitted through language. Because these points are either self-evident (like the final one), or deeply entrenched in Cognitive Linguistic thinking (like the other three), I do not think it is necessary to present them in more detail here. The consequences of these issues for diachronic metaphor research are however far-reaching, and they are not necessarily universally recognized. In the following pages, I will illustrate the impact of the four principles on diachronic metaphor research, and refer to the neglect of those principles – with a certain degree of rhetorical hyperbole – as four 'fallacies'. (The illustrations will predominantly come from studies that I published elsewhere over the last twenty years, supplemented with a few cases involving original materials. This inevitably entails that my own work will be disproportionately present in the bibliographical section of the paper. To be sure, this is not meant to diminish the value of other authors' work. For a more balanced account of recent work in historical cognitive semantics, see Geeraerts 2010.)

2 The 'dominant reading only' fallacy

The fact that meaning is prototypically structured implies that the prototypical semantic development of words needs to be taken into account when establishing the presence of a metaphor of a certain type (see Geeraerts 1997 for an extensive treatment of prototype effects in diachronic semantics). In a TARGET IS SOURCE pattern, the meaning that is selected as the Source is very often taken to be the currently dominant literal reading, but that is not necessarily historically correct. To achieve a historically adequate picture of the emergence of a metaphor, the birth of the metaphor needs to be checked against the individual word histories of the expression in question: the meaning of the Source item that provides the historical basis for the metaphorical expression may be a different one than the most readily available candidates.

A straightforward example may be found in the following use of the word *antenna*. The following quotation is taken from a web version of *How to Turn your Ability into Cash* by "master salesman and successful author" Earl Prevette.

> There are three separate Departments of the Mind which deal with ideas. The function of these Three Departments of the Mind bears a striking similarity to the three Departments of the Government. First: The Emotion is the Legislative Department of the Mind. The

Emotion is the antenna of the Mind radiating and emitting thoughts into space, and also receiving them from space (...) Second: The Judgment is the Judicial Department of the Mind. (...) Third: The Desire is the Executive Department of the Mind. (...)

The metaphor *emotion is the antenna of the mind* is echoed by other expressions. In a web text by the Rev. Tim Dean, chaplain of the Cayuga Medical Center, we note that *feelings are like the antennae of the soul,* and in the internet document *A Rhetoric of Objects,* Jonathan Price mentions that *attention is the antenna of the soul.* Further examples that can be found googling for the combination *sensitive antenna* include the following:

Artists are like sensitive antenna and pick up on things in the culture

I don't know, I thought it was fine and I have a pretty sensitive antenna for that type of stuff

With my sensitive antenna to sense the vibes from different people, I subconsciously tried to act and speak in a way to prove myself

What I am referring to are the early stages of panic that my sensitive antenna are picking up

Correct me if I'm wrong, but if there's no sex in your life, then my sensitive antennae are telling me that you're either resting or else you're recovering from a broken relationship

Up till now, for the sake of old times, when I cared less about what my sensitive antennas told me, I decided to remain acquainted with these people with devastating effects

Applying the standard argumentative format of Conceptual Metaphor Theory, examples such as these could readily lead to postulating a metaphor SENSITIVITY IS AN AERIAL, or more broadly, HUMAN COMMUNICATION IS A RADIO DEVICE. Beyond the word *antenna*, this pattern would seem to be supported by expressions like *we are on the same wavelength, he couldn't tune in to her reasoning, there is a lot of noise on our communication, they have to fine-tune their interaction, I am getting your point loud and clear, are we using the same frequency.*

However, the presence of the plural *antennae* in the examples invites a closer look at the semantics of *antenna*: next to the dominant 'aerial' reading (for which *antennas* is the regular plural), the interpretation 'feeler of an animal' occurs, with the plural *antennae*. But while the 'feeler' reading is synchronically the secondary meaning, it is diachronically primary: the 'feeler' reading occurs in English since the 17th century, when it is introduced as a loan from Latin; the radio antenna, on the other hand, was only invented by Marconi in the first years of the 20th century. The question then arises whether the association between emotional sensitivity and *antenna* might not also be older than the SENSITIVITY IS AN AERIAL metaphorical pattern assumes. And indeed, the OED includes the following relevant quotations for the figurative interpretation of the 'feelers' reading:

> O. W. Holmes, Poems 214 1855 "Go to yon tower, where busy science plies Her vast antennae, feeling thro' the skies"
>
> E. Pound, Pavannes and Divisions 43, 1918 "My soul's antennae are prey to such perturbations"
>
> Listener 17 Dec. 1959 1082/1 "This is where an author with sound learning, a seeing eye, and sensitive 'antennae' can be of great assistance

The first example predates the invention of the radio antenna, while the other two belong here on the basis of the plural form. The metaphorical pattern UNDERSTANDING IS A TACTILE EVENT that may be associated with the expression is further illustrated by words like *feeling, to feel, to touch, to grasp, to get (a point)*.

It follows that the examples cited earlier for a pattern SENSITIVITY IS AN AERIAL, or more schematically, HUMAN COMMUNICATION IS A RADIO DEVICE need to be revisited, and that, in fact, at least some of the examples would rather illustrate UNDERSTANDING IS A TACTILE EVENT than HUMAN COMMUNICATION IS A RADIO DEVICE. How to decide between the competing interpretations will not always be a straightforward matter. References to immaterial signals (like 'waves' or 'vibes') point towards the 'radio' interpretation, whereas the use of the plural (specifically in the form *antennae*) points towards the 'feelers' interpretation. Indications such as these do not necessarily decide the issue, though, because the individual quotations do not always contain such indices, and moreover, the indices themselves may be indecisive. The utterance *artists are like sensitive antenna and pick up on things in the culture* suggests, for instance, that *antenna* also appears as a plural: should we then assume that other instances of *antenna* may also be plurals, and that those plurals suggest a 'feeler' pattern?

The fundamental point to be made here is not so much the difficulty of deciding between the two interpretations, but the fact that a look at the history of the word *antenna* reveals the very existence of those interpretations. *Antenna* goes through a process of semantic change in which the original 'feeler' meaning gives rise, by a cognitive process based on visual and functional similarity, to the 'aerial' meaning. To be precise, this semantic shift primarily occurs in Italian, when Marconi adopted the term *antenna* for the new invention. In English, the radio *antenna* is a loan from Italian while the feeler *antenna* has a Latin origin. As such, the relationship in English is primarily homonymic, even though the semantic relationship between the two words will not go unnoticed for most speakers. Crucially for the argument that I am developing, both meanings of *antenna* go through a process of metaphorization targeting the domain of communicative sensitivity – but if the specific history of *antenna* were not taken into consideration, the metaphorical ambiguity of an expression like *my soul's antenna* would remain hidden.

3 The 'semasiology only' fallacy

The fact that meaning is structured both semasiologically and onomasiologically implies that both the semasiological and the onomasiological perspectives need to be taken into account when studying historical metaphorical patterns, i.e. establishing the importance of a TARGET IS SOURCE pattern is often done by merely charting the presence of Target in the semasiological range of Source, without checking the importance of Source in the onomasiological range of Target. This may hugely overestimate the importance of the pattern for the conceptualization of the target. Schematically, the relevant perspectives are presented in Table 1.

Tab. 1: Semasiological and onomasiological perspectives.

	semasiology of Source	
onomasiology of Target	TARGET IS SOURCE TARGET IS NOT-SOURCE	NOT-TARGET IS SOURCE

The dominant perspective in Conceptual Metaphor Theory is to look at the data along the horizontal dimension of Table 1: starting from the Source expression, it is established that TARGET IS SOURCE plays a significant role in the semasiological range of Source next to NOT-TARGET IS SOURCE, just like in the previous paragraph, for instance, we noted that the target domain of communicative sensitivity appears in the semasiological range of *antenna*. But how important that presence is for the conceptualization of communicative sensitivity cannot be established by only looking at the semasiology of Source: what one would really like to know is the importance of the pattern in the onomasiology of the Target, i.e. if we look along the vertical dimension of Table 1, what other conceptualizations of the Target do we find, and how strongly is TARGET IS

SOURCE represented within that onomasiological range, in comparison to TARGET IS NOT-SOURCE?

A concrete example of such a way of thinking is found in Geeraerts and Gevaert (2008). When we compare ANGER IS HEAT (a cherished metaphorical pattern in Conceptual Metaphor Theory) to other expressions for anger in Old English, it turns out that the literal expressions dominate, and that ANGER IS HEAT takes up only a minority position in the onomasiological range of anger. In Table 2, the most common Old English expressions are listed according to the conceptual theme that they illustrate. A specification of the semantic process behind the name, together with the frequency with which it occurs in the data (covering all available Old English sources) makes clear that metaphorical naming is proportionately not in the majority, and that an ANGER IS HEAT metaphor in particular is marginal.

Tab. 2: Old English expressions of anger.

Theme	Expressions	semantics	nº	
WRONG EMOTION	ire	literal	46	
FIERCE	gram, wrað	literal or hyperonymy	15	
INSANE	ellenwod	literal or hyperonymy	1	
STRONG EMOTION	anda	hyperonymy	2	
UNMILD	unmiltse	hyperonymy	1	65
AFFLICTION	torn, sare	metonymy	11	
SADNESS	unblide, gealgmode	metonymy	3	
SWELLING	belgan	metaphor	33	
SYNAESTHESIA	sweorcan, biter, hefig	metaphor	3	
FIERCE	reðe	metaphor	4	
HEAT	hatheort, hygewaelm	metaphor	2	56

4 The 'natural experience only' fallacy

The fact that meaning is embodied in natural and cultural experience implies that diachronic metaphor theory needs to take into account the cultural background of experience just as well as it physiological basis, i.e. diachronic metaphor theory should take into account the history of ideas, and the history of daily life (the point has been made before, see for instance Pagán Cánovas 2011). Because there are various aspects to this broader background, a number of illustrations may be mentioned here.

First, it was pointed out in Geeraerts and Grondelaers (1995; an article that was influential in bringing about the 'cultural turn' of Conceptual Metaphor

Theory described in Kövecses 2005) that the scientific conceptions of a given age – or more broadly, the scientific traditions of a given culture – may have an influence on the vocabulary of the common language. Specifically, we pointed out that there is plenty of evidence for the impact of the humoural theory of human physiology and psychology on natural language, as in the expressions brought together in Table 3. For each of the four basic physiological fluids that constitute the humoural theory, the table shows how it has left relics – with meanings in the physiological or the psychological domain – in English, French, and Dutch.

Tab. 3: Impact of the humoural theory on natural languages.

	ENGLISH	FRENCH	DUTCH
PHLEGM	*phlegmatic* 'calm, cool, apathetic'	*avoir un flegme imperturbable* 'to be imperturbable'	*valling* (dialectal) 'cold'
BLACK BILE	*spleen* 'organ filtering the blood; sadness'	*mélancolie* 'sadness, moroseness'	*zwartgallig* 'sad, depressed' (literally 'black-bilious')
YELLOW BILE	*bilious* 'angry, irascible'	*colère* 'anger'	*z'n gal spuwen* 'to vent (literally 'to spit out') one's gall'
BLOOD	*full-blooded* 'vigorous, hearty, sensual'	*avoir du sang dans les veines* 'to have spirit, pluck'	*warmbloedig* 'passionate' (literally 'warm-blooded')

We then argued that the ANGER IS HEAT metaphor could also be part of that humoural legacy. Rather than being directly motivated by universal physiological phenomena, as was initially suggested by Lakoff and Kövecses, the ANGER IS HEAT metaphor (or more precisely the ANGER IS THE HEAT OF A FLUID IN A CONTAINER metaphor as identifed by Lakoff and Kövecses) fits into the humoural framework. An analysis of anger expressions in literary texts like Shakespeare's *The Taming of the Shrew* supports such an analysis.

In the present context, the crucial feature of this story is the necessity of incorporating the history of ideas into the analysis of metaphorical expressions. Regardless of whether the ANGER IS THE HEAT OF A FLUID IN A CONTAINER metaphor is exclusively based on the humoural theory or whether it is a combination of the humoural theory and a physiological impulse, a proper understanding of conceptual metaphors implies an awareness of the cultural and scientific traditions that may have influenced the language.

Two points may be added to this general idea. To begin with, the historical influences are not restricted to the history of ideas: the history of the material culture may also leave its marks. One may notice, for instance, how successive technological (and not just scientific) developments provide source domains for conceptualizing human psychology. Taking our examples from Dutch (in most of the following expressions, the English translation exhibits the same figurative polysemy as the Dutch original), we identify the influence of clocks in expressions like *opgewonden* 'excited' (literally 'wound up'), *van slag zijn* 'be off one's stroke', *drijfveer* 'mainspring', *afgelopen* 'wound down'. Steam engines have left their mark in *stoom afblazen* 'to let of steam', *klaarstomen* 'to steam up, to make ready', *druk* 'pressure', and *onder stoom staan* 'to be steamed up'. Radio provides a source domain in *op dezelfde golflengte zitten* 'to be on the same wavelength', *onderling afstemmen* 'to tune in to each other', *ruis* 'noise' *stoorzender* 'jammer; (hence figuratively) nuisance' – and of course, *antenna*. Simply stating that these expressions illustrate a general THE MIND IS A MACHINE metaphor is not giving them their due: each technological source provides perspectives that seem to be specifically suited for conceptualizing specific target domains, or specific aspects of target domains. The radio metaphors favour a communicative target domain. The steam engine metaphors highlight power and pressure. The clock metaphors focus on precision and smooth operation. Moving beyond the schematic level of THE MIND IS A MACHINE and analyzing this specificity of the metaphorical expressions is an integral part of Conceptual Metaphor Theory, but it requires two things: a systematic analysis of the *ground* of the metaphor in the sense of Richards (1936), i.e. the quality that motivates the use of a source ('vehicle' in Richards' terminology) for a specific target ('Tenor' according to Richards), and a sensitivity for the history of the material culture that constitutes a part of the environment of a language.

A second point to be added involves the possibility of cultural changes of a more far-reaching, but at the same time less tractable nature than the changes in the immaterial and material context that we have illustrated by the humoural theory, and the technological domains of clocks, steam engines, and radiography. Cultural history distinguishes between major periods of development in which not just the material culture or the political and economical circumstances evolve, but in which people's outlook on life, in a broad and vague sense, change pervasively. For the history of the West, the succession from classical antiquity to the middle ages and then to the renaissance and the modern world is a case in point. To the extent that these shifts are real, we may expect them to have a bearing on the semantic changes, metaphorical and other, that the vocabulary of a language undergoes in a certain period. This is not an issue that is very systematically investigated, but if we stay in the domain of emotion terms, the following two examples may briefly illustrate the point.

Diller (1994) suggested that the Middle English emergence of the word *anger*, as against older *ire* and *wrath*, signals a sociohistorical shift towards the individualization of the emotion – precisely the kind of shift, in other words, that would correspond with a transition towards the individual self-awareness that is traditionally attributed to the post-medieval period. Diller's hypothesis was tested by means of a quantitative corpus-based analysis in Geeraerts, Gevaert and Speelman (2012). The results of the quantitative analysis support Diller's hypothesis.

For a second example we turn to the word *emotion* iself, or more precisely to the French verb *émouvoir* from which it derives. Geeraerts (2014) presents evidence, based on Bloem (2008), that the psychological interpretation of *émouvoir* (and, in fact, its near-synonym *mouvoir*) may have come about in the context of the theory of humours. When the psychological reading enters Old French, it does so indiscriminately in the verb *émouvoir* and in the verb *mouvoir*. For both verbs, the psychological reading seems to be a literal expression in the context of the theory of humours, referring to the movement of the humours in the body and their psychological side-effects. Without going into detail, an example like the following may illustrate the kind of bridging contexts in which the psychological reading emerges:

> Le roy demande: Felonnie de quoi avient? Sydrac respont: Des humeurs mauvaises qui aucune fois reflambent au cors comme le feu, et esmuevent le cuer et eschaufent, et le font par leur reflambement noir et obscur; et por cele obscurté devient mornes et penssis et melanconieus.
>
> 'The king asks: Where does felony come from? Sydrac replies: From the bad humours that at one point start burning in the body like fire, and that move the heart and heat it, and make it dark and black by their burning; and from this darkness it becomes sad and thoughtful and melancholy'

The movement in this example is primarily literal: the humours that fill the heart are agitated and heated, but this literal process has outspoken psychological side-effects. It can be shown that in the Old French period, both *émouvoir* and *mouvoir* exhibit the same range of readings: purely spatial ones, purely psychological ones, and bridging ones like in the example.

But in the course of time, this equivalence of the two verbs gives way to the current specialization, in which *émouvoir* is restricted to the psychological readings. Why there should be such a growing differentiation of both verbs is difficult to answer definitively, but it is not implausible that cultural history played a role. A structural explanation might refer to a principle of isomorphic efficiency, which in this case would imply a ban on superfluous synonymy. The general validity of such a principle is however debatable: see the discussion in Geeraerts (1997: 123–156). A functional explanation, by contrast, could assume that there is a diachronically growing need for concepts referring exclusively to psychological phenomena, i.e. for words that provide an independent lexicalization for individual mental experiences like feelings (and the generic notion of 'feeling'). In the terminology of Geeraerts, Grondelaers and Bakema (1994), the conceptual onomasiological salience or 'entrenchment' of a concept rises to the extent that the things that could possibly be identified by that concept are actually being identified by it. The rise, then, of a specialized, dedicated term for the concept 'to feel, in a psychological sense' can be seen as a structural analogy of growing conceptual onomasiological salience. The growing entrenchment of a concept is reflected, on the level of usage, in the increased frequency of words exclusively referring to that concept, and on the level of vocabulary structure, in the emergence of words specialized for that concept.

The growing structural independence of the concept of emotion is also reflected in the word *émotion* itself, which is added much later to the vocabulary than the verb *émouvoir*, but whose appearance as such contributes to the growing entrenchment of the concept of emotion in the structure of the lexicon. In addition, since its emergence in the late 15th century *émotion* enjoys a growing success at the expense of the verb (see also Bloem 2012). In the context of Cognitive Linguistics, the heightened nominal rather than verbal construal could again be seen as signalling the strengthened recognition of emotion as a thing in its own right.

In short, the diachronic differentiation of *mouvoir* and *émouvoir* (and hence, *émotion*) seems to fit into a longitudinal cultural development towards psychologization and interiorization of mental life, similar to Diller's hypothesis about the success of *anger* in contrast with older terms. The need for a dedicated term for the emotions, as inner mental experiences, increases; or, to put it in a slightly different terminology, the conceptual onomasiological salience of *émouvoir* and *émotion* in their psychological reading rises.

5 The 'metaphorization only' fallacy

The fact that meaning is transmitted through language implies metaphors do not just arise through original metaphorization, but that they may also arise through a 'deliteralizing' reinterpretation process: while a new TARGET IS SOURCE pattern is usually formed by figuratively categorizing the Target as Source, it may also happen that an existing literal categorization is reinterpreted as a figurative TARGET IS SOURCE pattern, because the literal motivation of the original expression is no longer accessible.

The concept 'emotion' provides an example of the process. (Again, see Geeraerts 2014 for more details.) Let us assume that French *émotion* or English *emotion* are currently perceived as metaphorically linked to the concept of movement. This will not generally be the case. For many language users, the words may well be basically opaque. But at least in some cases, a metaphorical association with the concept of movement is envisaged. The *Oxford English Dictionary*, for instance, explains the reading 'any strong mental or instinctive feeling, as pleasure, grief, hope, fear, etc.' as an extension of a reading 'an agitation of mind; an excited mental state', which itself seems to be analyzed as a metaphorical interpretation of the general literal meaning 'movement; disturbance, perturbation'. Now, if people indeed perceive such a metaphorical link, and if we further assume that the original historical motivation for the emergence of the term involves the humoural theory, then the metaphorical interpretation comes about in a different way from what we normally consider to be the process of metaphorical speech.

In fact, in the regular type of creative metaphor, an expression with reference A and sense α is applied with reference B and with an extended, figurative sense α'. Surely, this is a simplified picture of the relationship between α and α' (very often, the precise nature of α' is not as easy to determine as this simple variable suggests), but it helps to contrast the regular form of metaphor with reinterpretive deliteralization. In the latter, an expression with reference A and sense α is interpreted with the same reference A but with an extended, figurative sense α'. Comparing two examples may bring out the differences more clearly. A lover who addresses his beloved as *sparkles* triggers the implication that he sees her as lively, dynamic, vigorous and invigorating. In this kind of metaphor, which may be said to be based on 'figuration', the reference of *sparkles* shifts from small burning fragments and glittering points of lights to a person; at the same time, the sense of the word shifts from the material or optical field to a psychological one: the beloved person does not literally sparkle. The shift occurs, by and large, because there is a unique and forceful experience that calls for a singular and pithy expression. In comparison, thinking that emotion is a non-literal kind of motion does not change the reference of *emotion*, but merely reinterprets the link between the word and its referent. This reinterpretation is triggered by the fact that the original, literal motivation for the word is no longer available. In that sense we can say (with a little exaggeration) that metaphor based on figuration involves making sense of the world – 'what is this overwhelming experience that she invokes in me, and how shall I call it?' – whereas metaphor based on deliteralization involves making sense of the language – 'why is this thing called as it is?'.

In the larger scheme of things, deliteralization as defined here is part of a broad class of reinterpretation processes in which existing expressions are semantically reinterpreted when the original motivation of the expression is no longer available to the language user. Further examples (specifically in the field of idiomatic expressions and compound nouns) can be found in Geeraerts (2002). Deliteralization is a prime example of the integrated nature of culture and cognition in the realm of language: language users do not invent language from scratch, but they receive it as part of their cultural environment; at the same time, they cognitively process what is relayed to them, and that mental absorption may imply a partial reinvention of what is being reproduced. The relationship between culture and cognition is a dialectic one: language is a culturally transmitted and hence intrinsically historical phenomenon, but at each point in time, the transmission process requires cognitive reproduction.

6 Conclusions

To summarize and conclude, I have argued that there are four fallacies to avoid in diachronic metaphor research in Cognitive Linguistics: *the dominant reading only fallacy*, which neglects to have a closer look at the history of words; *the semasiology only fallacy*, which neglects the relevance of the onomasiological alternatives for Target; the *natural experience only fallacy*, which neglects the cultural background of cognitive processes; and *the metaphorization only fallacy*, which neglects processes of deliteralization and reinterpretation as sources of metaphoricity. Each of these points derives from a tenet taken for granted in Cognitive Linguistics: respectively, that meaning is prototypically structured; that meaning is structured both semasiologically and onomasiologically; that meaning is embodied in both natural and cultural experience; that meaning is transmitted through language. Beyond these specific backgrounds, the common denominator behind the identification of the four fallacies is the obvious recognition (perhaps so obvious that it tends to be forgotten) that historical metaphor research needs to take the historicity of language as its main starting-point.

References

Bloem, Annelies. 2008. *Et pource dit ausy Ipocras que u prin tans les melancolies se esmoeuvent. L'évolution sémantico-syntaxique des verbes 'mouvoir' et 'émouvoir'.* Leuven: Katholieke Universiteit Leuven dissertation.

Bloem, Annelies. 2012. (E)motion in the XVIIth century. A closer look at the changing semantics of the French verbs émouvoir and mouvoir. In Ad Foolen, Ulrike M. Lüdtke, Timothy P. Racine & Jordan Zlatev (eds.), *Moving ourselves, moving others: Motion and emotion in intersubjectivity, consciousness and language*, 407–422. Amsterdam & Philadelphia: John Benjamins.

Diller, Hans-Jürgen. 1994. Emotions in the English lexicon: A historical study of a lexical field. In Francisco Moreno Fernández, Miguel Fuster & Juan Jose Calvo (eds.), *English historical linguistics 1992*, 219–234. Amsterdam & Philadelphia: John Benjamins.

Geeraerts, Dirk. 1997. *Diachronic prototype semantics. A contribution to historical lexicology.* Oxford: Clarendon Press.

Geeraerts, Dirk. 2002. The interaction of metaphor and metonymy in composite expressions. In René Dirven & Ralf Pörings (eds.), *Metaphor and metonymy in comparison and contrast*, 435–465. Berlin & New York: Mouton de Gruyter.

Geeraerts, Dirk. 2010. Prospects for the past: Perspectives for diachronic cognitive semantics. In Margaret E. Winters, Heli Tissari & Kathryn Allan (eds.), *Historical cognitive linguistics*, 333–356. Berlin & New York: Mouton de Gruyter.

Geeraerts, Dirk. 2014. Deliteralization and the birth of 'emotion'. In Masataka Yamaguchi, Dennis Tay & Ben Blount (eds.), *Approaches to language, culture, and cognition. The intersection of cognitive linguistics and linguistic anthropology*, 50–67. London: Palgrave MacMillan.

Geeraerts, Dirk & Caroline Gevaert. 2008. Hearts and (angry) minds in Old English. In Farzad Sharifian, René Dirven, Ning Yu & Susanne Niemeier (eds.), *Culture and language: Looking for the mind inside the body*, 319–347. Berlin & New York: Mouton de Gruyter.

Geeraerts, Dirk, Caroline Gevaert & Dirk Speelman. 2012. How 'anger' rose. Hypothesis testing in diachronic semantics. In Kathryn Allan & Justyna Robinson (eds.), *Current methods in historical semantics*, 109–132. Berlin & New York: Mouton de Gruyter.

Geeraerts, Dirk & Stefan Grondelaers. 1995. Looking back at anger: Cultural traditions and metaphorical patterns. In John Taylor & Robert E. MacLaury (eds.), *Language and the construal of the world*, 153–180. Berlin & New York: Mouton de Gruyter.

Geeraerts, Dirk, Stefan Grondelaers & Peter Bakema. 1994. *The structure of lexical variation. Meaning, naming, and context.* Berlin & New York: Mouton de Gruyter.

Kövecses, Zoltán. 2005. *Metaphor in culture. Universality and variation.* Oxford: Oxford University Press.

Pagán Cánovas, Cristobal. 2011. The genesis of the arrows of love: Diachronic conceptual integration in Greek mythology. *American Journal of Philology* 132. 553–579.

Richards, Ivor A. 1936. *The philosophy of rhetoric.* Oxford: Oxford University Press.

Conceptual variation and change

Kathryn Allan
Lost in transmission? The sense development of borrowed metaphor

Abstract: Both metaphor and borrowing are generally acknowledged to be key processes in the enrichment of the English lexicon: metaphor is recognised as a trigger for the development of polysemy, and borrowing has been, and continues to be, a major source of new lexis. This paper considers the effects when these two processes coincide, when metaphorical sense developments are borrowed across language boundaries. As a starting point, it focuses on "dead" or "historical" metaphors in English which were "alive" in the donor language at the time of borrowing. Many of the examples of "dead" or "historical" metaphor that have been identified in the literature are lexemes that were borrowed into English. For example, the noun *pedigree* was borrowed into Middle English from Anglo-French *pé de grue* 'foot of a crane, pedigree', but only seems to be recorded in English with its "metaphorical" sense; the metaphor that existed in French is therefore opaque for most monolingual English speakers. *ardent* was also borrowed into English in the Middle English period, and might be expected to be more likely to retain its metaphorical polysemy, since it relates to a conceptual metaphor which is still found in English, INTENSITY (IN EMOTION) IS HEAT. Although both the literal sense 'burning' and figurative senses including 'passionate' are attested in English, the literal sense is archaic or obsolete in Present Day English, and evidence from resources such as the *Middle English Dictionary* and *Early English Books Online* suggests that it appears to be rare even in earlier periods. Where it is found in earlier documents, the 'burning' sense appears to be restricted to particular text types and contexts. Again, the historically metaphorical motivation for the meaning 'passionate' is not obvious to contemporary speakers unless they are familiar with the French or Latin etymons of the lexeme. The role of borrowing in the semantic development of non-native lexemes has been discussed by various scholars. For example, Durkin (2009) notes that borrowing sometimes only involves a component of the meaning of the donor form, and discusses later borrowing of additional senses from the donor language; in his classic account of language contact, Weinreich (1964) also discusses the impact of borrowing on the existing lexis of a language. However, the significance of borrowing in the histories of metaphors has not been considered in detail. This paper explores what the

---
Kathryn Allan: University College London

implications of borrowing are for diachronic metaphor studies, and for the term "metaphor" itself.

1 Introduction

Both metaphor and borrowing are generally acknowledged to be key processes in the enrichment of the English lexicon. Metaphor is recognised as a trigger for the development of polysemy, and is often listed as one of the best-attested tendencies in semantic change: for example, Ullmann includes metaphor as a one of four "cardinal types" of association "such as have proved their strength by initiating semantic changes" (Ullmann 1959: 79), and Traugott and Dasher note that "For most of the twentieth century metaphor(ization) was considered the major factor in semantic change" (Traugott and Dasher 2004: 28). Some linguistic metaphors are "alive" to contemporary speakers, in the sense that they are expressed by lexemes with both "literal" source senses and "metaphorical" target senses; others are "dead" or "historical" in that no corresponding "literal" sense is used (see for example Deignan 2005: 40). For some scholars, these cannot be considered metaphors, but from a historical point of view their metaphorical motivation is interesting and significant. Borrowing also has a major impact on the lexicon, as a major source of new vocabulary. It is generally accepted that modern English is a "lexical mosaic" (Katamba 2005: 135) which reflects a great deal of borrowing in earlier periods, especially from French and Latin in the period after the Norman Conquest. Core vocabulary has been the least affected, although it still seems to show considerable influence; borrowing has changed the shape of other areas of the lexicon, such as scientific vocabulary and many technical registers, even more dramatically. Scheler (1977: 72) examines the proportion of loanwords in the lexis of English, using a variety of sources[1]. In a basic list which concentrates on core vocabulary, he finds that approximately 50 % of items are borrowed. His figure for a longer list composed of data from a learner's dictionary is higher at approaching 70 %, and in a very large wordlist derived ultimately from the *Oxford English Dictionary* (*OED*) the total of loanwords reaches 70 %, with 56 % derived from French and Latin (although this list omits many rarer and obsolete words).

---

[1] See Durkin (2014: 22–24) for a longer discussion and updated figures based on revised material in *OED3*.

This paper considers the effects when borrowing and metaphor coincide, i.e. when metaphorical sense developments are borrowed across language boundaries along with the lexemes that express them. As a starting point, it focuses on "dead" or "historical" metaphors in English which were "alive" in the donor language at the time of borrowing. It considers what happened to the senses of a number of loanwords in their early histories in English, and how their etymologically "metaphorical" senses were lost. Two case studies will be presented: first, I will consider the verb *inculcate*, which is discussed by Goatly as an example of "dead and buried metaphor" (Goatly 2011: 32), and secondly, I will look in detail at the adjective *ardent*, also mentioned in the literature on historical metaphor (Deignan 2005: 39; see also Steen 2007: 95–96). The central question addressed in the paper is whether the process of borrowing itself is likely to result in metaphor "death": is it usual for both senses of a linguistic metaphor to be borrowed, and then for the "literal sense" to die out within the target language, or is it more likely that the metaphor will be "lost in transmission"?

2 Borrowed metaphor

In the literature on metaphor within cognitive linguistics, borrowing is rarely mentioned; metaphorical sense developments within a language are much more common as a focus of study. Where the etymologies of borrowed lexemes with metaphorical senses are discussed, there is usually little consideration of which senses in the donor language are borrowed along with the word form. A typical example can be found in an article on 'Metaphors in English, French, and Spanish Medical Written Discourse', which gives *muscle* as an instance of metaphor and briefly details its etymology:

> A frequently cited example [of metaphor] is 'muscle' (from the Latin word *musculus*, which means 'small mouse'). In this metaphor, 'muscle' is the Topic, 'small mouse' is the Vehicle ... (Divasson and Léon 2005: 58)

While it does acknowledge the history of the English lexeme, this kind of comment blurs the distinction between the forms that appear in different languages and their meanings. In this example, it is not clear in which language the linguistic metaphor is "alive": there is no information about whether the Latin term *musculus* means both 'little mouse' and 'muscle', or whether the loanword *muscle* has both senses in English (or had these senses in an earlier period), or both. A closer look at the history of *muscle* in *OED3* shows that the sense 'little mouse' is not recorded (or at least, not frequently enough to be included in the entry); *muscle* is only found in English with the sense 'part of the body' and related meanings, such as 'physical strength', 'power' (e.g. of a machine) and 'Threat of physical violence'. The entry also shows that *muscle* should not be regarded as a loanword borrowed solely from Latin; Middle French *muscle, muscule* is presented as a co-etymon of Latin *musculus*, indicating that both languages are likely to have influenced the establishment of the English lexeme and its semantic (and formal) development. The *Trésor de la Langue Française Informatisé* (*TLFi*) and the *Dictionnaire du Moyen Français* give more information about the senses of *muscle* in Middle French, and the account it presents suggests that it was not used with the sense 'mouse' or any related senses; the metaphor only existed linguistically in Latin, and the etymologically "literal" sense was not transmitted to French or English.

My intention here is not to single out Divasson and Léon's paper for criticism, since their focus is not historical. Their interest is in current lexemes in the medical terminology of different languages which evidence the same metaphorical mapping, and they give this example only to explain the different constituent parts of a metaphor and the kind of relationship these have. However, their comment is representative of the lack of attention that has been given to the issue of borrowing and its central importance in the lexical history of metaphorically motivated lexemes in English (and other languages). Traugott draws attention to borrowing in a 1985 paper which examines the metaphorical origins of a set of lexemes including illocutionary verbs, and notes that the "metaphoricity" of loanwords in the borrowing language should not be taken for granted.

> Whether they were considered metaphorical when they were borrowed from Latin into English, often via French, is another question which deserves investigation. While some, such as *insist*, were used with spatial as well as speech act verb meanings when they were borrowed, suggesting the relative transparency of the metaphorical process in sixteenth century English, it is possible that others were actually never thought to be metaphorical in English ... (Traugott 1985: 53, footnote 18).

As Traugott points out, from a synchronic point of view, it seems difficult to argue that the examples she considers can be regarded as metaphorical, and the same is true of *muscle*. Diachronically, it seems important to give prominence to borrowing as a key part of the semantic history of this lexeme and all etymologically metaphorical loanwords. Purely etymological metaphors, i.e. lexemes which have never been metaphorically "alive" in English, should perhaps be treated differently from linguistic metaphors which have been established in English but have "died out" over time.

3 inculcate

The first case study to be presented here discusses an example mentioned in the literature on historical metaphor, the verb *inculcate* (discussed in Goatly 2011: 32, using the term "dead and buried" rather than "historical"). In current synchronic dictionaries, *inculcate* is recorded with a single meaning 'instil (an idea, attitude, or habit) by persistent instruction' (*Oxford Dictionary of English*). Like *muscle*, *inculcate* is a Latin/Romance loanword, in this case borrowed directly from Latin in the Early Modern English period. The earliest attestation in *OED2* is dated to 1559, although examples can be found as early as the 1530s in *Early English Books Online*, so it seems likely that the revised entry in *OED3* will give slightly different dates[2]. The Latin etymon for the loanword is *inculcāt-*, the participial stem of *inculcāre*, itself derived from *in-* + *calcare* 'to tread'. *inculcāre* has physical literal senses, 'to trample or press down' and 'to tread or stuff in' (also used in a transferred sense), and a metaphorical sense which relates to mental processes, 'to impress (an idea, etc., upon a person's mind), din in, drive home' (*Oxford Latin Dictionary*[3]). It therefore provides evidence for a mapping between physical pressure and mental effect, which seems similar to that shown by expressions like Present Day English *make an impression* 'have a strong effect on people ... causing them to notice you ...' (*Collins COBUILD English Dictionary*). The mapping is also evidenced by an earlier phrase, *beat (a thing) into one's head/mind* (*OED2*), which is often used in a pair with *inculcate* and means something like 'Teach/persuade by repetition'. There is a parallel French form *inculquer, inculcer* which is found slightly earlier than the English borrowing, and although this is not noted in *OED2* it may have had some influence on the sense development of the English form.

A first look at *OED2* indicates that both literal and metaphorical senses were borrowed along with the form into English, and the meanings of *inculcate* are correspondingly divided into 2 separate senses. Sense 1 covers a range of meanings that clearly develop from the metaphorical mental sense in Latin, defined as 'to endeavour to force (a thing) into or impress (it) on the mind of another by emphatic admonition, or by persistent repetition; to urge on the mind, esp. as a principle, an opinion, or a matter of belief; to teach forcibly'. It is attested by 14 quotations, which show continuous use between the earliest and latest quotation dates of 1559 and 1874 (1874 indicating contemporary us-

---

[2] See Allan (2012: 20–21) for a discussion of the differences between *OED2* and *OED3*.
[3] The *Oxford Latin Dictionary* also records the sense 'to force or obtrude (services, etc., on an unwilling recipient)'.

age when this entry was published in *OED1*). Several of these quotations are from religious texts (in the broadest sense[4]), but they are also taken from other kinds of writing, including poetry and fiction, historical accounts, and the correspondence of Edmund Burke. The earliest example is taken from a text called *Annals of the reformation and establishment of religion, and other various occurrences in the Church of England, during queen Elizabeth's happy reign ...*, and gives a sense of this meaning in context:

> 1559 Bp. Scot *Speech* in J. Strype *Ann Reformation* (1824) I. ii. App. vii. 418 The aucthoritie of the bisshoppe of Rome ... some inculcate against us, as a matter of great weight.

OED2 sense 2 corresponds to the literal Latin sense, and is clearly physical, defined as 'to tread upon, trample, press with the feet'. However, this appears to be a much more minor sense, since only two attestations are listed, one from the end of the sixteenth century and the second from the middle of the seventeenth. In itself, the number of quotations supplied by *OED* is not necessarily indicative of frequency of use, but generally editors will aim to supply more than one for each century, as the quotations in sense 1 show. Where as few as two in total are included, it is reasonable to assume that no others had been found when the entry was written, and in this particular case the imbalance between the number of quotations at each sense suggests that sense 1 was much more common than sense 2. Furthermore, both quotations at sense 2 are from translations of medical texts, which might indicate that this is a restricted technical use of the lexeme. The earlier quotation has a French source text, and the later a Latin source text (by a French writer). In this later quotation, the form in the source text is supplied in square brackets after the translation, *inculcate*, and this shows that the translator was directly influenced by the lexeme used in the Latin original:

> 1657 R. Tomlinson tr. J. de Renou *Medicinal Dispensatory* iii. ii. v. 127 A certain Cloth ... is often dipped and inculcated [L. *inculcatur*] in a fit Emplaister already made up.

The evidence in *OED2* therefore suggests strongly that the etymologically literal sense of *inculcate*, 'to tread upon, trample, press with the feet', is both rare and highly restricted: in these quotations, it is used only by writers using a particular technical register who are clearly familiar with the Latin source form, and it appears to have a limited period of use. Additional evidence for the semantic range of the lexeme can be found in *Early English Books Online* (*EEBO*), which includes some material which was not available to *OED2* edi-

---

4 Including e.g. a 1593 text on ecclesiastical law.

tors. There are 1456 hits (from 939 texts) for *inculcate* in *EEBO*, although these include both the verb form and the derived adjective form. An examination of all of these hits confirms the impression given by *OED2*, since only three hits showing a physical sense of *inculcate* can be found. The first of these is the following, from a 1598 text:

> ... have vve not the earth it selfe vvhich vvith our feete vve inculcate, and treade one ...
> (Jacques Guillemeau, *The Frenche chirurgerye ... truelye translated out of Dutch into Englishe by A.M.*, 1598)

Like the attestations in *OED2*, this example and the other two in *EEBO* are from medical texts which involve translation. In this case, the text is a translation of a French work which has used a Dutch model; the other two hits are from a 1657 translation of a Latin work, and a 1678 text which collects together extracts from a wide range of medical authorities in various languages, including several Latin works. A further two hits are dictionary definitions which record both physical and mental senses, but these do not provide evidence of actual use of a physical sense. The remaining 1451 examples in *EEBO* show the mental sense of *inculcate*.

The quotations in *OED2* and *EEBO*, taken together, do not constitute an exhaustive corpus of all examples of the verb *inculcate*, but they do provide enough evidence to give an indicative picture of how and when the lexeme was used with different senses. They appear to demonstrate convincingly that although both the literal and metaphorical senses of the Latin etymon can be found in English, the literal sense is extremely rare and did not become well-established, even within medical discourse. In a sense, it does therefore seem to have been lost in transmission. It may be that its history in English is fairly typical, particularly for a Romance loanword borrowed in the Early Modern English period. Nevalainen discusses the "phenomenal growth-rate of the lexicon in the decades around 1600" (Nevalainen 1999: 348) which is particularly associated with borrowing from Latin and Romance languages, and points out that "The intensive period of neologising is followed by a corresponding increase in obsolete words" and in the loss of some senses of neologisms, including loanwords (ibid.: 349). Most importantly, she notes that "As [these neologisms] apparently do not form part of the current lexis at any time, one would feel disinclined to talk about obsoleteness proper" (ibid.: 349). The same can be said of senses of loanwords which are attested in English but with such a minimal level of use that they can barely be considered part of the lexis. It seems rather misleading to think of the literal sense of *inculcate* as "dying out" in English; rather, only a trace of this meaning can be found in English, and it never became properly established.

4 ardent[5]

A second example of a borrowed lexeme which has lost its etymologically "literal" sense is *ardent*, which is again found in the literature as an example of historical metaphor (see, for example, Deignan 2005 and Steen 2007, 2010). In present day English, *ardent* has the usual meaning 'very enthusiastic or passionate' (*ODE*), and this is the only sense recorded in many synchronic dictionaries (e.g. *Collins COBUILD English Dictionary*, the *Oxford Advanced Learner's Dictionary*). *ardent* is ultimately from Latin *ardēre* 'to burn', and therefore the mapping appears to relate to a conceptual metaphor which is discussed in a number of publications, INTENSITY (IN EMOTION) IS HEAT (Kövecses 2005: 262; see also Kövecses 2000a: 93, Kövecses 2000b: 84 and Goatly 2007: 238). This is expressed linguistically in a number of present day English expressions, such as *burning* or *flaming desire*, *fiery temper* or *relationship*, and *heated argument*[6].

According to *OED2*, *ardent* is borrowed into English in the Middle English period. Its immediate etymon is Old French *ardant*, and it seems likely that it is also influenced by Latin *ardentem* (the present participle of *ardere* 'to burn'), though this is not explicitly noted in *OED2*. The forms in both Old French and Latin show literal senses relating to burning and metaphorical senses relating to passion. *TLFi* records attestations for the sense 'qui brûle, éclatant, vif [which burns, brilliant, lively]' as early as the tenth century, along with related senses such as 'enflamme [burning, in flame]' in the following three centuries, and metaphorical senses such as 'passionné, vif, animé, violent [passionate, lively, animated, intense]' from the early 13th century. Similarly, the *Oxford Latin Dictionary* (under the headword *ardens*) includes senses relating to burning, heat and light, and two different senses relating to the emotions, 'eager, zealous, enthusiastic' and 'intense, passionate'. In *OED2*, both the etymologically literal and metaphorical senses are attested for the English form *ardent* (and variant spellings) in the Middle English period. The earliest attestations, from

---

5 Allan (2014) also discusses this example in relation to different treatments of historical metaphor.

6 The conceptual status of the mapping means that not all scholars consider it to be an instance of historical metaphor. For Lakoff (1987), only "one-shot metaphors" can be considered to be "historical". *Pedigree* is "dead" both linguistically, since the metaphorical source sense is not found in English, and conceptually, because the mapping from 'foot of a crane' to 'family tree' is not system-wide and is not expressed linguistically by other lexemes; by contrast, *ardent* only fulfils one of these criteria. See Allan (2014) for a fuller discussion of different treatments of historical metaphor.

the late fourteenth century[7], show the metaphorical sense 'Glowing with passion, animated by keen desire' (of both people and emotions), but these are not significantly earlier than attestations for physical senses. 'Burning, on fire, red hot' and 'inflammable' (senses 1 and 2 in the *OED2* entry) are both found in quotations from the fifteenth century, and the further physical senses 'glowing' (sense 4) and 'That burns like vitriol; corrosive' (sense 3, found only in the phrase *ardent water*) are also found from the beginning of the seventeenth century and at the end of the eighteenth century respectively. In contrast to the entry for *inculcate*, there are a number of examples of all of these physical senses taken together, although individually each sense appears to be fairly minor. Sense 1 'burning, on fire, red hot, parching' is attested by six quotations dated from c1440 to 1882, but there are four or fewer quotations for each of the others, and only a single example of *ardent water*. It is also noticeable that two of the texts quoted at sense 1 are translations, one from French and the other from Latin, and this may have influenced the choice of *ardent* used with its literal sense.

The *Middle English Dictionary* offers more evidence for the early history of the lexeme (using the headword form *ardaunt*) and gives a different picture for this period from *OED2*, a picture which suggests strongly that the metaphorical sense is the more established one. 'Burning with desire or passion; fervent, ardent, passionate' is the first sense presented, and is attested by eight quotations from six sources, including two of the same ones found in *OED2*. The sense 'burning, fiery; brilliant' is only shown in three quotations, and is separated from *eue ardent* and *water ardent* 'an alcoholic distillate, such as brandy', since both phrases are direct translations of Latin *aqua vita*, and from *goute ardaunt* 'inflamed gout' (attested in only one quotation). A closer look at the three quotations supporting the sense 'burning, fiery; brilliant' shows that they are not all straightforward literal uses. The second example describes eyes, which cannot literally burn, so this might be argued to be metaphorical. The third is perhaps more complex, since it describes something which can literally burn or glow, but in a context which is clearly figurative: it occurs with reference to the divine, in the phrase "Thow ordaunt lyght..The trust and hoppe of all that christien be" (a1500 *Add.Hymnal* (Add 34193) 456/16). Evidence for later uses of *ardent* in English can again be found in *EEBO*. An initial survey of the texts recovered in a search show that metaphorical uses of *ardent* to mean 'passionate' (or a related meaning) are the most common, but also that literal

---

[7] These are quotations from an edition of Chaucer's Boethius, dated to c1374, although these have a later manuscript date of a1425 (and composition date of c1380) in the *Middle English Dictionary*.

uses in figurative contexts like the example above are more common than clearly literal uses. Figure 1 shows the number of hits for five collocations in which *ardent* might be expected to show a literal sense. The number of hits of the synonym *burning* is given alongside these for comparison:

ardent fire(s)	32	burning fire(s)	1208
ardent flame(s)	61	burning flame(s)	585
ardent coal(s)	1	burning coal(s)	1277
ardent wood	0	burning wood	68
ardent log(s)	0	burning log(s)	5

Fig. 1: *Collocations with* ardent *in* EEBO[8].

The number of hits in each case must be treated with some caution, since *EEBO* searches are not totally reliable; although variant spellings and forms are recovered with accuracy, occasionally characters that look similar can distort the total number of hits (e.g. *s* for *f*, recovering *sire* rather than *fire*). As well as this, *EEBO* includes different editions of the same text, so that several hits may show the same example. The extent to which this affects the total number of hits in each case can be gauged from a closer examination of the results of the search for *ardent fire(s)*. In the 32 hits recovered, which are from 30 records, there is one false match (the phrase *ardent syres*); there are also three editions each of two different texts, and two editions of one other text, which slightly skews the total. The figures in Table 1 therefore give a strong indication of the relative frequencies of different collocations, but cannot be taken to be definitive. Looking again at *ardent fire(s)*, only nine hits appear to show a literal meaning in a literal context, and three of these are from the same text, giving a total of six examples. The remaining 22 hits (subtracting the false match) show 19 examples of literal uses in figurative contexts, which discuss for example the *ardent fire of love* or *valour*, or *Cupid's ardent fire*. In the 61 hits for *ardent flame(s)*, the dominance of figurative contexts of use is even clearer. Only four examples show a literal use in a literal context, and again, expressions like *Love's ardent flame* and the *ardent flames of charity, affection* or *war* account for a far greater number of examples. All of the purely literal uses of both *ardent fire* and *ardent flames* occur in similar text types, and all are from the seventeenth century; around half occur in poetry, and the others in medi-

---

[8] Allan (2014: 304) gives different figures for these searches; this is because new text collections were added to *EEBO* in December 2011.

cal, religious or historical texts. It is also striking that all of these texts are either translations from Latin or French, or show very clear classical influences, often quoting Latin phrases or citing classical authors or figures. In some cases, texts are also emulating the forms of classical poetry, in particular Virgil's pastoral poetry. The lower lines of Table 1 show that other collocations with *ardent* which seem likely to show a clearly literal use, such as *ardent coal(s)*, *ardent wood* and *ardent log(s)*, occur either once (in the case of *ardent coal*) or not at all.

All of this evidence suggests strongly that *ardent* 'burning' is highly restricted, and tends to be used with a relatively small set of collocates in semi-metaphorical use. Straightforward literal uses do occur, but rarely and in particular contexts, and in literary or scholarly texts for a learned audience by writers familiar with Latin and French. As in the case of *inculcate*, though, the literal sense does not seem to become properly established in widespread use. By contrast, the synonym *burning*, which also has both literal and metaphorical senses, is more frequent and does not seem to show the same kinds of restrictions. As Allan (2014) notes, this does not necessarily mean that *ardent* was not thought of as metaphorical by speakers in the Middle and Early Modern periods, or at least some speakers. Literate speakers in the medieval period would have used and understood French and Latin alongside English (see Rothwell 2005 for an account of multilingualism in this period). This perhaps makes it unsurprising that both literal and metaphorical uses are found when the lexeme is borrowed and in its early history; it seems natural for the full range of meanings in the source language to influence the meaning in the target language for these speakers. However, the relative frequency of the different meanings shows the semantic development of the lexeme in English, and the status of *ardent* as a loanword offers an explanation for the dominance of its metaphorical sense.

5 The semantics of loanwords

The absence or loss of etymologically literal senses of loanwords such as *muscle*, *inculcate* and *ardent* in English is perhaps unsurprising if we examine accounts of the process of borrowing, and consider the period in which each lexeme is first attested in English. Any loanword borrowed into a language is integrated into an existing system, and its range of meaning in the target language is potentially constrained by the existing lexis of that system. In his influential account of language contact, Weinreich suggests that loanwords have a number of typical impacts on the existing lexis of a source language, which also determines what happens to the loanwords themselves:

> Except for loanwords with entirely new content, the transfer or reproduction of foreign words must affect the existing vocabulary in one of three ways: (1) confusion between the content of the new and old word; (2) disappearance of the old word; (3) survival of both the new and old word, with a specialization in content. (Weinreich 1964: 54)

The third possibility mentioned here, "specialization in content", corresponds to the semantic histories examined above. In each case, there is an existing English synonym for the etymologically literal sense of the lexeme: *mouse* already covers one sense of *musculus*; there are various lexemes that express physical impact of the kind denoted by *inculcare*, such as *tread*, *stamp*, and *trample*; and *burning* is the central term to describe entities that are on fire or very hot, the main literal senses covered by French *ardant* and Latin *ardentem*. It is unlikely that a borrowed word would replace an existing lexeme to cover any of these meanings, because they relate to everyday, necessary concepts that are used often. This is the point made by Durkin (2009: 4–7) in a discussion of the specialized meaning of the loanword *friar* in English, where he notes that "It is very common for a borrowed word to show only a very restricted and possibly rather peripheral portion of its meaning when it is borrowed into another language" (ibid: 6). Durkin (2014) is a lengthier consideration of loanwords in English, which begins by suggesting that although it is difficult to divide the lexis of a language very neatly, "it can be useful to think of a (not very precisely defined) common core of basic vocabulary, including words in everyday use ... [which] generally shows relatively little variation within narrowly defined speech communities, or within standard varieties" (Durkin 2014: 19). Historically, the basic vocabulary of English has adopted far fewer loanwords than other areas of the lexicon. The evidence that Durkin discusses, and the conclusions he draws, are consistent with general statements such as Burnley's assertion that "despite the great numbers of lexical items borrowed from French, the most frequently used words continued to be those of English and sometimes Scandinavian origin" (Burnley 1992: 431–2). Durkin (2014: 41–44) goes on to say that the same kind of trend can be observed if we take a different perspective and consider basic meanings rather than basic (i.e. high-frequency) vocabulary; again, fewer basic meanings are expressed by loanwords (as the most usual or central word for the concept). Since the literal senses of metaphors are typically concrete and experientially basic (see e.g. Coulson 2006: 34), this might explain why the etymologically literal senses of loanwords such as *muscle*, *inculcate* and *ardent* do not become more generally established, even if they are attested occasionally in English.

Conversely, the etymologically metaphorical senses of these loanwords are quite different kinds of meanings, and in all three cases seem much more likely to become established in English, though for slightly different reasons. In the case of *muscle*, it seems as though there was not a central term to express the meaning 'body tissue' in the period it was borrowed, so that the loanword offered a label that was not in competition with others already in the language system. Section 01.02.05.13.03 (*n.*) of the *Historical Thesaurus of the Oxford English Dictionary* (Kay et al. 2009; henceforth *HTOED*) lists the terms for 'muscle' found through time[9]:

> banloca OE · lira OE · sinulira OE · mouse<mus OE; 1561 · lacert c1386-1586; 1696 (*Dict.*) · fillet 1533; 1543 · muscle 1533- · lizard 1574 · flesh-string 1587 · bower 1596; 1611 · thews 1818- · · thew c1863-

Some of the dates of attestation given here have been revised in *OED Online*: *muscle* now has additional attestations, giving an earlier first date of a1398, and the first attestation for *lacert* has been redated to c1400; however, this makes only a minimal difference to the picture presented by the section. As it shows, there are lexemes to express the sense 'muscle' in Old English, but these are not attested into the Middle English period. *mus* in Old English is occasionally found with this meaning, and its reflex *mouse* is subsequently attested once in the sixteenth century, showing the same metaphorical mapping as *musculus* in Latin, but this seems to be very rare, and may show a loan translation of Latin. The French loanword *lacert* is found a few times in the Middle English period, but the added attestations for *muscle* suggest that it is borrowed around the same time, and it appears to become much more widely established very quickly. There is only one *OED2* attestation for *lacert* after the mid-sixteenth century, indicating that it drops out of use, perhaps because of competition with *muscle*. *muscle* therefore does appear to fill some kind of need for a medical term, and is perhaps "new content" in Weinreich's sense, though he intends this phrase to describe the loanword as a whole. The other sense is in competition with an already established and common lexeme *mouse*, and therefore the lexeme loses this sense in transmission to English.

The etymologically metaphorical senses of *inculcate* and *ardent* seem to fulfil a different kind of function in the lexicon, since there are already existing partial synonyms for both at the time they are borrowed. According to *HTOED* (section 03.06.02.03), there are various lexemes that express the meaning 'in-

---

[9] There are also lower-level sections which list terms for 'Types of muscle' and 'muscles of specific parts'; very few entries in either of these sections are attested earlier than *muscle*.

stil ideas' in Early Modern English, including *impress*, *plant* and *instil*. Closer matches for the *OED2* definition, 'impress on the mind of another by emphatic admonition, or by persistent repetition', are found either in Old English only, or are attested first around the same time as *inculcate*, including the related form *inculk*, *whet* and *beat (a thing) into one's head/mind*. The most dominant lexeme to express the main sense of *ardent* is easier to identify, and seems to be *burning* used in a metaphorical sense (motivated by the same conceptual mapping, as noted above). In both cases, though, the loanword appears to provide an alternative that takes over from the existing synonyms to some extent, and this "success" relates to the nature of borrowed French and Latin lexis in English. As discussed above, Latin and French are the major sources of borrowed lexis in English over its history, and loanwords from both tend to reflect the prestige with which both languages have been viewed by English speakers across time. Typically, these loanwords are fairly formal and occur in high-register texts (although this may change over time), and they are also common in technical registers including scientific language, sometimes as highly specialized terms. Each of the three examples discussed here conforms to one or more of these tendencies. *inculcate* is still labelled as "formal" in both the *Oxford Advanced Learner's Dictionary* and the *Collins COBUILD English Dictionary*. *ardent* has arguably lost some of its stylistic "prestige", but in some collocations it is still relatively formal: for example, *ardent desire* sounds more formal than *burning desire*, and an *ardent admirer* seems more sophisticated than a *great* or *keen admirer*. *muscle* is also a typical Latinate loanword, in that it is a medical term in its early history, and has only subsequently spread into more general use.

On the other hand, loanwords from Latin and French seem more likely to express the kinds of meaning that metaphorical senses convey, i.e. more abstract and/or less experientially basic senses, and this suggests that many or even most historical metaphors may be borrowed lexemes. There are certainly other examples that show similarities to the cases considered here: *pedigree* and *comprehend* (discussed in Allan 2014) have comparable histories, and *fervent* may also be similar, although more examination of its early history and contexts of use in English is needed to establish this. Assessing whether these examples represent a more general pattern, and whether it is typical for loanwords to be borrowed principally with their etymologically metaphorical senses, seems problematic, particularly since it is difficult to find any systematic way to identify a representative sample of historical metaphors. However, a tool that may offer some clues about the likelihood of such a pattern is *HTOED*. Figures 2 and 3 present two of the sections of *HTOED* in which *ardent* occurs, and which correspond to its etymologically literal and metaphorical senses.

Figure 2 presents the sections *Hot, Very hot* and *Burning hot* (subsections of 01.04.03.03.02 *Of/pertaining to heat*), and Figure 3 presents *Ardent/fervent* and *Inflamed with passion* (subsections of 02.02.15.01 *Ardent/fervent*). These particular sections and subsections have been chosen because they yield a similar-sized sample for each semantic field (42 and 45 entries respectively), and therefore can be compared. In each table, borrowed words and their derived forms[10] have been emboldened, and constitute a significant percentage of the total number of entries.

01.04.03.03.02 *Of/pertaining to heat*
12 *Hot* hot<hat OE- · het c1375 scots&north · **chaud c1380**
12.04 *Very hot* weallende OE · wall-hot<wealhat OE-a1225 · walm-hot<wielmhat OE-a1225 · welling hot a1300-a1400/50 · **estuant c1420;1633** · burning 1483- · <u>**scalding 1500/20-1720**</u> · broiling 1555- · moultering 1606 · **boiling hot 1607;1862** · walming-hot 1610 · **aestuant 1633** · <u>**stewing-hot 1711-**</u> · <u>**roasting 1768/74-**</u> · baking 1786- · **grilling 1839** · seething 1848 · hot as blazes/hell 1849- · **stewing 1856-** · white-hot 1858rhet · **incandescent 1859** · swithering 1886-dl · **boiling 1930cq**
12.04.03 *Burning hot* biernende OE · brynehat OE · fyrhat OE · hatwende OE · sweoloþohat OE · fiery c1290- also fg · fire-hot 1398;1678 · <u>**fervent 1400/50-1874**</u> · **ardent c1440-** · firous 1503(2) · <u>**fervid 1599-now poet&rhet**</u> · <u>**torrid 1658-**</u> · flamatious 1688 · <u>**flaming 1697-**</u> · **phlogistic 1791-1855chief rhet**

Fig. 2: *Extracts from* HTOED.

In Figure 2, there are 42 entries in total, and 18 of these (43%) are loanwords or loanword-derived; however, many of these borrowed lexemes are supported by very limited quotation evidence in *OED2*. The case studies of *inculcate* and *ardent* above demonstrate that it is difficult to make a judgement about how established particular senses are without looking closely at available examples, but in order to look at a body of data it seems reasonable to assume that any entries with only one or two attestations show rare and infrequent uses (although this is fairly conservative). Lexemes which are attested more than twice (with the relevant sense) have therefore been underlined, and there are 10 of these (i.e. 24%). *ardent* has already been discussed, and a brief look at the quotation evidence shows that some others are found in fairly restricted

---

[10] I have included derived forms with loanwords, but this is somewhat simplistic: in some cases, new forms are derived from loanwords that have been borrowed much earlier, and it is difficult to classify these as either loans or derivations from the existing resources of the language.

contexts: *fervid* and *phlogistic* are labeled "now poetic and rhetorical" and "chiefly rhetorical" respectively, and *torrid* tends to be used in a slightly narrower sense than most of the other entries, specifically to describe the weather. Four of the remaining six entries in this group, *scalding, roasting, stewing* and *flaming*, are all derived from verbs that were borrowed into English earlier. Overall, the data presented from this semantic area seems to show a relatively low level of borrowing of lexemes which become established in the language beyond very infrequent and restricted use.

02.02.15.01 *Ardent/fervent*
brandhat OE · fyrenful OE · hatheort OE · weallende OE · hot<hat OE- · fired a1300-a1340 · burning a1340- · firely 1340 · **ardent c1374-** · fiery c1385- · warm 1390-now rare · **fervent c1400-** · fire-burning 1562 · glowing a1577- · **fervorous 1602-1669;1920** · **torrid 1646-** · **fervid 1656/81-** · candent 1723 · **ardurous a1770-chief poet** · **ferverous 1800-1820 also transf** · tropic 1802 · **tropical 1834-** · aestuous 1844 · thermal 1866 · thermonous 1888poet

04 *Inflamed with passion*
onbryrd/inbryrd OE · fire-hot<fyrhat OE-1605 fig · **eschaufed c1374** · on afire a1400/50 · **inflammate c1450** · **inflamed 1526-1746/7** · **enkindled 1549/62-** · on fire 1553 · burnt/burned a1564;1859 · **boiling 1579-** · seething 1588- · heated 1593- · red-hot 1608- · **incensed 1612-1694** · in a fire 1641 · **on flame 1656-** · **in a flame 1685-1790** · ablaze c1840- · **aflame 1856-** · **incandescent 1859-**

Fig. 3: *Extracts from* HTOED.

The data in Figure 3, from the section *Ardent*, seems to present a different picture, and one which is consistent with the idea that semantic fields which relate to less basic meanings associated with metaphorical senses are likely to show a higher proportion of established loanwords. There are 45 entries in this dataset, and 23 of these (i.e. just over half) are borrowed or loanword-derived. Again, some of these show very minor use, and subtracting all lexemes with only one or two attestations in *OED2* leaves a total of 16[11], 35.5% of this total

---

[11] It is notable that several of the lexemes in the section cluster into groups of related forms: for example, the group includes four entries ultimately derived from Latin *fervēre*, i.e. *fervent, fervorous, fervid,* and *ferverous*, and five from Latin *flamma*, i.e. *inflammate, inflamed, on flame, in a flame* and *aflame* (though in each case not all of these lexemes are borrowed directly from Latin). It seems likely that some of these forms had limited use, since they are likely to have been in competition to some extent. However, all are attested several times with this sense.

group. *ardurous* is the only one with a label showing restricted use, and is marked as "chiefly poetic".

In itself, this analysis of these sections of *HTOED* cannot be taken to be definitive; much more evidence is needed, ideally along with a full analysis of each lexeme. However, it seems to be consistent with the hypothesis that loanwords with metaphorical senses in the source language are most likely to retain these senses and to lose their literal senses in the process of being borrowed. It may also be true that most historical metaphors are also etymological, although again this cannot be asserted with certainty; almost all examples cited in the literature on historical metaphor are loanwords, but a larger survey is needed to provide more convincing evidence that these reflect a more general pattern.

6 Conclusion

The aim of this paper was to examine what happens to etymologically metaphorical loanwords in English, and to consider whether their semantic histories might show similarities. The histories of *muscle*, *inculcate* and *ardent* suggest strongly that the process of borrowing has a major effect on the meanings of loanwords, and makes it highly likely that not all senses of a metaphor will become established in a borrowing language (or at least in English, the focus of this paper). The systematic nature of the lexicon makes it unlikely that basic meanings will be conventionally expressed by loanwords where native lexemes already exist with these meanings; metaphorical senses, which are typically less experientially basic and more abstract, are much more likely to be borrowed and to become the dominant senses of borrowed lexemes. This explains why many historical metaphors are also etymological metaphors. As well as this, the relationship between English and the languages which it borrows from appears to have an effect on the semantic development of loanwords from these languages: all three lexemes discussed in this paper have Latin or French origins, like a significant proportion of loanwords in English, and their provenance makes it much more likely that they will become stylistically-marked, high-register lexemes. Such lexemes frequently belong to technical vocabularies or express abstract notions. A preliminary survey of data for two semantic fields in the *Historical Thesaurus of the Oxford English Dictionary* appears to corroborate the tendency for loanwords to retain metaphorical rather than literal meanings, and investigation of a number of different sections could provide further evidence.

The case studies presented here also show that it is not unusual for loanwords that show the kind of semantic development discussed above to be attested in English a relatively small number of times with their etymologically literal senses. This may be explained by the linguistic situation in England in earlier times: in both the Middle and Early Modern English periods, when large numbers of loanwords were borrowed from French and Latin, there was less separation between English and these languages, though for different reasons. In the Middle English period, the effects of the Norman Conquest meant that there was widespread contact between speakers of English and French; both had specific functions in medieval England, with French the more prestigious language, widely used in written contexts, including in the law and in record keeping. Latin was also widely used, including in the church, and (like French) in the law and in record keeping. A large proportion of speakers would have used or understood all three languages to some extent, and this led to large-scale borrowing into English. In the Early Modern period, contact between languages was not the result of contact between speakers, but a corollary of the status of French and Latin as international languages of culture and scholarship, and a revival of interest in classical learning which made Latin works particularly influential. By this time, English was taking over many of the roles that had been fulfilled by French and Latin in the Middle English period, and there was widespread agreement that the language needed to be improved and the lexicon enlarged; borrowing from French and Latin was an important source of new vocabulary. This was a period of great lexical experimentation, which was marked by "an overzealous desire to enrich the Early Modern English lexicon" (Nevalainen 1999: 349). This makes it unsurprising that lexemes like *inculcate* should be attested with the senses of their etymons, but equally unsurprising that not all senses attested in English should become conventional.

The case studies presented in this paper show the importance of fine-grained analysis of data. Both the contexts of use of the lexemes examined and the nature of the material in which they are found offer clues about why they show particular meanings in English. As well as this, their semantic histories need to be considered within a broader historical context which recognises broader trends in linguistic and cultural history: only then can their particular pathways of semantic development in English be fully understood.

References

Allan, Kathryn. 2012. Using *OED* data as evidence. In Kathryn Allan & Justyna A. Robinson (eds.), *Current methods in historical semantics*, 17–39. Berlin & New York: Mouton de Gruyter.

Allan, Kathryn. 2014. An inquest into metaphor death: Exploring the loss of literal senses of conceptual metaphors. *Cognitive Semiotics* 5(1–2). 291–311.

Burnley, David. 1992. Lexis and semantics. In Norman Blake (ed.) *The Cambridge history of the English language: Volume 2, 1066–1476*, 409–99. Cambridge: Cambridge University Press.

Coulson, Seanna. 2006. Metaphor and conceptual blending. In Keith Brown (ed.) *Encyclopedia of language and linguistics*, 2nd edn. Volume 8, 32–39. Oxford: Elsevier.

Deignan, Alice. 2005. *Metaphor in corpus linguistics*. Amsterdam & Philadelphia: John Benjamins.

Divasson, Lourdes & Isabel León. 2006. Metaphors in English, French, and Spanish medical written discourse. In Keith Brown (ed.) *Encyclopedia of language and linguistics*, 2nd edn. Volume 8, 56–63. Oxford: Elsevier.

Durkin, Philip. 2009. *The Oxford guide to etymology*. Oxford: Oxford University Press.

Durkin, Philip. 2014. *Borrowed words: A history of loanwords in English*. Oxford: Oxford University Press.

Early English Books Online. 1999–. http://eebo.chadwyck.com/home, accessed August 2012.

Goatly, Andrew. 2007. *Washing the brain: Metaphor and hidden ideology*. Amsterdam & Philadelphia: John Benjamins.

Goatly, Andrew. 2011. *The language of metaphors*, 2nd edn. London: Routledge.

Katamba, Francis. 2005. *English words*, 2nd edn. London: Routledge.

Kövecses, Zoltan. 2000a. *Metaphor and emotion: Language, culture, and body in human feeling*. Cambridge: Cambridge University Press.

Kövecses, Zoltan. 2000b. The scope of metaphor. In Antonio Barcelona (ed.), *Metaphor and metonymy at the crossroads: A cognitive perspective*, 79–92. Berlin & New York: Mouton de Gruyter.

Kövecses, Zoltan. 2005. *Metaphor in culture: Universality and variation*. Cambridge: Cambridge University Press.

Lakoff, George. 1987. The death of dead metaphor. *Metaphor and symbolic activity* 2(2). 143–147.

Nevalainen, Terttu. 1999. Early Modern English lexis and semantics. In Roger Lass (ed.), *The Cambridge history of the English language, Vol. 3, Early Modern English 1476–1776*, 332–458. Cambridge: Cambridge University Press.

Rothwell, William. 2005. Preface: Anglo-French and the AND. In *The Anglo-Norman Dictionary*, 2nd edn. Volume I A–C. London: Modern Humanities Research Association v–xx.

Scheler, Manfred. 1977. *Der Englische Wortschatz*. Berlin: Erich Schmidt.

Steen, Gerard. 2007. *Finding metaphor in grammar and usage: A methodological analysis of theory and research*. Amsterdam & Philadelphia: John Benjamins.

Traugott, Elizabeth Closs. 1985. "Conventional" and "dead" metaphors revisited. In Wolf Paprotté & René Dirven (eds.), *The ubiquity of metaphor: Metaphor in language and thought*, 17–56. Amsterdam & Philadelphia: John Benjamins.

Traugott, Elizabeth Closs & Richard B. Dasher. 2005. *Regularity in semantic change*. Cambridge: Cambridge University Press.

Ullmann, Stephen. 1959. *The principles of semantics*. Oxford: Basil Blackwell.
Weinreich, Uriel. 1964. *Languages in contact: Findings and problems*. The Hague: Mouton.

Dictionaries and Thesauri

The Anglo-Norman Dictionary. 1977–1992. Louise W. Stone, T. B. W. Reid & William Rothwell (eds.). London: The Modern Humanities Research Association (2nd edition online), www.anglo-norman.net, accessed August 2012.

Collins COBUILD English Dictionary (2nd revised edition). 1995. John Sinclair (ed.). London: Harper Collins.

Dictionnaire du Moyen Français. 2012. ATILF – CNRS and Université de Lorraine. http://www.atilf.fr/dmf/ accessed August 2012.

The Historical Thesaurus of the Oxford English Dictionary. 2009. Christian Kay, Jane Roberts, Michael Samuels & Irené Wotherspoon (eds.). Oxford: Oxford University Press.

The Middle English Dictionary. 1952–2001. Hans Kurath, Sherman Kuhn & Robert E. Lewis (eds.). Ann Arbor: University of Michigan Press. http://quod.lib.umich.edu/m/med/, accessed August 2012.

Oxford Advanced Learner's Dictionary of Current English (7th edition). 2005. Hornby, Albert S. (ed.). Oxford: Oxford University Press.

Oxford Dictionary of English. 2010. Catherine Soanes & Angus Stevenson (eds.). Oxford: Oxford University Press.

Oxford English Dictionary (OED) Online 2000– http://dictionary.oed.com, accessed August 2012.

Oxford Latin Dictionary. 1982. P.G.W. Glare (ed.). Oxford: Oxford University Press. *Le Trésor de la Langue Française Informatisé*. 2002. http://atilf.atilf.fr/, accessed August 2012.

Xavier Dekeyser
Loss of prototypical meaning and lexical borrowing:
A case of semantic redeployment

"To starve or to die?"

Abstract: Lexical loss in general is a well documented process, while loss of the core meaning of a word is less highlighted, or hardly so. This facet of lexical semantics very well fits in with the paradigm of prototype semantics, the main tenet of which is that the make-up of a lexical item consists of more or less polysemous clusters of meaning with blurry boundaries. These meanings are characterized by differences in prominence: so some have a central or so-called prototypical status, while others are rather peripheral components. What are the diachronic implications of these properties? Not only are the prototypical cores more salient, they also tend to subsist over longer periods of time; by contrast, peripheral meanings are less stable and often do not survive for very long. In diachronic studies that aim at an overall outline from the very beginning the oldest (ancestral) meaning is assumed to be the prototype, being the historical epicentre from which all the other meanings subsequently radiate. Yet, in the course of time this centre can recede into the background or even get lost throughout in particular onomasiological configurations. In my eyes prototype semantics seems to have overlooked this aspect of semantic change. In this paper, then, I will focus on two lexical sets: *deal*, noun and verb, and *starve* to demonstrate that prototypes can and do get lost. However, describing what happened is one thing, explaining it is another. Onomasiological availability of more prestigious or frequent loanwords may have prompted this semantic restructuring. But there is a more plausible motivation. Indeed, native speakers tend to prefer conceptualization by means of lexical items whose core meaning is more exclusively associated with a given concept rather than items characterized by marked, often dysfunctional, polysemy. Given the abundance of borrowed words in the English lexicon this is more often than not a loanword, but not necessarily so. This aspect of diachronic semantics is actually an instance of cognitively motivated semantic redeployment through time, aimed at increased semantic transparency. It will also be demonstrated that both metonymy and metaphor play a major role in this process.

Xavier Dekeyser: University of Leuven and University of Antwerp

1 Introduction

In the 1990's I did some research in the field of diachronic semantics, making use of prototype semantics as my paradigm (Dekeyser 1990: 35–48, Dekeyser 1991: 153–162, Dekeyser 1994: 289–299, Dekeyser 1995: 127–136, and Dekeyser 1998: 63–71). In the present paper my aim is to resume and further elaborate this matter. Lexical loss in general is a very common and well described linguistic process, while loss of the prototypical core of a word is less known, if known at all.

This facet of semantic analysis very well fits in with the paradigm of prototype semantics, as will be demonstrated in what follows. The main tenet of prototype semantics is that the make-up of a lexical item consists of more or less polysemous clusters of meaning with blurry boundaries. These meanings are characterized by differences in salience or prominence; so some have a central or so-called prototypical status, while others are rather peripheral components surrounding the core. See Geeraerts (1997: 10–11). What are the historical implications of these properties? Not only are the prototypical cores more salient, they also seem to subsist over longer periods of time, while peripheral meanings are more or less ephemeral and so tend not to survive for very long. Again see Geeraerts (1992: 186–187).

In diachronic studies like this, which aim at an overall outline from the very beginning, the oldest (ancestral) meaning, insofar as discoverable, is assumed to be the prototype: it can be seen as the historical epicentre from which all the other meanings subsequently radiate. Yet, in the course of time this centre may assume a marginal status or recede into the background. It is even possible for a prototypical meaning to get lost throughout in particular onomasiological configurations. It was argued in Dekeyser (1998: 63–71) that (diachronic) prototype semantics seems to have overlooked this aspect of semantic change. In this paper, then, I will focus on two lexical cases: *deal*, noun and verb, and *starve* to demonstrate, once more, that it is possible for prototype meanings to be infringed upon by borrowed more or less synonymous lexemes.

The approach we have adopted in this analysis is predominantly an **onomasiological** one: we start from a given concept, say "die", and try to find out what the lexical items are that actually express it. By contrast, **semasiology** is concerned with the analysis of the meaning(s) of a particular word, e.g. *starve*, often in terms of semantic polysemy. Whenever relevant, this type of semantic analysis will also be used occasionally. In other words, this paper actually constitutes an interface between two aspects of semantics. See also Geeraerts (1997): 17.

2 *DEAL* (noun and verb)

2.1 Old English

Onomasiologically the lexical set *dæl, (to)dælan* expresses the prototypical concept broadly related to "divide", as their analogues still do in present-day Dutch, *deel* and *(ver)delen* and German *Teil, (er)teilen*. For the sake of brevity, we will ignore a few minor phonological/ morphological variants, such as *dal* and *todal*.

Let us first adduce some examples for the noun. Unless stated otherwise, the examples and the sources referred to below can be found in Bosworth (1972: 194 and 995).[1]

(1) Ex. 29, 36, 40 *ðu offrast teoðan **dæl** smedeman*.
    Thou shalt offer a tenth part of flour.

(2) Bt. 33, 2; Fox 122, 26 *Hi heora god on swa manige **dælas todæleð***.
    They divide their goods into so many parts.

We should also note the peripheral meaning 'part of speech', as in:

(3) Aelfc. Gr. 2 *We **todælað** ða boc to cwydum, and siððan ða cwydas to **dælum**, eft ða **dælas** to stæfgefegum*.
    We divide the book into sentences, and then the sentences into words (parts), again the words into syllables.

The verbs *dælan* and *todælan* express the concept of "dividing", as in (2) and (3) above. However, more often than not this shades off into "distribute", i.e. to divide and give it to others; see also (2) above.

(4) Cd. 52 *Mathusal magum **dælde** gestreon*.
    Mathusalah distributed the treasures to/among his brothers.

Such examples nicely instantiate one of the major characteristics of prototype semantics, viz. that categories are non-discrete, i.e. blurred at the edges, as pointed out above (Geeraerts (1997: 25).

---

[1] In all of the quotations in this paper the relevant lexical items are printed in bold type so as to give them more prominence.

Todælan developed a great number of related peripheral meanings that we do not need to go into here, as we are not primarily concerned with detailed semasiological analyses. In what follows we will briefly deal with new semantic developments in ME and EMODE. We can leave *todelen* out of consideration, seeing that it got lost by the end of the ME period (see MED and OED).

2.2 Middle and (Early) Modern English

2.2.1 In this section all our quotations are taken from the MED. As a matter of fact, the meanings of OE *dæl/dælan* also occur in ME: language and language change is a continuum. Example (5) bears on the noun, while (6–7) bear on the verb.

(5) (a1387) Trev. *Higd.* (StJ-C H.1) *Temse departeð hem from ðe oðer dele of Engelond.*

(6) a1225 (c1200) *Vices & V.* (1) (Stw.34) *ðu dalst al ðat tu hafst.*

(7) (a 1387) Trev. *Higd.* (StJ-C H.1) *ðis werke I departe and dele in bookes.*

In (6) it is shown once again how the notion "divide" can shade into "distribute" or "share", while (7) is an example of ME *delen* occurring as a doublet by the side of the loan *departing*. The most dramatic innovation in Late ME is the emergence of the meaning "have to do with":

(8) (c1395) Chaucer *CT.CY* (Manly Rickert) *Noght wiste this preest with whom that he delte.*

Clearly, this category underlies most of the (Early) MODE meanings and as such seems to have acquired the status of a new prototype. However, its derivation from the OE prototypical meaning is anything but clear, at least at first sight. A plausible explanation could be that the concept of "distribute" is metaphorically generalized; indeed, if one distributes something, one has to do (deal) with someone else.

2.2.2 Semasiologically, the history of the items involved is marked by two opposite trends in MODE: semantic expansion on the one hand and loss on the other. The verb *deal* developed a variety of new meanings that are broadly related to the concept "have to do with", which emerged in Late ME, more particularly in Chaucerian English, as shown above in (8), and normally in collocations with the prepositions *with* or *in*. As a noun *deal* began to express new metaphorical meanings, such as "a particular type of treatment, an agreement, a bargain", etc. For more details see the relevant quotations in the OED.

However, the verb as well as the noun lost their (OE) prototypical meanings in the course of the same period. By and large, all but a few of the latest OED quotations date from Early MODE. A relic from the past can be found in the verb *deal* often with *out* in the meaning of "distribute", and transitive *deal* in the context of a card game, while the noun still occurs in its prototypical meaning in the grammaticalized quantifiers *a great/good deal of*.

2.2.3 In Late ME the onomasiological set expressing the concept "divide" was extended or enriched with a number of loanwords from French and/or Latin: *part* and *portion* as nouns, *divide* and also *depart* for the verb. Here follow a few of the earliest attestations: *part* (9 and 10), *portion* (10 and 11) and *partie*, a variant of *part* (12)

(9) (a1382) *WBible (1)* (Bod 959) Ecclus . 37.21: *A shrewde word schal change ðe herte of the whiche foure **partis** (L partes) springen: good and euel, lijf & deð.*

(10) (c1400) *Bk.Mother* (Bod 416) 99/4: *A man hadde two sones: and ðe younger seide, 'Fadir, yif me the **porcioun** of ðe substaunce ðat falleð to me.' And ðe fadur yaf to him his **part**.*

(11) (a1387) Trev. Higd. (St-C H.1) 1.99 *ðe norð est **porcioun** (L portio) of Arabia hatte Saba.*

(12) (c1385) Chaucer *CT.Kn.* (Manly Rickert) A 3008: *Nature hath nat taken his bigynnyng Of no **partie** of a thing.*

And here are a few examples to illustrate the borrowing of verbs. To begin with, "dividen" can occur in its mathematical sense (13), but mostly it is used in more comprehensive meanings, such as "divide" and "separate" (14–15).

(13) (c1450) *Art Number.* (Ashm 396) 43/21: *For to **dyvyde** oo nombre by a-nother.*

(14) (c1375) Chaucer *CT.Mk.* (Manly Rickert) B 3424: ***Dyvyded** is thy regne, and it shal be To Medes and to Perses yeve.*

(15) c1450 (1410) Walton *Boeth.* (Lin – C 103) p.162: *That þing may not be **devided** propirly.*

ME "departen", which in present-day English normally only occurs in the peripheral meaning of "leave, go away", peripheral from a historical point of view, was also used to express the prototypical concept of "divide". See (5) above and particularly (7), where it is clearly synonymous with native *delen*. And here is another example from Chaucer, in which both *depart* and *divide* occur:

(16) ?a 1425 (c1380) Chaucer *Bo.* (Benson – Robinson) 3.pr.11.166: *The thinges that ben softe and fletynge … **departen** lightly and yeven place to hem that breken or **devyden** hem.*

Let us now turn to *starve*, whose story is somewhat different, as a matter of course.

3 STARVE

3.1 Old English

It appears from the OE material collected by Malgorzata Klos in a paper which she presented for the "Medieval English Studies Symposium", November 20–21, 2010 Poznan, that all but a few lexical items to express the concept "die" are metaphorical (euphemistic) expressions and/or periphrases, such as *geendian lif*, *gast agiefan*, etc. By far the commonest is *forðferan/forðfaran*.

(17) Anglo-Saxon Chron. *Her Marcus se godspellere **forðferde**.*
In this year Marc the evangelist passed away.
(quoted by Margorzata Klos)

Typically, the "literal" expression *sweltan* is only scarcely attested, while *steorfan* does not seem to occur at all, at least not in the corpus involved, which proves it to be utterly uncommon.
Here are two examples from Bosworth, resp. anno 948 and 917:

(18) Bt. 18, 4 *Ealle men **sweltað**.*
Everybody dies.

(19) Lchdm. Iii 188, 21 *Se ðe gelið raðe he **styrfð** oððe genunge he ariseð.*
He that takes to his bed, soon he will die or he will be up again.

Considering the specific context of this study we will only briefly outline the lexico–semantic development of both *sweltan* and *steorfan* in ME/EMODE.

3.2 Middle and (Early) Modern English: lexical loss and semantic change

3.2.1 The relevant data in the MED indicate that *sterven* (20–21) is still commonly used in its literal meaning of "die, cease to exist". Note that in (21) it co-occurs with "dien", which proves it to be still (broadly) synonymous, even in very Late ME, with the Scandinavian loan; see 3.2.2 below.

(20) (c1390) Chaucer *CT.Mel.* (Manly Rickert) B 2231:*Ther is ful many a child vnborn of his modor that shal* **sterve** *yong by cause of thilke werre.*

(21) (a1500) (?1450) *Merlin* (Cmb Ff. 3.11) 401: *Kynge Claudas ... er he* **dyed** *... hadde euell myschef, ffor he* **starf** *in grete age disherited.*

The MED also contains a great many quotations related to *sterven* to express the concept of "die in a specified state or condition", such as "sterven in sinne", sometimes with a metaphorical connotation as in (22):

(22) (c1385) Chaucer *CT.Kn.* (Manly – Rickert) A. 1249: *Wel oghte I* **sterve** *in wanhope and distresse.*

In the same context, and in view of the topic of this paper, it should be stressed that the meaning "die from hunger" is frequently attested as well:

(23) a 1126 *Peterb.Chron.* (LdMisc 636) an. 1124: *Ful heui gær wæs hit se man þe æni god hæfde: him me hit be ræfode mid strange geoldes & mid strange motes: þe nan ne heafde* **stærf** *of hungor.*

(24) (c1300) *Sleg.Magd.* (2) (LdMisc 108) 244: *Muche me ðinchez wunder ðat ðou last Iesu cristes folk ðus* **steorue** *for hungur.*

The MED entry about *swelten* is considerably shorter and less elaborate than the one for its analogue *sterven*. Does this indirectly foreshadow the beginning of an ongoing demise in Late Middle English and afterwards?

(25) (? c1200) Orm. (Jun 1) 5833: *Crist ras upp off dæðe ... Fra ðatt he* **swalt** *o rode.*

(26) (a1450) *Yk.Pl.* (Add 35290) 428/56: *In to his harte thraly ðei thraste ... ðat swetthyng full swiftly he* **swelted.**

3.2.2 In large parts of England, mainly in the North, Scandinavian dialects had been co-occurring with English, so it is not surprising that some Scandinavian lexemes were increasingly used in the native language as well; see Dekeyser, Anglica (2011): 27–35. *Dien* is one of these (early) loans, which was added to the English onomasiological set expressing the notion of "cease to exist". Was there a lexical need for this borrowing? Gevaert (2007: 207–210) convincingly demonstrated that late ME could do without the loan *anger* in the semantic field of "ire" or "wrath". In much the same way our data seem to suggest that this also holds for *dien*, but a semasiological analysis of this matter, however concise, is clearly outside the scope of this paper.[2]

The MED quotation from *Holy Rood* apparently shows the very first occurrence of *dien* in the history of written English:

(27) c1175 (? OE) HRood (Bod 343) 14/25: *Forðan ðe ic nu **deghen** sceal*

The new lexical item must already have been firmly established in the lexicon of Early ME, seeing that in (28) it is used to gloss *gewiten* "pass over, depart" instead of the native verbs.

(28) c1225 Wor. Bod.Gloss. (Hat 115) 23: *Gewat: **deide**.*

The ascendance of the Scandinavian loan in EME, mainly in the North and Westmidlands and later in all the other dialects, is abundantly documented in the data in Klos (2010a).This expansion is matched by a gradual shrinking of the native verbs.

Examples like (21) above clearly demonstrate that the loanword had broadly become synonymous with *sterven*. Here follow two more instances, this time from Late ME:

(29) (a1470) Malory Wks. (Win-C) 21/4: *Ye shall **dey** other be prisoners.*

(30) c1475 (c1445) Pecock *Donet* (Bod 916) 8/36: *Schal ðe soule of a man **dye** and come to nought, whanne ðat we seen ðilk man **deie**?*

3.2.3 The development of *swelt* was characterized by lexical loss across the board in the course of Early MODE., probably ascribable to the co-existence of no fewer than three semantically related verbs expressing the notion of "die" (lexical redundancy).

---

[2] In this context, an interesting analysis of the pair *niman* vs. *taken* can be found in Toupin (2005: 13–38). For an overall survey of borrowing from Scandinavian the reader is referred to Dekeyser (2011: 27–35).

It still features in the OED, yet marked as dialectal. On this score the following OED quotation is very telling and significant:

(31) 1794 W. Hutchinson *Hist. Cumbld*. I. 220 *note: Provincial words:* **swelting** *for expiring.*

Apart from the metaphorical peripheral extension "die from hunger", the Scandinavian loanword *die* was and is typically associated with its prototypical meaning. By contrast, the crucial semantic innovations are to be found in *starve*.

For one thing, the core meaning got lost; one of the latest OED quotations is:

(32) 1590 Spenser *F.Q*. II. VI. 34: *These armes ... the which doe men in baleto* **sterue.**

Typically, in MODE "die from hunger" has assumed the status of a new prototypical meaning, extended to "be very hungry" and to the meaning of "to long for something or someone greatly wanted" (e.g. to starve for affection). See the OED or any modern scholarly dictionary for more details. The (new) core meaning is an example of semantic shrinking, while the second stage is an outstanding instance of metonymy: indeed, the underlying meaning shows a cause (hunger)- result (death) relationship shifting to cause, which can then assume a metaphorical dimension.

It is very remarkable that transitive *starve,* which emerged as late as ca. 1500 (see MED and OED on that score) but is now currently used in present-day English, roughly developed the same semantic pattern: "cause to die" (now lost just like the prototypical meaning of its intransitive analogue), then "cause to die of hunger" and mainly in the passive also metonymical/metaphorical "be deprived of" (e.g. to be starved of attention / for affection). Now the time has come to draw (tentative) conclusions.

4 Concluding remarks

The semasiological structures of the lexical items that have been highlighted in this paper exhibit, contrary to expectations, across-the-board loss of their prototype, while peripheral meanings and younger cores prove to be more resilient through time and often develop their full potential. What stands out is that the onomasiological configuration can and does have an impact on the semantic make-up of a lexical item: indeed, in each of the cases involved a core meaning is pushed aside when there is another suitable lexeme available that conceptualizes the same meaning more adequately, as shown in the following schematic representation, in which the onomasiological aspect is presented as horizontal, while the semasiological one can be inferred from the vertical arrangement:

THE SEMASIOLOGICAL/ONOMASIOLOGICAL INTERFACE			
1. DEAL (n.) and PART, etc.			
DEAL:	(a) "part", "portion" (b) "Transaction" (c) etc.	⟶	PART, etc.
2. DEAL (v.) and DIVIDE, etc.			
DEAL:	(a) "To divide", "To separate" (b) "To have to do with" (c) "To do business" (d) etc.	⟶	DIVIDE, etc.
3. STARVE and DIE			
STARVE:	(a) "To pass away", "perish" (b) "To die from hunger" (c) "To be very hungry" (d) etc.	⟶	DIE

This claim is further substantiated in a brief survey in Dekeyser (1998 : 69) for the sets: *haven* and *port* (involving metaphorization of the former), *harvest* and *autumn* (metonymy in *harvest*) , multifarious *fare* vs. *travel, journey* and *voyage;* for *seethe* and *boil* see Bator (2011); also in some native sets, such as the multal quantifier *much,* originally expressing "extent" in OE versus *large, great, big*; other cases include *sell* , which in OE meant both "give" and "sell" as opposed to unambiguous *give,* and some more. Recently (Dekeyser 2012) I have been concerned with the grammaticalization and, subsidiarily, also the metaphorization of Old English *butan* to present-day *but.* Once again it appears that the earliest layer (or the prototype) 'outside' got lost in the course of Middle English and was lexically replaced with *outside (of),* while initially peripheral (metaphorical) meanings like "except" and later the meaning of "contrast" fully developed their potential as essential semantic components.

A more fundamental question that needs to be addressed here concerns the cognitive motivation, if any, for such developments. Indeed, to merely describe what happened is one thing, to account for it is another. When loans are involved the presence of a prestigious or frequent variant may, at first sight, account for this phenomenon. But, of course, this does not hold for native sets. In addition, the semantic changes involved took place well after these foreign words got introduced.

Cross-linguistically, however, there is some evidence suggesting that loans may well have enhanced the tendency towards loss of the prototypical core in English. For one thing, the Dutch and German analogues *deel – delen* and *Teil – teilen* have preserved their original meaning, there being no loanwords available. Very remarkably, the same holds for Dutch *sterven* and German *sterben*. Though we should beware of a *cum hoc propter hoc* process of reasoning here, I wonder whether this is a matter of mere coincidence.

Yet, there is a more plausible motivation. Native speakers tend to prefer conceptualization by means of lexical items that are exclusively, or almost so, and unambiguously associated with a given concept rather than items characterized by marked (dysfunctional?) polysemy, as shown in each of the items we have examined, which seems to be an instance of what Geeraerts (1997: 125) calls "polysemiophobia". Given the impressive abundance of borrowed items in the English lexicon, this is mostly a loanword, initially more or less monosemous, but not necessarily so. As evidenced by the chronological data, this is a very gradual process difficult to trace exactly and taking several centuries before it is fully implemented; in the set *starve* and *die* even half a millennium is involved. Actually, this aspect of diachronic semantics is an instance of cognitively motivated semantic redeployment through time, aimed at increased semantic transparency.

The available data also suggest that loss of the core meaning and the resulting semantic redeployment are only possible in a particular onomasiological configuration, if the remaining meanings constitute a coherent semasiological cluster around (new) prototypes, which is clearly the case in each of the sets of lexical items analysed here and also in Dekeyser (1998). To conclude, the aim of this study is to draw attention to these and similar diachronic configurations and, above all, to outline an adequate descriptive model to accommodate them.

References

Primary sources

Bosworth, Joseph & T. Northcote Toller (eds.). 1972. (repr.) *An Anglo-Saxon Dictionary*. Oxford: Oxford University Press.
Middle English Dictionary Online (= MED). 2001. Ann Arbor: University of Michigan Press.
Oxford English Dictionary Online (= OED). 2008. Oxford: Oxford University Press.

Secondary sources

Bator, Magdalena. 2011. Boil vs. seethe in Middle English. Paper read at the 10th Medieval English Studies Symposium. Poznan 19–20 November.
Dekeyser, Xavier. 1990. The prepositions WITH, MID and AGAIN(ST) in Old and Middle English: A case study of historical lexical semantics. *Belgian Journal of Linguistics* 5. 35–48.
Dekeyser, Xavier. 1991. Romance loans in late Middle English: A case study. *Cahiers de l'Institut de Linguistique de Louvain* 17(1–3). 153–162.
Dekeyser, Xavier. 1994. The multal quantifiers *much/many* and their analogues: A historical lexico- semantic analysis. *Leuvense Bijdragen* 83(4). 289–299.
Dekeyser, Xavier. 1995. Travel, journey and voyage: An exploration into the realm of Middle English lexico-semantics. *North-Western European Language Evolution* 25. 127–136.
Dekeyser, Xavier. 1998. Loss of prototypical meanings in the history of English semantics or semantic redeployment". In Richard M. Hogg & Linda van Bergen (eds.) *Historical Linguistics 1995. Selected papers from the 12th International Conference on Historical Linguistics. Volume 2: Germanic Linguistics*, 63–71. Amsterdam & Philadelphia: John Benjamins.
Dekeyser, Xavier. 2011. The influx of Scandinavian loans into Middle English: A long-lasting process. *Anglica* 20. 27–35.
Dekeyser, Xavier. 2012. From Old English *butan* to present-day *but*: A textbook case of grammaticalization. In Joanna Esquibel & Anna Wojtys (eds.), *Explorations in the English language: Middle Ages and beyond. Festschrift for Professor Jerzy Welna on the occasion of his 70th birthday*, 297–308. Bern: Peter Lang.
Geeraerts, Dirk. 1992. Prototypical effects in diachronic semantics: A round-up. In Gunter Kellermann & Michael D. Morrissey (eds.), *Diachrony within synchrony: Language, history and cognition*, 183–203. Bern: Peter Lang.
Geeraerts, Dirk. 1997. *Diachronic prototype semantics. A contribution to historical lexicology*. Oxford: Clarendon Press.
Gevaert, Caroline. 2007. *The history of ANGER: The lexical field of anger from Old to early Modern English*. Leuven: Katholieke Universiteit Leuven dissertation.
Klos, Malgorzata. 2010a. 'to die' in Early Middle English: *Deien, swelten* or *sterven*? In. Jacek Fisiak (ed.) Studies *in Old and Middle English*, 155–164. Bern: Peter Lang.

Klos, Malgorzata. 2010b. The taboo of death as reflected in language: Old English terms denoting 'to die'. Paper read at the 9th Medieval English Studies Symposium, Poznan, 21–22 November 2010.

Toupin, Fabienne. 2005. A medieval linguistic puzzle: The displacement of Anglo-Saxon *nimen* by Scandinavian *taken*. *Bulletin des Anglicistes Médiévistes* 68. 13–38.

Roslyn M. Frank
A complex adaptive systems approach to language, cultural schemas and serial metonymy: Charting the cognitive innovations of 'fingers' and 'claws' in Basque

Abstract: The chapter opens with a series of theoretical considerations that will be employed in the analysis of a single polysemous lexeme in Basque, namely, *hatz*. The section begins with an introduction to one of the principal instruments of analysis, an approach that allows language to be viewed a *complex adaptive system* (CAS). Next the scope of the CAS approach is enlarged so that it incorporates the notion of cultural schemas and their heterogeneously distributed nature. Then, the role of *serial metonymy* in semantic innovation and change is examined. These conceptual tools are applied to the analysis of the Basque data and to the exploration of the factors that contributed to the development and structuring of the resulting semantic network, particularly, to new senses such as 'fingers' and 'claws'. Finally, in the concluding section it is argued that this approach to modeling language and semantic change represents a powerful conceptual tool for researchers working in usage-based frameworks, and more specifically, for those investigating topics in the field of cognitive diachronic lexical semantics.

1 Introduction

The present chapter examines the senses that have evolved over time from a single Basque lexeme and attempts to chart the cognitive mechanisms that gave rise to them, mechanisms of semantic extension that, as will be shown, result primarily from instances of *serial metonymy*. These innovations take place against a background of cultural schemas – encyclopedic knowledge – that was accessed by speakers previously and, for the most part, is still recognizable today.

Roslyn M. Frank: University of Iowa

Initially, the paper lays out the theoretical approach that will be employed in the analysis of the polysemous nature of the Basque data set. The discussion begins by highlighting the advantages that can be gained by viewing language as a *complex adaptive system* (CAS). It moves on to examine the role played by cultural schemas in the CAS framework and the concept of serial metonymy. These tools of analysis, when applied to the analysis of the Basque data set, demonstrate that language, particularly the lexicon, acts both as a memory bank and a fluid vehicle for the (re-)transmission of cultural cognition and its component parts across time and space. In short, the paper argues in favour of applying the concept of serial metonymy and the expanded CAS model to research in diachronic lexical semantics.

2 Language viewed as a Complex Adaptive System (CAS)

In recent years, the usage-based approach to language has gained significant momentum (Kemmer and Barlow 2000). And at the same time increased attention has been focused on understanding language as a *complex adaptive system* (CAS) (Beckner et al. 2009; Frank 2008a; Frank and Gontier 2010; Steels 2000, 2002). Both these theoretical approaches are ones that are particularly appropriate in terms of their applications to the field of diachronic cognitive semantics, particularly, lexical semantics. Indeed, they are complementary. Whereas those working in cognitive linguistics are familiar with the usage-based approach, they are far less acquainted with the other framework and the fact that human language represents one of the most pervasive examples of a complex adaptive system, even though such dynamic systems are ubiquitous in nature. Typical examples include social insects, the ecosystem, the brain and the cell, the Internet, and also, in general, any human group-based, multi-agent endeavor that takes place within a sociocultural environment.

Over the past two decades the study of complex adaptive systems, a subset of nonlinear dynamical systems, has become a major focus of interdisciplinary research in the social and natural sciences (Lansing 2003). However, it is only recently that its applications to the study of human language have started to attract the attention of cognitive linguists. Broadly defined, a complex adaptive system is one that is self-organizing in which there are multiple interactions between many different components while the components themselves can consist of networks that in turn operate as complex (sub)systems. The actions of the agents take place at the local or micro-level of the system, while their actions feed into the overall system producing global level structures. Since the global and local levels are coupled, this coupling also drives the system to be dynamic at the global level (Hashimoto 1998). In short, a complex adaptive system is self-organizing: it is constantly constructed and reconstructed by its users.

As a result, a complex adaptative system is characterized by distributed control, that is, control is distributed throughout the system. Since the system has no centralized mechanism of control, CAS thinking is concerned with understanding the global behavior arising from local interactions among a large number of agents. Very often, this global behavior or emergent dynamics is complex; it is neither specified by prior design nor subject to a centralized locus of agency. And, consequently, it is often difficult or impossible to predict solely from knowledge of the system's constituent parts what the emergent global level properties of the system will be. In other words, complex systems are systems that constantly evolve over time. Thus change is an integral element of their functioning. Complex adaptive systems are adaptive in that they have the capacity to evolve in response to a changing environment, a capacity also known as adaptability.

The CAS approach to language states that *global order* derives from *local* interactions. Language agents are carriers of individual linguistic and encyclopedic knowledge which becomes overt behavior in local interactions between agents. Through these *local level* (microscopic) interactions agents construct and acquire individual ontologies, lexicons and grammars. When the latter are sufficiently entrenched within the system, they become part of the *global level* (macroscopic) properties of collective ontologies, lexicons and grammars of the speech community. The latter could be viewed as being held collectively by the group or speech community, understood as a whole. Actually, the process is even non-linear in the sense that individual ontologies, lexicons and grammars continuously contribute to and, in turn, are influenced by the global level. This perspective allows us to view language as a constantly evolving system that defies simplistic taxonomic, essentialist categorization. In short, language is understood as a multiagent complex adaptive system in which emergent phenomena result from behaviors of embodied, (socioculturally) situated agents.

Consequently, language is an outstanding example of a complex adaptive system, constantly constructed and reconstructed by its users. It is an emergent phenomenon, the result of *activity*, the collective, cumulative behavior of language agents over time. Built into the system is a type of recursiveness consisting of feedback mechanisms that link the two levels of the system together. The feedback loops introduce what is referred to as *circular* or *recursive causality* into the system. At the local level the cumulative effect of individual language agent's choices can translate into global level structures, held by and accessible to the collective as a whole. Similarly, at the local level the resulting emergent global level structures of language co-determine the range of behaviors of the agents at the local level, that is, the range of possible interactions at the local or micro-level.

As is well recognized, one of the hardest problems we face when addressing the question of the way semantic change takes place is the difficulty in locating the site of agency. This issue has often been compared to the problem of agency associated with "the theory of the invisible hand" (Geeraerts 2010b: 232–233), while language itself has been categorized as "a phenomenon of the third kind", based on the fact that it looks like something that was brought about by prior design, but was not (Keller 1994: 61–107). According to Keller who was writing before the concept of complex adaptive systems theory had fully crystallized, "phenomena of the third kind" can be perceived and described on the micro-level as well as on a macro-level. He compares language itself to something much more highly complex than a system of footpaths, yet similar in its constitution, an analogy that resonates strongly with complex adaptive systems thinking and the notion of circular causality. Moreover, today many of the systems that Keller listed as belonging to this class of "phenomena of the third kind" are regularly modeled using a complex adaptive systems framework where agency becomes distributed throughout the system.

3 Defining context: The role of encyclopedic knowledge and cultural schemas

When addressing approaches used in diachronic lexical semantics, the following quote is often cited: "Words do not convey meaning in themselves, they are *invested* with meaning according to the totality of the context. They only *have* meaning in so far as they are interpreted as *meaningful*, in so far as *the hearer attributes meaning to them in context*" (Nerlich 1990: 181; emphasis in original). The question that is often left unanswered, however, is exactly what is meant by "the totality of context". From a synchronic point of view, the answer is relatively simple, the context of the speech act along with the encyclopedic knowledge of the interlocutors which is viewed as a relatively stable element. When we shift our focus to the diachronic axis of the semantic data and the motivation behind polysemous senses that have become associated with the lexeme, the notion of context becomes more complex. Yet even from a synchronic point of view, the assumption that this encyclopedic knowledge is evenly distributed throughout a given speech community needs to be brought into question.

At this juncture it should be noted that cognitive linguists conducting work on historical lexical semantics are confronted with a large number of competing terms and conceptual frameworks. In other words, although significant progress has been made with respect to methodology, the manner in which extralinguistic knowledge is treated still varies widely and the terms used to deal with this aspect of language are frequently tied to specific frameworks. At times the same term or a highly similar one is employed whereas the definitions and theoretical frameworks that they reflect can be incompatible. Examples of these competing expressions are schemas, frames, scripts, fields (semantic fields, conceptual fields), domains, domain matrix, cultural models, idealized cognitive models (ICMs), to name only a few (cf. Cienki 2010; Barsalou 1992; Croft 1993; Nerlich and Clarke 2000).

None of these frameworks, however, operate from within the CAS approach to language which includes a series of assumptions about the relationship between world-knowledge and the speakers themselves that are particularly germane to historical cognitive semantics. At the micro-level, individual speakers will have slightly different understandings of the lexicon and the background cultural schemas that inform it. This results from different histories of interaction with other members of the language community and the degree to which the speaker is familiar with the cultural conceptualizations that support (or once supported) the senses associated with a given lexical item. Therefore, at the micro-level, we are confronted with heterogeneously distributed understandings and, consequently, their exteriorization in linguistic practice.

Sharifian has discussed the relationship between 'cultural schemas' and language from within the framework of CAS. Cultural schemas, understood at the macro-level, are culturally constructed schemas that operate at the collective, global level, and consequently, are shared, albeit heterogeneously, by the members of the social group and, more particularly, they are held intersubjectively by the members a speech community.[1] At the macro-level, cultural sche-

---

[1] As Sharifian observes, cultural schemas are part of the framework used by cognitive anthropologists for whom "culture is a cognitive system, and thus the notion of 'cultural schema' provides a useful tool to explore cognitive schemas that are culturally constructed across different societies and cultural groups. A term that closely overlaps with cultural schema and has again received major attention in cognitive anthropology is that of the 'cultural model'" (Sharifian 2014: 106). Cf. also D'Andrade (1995); Holland and Quinn (1987). The latter term, initially intended to displace 'folk models' (Keesing 1987), has also been employed in the sense of "a cognitive schema that is intersubjectively shared by a social group" (D'Andrade 1987: 112). D'Andrade repeatedly refers to the notion of 'schema' to explain his use of the term 'cultural model' while he regards models as complex cognitive schemas. Strauss and Quinn (1997) also

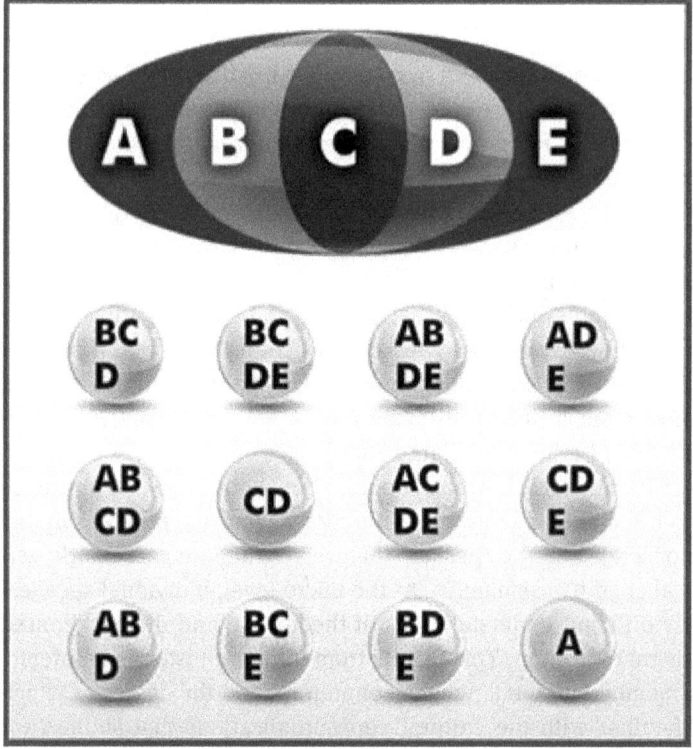

Fig. 1: Diagrammatic representation of a cultural schema (Sharifian 2014: 105).

mas emerge from interactions between the members of a cultural group, and they are constantly negotiated and renegotiated across time and space (Sharifian 2009, 2014).

At the micro-level, individuals have internalized their own version of these macro-level schemas, albeit in a heterogeneously distributed fashion. In other words individuals who belong to the same cultural group may share some, but not all, components of a given cultural schema. From this perspective, the way each person internalizes a macro-level cultural schema is to some extent col-

---

maintain that another term for cultural schemas (especially of the more complex sort) is 'cultural model'. Others such as Polzenhagen and Wolf (2007), however, have employed the term 'cultural model' to represent more general, overarching conceptualizations encompassing metaphors and schemas which are minimally complex (cf. Sharifian 2008, 2009, 2014).

lective and to some extent idiosyncratic.² This pattern is diagrammatically presented in *Figure 1*.

3.1 Interaction between macro-level cultural schemas and micro-level lexical schemas

Figure 1 shows how a cultural schema may be "represented in a heterogeneously distributed fashion across the minds of individuals. It schematically represents how members may have internalised some by not all components of a macro-level cultural schema. It also shows how individuals may share some, but not all the elements of a cultural schema" (Sharifian 2014: 106). In short, the features of these cultural schemas, instantiated globally at the macro-level, are accessed unevenly – heterogeneously – by individual members of the group.³

At the same time, because individual members of a speech community will not have internalized the macro-level cultural schemas exactly in the same way, it follows that the micro-level lexical networks associated with the schemas will not necessarily fully coincide. The differences, as will be shown in the case of the Basque data, can be influenced by variations in the lexical networks and cultural schemas entrenched in the particular dialect spoken by the language user. Over time, dialectal differences that have arisen locally can lead to innovations at the macro-level of the system, that is, when speakers of different dialects come into contact with each other.

As is well known, cultural variation in human behavior and linguistic expression depends on the wider sociocultural context. In fact, variation has long

---

2 These cultural schemas operate as cognitively backgrounded resources and are in some senses similar to Fillmore and Atkin's (1992: 76–77) notion of 'frames', which in turn have parallels with Lakoff's Idealized Cognitive Models: "[...] the notion of 'frame' [is used] to refer to the coherent set of beliefs and expectations that shape our way of thinking and talking about specific domains in the world [...]" (Geeraerts 2010b: 223). For a cogent overview of these competing terms and their corresponding theoretical frameworks, cf. Cienki 2010.

3 In a related fashion, although addressing the concept of prototypicality, Geeraerts (2010b: 188) states that "the clustering of meanings that is typical of family resemblances and radial sets implies that not every reading is structurally equally important (and a similar observation can be made with regard to the components into which those meanings may be analysed). If, for instance, one has a family resemblance relationship of the form AB, BC, CD, DE, then the cases BC and CD have greater structural weight than AB and DE." This model contrasts with the model proposed by Sharifian, described above, which speaks to the totality of the components of a cultural schema and their heterogeneous distribution throughout a speech community.

been recognized as the basis for the spread of change. As was argued in the well-known study by Weinreich, Labov and Herzog (1968: 188), no change is possible without variation and heterogeneity. From a CAS point of view, the inherent causal circularity of the overall system insures that the structured encyclopedic knowledge – the cultural schemas – are not only inextricably connected with what is sometimes referred to as "linguistic knowledge" (Cienki 2010: 170), they are also part and parcel of the internal dynamics of the system itself. Furthermore, they, too, undergo change to a greater or lesser degree, changes that are reflected in the choices made by speakers at the micro-level as they go about (re-)interpreting this reality linguistically.

4 Visualizing lexical semantic innovation and change

As a convenient means of visualizing the complex processes by which semantic change takes place, a rhizome-like structure is a helpful descriptive tool (*Fig. 2*).[4] The nodes of the rhizome represent the senses of the lexical item with the largest central node standing for the initial starting point for the discussion of the expansion or extension of meanings of a given lexical item. The node could be understood as the earliest identifiable prototypical or most salient meaning. Thus, the size of the node correlates to its importance in the overall network, its overall salience. Its salience, in turn, is explained by several interrelated factors, for example, by its frequency of use by the members of the speech community as well by its significance with respect to the role it plays within the larger network of cultural conceptualizations to which it belongs, conceptually speaking. Stated differently, the size of the nodes in the rhizome

---

4 The rhizome model was first elaborated by Deleuze and Guattari ([1980] 2005: 1–26) who used it to describe a kind of theoretical framework that allows for multiple, non-hierarchical entry and exit points in data representation and interpretation. More recently, the model has developed conceptual analogues in models which stress the notion of heterarchy and/or panarchy. Since these models represent a different type of network structure and connectivity, they stand in contrast to hierarchical, arboreal visual models of data representation. Consequently, they are more appropriate for describing the way that complex dynamic systems function and adapt, including multi-agent systems such as human language. To my knowledge, until now the rhizome model has not been applied as a visual support specifically for studies in the field of diachronic lexical semantics. For other applications of rhizome and heterarchical approaches to data representation, particularly of the use of Galois lattices (or conceptual lattices), cf. Roth (2005: 45–52), Holling and Gunderson (2002) and Holland (1995).

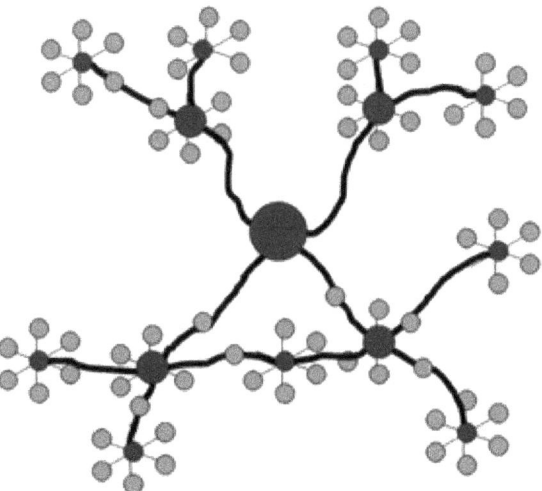

Fig. 2: Rhizome representation of a semantic network.

can be understood to stand for the salience of the various senses attached to the polysemous item at a given point. Moreover, the salience level of a term at a given point in time is determined by agent activities, past and present, and by a kind of erosion-propagation function of the past values of the node in question as well as, in some instances, the salience and connectivity of the neighboring nodes. In short, the cognitive pathways that link the various senses back to the central node are a multifactorial phenomenon.

At the same time, the dynamic nature of the system can give rise to changes in the rhizome structure, that is, at some point speakers may no longer have access to the cognitive pathways leading back to the central node. Indeed, in this process of restructuration of the network, the central node itself can be replaced by another one that results from the budding off of a node representing a secondary sense of the item. In this instance, the original central node is no longer accessible to speakers, although through recourse to written sources, e.g., the OED, or other means of reconstruction, the cognitive processes that led to the production of the secondary node can be recovered.

The chronological layering of material that entered a language at different times, in the more or less distant past, often acts as a record of prior sociocultural practices, ones that originally motivated and set in motion the semantic changes but which are no longer current or even accessible to the average speaker. That is, access to these bridging contexts has become blocked. Or stated differently, the well-trodden trails that were once available to the speakers are no longer fresh enough to be detected.[5] And when they have disappeared entirely, not only at the micro-level but also at the macro-level, leaving no written documentation, the task that falls to the investigator is that of identifying the cognitive pathways that once existed, by analyzing the semantic debris left behind and attempting to reconstruct the bridging mechanisms, albeit hypothetically, along with the cognitive processes that could have led to the sequence of semantic extensions that appear to be present in the network. When written documentation is lacking, one approach is to identify, albeit tentatively, the cultural schemas – the extralinguistic sociocultural understandings operating in the background – that were active in times past and that, therefore, might explain the senses which have become entrenched in the network.

Referring the way that semantic change takes place, Geeraerts' discussion brings into view an important aspect of the feedback loops that operate between the micro- and macro-levels of the system. But first, we need to examine the way the opposition outlined by Paul (1920) between *usuelle Bedeuung* and *okkasionelle Bedeutung* fits into a CAS approach to semantic change. As Geeraerts explains, for Paul the two terms imply a distinction between decontextualized, coded meanings (stored in the language user's memory) and contextualized readings that are realized in a specific discourse context. Or stated differently, the *usual* meaning is the established meaning as shared by the members of a language community whereas the *occasional* meaning involves modulations that the usual meaning can undergo in an actual speech act (Paul 1920: 75). When translated into the terms of the CAS model, we are looking at the novel contextualization of coded macro-level meanings – conventional meanings accessible to the speaker – which take on new meanings through *invited inferences*, interpretations that are not expressed explicitly but are nevertheless intended or at least allowed to happen by the speaker and are then decoded by the listener (Geeraerts 2010a: 337–343, b: 14–16, 231).

---

[5] In dynamic systems theory, this laying down of pathways by agents immersed in a multi-agent system is known as *stigmergy*. Steels (2000: 144) makes this observation concerning stigmergy and the kind of circular causality associated with it in the case of living systems: "For example, the path formed by an ant society is an emergent phenomenon of the actions of the individual ants. There is no global coordination nor supervision and the individual ants cannot oversee the total path. Nevertheless the path is more than an epiphenomenon. It plays a causal role in the behavior of the individual ants. The path is formed by pheromone deposited by the ants as they follow the trail already existing. The more ants deposit pheromone the stronger the path becomes and the more the path casually impacts the behavior of the individual ants." Cf. also Therauluz and Bonabeau (1999) and Susi and Ziemke (2001).

Speaking of Paul's distinction, Geeraerts makes this observation: "To begin with, let us note that there can be various usual meanings to a word: if a word is polysemous, the usual meaning involves a set of related meanings, a cluster of different well-established senses. The occasional meaning, on the other hand, is always a single meaning" (Geeraerts 2010b: 15). And this ad hoc meaning is often realized by the listener selecting the most appropriate reading based on the multiple already established macro-level senses of the word. That process, however, can give rise to a novel meaning that enters the system at the micro-level, that is, it is introduced by the individual language agents.

Whereas the usual meanings, the macro-level ones, are the basis for deriving occasional ad hoc meanings, over time, given the right circumstances, the novel contextualized meaning may become conventional and decontextualized and, therefore, end up being part of the macro-level of the system. Furthermore, "the utterance-type meaning may further stabilize into a new coded meaning, existing alongside the original one and sometimes replacing it. Note that the situation in which the inferences are activated together with the original meaning function as a bridging context between the new and the old meaning" (Geeraerts 2010b: 231). Determining the factors that contribute to the way in which novel meanings stabilize and eventually become part of the macro-level of system as well as the way a novel meaning can displace an established one are a central concern of diachronic lexical semantics.[6]

More concretely, when we project the polysemous meanings of a word visually onto a rhizome-like network, a number of questions arise. What motivates the branching processes? What factors contribute to the changing values of the nodes, e.g., their salience? And what are the mechanisms that allow a node to break free when it is already established on one of the branches of the network? When that happens, the speaker can no longer relate the new (novel) meaning node to the sense node that generated the branching in the beginning. There are various factors that can produce this type of blockage and, consequently, contribute to the reorganization of the rhizome-like mapping. These will be examined in more detail when we discuss the Basque examples.

For now let it suffice to say that the rhizome-like visual mapping of a semantic network has several advantages. On the one hand the visual model is not incompatible with prototype theory while on the other the same diagram

---

[6] While CAS oriented agent-based computer simulations of language have provided valuable information about the dynamics of the real world(s) that they emulate (Steels 2000; Hashimoto 1998), by applying this theoretical framework to topics in diachronic lexical semantics the researcher moves beyond the simulation of events to the description and modeling of the emergence and entrenchment of real-world linguistic data.

furnishes a visual representation that can be viewed as portraying either synchronic or diachronic processes. It also provides a means of expressing visually the structural stability, connectivity and the flexible extensibility of a polysemous network (cf. Geeraerts 1992: 192–193).

5 An instrument of analysis: Serial metonymy

Before entering into a discussion of the Basque examples, we will look at a mechanism known as *serial polysemy* and discuss the way it can help us understand the nature of the innovations – extensions – that have taken place in the case of the Basque term *hatz*, that is, how these extensions can be conceptualized as expanding out from the central node of the network. In this respect serial metonymy is a particularly useful instrument of analysis. Following the definition given by Nerlich and Clarke (2001), serial metonymy refers to metonymic chains that present themselves as either synchronic lexicalized chains, where all of senses associated with the polysemous lexeme are accessible to speakers, or diachronic chains where links in the series may be missing, i.e., no longer accessible to the members of the speech community. In line with Geeraerts' disussions of *invited inference* (cf. also Traugott and Dasher 2002), Nerlich and Clarke (2001) argue that it is the ability to infer the referential intentions of others that sets in motion the cognitive processes giving rise to serial metonymy. These inferences, however, draw on the knowledge of the background cultural schemas possessed by the speakers at that point in time. In other words, the relations that are exploited are well entrenched in our world-knowledge.

An example of a metonymic chain exhibiting synchronic polysemy is the word 'paper' where speakers are capable of retrieving and hence recognizing the cognitive links in the chain of semantic extensions: 'a substance made from pulp of wood or other fibrous material → something used for writing or drawing on → an essay or dissertation, a document → the contents of the essay'. In other words, the motivation behind this and other similar synchronic metonymic chains is still transparent. In contrast, it is not unusual for a diachronic metonymic chain to develop over time in such a way that speakers no longer can identify the connecting linkages. For example, we have the case of the innovations that the term 'shambles' has undergone: 'stools for sitting on → to display wares on → to display meat on → meat market → slaughterhouse → bloodshed, scene of carnage → mess'. This is an example of a diachronic metonymic chain that combines synecdoche (particularisation and generalisation) and hyperbole. "In this case, only the last member of the chain is linguistically available to present-day speakers when they say 'What a shambles!'. The motivation behind the metonymic chain, whose initial links at least were metonymically motivated (the relation between a piece of furniture, its function, and the objects on it), has become obscured" (Nerlich and Clarke 2001: 247). In other instances, a metonymic series can result in a situation in which only the first and last member of the chain are synchronically available, where the sense associated with the original central node of the lattice network is recognized, but the connecting nodes – the motivating links in the metonymical series – are obscured.

As Nerlich and Clarke have noted, the diachronic dimension of what they call serial metonymy has been studied to some degree in the past by historical semanticists, such as Darmesteter (1887) who distinguished between two long term semantic processes: *radiation* and *concatenation*. "In the case of radiation a word accumulated meanings around a core, that is, becomes polysemous; in the case of concatenation a word develops a polysemous chain of meanings, where the first links in the chain might be lost or forgotten" (Nerlich 2001: 1623). The advantage of a rhizome-like visualization is that both of these semantic processes can be mapped simultaneously.

From the perspective of historical lexical semantics, serial metonymy could be viewed as a particular type of cover term for the reanalyses taking place at the micro-level of the system in the case of (re)contextualizing potentially ambiguous strings (Fortson 2003: 660).[7] It is only when extralinguistic cultural factors, the background cultural schemas accessible to the speaker, are taken into consideration that certain patterns emerge and become entrenched. Indeed, Fortson goes so far as to allege that what are called "[m]etonymic changes are so infinitely diverse precisely because [...] the connections are not linguistic, they are cultural. This has in some sense always been known, but when metonymic extension is defined in terms of an 'association' of a word becoming the word's new meaning, we can easily forget that the 'association' in question is not linguistic in nature" (Fortson 2003: 659).

Keeping in mind that polysemy is the synchronic reflection of diachronic semantic change, from the perspective of CAS, the polysemous nature of a lexeme – the senses still accessible to the investigator – should be viewed as the cumulative result of a myriad of choices made by individual agents at the micro-level of the system which, when viewed synchronically, show up at the macro- or global level of the system. This is in line with the claim of Nerlich

---

[7] Cf. Koch (2011) for a detailed study of what he terms "the fundamental importance and the impressive range of metonymy".

and Clarke (2001: 248) "that diachronic metonymic chains deserve more attention, as they are the sedimentational residue of discursive metonymy and of synchronic metonymic polysemies, and might tell us something about the cognitive entrenchment of metonymic structures." The CAS approach also allows for an understanding of the feedback mechanisms inherent to a dynamic multi-agent system in which the agents influence the overall system by their individual choices and in turn are influenced by the system. In other words, the synchronic links that exist between the various senses of an item can be explained as coinciding with diachronic mechanisms of semantic extension (cf. Geeraerts 2010a).

In short, when analysed from a CAS perspective, there is a continual feedback loop in operation that connects language users, functioning at the micro-level of the system, to the macro-level of the system so that the individual choices feed into the macro-level of system and in turn influence the range of choices available to the speaker. When viewed diachronically, the micro-level choices take place against a background of cultural schemas and these in turn play a role in the choices and interpretations of speakers. On the one hand, it is clear that over time cultural schemas tend to evolve along with the real-world referents that are implicated by them. On the other hand, the stability of a cultural schema can contribute to situations in which aspects of the source meaning – the core or prototypical sense of the central node of a metonymical chain – are retained. In short, the circular causality intrinsic to CAS contributes to the system's overall resilience and stability as well as to its ability to adapt (Frank and Gontier 2010; Steels 2000).

6 Tracks to fingers: The case of *hatz*

Before addressing the subject of the polysemous senses associated with the Basque term *hatz*, several comments are in order concerning the data set being employed. First, it should be kept in mind that until the 1980s the vast majority of Basque speakers could not read or write in their own language, although by then bilingualism was already the norm so speakers were generally literate in Spanish or French. A few hundred years earlier, however, the situation was quite different with many geographical zones, especially rural areas, being populated by monolingual Basque speakers. Indeed, until quite recently, Basque speakers grew up speaking the language of their parents; they acquired their knowledge of the language orally and it was passed from one generation to the next almost exclusively in this fashion until after the death of Franco in

1975. It was only then that major efforts to create a literate generation of Basque speakers got underway and started to gain momentum. In summary, until the latter half of the 20th century, it could be argued that Basque survived in an almost exclusively oral environment.

At the same time, dialectal differences both contributed to and were a reflection of the isolation of the speakers. Today there are five major dialects, 11 sub-dialects which subdivide into 24 minor varieties. Historically, between 6 and 9 dialects were distinguished. The geographical distribution of the dialects, moving from west to east is: Biscayan, Gipuzkoan, Upper Navarrese (Northern and Southern), Lower Navarrese (Eastern and Western), Lapurdian and Zuberoan or Souletin (Souletin and the extinct dialect of Roncalese).

The strength and persistence of these dialects represented a challenge to Basque language planners who were concerned with the development and diffusion the unified standard (Batua), a process that was initiated in the 1970s and is still on-going (Zuazo 2003, 2010). Similarly, there have been efforts to standardize several of the dialects themselves, particularly Bizkaian and Zuberoan. Although from one point of view the persistence of the dialects might be viewed in a negative light, it is clear that they play an important role for any cognitive linguist interested in documenting semantic change since the variation that has resulted from their relative isolation from each other – obviously more so in times past than today – provides the researcher with a wealth of information, rich data sets that can be compared and contrasted.

We can now turn our attention to the Basque data and the senses that have grown up around the semantic core of *hatz*,[8] a polysemous lexeme, whose meanings include: 1) 'trace, imprint, track, print' 2) 'pawprint or footprint'; 3) 'paw of an animal'; 4) 'digits (fingers and toes)' as well as what might be viewed as more abstract notions, such as 5) 'an example to follow' (Michelena 1987: 257–260; Azkue [1905–1906] 1969, Vol. I, 101–103; Casenave-Harigile 1993: 171). The cultural schema that stands behind these meanings reflects the recognition that tracks – prints – are regularly left behind when an animal, human or other object passes by. Although the time depth that should be assigned to the schema is unclear, it is a schema that harkens back ultimately to a hunter-gatherer mentality, where being able to recognize signs in nature would have been particularly important. Focusing on the print left by animals or humans would have been a logical semantic extension. Indeed, the core meaning (1) is often modified by the addition of a prefixing element that indicates the type of

---

[8] Today the lexeme in question is sometimes written as *hatz* while at other times as *atz*, particularly in compound forms.

trace or print in question, that is, the entity that produced the print, e.g., *oinatz* (*oin* 'foot') 'footprint'.

The next step in the metonymic chain occurs when the focus shifts from the 'product', the print, to the object that 'produced' the print. Thus, it appears that early on *hatz* acquired the additional meaning of 'paw' or 'foot' of an animal. Through a similar process of reanalysis, the term gained the meaning of 'digits (fingers and toes), the physical entities that certainly would have been important in identifying the type of animal whose prints were left behind on the ground, e.g., in the snow or soft earth. Here it should be noted that in Basque there is another term for 'digit' or 'finger', namely, *erhi/eri*. But it is not polysemous which suggests that at some point, early on, when the secondary meaning of *hatz* as 'digit, finger' came into being, the term *erhi/eri* was already accessible to speakers. However, all indications are that the semantic extension from *hatz* understood as 'trace, print, vestige, etc.' to *hatz* as 'digit, finger' is not a recent one, as will be shown in the next section.

Turning now the what appears to be an abstract extension of the term *hatz*, 'an example to follow', a closer look at the contexts in which this interpretation developed will show that it started out as a reference to a concrete entity, namely, to the act of following in someone's footprints. At the same time, concrete expressions such as *gure atzean* 'in our print(s), footprint(s)', construed also abstractly as 'following our example', gave rise to inferences of a purely spatial nature. The cognitive motivation behind this link in the evolution of the metonymic chain is perhaps better captured by the expression: *bata bestearen atzean* 'one [person following] in the tracks, footprint(s), footstep(s) of another' (Azkue [1905–1906] 1969, Vol. I, 100). Or the imagistic content of the expression could be conceptualized more spatially as 'one after the other', which as we will see, eventually gave rise to a new spatially conceptualized term, namely, *atze*, understood today to mean 'after, behind, in back of', at least in many dialects as well as in Standardized Basque (Batua).

The end result of the processes that contributed to this shift in meaning was the false division of the original inessive form *atz-ean* 'in the track(s)/footprint(s)' and, hence, the new form *atze*. It appears that this particular meaning node, namely, *atze* ('behind, after, in back'), hived off from the main node of the network at a point when the speakers could no longer retrace its origins back to the core meaning of *hatz*. In short, one of the cognitive links in the metonymic chain had been broken. In contrast, in some eastern subdialects, in addition to meaning 'back, behind', it is still associated with concepts such as 'rastro' (Sp.) and 'trace' (Fr.) (Azkue [1905–1906] 1969, Vol. 1, 101).

To understand the sequence of events that produced the spatial meaning and the rupture of the connecting cognitive link in the network, we need to keep the following facts in mind. There is evidence that at some point in the past expressions such as *bata bestearan atzean* were reanalyzed by speakers of dialects in which the core meaning of *hatz* had been lost (or had shifted), that is, its meaning of 'trace, print, track' was no longer accessible to them. By the beginning of the 20th century, we find evidence that these dialectal differences were playing a role in the reanalysis, although the differences may well have arisen much earlier.

For example, Azkue, speaking of the dialectal distribution of *hatz*, indicates that it had retained the base meaning of 'track, trace, print' only in two eastern dialects, Lapurdian and Lower Navarrese (Azkue [1905–1906] 1969, Vol. I, 100). In the remaining dialects, *hatz* had kept its base meaning only in compounds, e.g., expressions with a prefixing element, such as *oinatz*. Moreover, Azkue places the core meaning first, listing senses such as 'finger' (understood as digits of hands and feet) as secondary, while the meaning 'paw, foot, hoof of an animal' is the third meaning given. Concretely, the terms employed by Azkue ([1905–1906] 1969, Vol. I, 100) are: 'rastro, vestigio, pisada' (Sp.) and 'trace, vestige, pas' (Fr.) whereas in the *Diccionario general vasco* (Michelena 1987, Vol. 3, 258), compiled nearly a hundred years later, essentially the same words are used to define the secondary meaning of *hatz*: 'vestigio, huella, rastro, pisada' (Sp.) and 'trace, marque, empreinte', i.e., 'vestige, empreinte qu'une chose laisse' (Fr.).

This reordering of the polysemous senses assigned to *hatz* is an example of how a semantic network can undergo restructuration which results in the reordering of the polysemous senses of the lexeme (Frank 2008a). Moreover, in dialects where the linkage between *atze* and *hatz* has been rendered totally opaque, speakers do not recognize semantic linkages connecting *atze*, i.e., in its meaning of 'behind, after, in back (of)', to the core meaning of the pre-existing network. However, in Basque even when this kind of network rupture takes place, the extended data sets, drawn from the various dialects, are sufficient to demonstrate 1) that the heterogeneously distributed nature of the meaning chains accessed at the micro-level have played a key role in the discontinuities found in the network and 2) that the earlier prototypical meaning at the center of the network, the core node, has been replaced by another in many dialects as well as in Standardized Basque.

Stated differently, utilizing a rhizome model as a visual aid to chart what has gone on, the original central node would need to be significantly reduced in size or it would disappear entirely, while what was a secondary node in the original network tightly connected to the main node, would need to be increased in size in order to reflect the fact that the meaning 'digit' (fingers and toes) now occupies the main node and hence is viewed as the 'conventional sense' of the term. When this restructuring takes place, however, the original semantic network is thrown into disarray and the original metonymical chains – as well as the cognitive motivations that produced the connections – are no longer accessible to the speaker or at least not to all speakers in the speech community.[9] However, this process of restructuration of the network cannot be attributed to a break down in the cultural schemas that originally gave rise to it. Those schemas and accompanying encyclopedic knowledge are still accessible to speakers, i.e., encounters with 'tracks' and 'footprints' continue to be part of human experience.

One final comment needs to be made concerning the role of metonymy in the restructuration of the network. There is little doubt that when viewed from a certain perspective – that is after the fact – development of the sense associated with *atze* 'behind, after, in back (of)' could be seen as part of a metonymic chain in which the referentiality of the base lexeme undergoes reanalysis and the spatial dimension, implicit earlier, becomes highlighted. Consequently, when hearing the aforementioned expression, namely, *bata bestearen atzean*, there are two possibilities with respect to the 'scene' that comes to the mind of the speaker. In the case of Basque speakers who recognize *(h)atz* 'trace, print, footstep' as the base of *atzean*, for them the inessive form consists of *(h)atz-e-an* ('in the track(s)'). Here attention should be paid to the fact that an epenthetic *e* regularly appears before inessive endings when the stem itself terminates in a consonant as is the case of *h)atz* (Rijk 2008: 50–51. In this instance, cognitively, the 'scene' in question has one person walking in the 'footprints' of the other. In contrast, in the case of speakers who no longer recognize the base meaning of *hatz*, the scene that they visualize is different: the 'footprints' are not visible. All that they 'see' is one person walking 'behind' the other. For them the inessive form *atzean* is reanalyzed and understood as *atze-an* in which the epenthetic *e* becomes part of the stem.[10] Only the spatial relationship remains. We might say that a shift in focus has occurred and one element

---

9 It should be emphasized that the lexemes analyzed in this study, while they represent the primary senses associated with *hatz*, i.e., situating it as the primary node in the rhizome network, there are literally dozens of expressions that derive from this polysemous semantic base. Consequently, examining the full richness and complexity of these other meaning extensions would far exceed the scope of the present chapter.

10 Azkue ([1905–1906] 1969, Vol. I, 214) discusses the instance of *(h)atz > atze*, citing it along with various other examples of reanalysis in which the epenthetic *e* ends up forming part of a new lexeme: "Cette épenthétique est si usuelle dans la déclinaison des noms communs terminés par une consonne, qu'elle est reste comme faisant intégrante des mots appelés, dans le langage technique des grammairiens, adverbes de lieu: *aurre* pour *aur*, *urre* pour *ur*, *atze* por *atz* [...]."

implicitly present earlier now becomes highlighted, through a kind of metonymic extension. Or we can conceptualize the cognitive process as a more involved systemic one, affecting the semantic network as a whole.[11] Hence, in the first instance we might say that, cognitively, the scene is more complex in terms of its component features than the second one which now lacks the defining feature found in the original scene.

Geeraerts makes a similar kind of generalization, although from within the framework of prototype theory and without mentioning the role of cultural schemas, starting from the premise that the phenomenon of change can be related to highlighting aspects of the referential subsets of the lexeme; that the reanalysis can come about in a referential subset that, is not yet itself, synchronically speaking, a distinct meaning of term: "New meanings are not necessarily derived from an existent meaning in its entirety; they may also represent an extension from a referential subset of any such meaning [...] in fact, the new meaning arises when a characteristic typical of a salient individual or a salient subset of a category is overgeneralized to the category as a whole" (Geeraerts 1992: 189).

In summary, this review of the polysemous nature of *hatz* demonstrates the dynamic nature of a semantic network, the changing strength and weakness of the connections between the nodes that make up the overall configuration as well as the way the nodes themselves react, increasing or decreasing in size due to the frequency with which the particular sense associated with each node is evoked by speakers at the local-level. Consequently, any attempt to describe these processes by merely assigning to them a classificatory term such as serial metonymy will fail to capture the complexity of the diachronic axis of the data, what has gone on previously, and the way that the nodes of the overall network, their interconnections and relative weights or sizes interact and have been affected across time.[12]

Finally, as has been noted, the 'invisible hand' metaphor (Keller 1994) stops short of indicating precisely how the transition from the individual level to the global level occurs. So we are confronted with this question: what exactly are the mechanisms that enable the cumulative effects? Logically speaking,

---

11 Such a bridging context – where both the old and the new meanings are in play – might be compared to what have been called "switch-and-trigger mechanisms" that can act to drive evolutionary processes into new trajectories (cf. Lansing 2003: 186).

12 The interactions between the meaning nodes or loci in the network, rather than being linear, are frequently *epistatic*, that is, the interplay between several nodes can contribute to the semantic pathway or trajectory taken, and hence to the emergence and entrenchment of a given sense at the global level of the system (cf. Carlborg and Haley 2004).

two situations may occur: the particular innovation can occur *in parallel*, more or less simultaneously, where the same type of inference is made across the board by speakers within a given speech community and/or a subgroup of that community, e.g., the meanings accessible to speakers of a given dialect can set in motion the change (Geeraerts 2010b: 232–233). The second type, which Geeraerts describes as taking place 'serially', assumes that the innovation is introduced by one speaker and/or one specific subgroup and that, subsequently, the other members of the larger speech community come to imitate it.

The Basque data suggests that both cognitive mechanisms were operating. The innovations that affected the senses of *hatz* and its associated semantic network can be viewed as having occurred in parallel and that they propagated through the system as multiple agents made similar interpretations at the micro-level of the system. In other words, while it appears that the two models of parallel and serial development are entirely plausible and in theory can be viewed as separate entities, in actual practice they also can operate in tandem as the Basque data demonstrates. In this respect, it is important, although difficult, to separate the motivation(s) behind the innovation and those that lead to the diffusion of the innovation across the system, its subsequent entrenchment and instantiation as a 'change' within the system, that is, as a structure operating at the global level.

7 Fingers to claws: The case of *hatzamar*

At this juncture, we will turn our attention to the analysis of *hatzamar (hatz-(h)amar)*, a compound form in which the first element is based on a secondary meaning node of *hatz*, i.e., the sense of 'digits'. As noted, the serial metonymy associated with *hatz* forms a meaning chain which allows the referential object, the 'imprint, track' or 'trace', to be reanalyzed so that the focus is on the body part, the entity that produced the 'track', whether human or animal. As will be shown, the expression *hatzamar* (Michelena 1987, Vol. 3, 261–264) begins at a point in the metonymic series when this first change was available to speakers at the global level of the system.

The second element of the compound is clearly recognizable as the Basque numeral ten *(h)amar*. At first glance, one might assume that the two terms in combination refer to nothing more than the concept of 'ten fingers'. However, this assumption is not supported by the evidence. For example, the expression in Basque that translates as 'ten fingers' is *(h)amar hatz*, not *hatz-amar* (Trask 1997: 284). Consequently, something else appears to be going on in terms of the referentiality of the expression *hatzamar*, a suspicion reinforced by the fact that the term used to translate it into Spanish, is 'zarpa' (Michelena 1987, Vol. 3, 261; Frank 2011: 25–36). While 'zarpa' is often translated into English simply as the 'paw of an animal', this does not convey the full referentiality of the expression for the paw in question must be equipped with 'claws'. The visual equivalent of the expression is best rendered by imaging, not a human hand, but rather an animal's paw, such as a bear paw.[13] At times it is associated with the notion of 'curved' or 'bent fingers'. When *hatzamar* is applied to refer to the hand of a human being, it conveys an augmentative, scornful stance and hence a negative attitude on the part of the speaker.

Today the term has two senses, the first and primary one being 'a paw equipped with claws' while a second meaning has developed in several dialects. It results from a reanalysis of the compound giving rise to what appears to be a rather ingenious folk etymology in which *hatzamar* ends up being understood in the sense of 'finger' and interpreted as the singular form of *hatzamarrak* which, in turn, is understood to be the plural, meaning 'the ten fingers'. The odd nature of assigning the meaning of 'the ten fingers' to *hatzamarrak* has been noted by Trask (1997: 284). Moreover, at the beginning of the 20th century, Azkue ([1905–1906] 1969, Vl. I, 100) complained that "the coarse term *hatzamar*" was being used to mean 'finger', rather than the word *hatz*. To emphasize the oddness of this interpretation, Azkue's gives his own much more accurate translation of the compound: 'a ten-finger'.[14] The secondary meaning of 'finger' appears to have developed through attempts to make sense out of the compound, even though the result is still etymologically opaque.

In this section two of the readings that could be proposed to explain compound term's meaning as an animal paw equipped with claws will be described. The first is the simplest, although not necessarily the most convincing, namely, that the concept conveyed by 'a ten-finger' comes from the similarity holding between the shape of a human hand with the ten fingers fully extended and the shape of an animal's paw equipped with claws. There is a second possibility, more cognitively complex but at the same time quite intriguing, which argues that a hand-count gesture was the bridging context for the development of *hatzamar*. As Ifrah (1985: 26–29) has noted, there are two basic ways

---

13 This compound has developed a phonological variants, the most common being *hatzapar* which in some dialects is associated also with the claws of birds, more specifically, an avian foot equipped with claws.

14 "Hoy, fuera de los derivados, se usa [*atz, hatz*] más bien como 'pulgada' que como 'dedo', habiendo usurpado su puesto en esta significación la burda palabra *atzamar*. *Atzamar bat*, literalmente, es 'un diez-dedo'" (Azkue [1905–1906] 1969, Vol. I, 100).

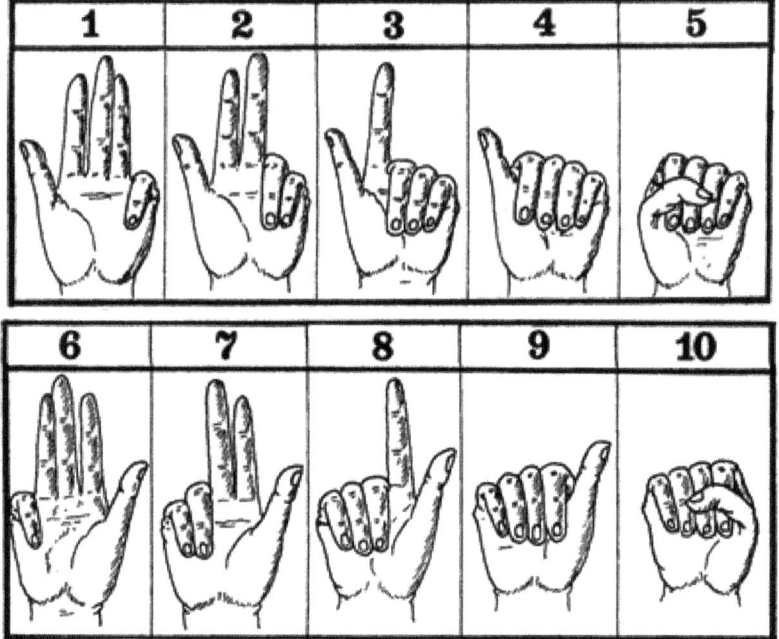

Fig. 3: Manual down-count gestures: Left hand and right hand. Adapted from Ifrah (1985: 28–29).

of doing hand-counts using the digits on one's hands: an up-count and a down-count. For many in the West the up-count is somewhat more familiar where the count starts with a clenched fist, and is then based on the number of fingers raised. Hence, one raised finger, stands for 'one'. According to Ifrah, the down-count operates by counting the number of fingers bent downwards or clenched, starting with the fingers on the left hand (*Fig. 3*).

In fact, when counting, it is not unusual for the thumb to touch the tip of the finger as it is being counted, that is, as it is bent downwards. Consequently, when all the fingers are clenched on the right hand, we have a hand gesture that stands for the number ten. At the same time, by bending or clenching of the fingers the result could also be viewed as a paw with curved claws, similar to that of an animal, e.g. a bear paw.[15] However, the hand gesture that stands (or stood) for each of the numerals in such a down-count is less well known.

---

15 Although beyond the scope of this chapter, until relatively recently, in Basque folk belief bear paws played an important prophylactic and protective role while their symbolism appears to be connected to the archaic belief that humans descended from bears. Evidence for the belief in this ursine genealogy was documented as late as 1987. Hence, a hand gesture that

While the second approach is speculative in that it draws on background knowledge of an ethnographic nature, specifically, a reading that involves cultural schemas related to a gesture linked to this manual down-count, there is another reason to suspect that such knowledge schemas might have guided and structured the formation of Basque numerals. Before examining that evidence, we need to look more closely at cross-linguistic data concerning the semantic structure of numerals. For example, Heine (2004: 108) has observed that the "human hand provides the most salient model for structuring numeral systems." In his study concerning generalizations that relate to numerals, Greenberg observes that it is commonplace for numerals to be used with accompanying gestures, and that the gestures are often used without verbalization. Moreover, there are "other indications that some of the numerical systems recorded in the literature are simply the names for gestures used in counting" (Greenberg 1990: 277). In the instance of lower numerals, particularly those from 1 to 6, there is a tendency for them to be monomorphemic, whereas "[n]umerals from '6' to '9' are likely to be created as predications about fingers and hands: they tend to refer to individual fingers and to be expressed by means of propositional structures having predications like 'Take the index finger off', 'add the big finger', 'put the thumb on top of X;, 'jump from one hand to the other' as a source" (Heine 204: 109).

In the case of Basque, the numerals from 1 to 6 appear to be monomorphemic, although their motivation is opaque rather than transparent. The semantic structure of the numerals from 7 to 9, however, is more complex. Of these, the numeral that has received the most attention from linguists is 9: *bederatzi*. The reason for this lies in the fact that the numeral is composed, rather transparently, of two elements. The first element is *bedera* which is alive and well today, a compound composed of *bat* 'one' and *bera* 'same, itself, himself, herself'.[16] When *bat* and *bera* are combined, the result *bedera* is read as

---

mimicked a bear paw, i.e., one's hand with fingers clenched as if they were claws, might have had a symbolic value (cf. Frank 2005, 2008b, 2011). Cross-culturally, there is clear evidence that where the religious belief in a bear ancestor is present, humans dressed as bears often hold out their hands so that they mimic the bear's paws, i.e., the fingers are slightly curved downwards as if they were claws. A similar a hand gesture is utilized when calling on the bear ancestor in the act of praising or cursing others, while in acts related to taking the 'bear oath', that is, swearing by the bear to tell the truth, a real bear paw is often employed (Mathieu 1984; Lajoux 1996; Von Sadovsky 1994).

16 For a fine-grained analysis of the interpretations that have been put forward over the years to explain *bederatzi* as well as for a detailed discussion of the compound *bedera*, cf. Frank (2011: 32–34). It should be noted that all Basque linguists are in agreement that the first element of *bederatzi* contains the Basque numeral referring to 1.

meaning 'one itself, each one, one each' (Michelena 1987, Vol. 4, 170–173, 359–363). If we keep in mind that in a manual down-count the gesture that corresponds to the number 9 consists of a hand with only one finger raised, this would suggest that the second element in the compound might be *atzi*. This interpretation would bring *atzi* into the semantic network emanating from *hatz*, particularly from its secondary meaning node of 'finger'.[17]

This possibility is strengthened by the fact that several variants in *atzi* are recorded, however, usually in compounds where *atzi* is the first element, such as the verbal form *atzitu* (*atzi-tu*) 'to trap, grab hold of, capture, catch, seize, grasp'. This is a verb with meanings closely replicating those of the compound verb *atzeman* (*atz-eman*) "to seize, grab, grab hold of, capture, catch" in which the second element is the verb *eman* 'to give, strike, clobber, hit' (Michelena 1987, Vol. 3, 280) while the first element is readily identified as *(h)atz*. There are phonological variants of the verb *atzitu* without the relatively modern suffixing element *-tu*, verbs such as *atzi* and *atxi*. Their presence might suggest that *atzi* is an old synthetic verbal form based on *atz*, that is, on *hatz*. Trask has shown that in the case of synthetic verbs, the oldest stratum of Basque verbs, such as *ikusi* 'to see', it is the suffix *i* that forms participles from verbal radicals. He concludes that earlier "the suffix *i* formed participles from nouns" (Trask 1995: 218).

While the etymology of *bederatzi* outlined here is plausible given the evidence currently available, it not a proven fact. When taken in conjunction with cultural schemas linked to the meaning of *hatzamar*, the resulting data set exposes the possible culture-dependent character of the content side of the lexemes: that gestures associated with a down hand-count could have been a factor in the naming processes. On the assumption that the etymologies outlined here with respect to *hatzamar* and *bederatzi* are correct, it would follow that we could be talking about linguistic events that have a significant time depth, that is, with respect to the point in time when the extension of the metonymic chain – from the core meaning of *hatz* as 'trace, print' to its sense of 'finger' – would have taken place. The resilience and stability that this interpretation implies for certain aspects of the diachronic axis of the Basque numeral system is quite remarkable. However, this kind of the persistence of archaic cultural schemas in the Basque language is not unique nor is it phenomenon limited to a single semantic domain (Frank 2008b, 2009, 2013; Elexpuru 2009).

---

17 Zytsar (1983: 710) has argued that there is cross-linguistic evidence for the numeral 9 being construed as 'one less (than) ten' and hence he decomposes *bederatzi* into *bedera* and **(a)tzi* where for him the second element represents a lexeme meaning 'ten' which has been lost.

8 Concluding remarks: Words as 'memory banks'

As is well recognized, language is a central component of cultural cognition. Similarly, as has been demonstrated in the case of the polysemous senses entrenched in the semantic network of *hatz*, we can see that the lexicon serves as a "collective memory bank" of the cultural cognition of a group (Ngugi wa Thiong'o 1986). Moreover, as Sharifian has noted: "Many aspects of language are shaped by the cultural cognition that prevailed at earlier stages in the history of a speech community. Historical cultural practices leave traces in current linguistic practice, some of which are in fossilized forms that may no longer be analysable. In this sense language can be viewed as storing and communicating cultural cognition" (Sharifian 2014: 104). From this perspective, we can argue that language, particularly the lexicon, acts both as a memory bank and a fluid vehicle for the (re-)transmission of cultural cognition and its component parts, cultural conceptualizations and schemas, across time and space. Consequently, cognitive approaches to diachronic lexical semantics afford us a way of documenting and, therefore, recuperating, albeit tentatively, prior cultural practices that have left only faint traces in the record of the speech community in question.

In this chapter, it has been argued that the CAS theoretical framework affords a tool for conceptualizing and analyzing the motivation(s) behind semantic innovations and change. The framework stresses the dynamic and highly complex nature of the mechanisms operating inside a multiagent system. Emphasis is placed the circular causality intrinsic to its functioning and, hence, the way in which the interaction between the micro- and macro-levels of the system contribute to the resilience and stability of the subsystems as well as to their ability to adapt. The CAS framework has been expanded conceptually so that it integrates and internalizes extralinguistic knowledge in the form of cultural schemas, making them an intrinsic, inseparable part of the multiagent system itself.

At the same time, visualizing the polysemous senses of *hatz* as mapped conceptually onto a rhizome-like structure has several advantages. It makes visible the connections established across time between the nodes or senses of the semantic network, while the nodes themselves can be conceptualized as increasing or decreasing in size, or even becoming disconnected from the base node and the rest of the semantic network. The model is also compatible with discussions of serial metonymy and to a certain extent with prototype theory. In short, it is argued that this model is particularly helpful when attempting to bring a more cognitively oriented framework to bear on topics in diachronic lexical semantics.

Moreover, by expanding the theoretical model, the notion of 'context' is redefined so that it encompasses the extralinguistic knowledge of the speaker, the sociocultural 'context'. Therefore, in this model the cultural schemas accessible to the speakers, are internalized to the system. While intricate and often quite unpredictable, the connections between semantic innovation and changes taking place in the extralinguistic sphere of knowledge need to be taken carefully into consideration. Even though they can make the description of lexical meaning difficult, the connections and the motivations behind the diverse ways that these cognitive pathways have been laid down need to be explored and addressed. As Cruse comments: "[a] contextual approach to word meaning [...] has certain inescapable consequences that some might consider to be disadvantages. One is that any attempt to draw a line between the meaning of a word and 'encyclopedic' facts concerning the extra-linguistic referents of the word can be quite arbitrary" (Cruse 1986: 19).

In conclusion, while the analysis carried out on the Basque data is not as fine-grained or comprehensive as it could be, the approach used does assign, albeit tentatively, a significant time depth for certain nodes of the semantic network. Consequently, the results reaffirm the following observation by Radden and Panther (2004: 26): "Just as present-day human behavior is the result of past motivations, present-day language behavior (and we might add, the products of this behavior, language structures) is motivated by factors that were operative a long time ago but whose effects are still visible today."

References

Azkue, Resurreccion Maria. [1905–1906] 1969. *Diccionario vasco-español-francés, Vol. 1.* Bilbao: La Gran Enciclopedia Vasca. http://archive.org/details/diccionariovasco01azku.

Barsalou, Lawrence W. 1992. Frames, concepts and conceptual fields. In Adrienne Lehrer & Eva Feder Kittay (eds.), *Frames, fields and contrasts: New essays in semantic and lexical organization*, 21–74. Hillsdale, NJ/London: Erlbaum.

Beckner, Clay, Richard A. Blythe, Joan Bybee, Morten H. Christiansen, William Croft, Nick C. Ellis, John Holland, Jinyun Ke, Diane Larsen-Freeman & Tom Schoenemann. 2009. Language is a complex adaptive system. In Nick C. Ellis & Diane Larsen-Freeman (eds.), *Language as a complex adaptive system. Language Learning* 59. Special Issue. Supplement 1, 1–26. Hoboken, NJ: Wiley-Blackwell.

Casenave-Harigile, Junes. 1993. *Hiztegia II Eüskara-Français: Xiberotar eüskalkitik abiatzez [Dictionary II Basque-French: Based on the Zuberoan dialect].* Editions Ossas-Suhare: Hitzak Argitaldaria.

Cienki, Alan. 2010. Frames, idealized cognitive models and domains. In Dirk Geeraerts & Hubert Cuyckens (eds.), *The Oxford handbook of cognitive linguistics*, 170–187. Oxford: Oxford University Press.

Carlborg, Örjan & Chris S. Haley. 2004. Epistasis: Too often neglected in complex trait studies? *National Review of Genetics* 5(8). 618–625.

Croft, William. 1993. The role of domains in the interpretation of metaphors and metonymies. *Cognitive Linguistics* 4. 335–370.

Cruse, D. Alan. 1986. *Lexical semantics*. Cambridge: Cambridge University Press.

Darmesteter, Arsène. 1887. *La vie des mots étudiée dans leurs significations*. Paris: Delagrave.

D'Andrade, Roy G. 1987. A folk model of the mind. In Dorothy Holland & Naomi Quinn (eds), *Cultural models in language and thought,* 112–148. New York: Cambridge University Press.

D'Andrade, Roy G. 1995. *The development of cognitive anthropology*. Cambridge: Cambridge University Press.

Deleuze, Gilles & Félix Guattari. [1980] 2005. *A thousand plateaus: Capitalism and schizophrenia*. Trans. Brian Massumi. Minneapolis/London: University of Minnesota Press.

Elexpuru, Juan Martin. 2009. *Iruña-Veleiako euskarazko grafitoak [The Basque language inscriptions of Iruña-Veleia]*. Gasteiz: Arabera.

Fillmore, Charles & Beryl T. Atkins. 1992. Toward a frame-based lexicon: The semantics of *risk* and its neighbors. In Adrienne Lehrer & Eva Feder Kittay (eds.), *Frames, fields and contrasts: New essays in semantics and lexical organization,* 75–102. Hillsdale, NJ: Edbaum.

Fortson, Benjamin W. 2003. An approach to semantic change. In Brian D. Joseph & Richard D. Janda (eds.), *The handbook of historical linguistics*, 648–666. Oxford: Blackwell Publishing Ltd.

Frank, Roslyn M. 2005. Shifting identities: A comparative study of Basque and Western cultural conceptualizations. *Cahiers of the Association for French Language Studies* 11(2). 1–54.

Frank, Roslyn M. 2008a. The language-organism-species analogy: A complex adaptive systems approach to shifting perspectives on 'language'. In Roslyn M. Frank, René Dirven, Tom Ziemke & Enrique Bernárdez (eds.), *Body, language and mind. Vol. 2. Sociocultural situatedness,* 215–262. Berlin & New York: Mouton de Gruyter.

Frank, Roslyn M. 2008b. Recovering European ritual bear hunts: A comparative study of Basque and Sardinian ursine carnival performances. *Insula: Quaderno di Cultura Sarda* 3. 41–97. http://tinyurl.com/Hamalau.

Frank, Roslyn M. 2008c. Evidence in favor of the Palaeolithic Continuity Refugium Theory (PCRT): *Hamalau* and its linguistic and cultural relatives. Part 1. *Insula: Quaderno di Cultura Sarda* 4. 61–131. http://tinyurl.com/Hamalau.

Frank, Roslyn M. 2009. Evidence in favor of the Palaeolithic Continuity Refugium Theory (PCRT): *Hamalau* and its linguistic and cultural relatives. Part 2. *Insula: Quaderno di Cultura Sarda* 5. 89–133. http://tinyurl.com/Hamalau.

Frank, Roslyn M. 2011. Repasando a Joseba Lakarra: Observaciones sobre algunas etimologías en euskera a partir de un acercamiento más cognitivo. *ARSE* 45: 17–64. http://tinyurl.com/Repasando-a-Joseba-Lakarra.

Frank, Roslyn M. 2013. Body and mind in Euskara: Contrasting *dialogic* and *monologic* subjectivities. In Rosario Caballero-Rodríguez & Javier E. Díaz-Vera (eds.), *Sensuous cognition – Explorations into human sentience: Imagination, (e)motion and perception*, 19–51. Berlin & New York: Mouton de Gruyter.

Frank, Roslyn M. & Nathalie Gontier. 2010. On constructing a research model for historical cognitive linguistics (HCL): Some theoretical considerations. In Margaret E. Winters, Heli Tissari & Kathryn Allan (eds.), *Historical cognitive linguistics*, 31–69. Berlin & New York: Mouton de Gruyter.

Geeraerts, Dirk. 1992. Prototypicality effects in diachronic semantics: A round-up. In Günter Kellermann & Michael D. Morrissey (eds.), *Diachrony within synchrony: Language, history and cognition*, 183–203. Frankfurt/New York: Peter Lang.

Geeraerts, Dirk. 2010a. Prospects for the past: Perspectives for cognitive diachronic semantics. In Margaret E. Winters, Heli Tissari & Kathryn Allan (eds.), *Historical cognitive linguistics*, 333–350. Berlin & New York: Mouton de Gruyter.

Geeraerts, Dirk. 2010b. *Theories of Lexical Semantics*. Oxford: Oxford University Press.

Greenberg, Joseph H. 1990. Generalizations about numeral systems. In Keith Denning & Suzanne Kemmer (eds.), *Selected writings of Joseph H. Greenberg*, 271–309. Stanford: Stanford University Press.

Hashimoto, Takashi. 1998. Dynamics of internal and global structure through linguistic interactions. In Jaime S. Sichman, Rosaria Conte & Nigel Gilbert (eds.), *Multi-agent systems and agent based simulation*, 124–139. Berlin: Springer-Verlag.

Heine, Bernd. 2004. On genetic motivation in grammar. In Günter Radden & Klaus-Uwe Panther (eds.), *Studies in Linguistic Motivation*, 103–120. Berlin & New York: Mouton de Gruyter 2004.

Holland, Dorothy & Naomi Quinn (eds.). 1987. *Cultural models in language and thought* Cambridge: Cambridge University Press.

Holland John H. 1995. *Hidden order: How adaptation builds complexity*. New York: Helix Books (Addison Wesley).

Holling, C. S. & Lance H. Gunderson. 2002. Resilience and adaptive cycles. In Lance H. Gunderson & C. S. Holling (eds.), *Panarchy*, 25–62. Washington, D.C.: Island Press.

Ifrah, Georges. 1985. *From one to zero: A universal history of numbers*. Trans. Lowell Bair. New York: Viking Penguin, Inc.

Keesing, Roger M. 1987. Models, "folk" and "cultural": Paradigms regained? In Dorothy C. Holland & Naomi Quinn (eds.), *Cultural models in language and thought*, 369–393. Cambridge: Cambridge University Press.

Keller, Rudi. 1994. *On language change: The invisible hand in language*. London: Routledge.

Kemmer, Suzanne & Michael Barlow. 2000. Introduction: Usage-based conception of language. In Michael Barlow & Suzanne Kemmer (eds.), *Usage-based models of language*, vii–xxviii. Stanford, Calif.: CSLI Publications.

Koch, Peter. 2011. The pervasiveness of contiguity and metonymy in semantic change. In Kathryn Allan & Justyna A. Robinson (eds.), *Current methods in historical semantics*, 259–311. Berlin & New York: Mouton de Gruyter.

Lajoux, Jean-Dominique. 1996. *L'homme et l'ours*. Grenoble: Glénat.

Lansing, J. Stephen. 2003. Complex adaptive systems. *Annual Review of Anthropology* 32. 183–204.

Mathieu, Rémi. 1984. La patte de 'ours'. *L'Homme* 24. 5–42.

Michelena, Luis. 1987. *Diccionario general vasco = Orotariko euskal hiztegia*. Bilbao: Euskaltzaindia/Desclée de Brouwer. http://www.euskaltzaindia.net/oeh.

Nerlich, Brigitte. 1990. *Change in language: Whitney, Bréal and Wegener*. London/New York: Routledge.

Nerlich, Brigitte. 2001. The study of meaning change from Reisig to Bréal, In Sylvain Auroux, E. F. K. Koerner, Hans-J. Niederehe & Kees Versteegh (eds.), *International handbook on*

the evolution of the study of languages from the beginnings to the present, 1617–1628. Berlin & New York: Mouton de Gruyter.
Nerlich, Brigitte & David D. Clarke. 2000. Semantic fields and frames: Historical explorations of the interface between language, action and cognition. *Journal of Pragmatics* 32. 125–150.
Nerlich, Brigitte & David D. Clarke. 2001. Serial metonymy: A study of reference-based polysemisation. *Journal of Historical Pragmatics* 2(2). 245–272.
Ngugi wa Thiong'o. 1986. *Decolonising the mind: The politics of language in African literature*. London: Heinemann.
Paul, Hermann. 1920. *Prinzipien der Sprachgeschichte*. 5th ed. Halle: Niemeyer.
Polzenhagen, Frank & Hans-Georg Wolf. 2007. Culture-specific conceptualisations of corruption in African English: Linguistic analyses and pragmatic applications. In Farzad Sharifian & Gary B. Palmer (eds.), *Applied cultural linguistics: Implications for second language learning and intercultural communication*, 125–168. Amsterdam & Philadelphia: John Benjamins.
Radden, Günter & Klaus-Uwe Panther. 2004. Introduction: Reflections on motivation. In Günter Radden & Klaus-Uwe Panther (eds.), *Studies in Linguistic Motivation*, 1–46. Berlin & New York: Mouton de Gruyter.
Rijk, Rudolf P. G. de. 2008. *Standard Basque: A progressive grammar*. Cambridge/London: The MIT Press.
Roth, Camille. 2006. Co-evolution in epistemic networks: Reconstructing social complex systems. *Structure and Dynamics: eJournal of Anthropological and Related Sciences* 1(3). Article 2. http://repositories.cdlib.org/imbs/socdyn/sdeas/vol1/iss3/art2.
Sharifian, Farzad. 2008. Distributed, emergent cultural cognition, conceptualisation and language. In Roslyn M. Frank, René Dirven, Tom Ziemke & Enrique Bernárdez (eds.), *Body, language, and mind. Vol. 2: Sociocultural situatedness*, 109–136. Berlin & New York: Mouton de Gruyter.
Sharifian, Farzad. 2009. On collective cognition and language. In Hanna Pishwa (ed.), *Social cognition and language*, 163–177. Berlin & New York: Mouton de Gruyter.
Sharifian, Farzad. 2014. Advances in cultural linguistics. In Masa Yamaguchi, Dennis Tay & Benjamin Blount (eds.), *Towards an integration of language, culture and cognition: Language in cognitive, historical, and sociocultural contexts*. 99–123. London: Palgrave McMillan.
Steels, Luc. 2000. The puzzle of language evolution. *Kognitionswissenschaft* 8(4). 143–150.
Steels, Luc. 2002. Language as a complex adaptive system. In Frank Brisard & Tanja Mortelmans (eds.), *Language and evolution*, 79–87. Wilrijk: UIA. Antwerp Papers in Linguistics 101.
Strauss, Claudia & Naomi Quinn. 1997. *A cognitive theory of cultural meaning*. New York: Cambridge University Press.
Susi, Tarja & Tom Ziemke. 2001. Social cognition, artefacts and stigmergy. *Cognitive Systems Research* 2: 273–290.
Theraulaz, Guy & Eric Bonabeau. 1999. A brief history of stigmergy. *Artificial Life* 5(2). 97–116.
Trask, R. L. 1995. On the history of non-finite verb forms. In José Ignacio Hualde, Joseba A. Lakarra, & R. L. Trask (eds.), *Towards a history of the Basque language*, 207–274. Amsterdam & Philadelphia: John Benjamins.
Trask, R. L. 1997. *The history of the Basque language*. London & New York: Routledge.

Traugott, Elizabeth Closs & Richard B. Dasher. 2002. *Regularity in semantic change*. Cambridge: Cambridge University Press.

Von Sadovszky, Otto J. 1994. Personal communication (April 4).

Weinreich, Uriel, William Labov, & Marvin I. Herzog. 1968. Empirical foundations for a theory of language change. In Winfred P. Lehmann & Yakov Malkiel (eds.), *Directions for historical linguistics: A symposium*, 95–195. Austin: University of Texas Press.

Zytsar, Yuri Vladimir. 1983. Los numerales del vascuence (problemas etimológicos). In Euskaltzaindia (ed.), *Piarres Lafitte-ri omenaldia [A Tribute to Piarres Lafitte]*. IKER-2, 709–729, Bilbao: Euskaltzaindia.

Zuazo, Koldo. 2003. *Euskalkiak: Herriaran lekukoak [Basque dialects: Documentation]*. Donostia: Elkar.

Zuazo, Koldo. 2010. *El euskera y sus dialectos*. Irun: Alberdania.

Richard Trim
The interface between synchronic and diachronic conceptual metaphor: The role of embodiment, culture and semantic field

Abstract: A large number of relatively recent studies have been carried out on synchronic, cross-cultural studies of metaphor. Many of these have been listed and described by Kövecses (2005, 2006). A far smaller number of studies have involved the investigation of diachronic trends, (Allan 2003, 2008); Geeraerts and Gevaert (2008); Geeraerts and Grondelaers (1995); Trim (2007, 2011); Winters (1992), among others). Until now, it appears that no studies have fully dealt with the interface between the two. The distinction made between the two dimensions in this study is that synchronic conceptual metaphor refers to models which exist at a fixed point in time but varies across languages/cultures whereas diachronic metaphor varies through time in one language/culture. The latter is reflected in different synchronic layers in time but, in reality, diachronic changes usually operate as an ongoing continuum. This analysis raises the question as to how universal trends may match up in both dimensions and thus to what extent the two may be similar. The answer to this question depends on the available synchronic and diachronic data being collected in different cultures. A large number of relevant studies are being made available but since more information is still required from an empirical point of view, the following analysis will be based on a number of hypothetical issues. There are several potential scenarios in which conceptual metaphor models match up along the synchronic and diachronic dimensions. Similar structures in conceptual models depend on various factors. This study will look at several of these factors which appear to play a major role in the patterns concerned. Among these are the distinction between potential creation and wide distribution of similar metaphor models in time and cultural space. It suggests that this factor depends on the level of abstraction in mappings, the structure of conceptual systems, the embodiment/culture ratio and the semantic field in which corpus data is collected. The results show that diachronic conceptual metaphor may often be similar to synchronic structures but that the causes are mixed. The following hypotheses are based on data drawn primarily from empirical studies in the semantic fields of the emotions and colour. These

---

Richard Trim: University of Toulon

fields are discussed with particular reference to English and Oriental languages in order to compare very different cultural histories.

1 Universal trends: Potential creation versus wide distribution

It has been suggested in the past that universal trends in metaphor patterns are due to the role of embodiment. Two examples of embodiment would be, on the one hand, physiological influence such as spatial orientation. Direction upwards is normally positive, as in "happy is up", and the reverse would be negative as in "sad is down". Other spatial forms would involve "source-path-goal", "part-whole", "centre-periphery" constructs, etc., (Lakoff 1987: 283; Lakoff and Johnson 1980: 24). On the other, basic-level concepts which are at an intermediate stage between superordinate and subordinate items of a semantic category in protypical analysis (Rosch 1975), are easier to discern and probably more universal. These would include actions and properties such as *running, walking, eating* and *hot, cold, hard, soft*, etc., (Lakoff 1987: 271). However, an analysis of the frequency of similar conceptual metaphor patterns at the synchronic and diachronic levels reveals a fact that may not be evident at first sight. Uniformity in cross-cultural or long-term patterns is not simply due to embodiment. Culture may play a major part in maintaining stability. The dividing-line between the types of universal trends outlined above and cultural influence is often difficult to determine and the delimitation of cultural thought likewise presents problems of definition. Kövecses (2005, 2006) attempts to give definitions of embodiment and culture.

The former appears to be related to recurring bodily experiences that get a structure through constant repetition. These are referred to as *image schemata* in the relevant cognitive linguistic literature and include areas such as spatial orientation that provide and an understanding for abstractions such as states, emotions and life. This represents one basic explanation of embodiment in the literature (Kövecses 2005: 18–19).

The latter concept of culture is defined by Kövecses (2005: 1):

> In line with some current thinking in anthropology, we can think of culture as a set of shared understandings that characterize smaller or larger groups of people (...). This is not an exhaustive definition of culture, in that it leaves out real objects, artefacts, institutions, practices, actions, and so on, that people use and participate in any culture, but it includes a large portion of it: namely, the shared understandings that people have in connection with all of these 'Things'.

A broad distinction which will thus be made between the two in this study is that the conceptualisation of metaphor may, on the one hand, be influenced by physiological features and, on the other, by "a set of shared understandings about the world". The latter are either independent of physiology or add non-physiological, conceptual features to a metaphor model, even when core physiological concepts are involved, as in humoral theory discussed below. Any terms such as *cultural thought* or *cultural conceptualisation* used in the following discussion will therefore refer to this non-physiological, or non-embodied, aspect.

With regard to culture playing a major role in stability, the issue raised here is that a distinction also needs to be made between potential creation at any point in time and wide distribution in cultural space. The first indeed normally concerns embodiment in universal trends while the second may involve entrenched or flexible cultural thought as well as embodiment. It will be seen in the ensuing discussions that similar patterns at the synchronic/diachronic interface draw on both of these processes. It will also be suggested in the discussion on culture that there may be a certain, albeit limited, degree of potential creation across cultures in specific forms of cultural conceptualisation.

A further issue is the attempt to define the extent to which any given mapping, be it embodied or cultural, will be created in a conceptual environment. In other words, how far does an embodied mapping extend or where are the limits to a culture?

2 Defining conceptual systems

An easier way of viewing this question is perhaps to consider conceptual settings in time and cultural space in which a given metaphor is unlikely to be created or interpreted. If a mapping is truly universal both synchronically and diachronically, the conceptual system in which it is located would presumably have no limits. This situation is probably quite rare or, at least, very difficult to verify according to definitions used. In order to illustrate the diachronic and synchronic structure of a conceptual system, one analogy is that of an ice sample taken in polar regions to analyse long-term climate change (Trim 2011: 74–75). If the sample is in the form of a cylinder, the upper surface of the cylinder would represent the present, synchronic situation, the outer limit of the surface the extent to which an embodied or cultural metaphor is likely to be created and/or interpreted and, finally, the greater the distance from the upper surface, the further back in time the metaphor was created or existed. In order to incorporate the variable of potential creations in a conceptual system, in line with mapping abstractions outlined above, the notion of prototypicality (Rosch 1975: 192–233), and "fuzzy edges" (Johnson-Laird 1983), may be included in the model.

Synchronically, the closer the metaphor is to the centre of the cylinder, the greater the potential for creation in a given culture and the higher the level of salience. The more it moves towards the edge, the less salient it becomes and the more its meaning becomes unclear. Diachronically, creative potential and salience is subject to considerable fluctuation through time. This would mean that the location of an existing or potential metaphor in the "ice sample" moves either towards the centre or the edge as it moves up through the cylinder. If it theoretically moved its position to a point outside the conceptual system, it would be extremely difficult, if not impossible, to interpret the metaphor by any speakers of the language community.

An example of a move towards the edge of the cylinder through time would be colour symbolism as in the Shakespearian notion of "green minds":

(1) *Beside, the knave is handsome, young, and hath all those requisites in him that folly and **green minds** look after.*
(*Othello*, [II, 1], 1044–77)

Although the term "green minds" may have been readily understood in Shakespeare's time, it is arguably less clear today. Further references tend to indicate that Shakespeare's interpretation was probably that of love sickness (Trim 2011: 122). The opposite would be where green signifies "ecological" which has gained in momentum in different applications since its introduction with the term 'green party' in the 1970's (see below). This model is dependent on a number of features which are present in mapping processes: among these are the role of the abstraction and its implication in both embodiment and culture.

3 Abstraction levels and the embodiment/culture ratio

A starting point in the investigation of the synchronic/diachronic interface may be based on the following observation according to available data in both dimensions. Patterns of similar conceptual metaphor models appear to follow at least four different trends (Trim 2011: 60–61). First, there are those mappings which can be seen in a large number of cultures as well as representing long-term paths in language histories (trend a); second, conceptual metaphors appear to exist in varying cultures at different times (trend b); third, there are long-term mappings which are restricted to one particular language or group of languages (trend c); and, fourth, metaphors may be similar synchronically but it is unlikely, or uncertain, as to whether they exist on any long-term, diachronic scale (trend d).

Two major problems appear at the outset when attempting to explore universal trends, or levels of uniformity in patterns, at the synchronic/diachronic interface. The first difficulty is that, without an investigation into every language in the world, synchronic investigation cannot fully cover all the possible evidence. Likewise, historical research becomes limited at the very early stages of a language or culture due to a lack of written documents. Two hypothetical concepts will be discussed in this analysis: a) the abstraction level in any given mapping and b) the embodiment/culture ratio.

The first term refers to how wide the reference of the source and target domains may be. The second term concerns the proportion of embodiment or culture, as defined in the proposals outlined in section 1 above, in the mapping process. An example of the combination of both features would be the expression: "our marriage has been a long, bumpy road". According to a cognitive approach, the notion of a road stems from a spatial "life is a journey" model based on the "source-path-goal" construct proposed above. Different aspects of human experience start at a specific point and usually go towards a final destination. This would represent an embodiment feature. However, the source-path-goal model also includes different cultural features. Not all languages have the "journey" model, as in the Hmong language of Laos and Thailand, which uses a "life is a string" structure (Kövecses 2005: 71; Riddle 2000), and the item "road" is in itself a cultural concept.

With regard to the abstraction level, this aspect may vary considerably within the same conceptual category or mapping domain. For example, Lakoff's "source-path-goal" image schema would have a very wide reference, i.e. it can refer to a large variety of human activities and experience, and may therefore be found in a large number of categories of languages. Related to this image schema is the "life is a journey" metaphor in which there is a beginning and an end, (Lakoff and Johnson 1980). It has a narrower reference in the sense that it only concerns the concept of life. Even more specific in this time/space mapping is "Time is a road" (Lakoff and Johnson 1999: 140) which incorporates a more culturally-based concept in the form of the "road" image. The abstraction level is thus different between the "goal", "journey" and "road" mappings with an increasingly specific reference respectively. The abstraction potential may also be placed on a vertical scale so that the above order of mappings would represent a gradually *lowering* (i.e. decreasing) level of abstraction. This example will be taken up again below with reference to cultural mappings.

In many ways, the abstraction level, or range of reference, is similar to other terms given in the past to conceptual accessibility. These include notions such as *conceptual distance* (Traugott 1985:23). Citing Brown and Witowski (1981), Traugott suggests that the degree of naturalness within a domain can determine distance. These would cover figurative expressions as in the reference to the centre of the eye in kinship terms. The *father of the eye* would be conceptually closer, and therefore more accessible, than *uncle of the eye*. In abstraction terms, the concept FATHER in this mapping would thus be at a higher level than the UNCLE reference. According to Traugott, a *corner in time* in time/space mappings would be more distant than a *path of time* since time is usually conceived in terms of a front-back, up-down axis rather than in geometric ways. Other terms have also been given to the conceptual distance variable in the past such as *semantic relatedness* in Katz et al. (1988). Similar discussions on the role of cognitive distance, particularly in the field of cultural mappings, have been proposed in relation to prototype metaphor (Tourangeau and Sternberg 1982: 203–244).

As far as the embodiment/culture ratio is concerned, its fluctuating position would be partly influenced by the abstraction level in the mapping. It can be seen that the orientational structure in the "goal" image, as in the physiological sources of orientation described above, implies a greater degree of embodiment than the "road" metaphor. There is thus a difference in the abstraction level between the two mappings. In many cases, the higher the level of abstraction in a mapping, particularly with reference to embodiment, the more likely the conceptual metaphor constitutes a universal trend. However, the discussion below will also include the distinction between the wide distribution of similar metaphor models and the potential for universal creation. It will be seen that a high proportion of culture, i.e. the set of shared understandings that characterize smaller or larger groups of people as outlined in the definition above, which may be established in the embodiment/culture ratio, can also be responsible for wide distribution both synchronically and diachronically.

Although mappings are usually mixed at differing levels of the embodiment/culture ratio, the two components of the latter need to be analysed separately in order to attempt to define their roles in creation and wide distribution. Embodiment will be discussed in relation to trends (a) and (b) outlined above and culture to trends (c) and (d).

4 Embodiment and synchronic/diachronic universal trends

What kind of embodied conceptual metaphor is likely to be created in any culture or at any point in time? This feature usually springs to mind when discussing trend (a) above in the case of matching synchronic and diachronic patterns. One particular embodied mapping, "anger is a pressurised container", (Lakoff 1987), and which appears to be a potentially universal trend at the synchronic level (Kövecses 2005, 2006), may fit trend (a) since it could include long-term models that can potentially be found in all conceptual systems.

Within the "pressurised container" mapping, the "anger is heat" metaphor has been described in great detail by Lakoff (1987) with numerous expressions such as "he blew his top", "she got all steamed up", etc. Due to the presence of this model in very different languages, it would appear at first sight that the model must be potentially creative across a wide range of time and cultural space. Similar conceptual metaphors are indeed found in languages that have very different cultural histories. European, African and Oriental languages are a case in point. The "heat" mapping and, according to Kövecses (2005: 39), the "angry person is a pressurised container" mapping at a higher level of abstraction, can be seen in languages such as: Chinese, (Yu 1995, 1998); Japanese, (Matsuki 1995); Hungarian (Bokor 1997); Polish (Micholajcuk 1998); Wolof, (Munro 1991) and Zulu, (Taylor and Mbense 1998). Although the six languages cited here are relatively limited in number, further studies may show that differing cultural histories may, nevertheless, contain similar conceptual models. There are, of course, variants within the pressure model. According to Yu, Chinese uses a "gas" concept rather than "fluid" in English for this particular "container" structure. This is due to the fact that the *ying* and *yang* conceptualisation of fluid substances is linked to cold temperatures and gas is linked to the notion of heat. However, the pressure concept covers these variants.

The diachronic dimension reveals a number of problems when suggesting these models are long-term paths due to the precise definition of the mappings concerned. To take the last example of Chinese, online studies such as those conducted by Chen, (University of Taiwan: www.ntnu.edu.tw/acad/rep/r97/a4/a404-1.pdf), claim that original mappings of the "anger" metaphor in Chinese did not actually involve the "gas" concept and "heat" but rather the notion of *qi* (a form of energy). This lexeme can be traced back to the era of the Warring States (403–221 B.C.). According to Chen, the relation to "heat" only developed later during the Han Dynasty (206 B.C.–220 A.D.) and the "anger is qi" model continued up until 500 A.D. The notion of *qi* had a polysemous form during the Warring States which entailed: a) energy in the universe, b) an element which influences a person's cultivation of righteousness, c) the essence of the body influencing physiological states and d) the essence of the body influencing emotional states. The role of this essence can thus be seen in the Yellow Emperor's Classic of Internal Medicine (Veith 1982):

(2) *bai bing sheng yu* **qi** *ye ' nu ze* **qi** *shang*
 'Every kind of sickness results from **qi**; anger causes **qi** to rush upwards'

Metaphorically, anger is represented by this essence in the body:

(3) *fen xin zhang dan'* **qi** *ru yong quan*
 'The heart is filled with hatred; **anger** comes up like a spring'

In order to calm down emotional feelings such as anger, this essence has to be reduced. Arguably, the concept was not related to heat, fluids or gas at that time in Chinese history. The question which now arises is whether this essence, in whatever form it may be, has a parallel of filling the body like the "container" model. If this is the case, could this interpretation be taken one step further and compared to some kind of pressure in the body? This deduction would suggest that the definition of the "pressure" model does indeed cover a mapping of this category and considerably increase its range of universality.

On the other hand, this is a speculative point since other kinds of examples given by Chen do not necessarily give that impression: *the mother of emperor is full of anger-qi, anger-qi is possessed by heaven and human beings*, etc. There is the notion of filling up a container but not necessarily pressure as in the English expression *he blew his top*. The "container" image may, however, represent one diachronic path among others. If the "anger is pressure" mapping is not implied, it could represent a synchronic universal trend today but not necessarily along the diachronic dimension. A similar problem can be seen in the history of English.

As far as embodiment in "heat" and "pressure" is concerned, Gevaert (2001, 2002) points out that there is evidence for the fact that the "heat" metaphor was a cultural borrowing in English from Latinate sources during the 9th and 10th centuries AD. Although the influence may be in the form of loan translations conventionalised in late Old English, and more textual information would be needed to verify this point, it is possible that a new cultural form was introduced at that time. Before then, English had, among other "anger" mappings, an "anger is swelling" metaphor that does not represent a normal collocation in Modern English. It can be found in Old English lexemes denoting "swell" such as *þrutian* and *abelgan*. Indeed, the *Beowulf* manuscript in Old English contains references such as *waes ða gebolgen beorges hyrde,* i.e. 'by then the barrow-snake (dragon) was swollen with rage', (*Beowulf*, l. 2304; trans. Chickering 1977). This would indeed indicate that some form of pressure was involved.

Within the framework of further research in this field based on the Thesaurus of Old English and the Anglo-Saxon Dictionary, Geeraerts and Gevaert (2008: 319–347) suggest that the notion of anger in Old English is not limited to swelling or pressure. There appears to be a range of etymological themes of which swelling is just one. An item such as *sare* ("affliction"), i.e. anger being related to pain, does not seem to be associated with a "pressurised container" image. This would support the hypothesis that an emotion such as anger may have other etymological themes in a concept such as Chinese "qi". Furthermore, the findings of the Old English study even claim that many metaphors for anger may not be embodied. According to contextual information, a compound such as *hatheort* ("hotheart") may not be physiologically grounded in the history of English, despite the fact that "heat" and "heart" images are used. According to Geeraerts and Gevaert, the compound appears in a letter from Saint Boniface to abbess Eadburga. It involves a passage translating a verse from a Latin psalm, in which it translates Latin *furor*. The metaphor has therefore followed a Latinate route, rather than Germanic, and supports the theory that the "heat" image was introduced into English via translation, rather than existing since the beginning of Old English. Images which are normally considered to be related to embodiment may therefore actually have a high cultural input transmitted from another language.

Another case in point is the claim that cultural influence from humoral theory rather than embodiment has a major influence on the "anger" metaphor in European languages (Geeraerts and Grondelaers 1995: 153–180). Although humoral theory is ultimately based on embodiment, the original theory may possibly become a cultural construct. Geeraerts and Grondelaers argue that, without totally rejecting the physiological aspects, the source of metaphorisation in anger in English and other European languages is motivated to a large extent by the reinterpreted legacy of humoral theory. This school of thought goes back to Hippocrates in Ancient Greece and became a dominant way of thinking in the Middle Ages. It was a common belief before the advances made in science after the medieval period that the four humoral fluids of the body regulate characters and emotions. Geeraerts and Grondelaers maintain that the conceptualisation of humoral theory continued to exist in language after such claims were only finally rejected by scientists in the nineteenth century, and in particular, Rudolf Virchow's *Die Cellularpathologie* in 1858. Parallel to this hypothesis, the QI concept also appears to have a cultural input.

5 Embodiment and diachronic variability

Some embodiment features appear to be long-term but may vary in duration and appear at different historical periods from a cross-cultural point of view (trend b). Lakoff's suggestion (1987: 310) that Japanese has a different conceptual system to European languages with regard to the belly ('*hara*') being the physiological focus of feeling has been supported by empirical evidence provided by Matsuki (1995: 144). According to Matsuki, the conceptualisation of *hara* in Japanese implies the notion of rising when a person gets angry:

(4) *hara ga tatsu*
    'hara rises up'

The container image of the body used to express anger in English has a correlation with the belly image in Japanese. The "bottling up" of anger in English is reflected in Japanese in the attempt to hold anger in the belly or when a person is unable to control his or her anger:

(5) *hara ni osameteoku*
    'hold it in *hara*'

(6) *hara ni suekaneru*
    'cannot lay it in *hara*'

According to Padel (1992: 12–13), the Ancient Greeks' understanding of thought and feeling was also in the belly: "in ordinary fifth-century life, when people wondered what was going on inside someone, what mattered was that person's *splanchna* 'guts'". Parallels may be seen in European languages. The notions of rising in anger and a feeling in the belly are also found in the German expressions: *Da kommt mir die Kotze [aus dem Magen] hoch* (my puke rises [from the belly]) and *Bauchgefühl* (belly feeling). Certain personal attributes are also associated with "guts" in modern English such as "he hasn't got the guts to do it", i.e. not being courageous enough to do something. However, the physiological centre of very many feelings in European languages – including bravery – appears to be associated with the heart.

The conclusion that can be drawn is that in the history of Western society there might have been a shift from the belly at some stage after the period of Antiquity. More evidence on this hypothesis is needed but, if it was the case, the shift probably occurred fairly early on. Jager (1990: 845–859) suggests that chest swelling, or pectorality, in the emotions, was common in Old English literature and well established by the end of the Middle Ages. This can be seen in the writings of medieval European literature such as Chaucer and Boccaccio:

(7) *Servant in love and lord in marriage*
 Love hath his fiery dart so brenningly
 Y-striked thurgh my trewe careful **herte**
 (Chaucer: Knight's Tale, *Canterbury Tales*)

(8) *Quando Bernabo udi questo, parve che gli fosse dato d'un coltello al* **cuore** *si fatto dolore senti*
 (When Bernabo heard this, it was as if a knife pierced his **heart**, so great was the pain he felt)
 (Boccacio: *Decameron*, Second Day, Novel IX)

The reason why there was a shift is probably due to the importance in the history of Western society of mental thinking in the emotions. Indeed, there also appeared to be an extension of pectorality from the physical to the psychological domain. Le Goff (1989: 13–26) suggests that this process was aided by the fact that medieval psychology situated various mental and affective functions in the thoracic region. At this stage of research, these ideas remain speculative and more historical data would be needed to trace evolutionary processes.

In the case of Japanese, it would appear that this major shift has not taken place and that this embodied model has remained a long-term diachronic feature. Matsuki's findings not only provide evidence for the fact that the *hara* concept is common today, other studies also imply that this form of conceptualisation has always existed in Japanese culture and Eastern philosophy in general. As Egli (2002: 49 ff.) points out: "Historically the *hara* was integral to Eastern philosophy that taught that the physical body is an essential part of what it means to be human. As such, traditional Japanese culture believed that the correct posture is focussed in the lower belly or hara, which is the center of gravity in the body. (...) The predominant Western perspective values rational thought above all else". The firm place of the conceptualisation of the *hara* image in traditional Japanese culture would therefore represent a long-term form. Synchronically, this embodiment structure does not match between Western and Japanese culture but they do match up at different historical periods. In this case, interchanging diachronic and synchronic equivalence is due to shifting conceptualisation in one culture.

It may be summarised at this point that mappings which appear to be clear cases of embodiment at first sight may actually have a certain amount of cultural input in accordance with the norms of mapping structures. It could be said that the *hara* concept has become a part of Japanese or Oriental culture in general. Not only cross-cultural studies can highlight such variants, long-term diachronic paths also suggest that cultural history modifies embodied mappings in domains such as the emotions. The following discussion will now turn to the cultural component of mappings.

6 Culturally-related systems

In accordance with the definitions of culture proposed above, the limits of any system related to the attributes of such categorisations are equally difficult to discern with regard to time or cultural space. This is not only due to the problem of deciding which aspects belong to one culture rather than another but also due to the heterogeneous nature of cultural systems themselves. Furthermore, such systems may overlap or share certain features but not others. This discussion will focus on just two aspects of culture with regard to conceptual systems. The first concerns 'global' structures involving different levels in the embodiment/culture mix. The example of the "goal-journey-road" sequence illustrated above will be analysed from the synchronic and diachronic angles in relation to the mapping of time and cultural space. The second aspect will examine internal variability in a cultural system.

Instantiations of the "Time orientation" metaphor (Lakoff and Johnson 1999: 140), which maps time onto space, can be seen in: *that's all behind us now* or *we're looking forward to the future*. The aspect of time and space metaphorisation has received much attention in the relevant literature, (Evans 2013; Trim, forthcoming). Chinese has the same mapping procedures, according to studies by Yu (1998: 92–95): *quian-chen* ('behind-dust/trace' = past); *jiao-xia* ('foot-under' = at present, now); *quian-tu* ('front/ahead-road' = future, prospect). The last example shows that Chinese uses the related "Time is a road" image as in the English expression, *it's a long and winding road in life*, that combines both the "life is a journey" and "road" metaphors.

However, cross-cultural variation can arise in other Oriental languages at the "life is a journey" level since, according to Kövecses (2005: 83), the equivalent in Hmong (Laos) is "life is a string". Furthermore, the concept of "road" has a greater number of variants. To take a diachronic example, the notion of a road, or crossroads, in the Crusades sermons of the Middle Ages was chosen to designate the "right" or "wrong" way for a choice of direction in life, according to whether potential recruits for the war effort decided to "Take the cross" or not. This can be seen in the Latin text below with a possible translation as follows:

(9) *Signum directivum ponitur in **biviis** sicut cruces, ut **viam rectam** ostendant, et si erratum est **ad crucem rectam viam** resumant ...,*
'A sign of direction is put at a **crossroads**, like crosses, **to show the right way**, and if one has taken a wrong turn, one can resume **the right way at the cross**' ...
(Gilbert of Tournai, cited in Maier 2000: 180–181)

This example suggests that the notion of a path or road in decision-making does appear to be firmly integrated into European cultural history. Left/right orientation appears to go a long way back in European history, at least to Leo the Great: *Unde autem populosior est via **laeva** quam **dextera**, nisi quia ad mundane gaudia et corporalia bona multitude proclivis est?*, 'And wherefore is the **left** road more thronged than the **right**, save that the multitude is prone to worldly joys and carnal goods?' (SERMO XLIX De Quadragesima XL). Left/right orientation is therefore apparent as respectively negative and positive in cultural history and suggests that direction has played a large part in conceptualising choices in life.

However, it should be pointed out that the exact interpretation of metaphorical senses in the example above is variable and made more complex with when relevant etymological data is taken into consideration. The modern English word "right" has the two senses of a) direction being opposite to left and b) the connotation of being correct. These two senses have two words in Latin, the first being *dexter* and the second *rectus*. The latter is used in the example above with the sense of the "correct thing to do" but does not presumably entail a direction to the right as opposed to the left. Nevertheless, it would appear that linear shape plays a role in metaphorisation in the origin of Latin *rectus*. This term is linked to the Proto-Indo-European root **reg-* (to move in a straight line). The spatial orientation of "straight" was therefore probably associated metaphorically with "correct" very early on and has remained so today.

Cultural notions of paths and roads change through time. The concept of a path as in the sermon above has culturally different features from the images of modern streets today. The arrival of car traffic led to "Two-way streets", as in political rhetoric:

(10) **Moving forward**, *we are committed to a partnership with Pakistan.* **Trust is a two-way street.**
(Barack Obama, 1 December, 2009: www.whitehouse.gov)

The mapping levels in the GOAL-JOURNEY-ROAD sequence involve a change in the embodiment/culture ratio to the extent that the cultural aspect may have far more weight in the mapping. The type of cultural concept such as "Two-way street" makes it specific to time and cultural space constraints.

Variation in internal structures creates other types of patterns. Kövecses (2005: 88) refers to intra-systemic categories as within-culture variation. Apart from standard metaphors used by the whole language community, other aspects such as sociolects, regional variants, technical jargon or the vast range of individual creations, are used by different sections of the language community. The characteristics of these intra-systemic categories also vary between each other. Sociolectal metaphors would normally be understood by all users of the sociolect and, in translation or by direct loaning in particular international sociolects, by speakers of other languages. This would also be the case of technical jargon or terms used in the business or media world. Regional variants would normally be restricted to one language, or possibly group of languages, if in contact. Individual creations, as in literature or poetry, may not be understood by all speakers of the language community. In the latter case, the degree of salience would play a large part in either the correct interpretation of the metaphor or its adoption by other speakers.

The limits of interpretation in a cultural system would depend partly on the level of abstraction and partly on cultural input. As in the case of abstraction in embodiment mapping, this implies the range of possible interpretations in the cultural system given the interlocutor's knowledge of the cultural signs used in the mapping. A fundamental question which arises here is whether, even in literary discourse, a mapping would be located outside the normal conceptual system of the language involved. In other words, can mappings be totally incomprehensible to everyone except the person who has created the mapping? Aitchison (1989: 146) raises this question in a mapping such as "cheeks are typewriters", a reference to technology used before the arrival of computers. She suggests that almost any mapping may be possible with a certain stretch of the imagination. This forms the crucial point in defining the limits of a conceptual system in metaphor creation. A limit would probably be a point at which a mapping becomes either a contradiction or nonsensical according to the average person's conceptual and encyclopaedic knowledge of the environment, as in a mapping such as "jam is coffee".

Even with the related cultural background, some individual creations in literary discourse may be difficult to interpret. This can be seen in the following lines from the poem entitled *Hornpipe* by Edith Sitwell (Roberts 1965):

(11) *And the borealic **iceberg**; floating on they see*
New-arisen Madam Venus for those sake from afar
Came the fat and zebra'd emperor from Zanzibar

Where like golden bouquets la far Asia, Africa, Cathay,
All laid before that **shady lady** *by the* **fibroid Shah** ...

Cultural information gives a certain understanding to the title of the poem since a hornpipe was a form of traditional dance invented on British ships in past centuries to keep sailors physically fit and the iceberg metaphor refers to a ship. *Shady lady*, which is partly based on Sitwell's typical play of words using similar phonetic patterns, may refer to a lady under a parasol evoked by the hot climates of the geographical locations mentioned in the previous line. However, *fibroid Shah* would require a further stretch of the imagination.

These mappings show how they can only be created within one particular culture. They could be temporary creations but cultural mappings, like embodiment, can also be very long-term. This is particularly the case of features such as symbolism, as can be seen in animal and colour symbolism with respect to the histories of Chinese and English.

7 Culture and long-term diachronic mappings in one conceptual system

In a diachronic study of dragon lexemes in Mandarin Chinese, Hsieh (2007) dates their appearance in the records of historical events as far back as the Chunqiu Dynasty (770–476 B.C.). As Hsieh (2007: 3) points out, the Chinese and Western values of dragon symbolism have always been in opposition: "The Chinese dragon was created to be used as an icon, whereas the present-day, negative image of the Western dragon may have been popularised by the Bible, such as in Revelation 12:9, 'The great dragon was hurled down – that ancient serpent called the devil or Satan' ". However, it should be added that the negative reputation of a dragon may go back long before, as in the two dragon-like creatures Faruir and Nidhögg in early Germanic literature.

Hsieh further points out that the positive value of the dragon has continued since early records up until modern usages in the media. Early attestations include the relics of customs: *long chuan* ('dragon boat') being a long, narrow boat often decorated with dragon images. These boats traditionally sail on 5 May (of the Chinese lunar calendar) in vain attempts to save the patriot and poet Qu Yuan (340–278 B.C.). They also include expressions used in historical events such as *Ye gong hao long* ('Yegong-favour-dragon'), in which the noble Yegong (Chunqiu Dynasty) decorated his house with dragon carvings. In modern times, the positive aspects of the dragon can be seen in the Bruce Lee movie (1971): *meng long guo jiang* ('The Way of the Dragon' = strongmen). The contrast to these values in Western history is seen not only in the Bible but also the example of *Beowulf* in Old English literature in which the dragon is a symbol of terror and evil. The histories of Chinese and English thus no doubt lead to more metonymic expressions such as "strongmen" in the former or the rather negative connotation of an "aggressive housewife" in the latter.

Long-term cultural conceptualisation restricted to one cultural system can also be seen in colour symbolism in English. In contrast to the clear-cut symbolism of the dragon, a more extensive analysis of colours reveals that a certain degree of ambivalence becomes apparent within cultures and therefore an aspect of metaphorical polysemy is visible in certain colour projections. Two long-term paths in English are represented by the more specific projection "nobility is blue" and the more general mapping "negative is yellow" (Trim 2011: 124). A reference to colour symbolism in Shakespeare, implying a 400-year span in this corpus, indicates that blue was associated with the nobility at that time, in the same way as the term "blue blood" is used in British English today:

(12) *If thou so yield him, there is gold, and* **here my bluest veins to kiss; a hand that kings have lipp'd**, *and trembled kissing*
(Anthony and Cleopatra [II,5], II, 1084–6)

According to Kiernan (1993: 219), this conceptual metaphor went back to the feudal times of the Middle Ages and would therefore constitute long-term, diachronic distribution. The reference to blue veins tends to be more metonymic. The veins were probably more visible among non-labouring aristocrats who had a pale skin. It would, however, represent only one path in the conceptualisation of blue since many others have been mapped in English such as in the case of indecency, e.g. *blue joke*, or being of low spirits, as in *the blues*. The latter tend to have varied cultural origins which are speculative. The attribute of indecency is attested in different ways in various etymological dictionaries. For example, John Mactaggart's *Scottish Gallovidian Encyclopedia* (1824) records an entry for Thread o'Blue as "any little smutty touch in song-singing, chatting, or piece of writing". Farmer's *Slang and Its Analogues Past and Present* (1890) suggests that this meaning derives from the blue dress uniforms issued to harlots in houses of correction. However, he writes that the earlier slang authority, John Camden Hotten, "suggests it as coming from the French *Bibliothèque Bleu*, a series of books of very questionable character".

The metaphorical polysemy of blue can also be seen in the colour yellow. However, one long-term path in English is the "negative is yellow" mapping that has consistently referred to human behaviour such as adultery, treachery and cowardice. This may, to a large extent, be due to religion since Judas is traditionally dressed in yellow, as depicted in paintings. It may also be associated with yellow bile. It has repeatedly been used to denigrate certain sections of the society such as the Jews who were forced to wear yellow insignia in the 13th century (by order of the Fourth Lateran Council 1215) and to wear yellow stars in the early 20th century (by order of the Third Reich). The colour was used in the 19th century to denigrate strike pickets by unionists, a term that is still used in reference to cowardice. The same conceptual metaphor was used by Shakespeare:

(13) *O vengeance, vengeance! Me of my lawful pleasure she restrain'd and pray'd me oft forbearance did it with a pudency so rosy the sweet view on't might well have warm'd old Saturn; that I thought he as chaste as unsunn'd snow. O, all the devils!* **This yellow Iachimo,** *in an hour, – wast not? – Or less*
(Cymbeline [II,5], ll. 1379–86)

This negative trend in colour symbolism does not appear to exist in the history of other cultures such as Chinese, according to comparative lists drawn up by Xing (2009), except perhaps for the sense of "pornographic" in the lexeme *huangshu*, which she suggests may have been borrowed from other languages. The metaphor path in English would therefore represent trend (c) of the four-directional model, outlined above in section one, which entails long-term paths in one culture.

8 Culture and short-term synchronic uniformity

The fourth trend in which cultures match up synchronically in a conceptual model, but for which there is no long-term distribution, often concerns the borrowing of culture at a given point in time. The borrowing of cultural models may be more frequent than embodiment constructs, such as the centre of thought and feeling, but the borrowing of a linguistic metaphor can result in the transfer of a new conceptual metaphor as in the ECOLOGICAL IS GREEN metaphor described below. The lack of long-term distribution is often due to the fact that cultural borrowing can be fairly recent in language history, in the same way as the introduction of new ideas into politics and society. This aspect will again be analysed with respect to colour symbolism in English and Chinese.

The colour green and the binary concept black/white, for example, are symbolically very rich in both languages but vary in their historical evolution. The conceptual metaphor "ecological is green" is a relatively new form of conceptualisation. Originating in Germany in the 1970's, it had spread worldwide by the 1980's, the colour being adopted by many different ecological parties ranging from Tasmania to Canada. A glance at Hong Kong business websites also reveal that the notion of ecology associated with this colour has spread to Chinese culture, (at least, in this particular geographical location):

(14) *Dali wins the title of Outstanding Green Ecological City in the award ceremony of Green China 2011 held in Hong Kong on November 28, 2011*
(www.in.kunming.cn)

The spread to Chinese culture would imply that both the new conceptual metaphor "ecological is green", as well as a linguistic metaphor such as *green political party*, would have been borrowed even if there is no preceding conceptual link in the diachronic dimensions of both languages. In the case of green, it could be said that there is a natural association between green and the colour of nature. Xing (2009) points out that English and Chinese have similar semantic functions in the sense of "natural", citing the examples of *green/organic food* as in *luse shipin* in Chinese and *green energy* in English. However, colour labels for political concepts may be borrowed without a matching conceptual structure in the target language and the notion of ecology is a recent development which has arguably created a new conceptual metaphor. Fairly arbitrary colours such as red for communism may be adopted on the symbolic relation with the founding political party.

One idea that may be introduced here in relation to abstraction in the embodiment/culture ratio outlined above is that there may be a certain level of abstraction in cultural mappings well as in embodiment. This can be seen in the comparison between "negative is yellow" and "ecological is green". The first may be at a lower level of abstraction, since the choice of the mapping appears to be relatively arbitrary, unless some cultural form such as yellow bile is well established, whereas the second has a natural link to the green of nature. In other words, had the ecological movement started in China, there may have been the choice of this colour for the ecology movement. In certain circumstances, there may therefore be a degree of universal potential creation in cultural conceptualisation that is not directly linked to embodiment. The example of green is not an ideal one since distribution may nevertheless be restricted. Geographical areas such as desert regions or the Arctic may logically not have this type of colour association unless it has been imported. However, there might theoretically be certain mappings in visual perception, for example, that are worldwide due to uniform features of the environment and this would represent an important avenue of research if such features had a parallel development to embodiment.

With regard to the black/white opposition, there are also resemblances at the conceptual metaphor level between English and Chinese but some clear differences as well. Black and white are similar to the notions of dark and light, closely associated with physiological embodiment, and tend to conceptualise negative and positive values respectively. At the same time, the histories of these two colours reveal that attributes may vary considerably from a cross-cultural point of view. The contrast of black being associated with funerals in English and white in Chinese is clearly a cultural feature, rather than an embodied one. Xing (2009) cites Tao (1994) in suggesting that the link between white and funerals in Chinese culture originated in the Oracle Bone script (1200–1050 B.C.) which documented white as the colour of sacrificial offerings. At a later stage, white (*bai*) became the colour of funeral clothing and then, through metonymy, developed into *baishi* ('white event', i.e. funeral).

Certain conceptual level mappings appear, nevertheless, to be similar in the histories of the two languages. According to Xing (2009), the term *black heart*, in the sense of having an evil nature, has a correspondence in Chinese *heixinyan* (*hei* = black; *xinyan* = heart). The "evil is black" mapping must therefore have traditionally existed in both languages, as can be found in other Chinese examples listed by Xing such as *black road, black elements, black/illegal child* (i.e. a child who has not been registered with the authorities). However, another item in the Chinese list includes *black market* which, according to lexicographical studies, would clearly be a loan. The exact origin of the term is not clear but Ayto (1999) suggests that the English lexeme either originated from German *Schwarzmarkt* during World War I or from the buying and selling of (possibly military) supplies during World War II. Whatever the exact origin is, it is clear that it is used worldwide today and has also entered the Chinese language as the term *heishi*. One relevant difference here is that, in contrast to the new idea of "ecology is green" at the conceptual metaphor level, *black market* may have been loaned at the linguistic metaphor level and matched an existing conceptual system in the mapping of 'illegal'. This would depend on the origin of metaphors for 'illegal' in Chinese but, whatever the case may be, it is likely that the loaning at both the levels of conceptual and linguistic metaphor are possible. This is also likely in the embodiment category. As outlined above, the conceptual metaphor "anger is heat" was probably loaned into Old English from Latinate sources. The extent to which a loaned metaphor model matches a pre-existing conceptual system in the target language would probably influence post-loaning conceptual productivity rather than the loaning process itself.

The different examples given therefore appear to create at least four possible corresponding patterns when comparing the synchronic and diachronic dimensions. Examples of embodiment have been chosen to describe the first two trends (a–b) and cultural conceptualisation for the second two (c–d). The question now arises as to the role that the semantic field may play in the formation of these patterns or, in other terms, the nature of the source and target domains in the mapping. Does the type of semantic field in metaphor analysis, as in the choice of a corpus, play a role in how similar metaphors are either synchronically or diachronically?

9 Conceptual system and semantic field

By definition, a corpus or data-set usually entails a collection of items involving mappings in which one particular source or target semantic field is analysed. The corpus aims at finding out which target domain images result from source domain concepts or vice versa. For example, how the emotions (source domain) are conceptualised in terms of metaphoric images. In the case of some semantic fields, such as colour, the objective of a study may be to look at colour metaphors from the opposite angle, i.e. from the point of view of the target domain, and see what items colours represent. The structure of mappings may vary according to the particular domains concerned. Not all are likely to be bi-directional, i.e. "love is war" is perfectly feasible, as in *he is known for his many rapid conquests*, (Kövecses 1988: 72), but the reverse is less likely. It does, however, apparently appear in reference to specific societies or legends such as the war-faring Amazons in Greek mythology who regarded war against men as love, (Die Welt, 15 March 2013). Whichever the direction of mapping may be, the problem also arises as to the definition of a semantic field in relation to its conceptual system. The nature of the semantic field, however, may have an impact on the embodiment/culture ratio and therefore the patterns of trends (a–d) highlighted above.

Some semantic fields are more clear-cut than others while some are very heterogeneous in the types of concepts used. Different types of domains, as for example the emotions, colours and war, reveal considerable diversity between them (Trim 2011: 109). If these three domains are considered to be independent semantic fields, and the types of cognitive domains used in mapping structures tend to suggest this, a breakdown of their mappings vary considerably according to the embodiment/culture ratio. The emotions and colour tend to be relatively homogeneous from the point of view of the types of concepts involved, whereas war incorporates a vast domain of concepts. However, the first two differ in their embodiment and cultural components.

The emotions tend to be based on physiological concepts that have a relatively uniform type of structure such as anger, hate, pride, humility, etc., even though the form of certain emotions may vary between languages and cultures. This type of variability would include the example of love whose conceptualisation appears to vary synchronically with respect to a lack of fondness attested in certain African cultures (Kövecses 1988: 11). In the same way, love appears to have varied diachronically in Western society with regard to modern interpretations of medieval courtly love (Trim 2007: 169). Nevertheless, there are a high proportion of physiological mappings in love which may be of a universal nature: "love is unity" as in *the perfect match*; "love is blindness" as in *he was blinded by love*; "love is madness" as in *she drives me out of my mind* (Kövecses 1988).

The domain of colours has a relative degree of uniformity since it involves only one type of concept, i.e. colour, even though different colours are involved and the literal perception of colours may also vary between languages, e.g. Welsh *glas* that can represent English blue, green or even grey (Taylor 1989: 3). Returning to historical aspects of the colour blue, English *blue* was borrowed from Old French *blo* which had a variety of shades such pale, wan, light-coloured, blond, discoloured and blue-grey. Despite the possibility of abstraction levels in culture, there tends to be more cultural heterogeneity in figurative language along the synchronic scale. This can be seen in many of the English and Chinese examples cited above due to varying visual conceptualisation in the vast range of colour symbolism. Even within European languages, the conceptualisation of human emotions and qualities vary, as in the following examples: "cowardice is yellow" (English); "wryness is yellow" (French and Dutch); "envy is green" (English and Dutch); "strength is green" (French); "sadness is blue" (English), (Trim 2007: 61).

The uniformity of concepts in a semantic field becomes considerably more varied in a category such as war. If war is defined as one semantic field in corpus analysis, is it feasible to analyse homogeneity or heterogeneity of metaphor mappings according to embodiment and culture? Where are the limits of the semantic field of war? A long list of concepts ranges from military campaigns and personnel to all the types of weaponry used in armed conflict.

Furthermore, a vast category such as war would contain concepts that are not solely limited to its own category in the same way as the concept of colour is considered to be limited to one category. A concept such as *alliance* may be related to war but also belong to other cognitive domains and this pattern is no doubt typical of many other heterogeneous semantic fields. It leads not only to problems in defining the conceptual system relating to war, the variety of its concepts creates considerable cultural variation in contrast to the more uniform embodiment structures used in a field such as the emotions.

On this basis, one hypothesis that could be put forward is that the embodiment/culture ratio varies according to semantic field. This may be more easily quantified in domains whose limits are more easily defined such the emotions and colour. In other words, the emotions, due to their internal physiological characteristics, may have a higher level of embodied mapping than a domain such as the colours which is more dependent on cultural interpretation via visual perception. This would influence the embodiment/culture ratio. On a qualitative basis, the two semantic fields as source domains would have different amounts of conceptual metaphor mappings involving the level of potential internal creation. Universal types of mappings such as "anger is pressure" would thus be more dominant in the field of the emotions than culturally-specific mappings such as "yellow is negative" in the domain of colour. This hypothesis would be based on the fact that, even if there is a certain degree of abstraction in culture as in the conceptual metaphor "ecology is nature and therefore green", potential universal creation is still more apparent in embodiment than culture.

10 Conclusions on similarity and variability in synchronic and diachronic metaphor

The preceding discussions have suggested that metaphors can have wide distribution of matching conceptual models across time and cultural space according to at least four main trends: a) diachronically and synchronically in different cultures, b) cross-culturally at different historical periods, c) diachronically in one culture and d) synchronically on a short-term basis. Two major components in mappings influence this distribution: embodiment and culture which tend to be mixed at varying levels according to the semantic field of the corpus concerned. In addition, it is highly likely that the extent of distribution along the synchronic and diachronic dimensions depends on the level of abstraction of the mapping.

The first two trends were described on the basis of embodiment constructs, the last two on culture. However, on the basis of the different examples discussed, and pending additional information which would confirm all hypotheses, it could be postulated that embodiment may be found in all four trends. ANGER IS PRESSURE could relate to (a) and the *hara* concept to (b) and (c). More data would be needed to confirm (d) but if the ANGER IS HEAT embodied concept was loaned into Old English, it may be assumed that such constructs may be loaned on short or long-term bases.

The cultural component differs to the extent that it is unlikely that cultural concepts follow the pattern in trend (a), unless the claim could be proved that there are certain types of cultural conceptualisation that have a high level of abstraction and are therefore potentially creative in all cultures. Otherwise, they would normally appear in the other three trends. More data would be required to confirm trend (b), although this is hypothetically possible. The examples above show that they are present in trends (c) and (d) with regard to colour symbolism.

These findings highlight an important feature in the distribution levels: wide distribution both synchronically and diachronically normally reflects two processes: potential internal creation (embodiment) and the maintenance or extension of cultural thought (culture). Embodiment, at a high level of abstraction, is likely to create similar patterns at any given point. Culture appears to increase synchronic/diachronic distribution as a result of the extension of mappings in time or via language contact.

The abstraction level in the embodiment/culture mix tends to be graded in the overall mapping: both within conceptual metaphors and between conceptual and linguistic metaphors. This can be seen in the "goal-journey-road" sequence. These concepts represent lowering levels of abstraction respectively from: a) the "source-path-goal" image schema that may represent a universal trend in embodiment to b) the more cultural "life is a journey" conceptual metaphor and to the c) *moving forward ... trust is a two-way street* linguistic metaphor that forms part of the overall "goal" image schema. Furthermore, the embodiment/culture ratio may vary according to the semantic field or corpus under study and this may have an influence on potential creation and cultural maintenance/extension. It can be seen from the discussion above that this distinction is apparent in the fields of the emotions and colours respectively.

A conclusion that can be put forward here is that the embodied component of a mapping tends to be potentially creative at both the synchronic and diachronic levels, whereas the wide or extended distribution of the cultural component appears to be either within the synchronic dimension on the one hand, or within the diachronic dimension on the other. Cultural mappings are unlikely to be within both at the same time and distribution tends to vary according to their weighting in the conceptual structure of any given semantic field. Thus, the potential internal creation of "anger is pressure" in the emotions may be widespread along both dimensions, as in English and Chinese. Depending on how Chinese "qi" is interpreted, this may represent trend (a), i.e. the underlying conceptual metaphor can be found both synchronically across languages as well as diachronically. On the other hand, culturally motivated conceptual metaphors such as colour symbolism tend to be extensive either synchronically or diachronically. For the reasons outlined above, "ecology is green" is thus widespread synchronically and "negative is yellow" diachronically. More empirical data would help verify these hypotheses but the models suggested in this analysis may go some way to defining which types of conceptual metaphor can be found at different points in both time and cross-cultural space.

References

Allan, Kathryn. 2003. A diachronic approach to figurative language. In John A. Barnden (ed.), *Proceedings of the Interdisciplinary Workshop on Corpus-Based Approaches to Figurative Language, 27 March, 2003*, 1–8. Lancaster: UCREL Technical Papers.

Allan, Kathryn. 2008. *Metaphor and metonymy: A diachronic approach.* Chichester: Wiley & Blackwell.

Aitchison, Jean. 1989. *Words in the mind: An introduction to the mental lexicon.* Oxford: Blackwell.

Ayto, John. 1999. *20th century words: The story of new words in English over the last 100 years.* Oxford: Oxford University Press.

Bokor, Zsuzsanna. 1997. Body-based constructionism in the conceptualization of anger. C.L.E.A.R. series, no. 17. Budapest: Department of English, Hamburg University and the Department of American Studies, ELTE.

Brown, Cecil H. & Stanley R. Witkowski. 1981. Figurative language in a universalist perspective. *American Ethnologist* 8. 596–615.

Chickering, Howell D. 1977. *Beowulf. A dual-language edition.* Anchor Books, New York.

Egli, Sandra R. 2002. *A study of equivalence in Hara assessments using the Brennan Healing Science model.* Phoenix Holos University dissertation.

Evans, Vyvyan. 2013. *Language and time: A cognitive linguistics approach.* Cambridge: Cambridge University Press.

Geeraerts, Dirk & Caroline Gevaert. 2008. Hearts and (angry) minds in Old English. In Farzad Sharifian, René Dirven, NingYu & Susanne Niemeyer (eds.), *Culture and language: Looking for the mind inside the body*, 319–346. Berlin & New York: Mouton de Gruyter.

Geeraerts, Dirk & Stefan Grondelaers. 1995. Looking back at anger: Cultural traditions and metaphorical patterns. In John R. Taylor & Robert E. MacLaury (eds.) *Language and the cognitive construal of the world*, 153–180, Berlin & New York: Mouton de Gruyter.

Gevaert, Caroline. 2001. Anger in Old and Middle English: a 'hot' topic? In *Belgian Essays on Language and Literature*, Belgian Association of Anglicists in Higher Education, University of Liège, Belgium, 89–101.

Gevaert, Caroline. 2002. The evolution of the lexical and conceptual field of anger in Old and Middle English. In Javier E. Diaz-Vera (ed.) *A changing world of words: Diachronic approaches to English lexicology, lexicography and semantics*, 275–299. Amsterdam: Rodopi.

Hsieh, Shelley Ching-yu. 2007. A diachronic study of dragon lexemes in Mandarin Chinese: Lexical change and semantic development. *Intergrams* 8.1. http://benz.nchu.edu.tw/intergrams/081/081-hsieh.pdf

Jager, Eric. 1990. Speech and the chest in Old English poetry: morality or pectorality? *Speculum* 65(4). 845–859.

Johnson-Laird, Philip N. 1983. *Mental models*. Cambridge: Cambridge University Press.

Katz, Albert N., Allan Paivio, Marc Marschark & James M. Clark. 1988. Norms for 204 literary and 260 nonliterary metaphors on 10 psychological dimensions. *Metaphor and Symbolic Activity* 3(4). 191–215.

Kiernan, Ryan. 1993. *Shakespeare: Poet and citizen*. New York: Routledge.

Kövecses, Zoltán. 1988. *The language of love*. London & Toronto: Associated University Presses.

Kövecses, Zoltán. 2005. *Metaphor in culture: Universality and variation*. Cambridge: Cambridge University Press.

Kövecses, Zoltán. 2006. *Language, mind and culture*. Oxford: Oxford University Press.

Lakoff, George. 1987. *Women, fire and dangerous things. What categories reveal about the mind*. Chicago: University of Chicago Press.

Lakoff, George & Mark Johnson. 1980. *Metaphors we live by*. Chicago: University of Chicago Press.

Lakoff, George & Mark Johnson. 1999. *Philosophy in the flesh: The embodied mind and its challenge to Western thought*. New York: Basic Books.

Le Goff, Jacques. 1989. Head or heart? The political use of body metaphors in the Middle Ages. In Michel Feher (ed.), *Fragments for a history of the human body*, 3, 13–26. New York: Zone.

Maier, Christophe. 2000. *Crusade ideology and propaganda*. Cambridge: Cambridge University Press.

Matsuki, Keiko. 1995. Metaphors of anger in Japanese. In John R. Taylor (ed.), *Language and the cognitive construal of the world*, 137–151. Berlin & New York: Mouton de Gruyter.

Micholajczuk, Agneszka. 1998. The metonymic and metaphoric conceptualization of anger in Polish. In Angeliki Athanasiadou & Elżbieta Tabakowska (eds.), *Speaking of emotions: Conceptualization and expression*, 153–191. Berlin & New York: Mouton de Gruyter.

Munro, Pamela. 1991. ANGER IS HEAT: Some data for a cross-linguistic survey. Manuscript, Department of Linguistics, UCLA.

Padel, Ruth. 1992. *In and ut of the Mind. Greek images of the tragic self*. Princeton: Princeton University Press.

Riddle, Elizabeth M. 2000. The "string" metaphor of life and language in Hmong. Paper presented at the International Pragmatics Conference, Budapest, Hungary.

Roberts, Michael (ed.). 1965. *The Faber book of modern verse*. London: Faber & Faber.

Rosch, Eleanor. 1975. Cognitive representations of semantic categories. *Journal of Experimental Psychology* 104(3). 192–233.

Taylor, John R. 1989. *Linguistic categorization: Prototypes in linguistic theory*. Oxford: Clarendon Press.

Taylor, John R. & Thandi Mbense. 1998. Red dogs and rotten mealies: How Zulus talk about anger. In Angeliki Athanasiadou & Elżbieta Tabakowska (eds.), *Speaking of emotions: Conceptualisation and expression*, 191–226. Berlin & New York: Mouton de Gruyter.

Traugott, Elizabeth Closs. 1985. "Conventional" and "dead" metaphors revisited. In Wolf Paprotté & René Dirven (eds.), *The ubiquity of metaphor: Metaphor in language and thought*, 17–56. Amsterdam & Philadelphia: John Benjamins.

Trim, Richard. 2007. *Metaphor networks. The comparative evolution of figurative language.* Basingstoke: Palgrave Macmillan.

Trim, Richard. 2011. *Metaphor and the historical evolution of conceptual mapping.* Basingstoke: Palgrave Macmillan.

Trim, Richard. Forthcoming. Abstraction levels in the universality of time and space in metaphorisation. Proceedings of the 27th International Summer School for Semiotic and Structural Studies, Imatra, Finland, 2012.

Veith, Ilza. 1982. HUANG TI NEI CHING SU WEN: The Emperor's Classic of Internal Medicine. Tapei: Southern Materials Center, Inc.

Winters, Margaret. 1992. Schemas and prototypes: Remarks on syntax change. In Gunter Kellermann & Michael D. Morrisey (eds.), *Diachrony within synchrony: Language history and cognition,* 265–280. Bern: Peter Lang.

Xing, Janet Zhiqun. 2009. Semantic and pragmatics of color terms in Chinese. In Janet Zhiqun Xing (ed.) *Studies of Chinese linguistics: Functional approaches*. Hong Kong: Hong Kong University Press.

Yu, Ning. 1995. Metaphorical expressions of anger and happiness in English and Chinese. *Metaphor and Symbolic Activity* 10. 223–245.

Yu, Ning. 1998. *The contemporary theory of metaphor: A perspective from Chinese.* Amsterdam & Philadelphia: John Benjamins.

Figuration and grammaticalization

Andrew D. M. Smith and Stefan H. Höfler
The pivotal role of metaphor in the evolution of human language

Abstract: There is broad agreement among evolutionary linguists that the emergence of human language, as opposed to other primate communication systems, is characterised by two key phenomena: the use of symbols, and the use of grammatical structure (Tomasello 2003). In this paper, we show that these two defining aspects of language actually emerge from the same set of underlying cognitive mechanisms within the context of ostensive-inferential communication. We take an avowedly cognitive approach to the role of metaphor in language change, setting out how general capacities such as the recognition of common ground, the inference of meaning from context, and the memorisation of language usage, can together lead to the conventionalisation of metaphors, and thence to systematic changes in language structure, including the development of grammatical linguistic units from formerly meaningful elements through grammaticalisation (Hoefler and Smith 2009). We show that the relevant cognitive competences are general-purpose mechanisms which are crucially not specific to language; they also underpin non-linguistic communication, where the same processes lead to the emergence of apparently arbitrary symbols.

1 Introduction

The fundamental problem of human language evolution is concerned with providing explanations of how a linguistic communication system emerged from a non-linguistic state. Although there are deep and ongoing controversies over the precise nature of human language (Chomsky 1995; Hauser Chomsky, and Fitch 2002; Jackendoff 2002; Langacker 1987; Tomasello 2003a), the wider evolutionary problem is almost always, even by otherwise bitter opponents (e.g. Bickerton 2003; Tomasello 2003b), operationalised into two distinct sub-problems, namely the emergence of symbolism and the emergence of grammar. Tomasello suggests, for instance, that:

Andrew D. M. Smith: University of Stirling
Stefan H. Höfler: University of Zurich

> [l]anguage is a complex outcome of human cognitive and social processes taking place in evolutionary, historical and ontogenetic time. And different aspects of language – for example, symbols and grammar – may have involved different processes and different evolutionary times. (Tomasello 2003b: 109)

In contrast to this common bifurcation of the problem, we claim instead in this article that the cognitive mechanisms underlying metaphor can provide a *single* solution to the two evolutionary sub-problems. We thus suggest a unified explanation of how human language could have initially emerged from 'no language' and then developed complex grammatical structures. We further argue that these mechanisms actually underpin all human communication, both linguistic and non-linguistic, from its pre-historical beginnings to the present. The paper is divided into three main sections: in section 2 we identify the two fundamental cognitive mechanisms on which metaphor is built, and which form the foundations of our analysis, namely ostensive-inferential communication and conventionalisation. We then apply these same mechanisms to explain both the emergence of symbols (in section 3) and of grammatical structures (in section 4), before presenting our conclusions in section 5.

2 The cognitive underpinnings of metaphor

Metaphor is a creative process in which an existing linguistic form is used to express a meaning similar, but not identical, to its conventional meaning (Kövecses 2002). Individual metaphors are built on an inferable analogy between the original and the novel meanings, or the 'source' and 'target' meanings in Lakoff and Johnson (1980)'s terms. Importantly, however, metaphor is not a deviant special case of language use, nor is literal use the default setting for language; metaphorical language use is often speciously considered exceptional only because of the seductively erroneous assumption that language is a tool which enables the speaker to encode meaning and the hearer to decode it (Wilson and Sperber 2012). Linguistic communication is, however, not simply an encoding-decoding process, nor is it even a process of reverse-engineering in which the hearer puts the speaker's original meaning back together again (Mufwene 2002; Brighton, Smith, and Kirby 2005); rather it is best characterised by the complementary processes of ostension and inference (Sperber and Wilson 1995).

The mutual recognition of common ground between interlocutors is the crucial cognitive mechanism which underpins ostensive-inferential communication; it both forms the foundation for the key processes of ostension and inference, and enables the use of existing conventions in novel ways. Common ground, the knowledge the interlocutors assume they share with each other, has a number of key aspects, including: shared recognition of each other as potential interlocutors; shared understanding of the goal of the communicative episode, built on an understanding of the other's intentions (Tomasello, Carpenter, Call, Behne, and Moll 2005); the recognition of relevant content from the context of the shared communicative episode; and shared conventions, including existing form-meaning mappings. On the basis of this shared knowledge, communication can be established as follows. The speaker[1] executes an ostensive act whose deliberate and atypical nature marks it as potentially relevant, and thus establishes the speaker's communicative intention. Furthermore, the ostensive act also invites the hearer to inferentially construct a relevant meaning, using as evidence the ostensive act itself, the context in which the act is performed, and the existing conventions shared by the interlocutors. This inferential construction of meaning by the hearer is a fundamentally uncertain and approximate process, which relies on highly idiosyncratic systems of knowledge, individually created by the interlocutors from their different cognitive representations of the world and of the context in which the ostensive act is made, and from their different representations of existing linguistic and cultural conventions. In such inexact circumstances, non-conventional (i.e. metaphorical) use of language is inevitable and ubiquitous, and this leads inexorably to the fluidity and variability characteristic of language.

Metaphors are defined by the analogical connections which can be drawn between the source and target meaning, and are interpreted in the same way: the hearer infers the parts of the source meaning relevant in the communicative context, and constructs an ad-hoc interpretation based on these relevant semantic fragments. The simple metaphor "John's a real pig", for instance, might be interpreted in various ways, depending on the context in which it is uttered: it might suggest that John is very messy, that he is very fat, that his eating habits are messy or gluttonous, or that he behaves very badly, among many others. The actual meaning constructed by the hearer would depend on which of these properties, which are conventionally associated with the source (pigs), appear most relevant and appropriate to the hearer in the current context. The use is clearly metaphorical because the inferentially constructed meaning is only similar, rather than identical, to the conventional meaning of 'pig'. In metaphorical usage more generally, the conventional meaning con-

---

1 Note that we use the terms *speaker* and *hearer* in a general sense to denote the communicator and the addressee, independently of whether the mode of communication is vocal or gestural.

tains more information than the meaning which is intended to be communicated; its less relevant meaning components (for instance, having a curly tail or four toes) must be ignored for the communicative episode to succeed. This very abandonment of the less relevant parts of the conventional meaning during the ostensive-inferential process, of course, is the key action which renders the use metaphorical. This ostensive-inferential view of metaphor leads to two interesting conclusions. Firstly, as Deutscher (2005) points out, there are almost always some aspects of conventional meaning which are ignored in a particular communicative episode, because they are irrelevant in the context; metaphor is therefore effectively ubiquitous in human communication. Secondly, we can see that every instance of language use can be placed on a figurative continuum, which runs from true literalness to traditional poetic metaphor (Sperber and Wilson 1995). This continuum from literal to figurative, metaphorical language use also encompasses phenomena such as metonymy, in which an object may be identified by one of its most salient properties, e.g. reference by a waitress to a particular diner as "The ham sandwich", cf. Sag (1981). In such cases the appropriate non-conventional meaning, namely the identification of a specific individual, is inferred by the hearer as the most relevant use of the metonymic expression, while the conventional, less relevant, components of its meaning must be ignored (Papafragou 1999). The figurative continuum can therefore be defined in terms of how much of the conventional meaning is disregarded, and how flagrantly these disregarded components clash with the actual meaning communicated.

Successful metaphors, though, are not ephemeral, but rather repeatedly used and adopted by other speakers. A vital part of our account of the evolution of both symbols and grammar, indeed, is the process of *conventionalisation* through which the originally novel usage of a form becomes conventional through repeated use. The cognitive process underlying this transformation is the simple assumption that interlocutors can remember their language use: whenever a form is used metaphorically, both speaker and hearer can add the novel form-meaning mappings to their linguistic repertoire. This memorisation of usage has two important effects: the entrenchment of the new association between form and meaning in the interlocutors' individual linguistic knowledge, and the establishment of new common ground between them. Expressions become entrenched in people's knowledge in proportion to their frequency of use: the more often a form-meaning mapping is used, the more readily accessible it becomes to the user, so that it can become invoked without the potentially complex reasoning which allowed its creation in the first place (Langacker 1987). A successful metaphorical usage is also new information which can itself be added to the common ground shared by the interlocutors and thus be used as background knowledge in future interactions: this not only allows the metaphor to be subsequently more easily interpreted, but more importantly it may also allow the metaphor to be used without its original licensing context. Both entrenchment and the establishment of new common ground, therefore, can allow specific metaphorical mappings to become increasingly independent of the context in which they were created. This is equivalent to the linguistic phenomenon of context-absorption (Kuteva 2001; Traugott and Dasher 2005), in which a meaning which originally had to be inferred pragmatically from the context comes to be semantically encoded. Once the meaning is part of the conventional meaning, we can regard the original metaphor as having been conventionalised; clear examples of this abound throughout language and are often dubbed 'dead metaphors' (Deutscher 2005: 118). Our claim in this article, however, is that *all* linguistic constructions derive from conventionalised metaphors; they are the culmination of originally ad-hoc ostensive acts whose meanings were inferred from context, memorised and subsequently entrenched through repeated use.

3 The evolution of symbols

Metaphor is usually considered as a linguistic phenomenon, as the use of a linguistic symbol in a non-literal manner. We agree with this characterisation of metaphor – metaphor can act on linguistic symbols – but argue that metaphor actually pre-dates symbolism. In this section, we intend to show that metaphor is involved in the processes of ostensive-inferential communication that lead to both (i) the emergence of iconicity and (ii) the emergence of symbolism.

3.1 Iconicity

In a first step, we intend to show that the cognitive mechanisms underlying the ad-hoc creation and use of an icon in an episode of ostensive-inferential communication are the same as the ones employed in the creation and use of an ad-hoc metaphor in present-day linguistic communication. To this aim, we will first have a closer look at the cognitive mechanisms involved in ostensive-inferential communication.

The most basic mode of ostensive-inferential communication is that of *direct ostension*. In this mode, the speaker creates a physical stimulus that allows the hearer to acquire the information that the speaker intends to communicate. If it is understood between the speaker and the hearer that, in the given situation, it is relevant for the hearer to know whether A or B, then the speaker, who knows that A, can provide the hearer with the information she requires simply by showing her that A. If, for instance, a father asks his daughter, upon her leaving the house, whether she has got her keys, then the daughter can provide her father with the required information simply by making him see how she takes her keys out of her pocket and puts them back in.[2]

Direct ostension does not require that the hearer recognises the communicative intention of the speaker: the hearer will acquire the information that the speaker wants to pass on to her by observing the speaker's ostensive act anyway. The speaker, on the other hand, does need to have an understanding of the hearer's communicative needs if he is to produce the right ostensive stimulus under the right circumstances. Note that in some situations, more than one ostensive stimulus may be available to make the intended information available to the hearer. If, in such situations, one of these stimuli is chosen more frequently than the others, the association between this particular stimulus and the respective meaning may become entrenched to a point where the stimulus will become the conventional way of communicating that meaning. The deeper the entrenchment becomes, the less important the original connection between the produced form and the communicated meaning will be: "association [which has] become habitual ceases to be association" (Keller 1998: 110). The conventionalisation of the use of a particular ostensive stimulus for conveying a particular meaning – possibly accompanied by a frequency-induced change in the form of the stimulus – is one path that can lead to the emergence of symbolic form-meaning associations. However, this path alone would not allow a simple communication system to become much more expressive over time; for a communication system to reach the level of expressivity that one finds in present-day human language, the cognitive mechanism of metaphorical extension, as it can be first observed in the emergence of iconicity, has to be in place.

In the *iconic* mode of ostensive-inferential communication, the speaker produces a stimulus that does not provide the intended information directly but whose form shares some conceptual properties with that information: "[t]he relation between an icon and its denotatum is that of similarity" (Keller 1998: 102). Suppose, for instance, a young woman asks a fellow student if this week's sports practice will include jumping or football, and that fellow student responds by drawing a circle in the air with his hand. The young woman will soon realise that a "literal" interpretation, i.e., taking the fact that her friend

---

[2] Keller (1998) calls stimuli that are used for direct ostension *symptoms*, Deacon (1997) refers to them as *indexes*.

Tab. 1: Comparative schematic analysis of pre-symbolic metaphor and symbol-based metaphor.

	Pre-symbolic metaphor	Symbolic metaphor
Example		
Communicative Situation	A gesture drawing a circle in the air with one's hand is produced in a context where a type of sport (football or running) needs to be identified.	The utterance "Sally is a chameleon" is produced in a context where one refers to a girl named Sally.
Analysis		
Signal (form)	round manual gesture	/kəˈmiːljən/
Signal meaning	round manual gesture (by ostension)	small appearance-changing reptile (by convention)
Relevant aspect	round	appearance-changing
Ignored aspects	manual gesture	small reptile
Inferred speaker meaning	football	appearance-changing person

has made said gesture at face value, does not provide her with any relevant information: communication, in this case, does not happen via direct ostension alone. However, as the young woman also realises that her friend would be cooperative (Grice 1957), and that he knows that she realises this, she can assume the produced cue to be there to point her to a relevant bit of information. In the present case, she may come to the conclusion that the shape of her friend's gesture resembles the shape of a football (they are both round) but does not resemble anything related to jumping; she will thus infer that the meaning her friend intended to communicate is the concept of football rather than that of jumping.

In an episode of iconic ostensive-inferential communication, the concept represented by the produced cue does not itself constitute the meaning intended by the speaker; it is rather transferred, by means of analogy, to the domain of potentially relevant meanings. An icon is thus an ostensive stimulus used metaphorically: some aspect of the signal meaning (here, the signal meaning is the concept represented by the signal itself: a manual gesture in the shape of a circle) is ignored because it is mutually recognised as irrelevant by the two interlocutors, while some other aspect of it also occurs in the speaker meaning and thus serves as a cue that helps the hearer identify the meaning that the speaker intends to communicate. The schematic comparison given in Table 1 illustrates that icons are pre-symbolic metaphors, i.e., metaphors created before the produced signal has been paired, through entrenchment, with a conventional meaning and thus become dissociated from the immediate information its form conveys. This analysis suggests that metaphor is a capacity that pre-dates symbolic communication: as it is grounded in the cognitive mechanisms of ostensive-inferential communication, its use is not limited to symbolic communication.

3.2 Symbolism

In a second step, we now turn to the role that metaphor plays in the emergence of a symbolic communication system. Symbols have frequently been described as conventionalised associations between forms and meanings where the relationship between form and meaning appears to be arbitrary.[3] We have already discussed how conventionalised form-meaning associations come about: they emerge if a particular signal is repeatedly used to express a particular meaning, so that the respective communicative behaviour becomes ritualised and entrenched in the collective memory of a population of interlocutors. The question that remains to be answered then is how form-meaning associations can become arbitrary. We contend that metaphor plays a crucial role in this process.

In principle, there are two pathways along which a non-arbitrary form-meaning association can become arbitrary: either the form changes or the meaning changes. Metaphor is the key to the second pathway: the mechanisms of ostensive-inferential communication make it possible for a speaker to use an extant form-meaning association to convey a novel, metaphorical meaning. The example given in Table 1 illustrates the difference between the use of a non-symbolic and a symbolic metaphor: while in the case of the former, the signal meaning that the metaphor exploits is created by means of ostension and thus coincides with the conceptual properties of the produced signal itself, in the case of the latter, it falls from an extant convention that associates the produced signal with a specific meaning. The actual metaphorical process, however, is the same in both cases: the hearer observes that the speaker has expressed a signal meaning which, if taken literally, does not seem to contribute in a relevant way to the present interaction. The hearer, presupposing the speakers' co-operativeness, then realises that some aspects of the signal mean-

---

[3] We say that the form-meaning association *appears* to be arbitrary because it is evidently not arbitrary from a diachronic perspective, i.e., if one knows the causal chain of events that has led to a symbolic form-meaning association.

ing do also occur in a potential speaker meaning that would be relevant in the given context. She thus ignores all irrelevant aspects of the signal meaning and uses the relevant aspect to infer the presumably intended speaker meaning. In the given example, the hearer observes the speaker stating that a human girl called Sally is a chameleon. She realises that, Sally being human, the fact that chameleons are small reptiles cannot constitute relevant information in the present context. She then infers that the speaker rather intends to point to some characteristics that chameleons and Sally share, namely that they both frequently change their appearance or that they easily blend in with their surroundings.

Once an extant form is used in the same metaphorical sense frequently enough, the association between that form and its new, metaphorical meaning will itself become entrenched and conventionalised. The new convention can then serve again as the starting point for the creation of yet another metaphor. Repeated metaphorical extension and conventionalisation may thus ultimately lead to an obfuscation of the original link between the form and the meaning it is associated with: the relationship between form and meaning becomes arbitrary. Metaphor thus allows interlocutors to use extant form-meaning associations as stepping stones to reach meaning spaces that were so far not covered by their communication system. In this way, the repeated conventionalisation of originally metaphorical extensions makes ever new meaning spaces accessible. This cumulative application of metaphor to conventionalised associations allows the expression of meanings which could potentially not have been reached in a single inferential step, thus greatly expanding the communicable meaning space. In present-day linguistic communication, the use of an ad-hoc metaphor may most often not be motivated by the problem that the intended meaning could otherwise not be expressed, but rather by pragmatic factors such as a need for brevity or social aspects such as the wish to attract attention, establish prestige by displaying one's eloquence, or avoid committing oneself (Pinker, Nowak, and Lee 2008). In the evolution of human language, however, the creative function of metaphor has played a pivotal role, without which the emergence and evolution of a symbolic communication system as expressive as human language may not have been possible.

In summary, our analysis so far suggests that the cognitive and communicative mechanisms involved in metaphor not only pre-date symbolic communication, but that they also constitute key prerequisites for (i) conventional form-meaning associations to become arbitrary over time, (ii) for new meaning spaces to become expressible and thus (iii) for originally simple symbolic communication systems to eventually reach the expressivity that we find in present-day human languages.

4 The evolution of grammar

Our analysis has taken an avowedly cognitive approach to language, which ultimately relies on two principal assumptions, commonly called the symbolic and usage-based theses (Evans and Green, 2006). The symbolic thesis holds that language has a fundamentally symbolic function, and therefore that the central unit of language is an association or mapping between a form and a meaning, and that an individual's linguistic knowledge can be described as a "structured inventory of conventional linguistic units" (Langacker 2008: 222). The usage-based thesis considers that there is no distinction between linguistic 'competence' and 'performance', rather that knowledge of language consists simply of abstractions of these form-meaning associations from the situated instances of their use in language. Crucially for our account, the symbolic thesis assumes that meaning is central to *all* linguistic units, including not only lexical items, but also grammatical schematic constructions such as 'the passive construction' or 'the intransitive construction'. The idea that both grammatical constructions and lexical items are inherently meaningful leads inevitably to the fact that the lexicon and grammar should not be considered as distinct entities, as in traditional generative grammar, but rather that they are, in a fundamental sense, the same. Given their common symbolic nature, it might also therefore be parsimonious to assume that their origins might be similarly accounted for by the same set of cognitive capacities.

Although there is no fundamental distinction between grammatical and lexical items in cognitive linguistics, they can nevertheless differ *qualitatively* in both form and meaning: whereas a prototypical lexical item has a monomorphemic form expressing a concrete, basic-level meaning (such as 'cat'), grammatical items typically have abstract schematic forms which express functional, schematic meanings. The passive construction, for instance, has its own abstract form which specifies both the types of its components and the order in which they are put together (X be VERB-ed by Y) associated with its own very general meaning, roughly focusing attention on the PATIENT (X) affected by the action described by the verb rather than the AGENT (Y) who actually carries out the action. The linguistic process through which grammatical structure is created is traditionally called grammaticalisation, and involves a number of changes through which lexical items gradually lose their independence of use and their meanings become more functional (Givón, 1979; Haspelmath, 1998). If we accept the symbolic thesis, then grammaticalisation can be conceptualised simply as a process of a symbol moving towards the grammar end of the lexicon-grammar continuum. The continuum itself is often conceptualised in traditional grammaticalisation theory using the metaphor of a cline, or a natural pathway along which linguistic items 'travel' as they become grammaticalised (Hopper and Traugott 2003). With this idea in mind, the focus of our enquiry now shifts to *how* items move towards the lexicon end of the lexicon-grammar continuum: in particular, how do schematic forms emerge, and where do abstract, functional meanings come from? We suggest that the cognitive capacities which enable metaphor also play a pivotal role in both these issues.

4.1 Schematic forms

The defining characteristic of schematic forms is that they contain variable slots which can be filled by multiple possibilities, such as the variables X, VERB and Y in the form of the passive construction described above. Schematic forms arise from the process of memorisation, the way in which constructions are stored, analysed and compared with each other. When a linguistic form is interpreted, the hearer constructs a meaning from context, and remembers the connections between form and meaning. These connections can be of essentially arbitrary complexity, depending on how form and meaning are analysed: the whole form may be mapped to the whole meaning; individual components of the form may also be mapped to individual semantic components.

But linguistic forms are inevitably structured in a linear fashion with items being expressed in sequence: this structure itself (the order of the items being produced) can also be mapped to parts of the constructed meaning. For example, the expression of one form *a* followed by another form *b* to invite the inference that the speaker wishes to draw attention to a state of affairs A and provide further information B about A allows the hearer to infer not only the mappings $a \leftrightarrow A$ and $b \leftrightarrow B$ but also that in a form containing two components, the first component refers to the topic of communication and the second to comment about that topic. It is, of course, no coincidence that the resulting construction in this case is the basis of the topic/comment and subject/predicate structures which are so pervasive in human languages.

Complex forms (those with multiple components) allow not only this kind of internal analysis of their own structure, but also external analysis in comparison with other complex forms. Two forms *ab* and *ac* sharing a sub-component *a* can easily be reanalysed with the shared component as a fixed item, combined with a variable slot which can be filled with either *b* or *c*. Tomasello (2003a) describes how children's language emerges in exactly this way, as children construct their language from analyses of the language they hear, with their emergent languages passing through a number of distinct stages. Initially, children's two-word combinations contain two roughly equivalent words under one intonation contour (e.g. *ball table*), but they soon develop a more systematic pattern, or pivot schema, in which one fixed item determines the function of the utterance and the other fills in a variable slot (e.g. *more juice, more milk*). These basic schemas develop into item-based constructions, frequently based around verbs, where the roles played by the participants are marked (by word order, morphology or syntactic markers), but only for individual items; there are no generalised 'thematic roles' like agent or instrument, rather a particular role might be marked with a preposition in one verb construction, for instance, but by word order in another verb construction. Tomasello (2003a) suggests that more general constructions are then created by children from these item-based constructions, as cross-construction patterns are found and analogies made, yielding abstract, adult-like constructions such as the transitive (X VERB-s Y), where the AGENT carries out the action of the verb on the PATIENT. Such abstract schemas can only be constructed because of humans' prodigious ability not only to infer the meaning associated with ostensive linguistic behaviour, but also more generally to find patterns and make analogies between existing symbols: these are the very cognitive capabilities which underlie the creation of metaphor.

Although the examples given show the emergence of relatively simple schematic forms, there is no reason to doubt that the same process is not implicated in the emergence of more general syntactic patterns from discourse strategies. We thus agree both with Tomasello (2003a) that similar processes, underpinned by the same cognitive capacities, are likely to have occurred in the evolution of language, and, more generally, with Hopper (1987)'s suggestion that all grammatical structures emerge from the pragmatic strategies employed by speakers in discourse.

4.2 Functional meaning

Although much of the literature on grammaticalisation refers to the idea of semantic loss or bleaching, e.g. "weakening of semantic content" (Givón 1973) or "desemanticization" (Heine and Kuteva 2002), it is probably more accurate to say that although concrete meanings are lost, there is also a somewhat compensatory gain of abstract meanings which provide more information about grammatical function, and which of course is the major result of grammaticalisation. Heine and Kuteva (2002)'s detailed analysis of grammaticalisation across a wide sample of the world's languages shows clearly that unambiguous patterns of grammatical development recur repeatedly in multiple unrelated languages. For instance, forms originally meaning BACK have independently developed into locational adpositions denoting BEHIND in languages as diverse as Icelandic, Halia, Moré, Kpelle, Baka, Aranda, Welsh, Imonda and Gimira (Smith 2011). Moreover, these developments are themselves instances of more general, frequent metaphorical shifts which use the human body as a basic template to express location; Heine and Kuteva (2002) present examples from various languages showing the development of adpositions from words meaning BELLY, BOWELS, BREAST, BUTTOCKS, EYE, FACE, FLANK, FOREHEAD, HEAD, HEART, MOUTH, NECK, SHOULDER and SIDE. Although the specific metaphors used vary from language to language (Heine, Claudi, and Hünnemeyer 1991), the most striking feature of these networks is their overwhelming unidirectionality; the conceptual shifts are consistently from concrete to abstract, as the linguistic associations move along the lexical-grammatical continuum described above.

The emergence of such grammatical meanings has traditionally been explained in two different ways in the literature, either via metaphorical extension (Heine et al. 1991) or via reanalysis (Hopper and Traugott 2003). We have, however, previously presented a unified account of grammaticalisation which characterises both the metaphor- and reanalysis-based approaches in terms of their underlying general cognitive mechanisms (Hoefler and Smith 2009), the now familiar foundations of ostensive-inferential communication and memorisation. We now turn to probably the most famous example of grammaticalisation in the literature, the development of the English construction *be going to* (Heine et al. 1991; Kuteva 2001; Hopper and Traugott 2003; Evans and Green 2006; Hoefler and Smith 2009), and explore how metaphorical extension can explain the historical grammaticalisation it has undergone. The *be going to* construction's original transparent meaning was MOTION, but it has gained additional meanings through the centuries, from INTENTION to a grammatical marker of FUTURITY, as shown in Example 1. Similar changes (GO TO > FUTURE in Heine and Kuteva (2002)'s terms) are attested in many languages across the world and throughout history. They appear, moreover, to form part of another very general grammaticalisation process in which certain verbs come to be used to mark specific tense or aspect functions (Heine and Kuteva 2002).

(1) a. I am going to play football.
    b. I am going to stay at home.
    c. It is going to rain.

The historical development of *be going to* shown in Example 1 also clearly illustrates one of the consequences of metaphor conventionalisation, that of layering (Hopper and Traugott 2003). When a metaphor is newly memorised, the form inevitably becomes part of two competing conventions: the original association and the new metaphorical association. In addition to their different meanings, these competing layered associations may differ in their level of entrenchment and in their syntactic properties. Indeed, form-meaning associations are internal to individuals' linguistic knowledge, and thus only indirectly observable through usage. The existence of a truly new association is therefore only exposed through actualisation (Trask 1996), when the construction is used in a context which is only interpretable using the new form-meaning mapping. Both layering and actualisation can clearly be seen in Example 1. In 1(a), *be going to* can be interpreted freely as any of the three historical meanings we are considering, as follows: (i) MOTION: 'I am moving somewhere to play football'; (ii) INTENTION: 'I intend to play football'; (iii) FUTURITY: 'In the near future, I will play football'. In 1(b), however, the clear contradiction between the meanings of *go* and *stay* ensures that the motion reading is unavailable, and only the latter two are possible; the inanimate dummy subject *it* in 1(c), meanwhile, renders both MOTION and INTENTION impossible, and obliges a FUTURITY reading. In modern English, therefore, we can consider that there is layering of three different *be going to* constructions, which differ both in their meanings and in the properties required of their subjects and associated main verbs. In the earliest, most lexicalised construction, *be going to* can be used only in conjunction with main verbs whose meaning is consistent with actual movement, and with subjects who represent animate beings. In the most recent, most grammaticalised construction, on the other hand, it is now solely a tense marker, and as such it can be used with any kind of subject and any main verb without restriction.

So how does metaphor allow the creation of new associations and their entrenchment? Let us consider first how the construction which meant MOTION could be used metaphorically to mean INTENTION. We must assume that speaker and hearer already share the construction, including its conventional meaning of MOTION, and that they are aware that the convention is shared. The key additional properties of the situation which are necessary to make the metaphor interpretable are twofold: (i) that INTENTION is associated with MOTION; (ii) that MOTION is not relevant in the current communicative context. These are shown in the first column of Table 2. Because the interlocutors' shared contextual knowledge shows that MOTION is irrelevant, all aspects of the conventional meaning are ignored. Another meaning must be sought, which must be both sufficiently relevant in the context, and associated with aspects of the conventional meaning; this association allows the non-conventional (and thus metaphorical) usage to be successfully inferred through analogy.

The newly conventionalised INTENTION sense of *be going to* can then act as a stepping stone for further metaphorical derivation, in the scenario present-

Tab. 2: Comparative schematic analysis of the metaphorical derivations of, first, INTENTION, and then, FUTURITY meanings for *be going to*.

	Intention	Futurity
Example		
Communicative context	Meaning of main verb (e.g. stay) inherently contradicts motion meaning.	Subject is inanimate, so motion and intention meanings are impossible.
Analysis		
Signal (form)	/bɪgoʊɪntu/	/bɪgoʊɪntu/
Signal meaning	motion (by convention)	motion, intention (by convention)
Shared association	motion → intention	intention → futurity
Relevant aspect	intention	futurity
Ignored aspects	motion	motion, intention
Inferred speaker meaning	intention	futurity

ed in the second column of Table 2. This shows the increased grammaticalisation of *be going to* through the development of the abstract grammatical meaning FUTURITY. In this scenario, the same reasoning applies, but the interlocutors take advantage of slightly different contextual and shared knowledge: (i) that INTENTION is associated with FUTURITY, because the things we intend to do happen in the future; (ii) that INTENTION is not relevant in the current communicative context, because there is no intentional, animate being in the scenario. Again, all aspects of the conventional meaning (both MOTION and INTENTION) are ruled out, but another meaning (FUTURITY) is inferred. The inference of this meaning can take place because FUTURITY is both associated with an aspect of the conventional meaning and relevant in the current non-intentional context. This new, even more abstract, meaning is then associated with *be going to*, memorised by the interlocutors, and, over time, conventionalised.

We have argued in this section that the cognitive mechanisms required for grammaticalisation to take place are that interlocutors share common ground, and that they can memorise the linguistic usage they experience. If they entertain sufficiently similar assumptions about the constitution of their common ground, then they will make the same inferences about what is most relevant in the communicative context, and thus understand the creative meanings which are expressed metaphorically. If they remember these new associations, and use them sufficiently frequently, then the new associations can also become conventionalised, and potentially act as the source for further metaphorical extensions. The cognitive mechanisms required for the development of grammatical structure, therefore, are exactly the same as those we described in section 3 as pre-requisites for the emergence of arbitrary symbols and their subsequent development into massively expressive communicative systems.

5 Conclusion

The problem of language evolution is generally divided into two distinct issues: the emergence of an arbitrary symbolic communication system and then the emergence of grammatical structure. We have examined these issues in detail in this paper, and have described in sections 3 and 4 how the same underlying cognitive mechanisms are required in both cases. These capabilities, namely the assumption of common ground between interlocutors, and the memorisation of experience, are the fundamental components of all ostensive-inferential communication, and provide the foundation on which the creative power of metaphor is built. We suggest therefore that metaphor, or rather the cognitive properties on which metaphor's creativity depends, may have played a pivotal role in enabling the origin and evolution of human language.

References

Bickerton, Derek. 2003. Symbol and structure: A comprehensive framework for language evolution. In Morten H. Christiansen & Simon Kirby (eds.), *Language evolution*, 77–93. Oxford: Oxford University Press.
Brighton, Henry, Kenny Smith & Simon Kirby. 2005. Language as an evolutionary system. *Physics of Life Reviews* 2(3). 177–226.
Chomsky, Noam. 1995. *The minimalist program*. Cambridge, MA: MIT Press.
Deacon, Terrence. 1997. *The symbolic species*. London: Penguin.
Deutscher, Guy. 2005. *The unfolding of language: An evolutionary tour of mankind's greatest invention*. New York: Metropolitan Books.
Evans, Vyvyan & Melanie Green. 2006. *Cognitive linguistics: An introduction*. Edinburgh: Edinburgh University Press.
Givón, Talmy. 1973. The time-axis phenomenon. *Language* 49. 890–925.
Givón, Talmy. 1979. *On understanding grammar*. New York: Academic Press.
Grice, Herbert Paul. 1957. Meaning. *Philosophical Review* 66. 377–388.
Haspelmath, Martin. 1998. Does grammaticalization need reanalysis? *Studies in Language* 22(2). 49–85.
Hauser, Marc D., Noam Chomsky & W. Tecumseh Fitch. 2002. The faculty of language: what is it, who has it and how did it evolve? *Science* 298. 1569–1579.
Heine, Bernd, Ulrike Claudi & Friederike Hünnemeyer. 1991. *Grammaticalization: A conceptual framework*. Chicago: University of Chicago Press.

Heine, Berd & Tania Kuteva. 2002. *World lexicon of grammaticalization*. Cambridge: Cambridge University Press.
Hoefler, Stefan & Andrew D. M. Smith. 2009. The pre-linguistic basis of grammaticalisation: a unified approach to metaphor and reanalysis. *Studies in Language* 33(4). 883–906.
Hopper, Paul J. 1987. Emergent grammar. *Berkeley Linguistics Conference* 13. 139–157.
Hopper, Paul J. & Elizabeth Closs Traugott. 2003. *Grammaticalization*, 2nd edn. Cambridge: Cambridge University Press.
Jackendoff, Ray. 2002. *Foundations of language: Brain, meaning, grammar, evolution*. Oxford: Oxford University Press.
Keller, Rudi. 1998. *A theory of linguistic signs*. Oxford: Oxford University Press.
Kövecses, Zoltan. 2002. *Metaphor: A practical introduction*. Oxford: Oxford University Press.
Kuteva, Tania. 2001. *Auxiliation: An enquiry into the nature of grammaticalization*. Oxford: Oxford University Press.
Lakoff, George & Mark Johnson. 1980. *Metaphors we live by*. Chicago: University of Chicago Press.
Langacker, Ronald. 1878. *Foundations of cognitive grammar: Theoretical Prerequisites* (Vol. I). Stanford, CA: Stanford University Press.
Langacker, Ronald. 2008. *Cognitive grammar: A basic introduction*. Oxford: Oxford University Press.
Mufwene, Salikoko S. 2002. Competition and selection in language evolution. *Selection* 3(1). 45–56.
Papafragou, Anna. 1999. On metonymy. *Lingua* 99. 169–195.
Pinker, Steven, Martin A. Nowak & James J. Lee. 2008. The logic of indirect speech. *Proceedings of the National Academy of Sciences*, 105(3). 833–838.
Sag, Ivan A. 1981. Formal semantics and extralinguistic context. In Peter Cole (ed.), *Radical pragmatics*, 273–294. New York: Academic Press.
Smith, Andrew D. M. 2011. Grammaticalization and language evolution. In Heiko Narrog & Bernd Heine (eds.), *Oxford handbook of grammaticalization*, 142–152. Oxford: Oxford University Press.
Sperber, Dan & Deirdre Wilson. 1995. *Relevance: Communication and cognition*. Oxford: Blackwell.
Tomasello, Michael. 2003a. *Constructing a language: A usage-based theory of language acquisition*. Cambridge, MA: Harvard University Press.
Tomasello, Michael. 2003b. On the different origins of symbols and grammar. In Morten H. Christiansen & Simon Kirby (eds.), *Language Evolution*, 94–110. Oxford: Oxford University Press.
Tomasello, Michael, Malinda Carpenter, Josep Call, Tanya Behne & Henrike Moll. 2005. Understanding and sharing intentions: The origins of cultural cognition. *Behavioral and Brain Sciences* 28. 675–735.
Trask, R. Larry 1996. *Historical linguistics*. London: Arnold.
Traugott, Elizabeth Closs & Richard B. Dasher. 2005. *Regularity in semantic change*. Cambridge: Cambridge University Press.
Wilson, Deirdre & Dan Sperber. 2012. *Meaning and relevance*. Cambridge: Cambridge University Press.

Miao-Hsia Chang
Two counter-expectation markers in Chinese[1]

Abstract: This study investigates the emergence and diachronic development of two markers of counter-expectation (CE) in Chinese: *sha4* 'evil spirit' and *jieguo* 'to yield fruit'.[2] The markers are compared with their counterparts in Taiwanese Southern Min (TSM), *soah* and *kiatko*. The results show that *sha4* 'evil spirit' emerged in the 7th century as an alternate form of *sha1* 'to kill'. Through metaphorical and metonymic changes, it evolved to include senses associated with suppression, destroying, and intensification. After the 11th century, it further evolved to have a concessive and CE sense in the predicate-initial position. The CE meaning is also pervasive in contemporary TSM *soah*. *Jieguo* emerged as a compound of *jie* and *guo* through reanalysis. Later, through the process of metaphorical change, its meaning was extended to 'end; result', used as either a noun or verb. On the other hand, the intransitive *jieguo* was transitivized to a verb of killing in the 14th century. In modern Chinese, it further underwent metonymic change and was reanalyzed as a linking adverbial indicating counter-expectation in contemporary Chinese. An identical use is observed in contemporary TSM. The evolutions and changes of *sha4* and *jieguo* in the history of Chinese are indicative of the effect of metaphor and metonymy on the semanticization and adverbialization of a verbal morpheme from a content word to a highly grammaticalized sentential adverb in different Chinese dialects. An understanding of the evolution of meaning can only be achieved by a close scrutiny of the situated meanings and communicative functions of the two forms in context.

1 Introduction

The 1980s has witnessed a shift of paradigm in linguistics to the study of the interactional aspects of language (e.g., Schiffrin 1987; Tomlin 1987; Taavitsain-

---

Miao-Hsia Chang: National Taiwan Normal University

---

1 This research project has been funded by the National Science Council, Taiwan, Republic of China, under grant number NSC 91-2411-H-003-045. An earlier version of this paper was presented at *New Reflections on Grammaticalization 3*, Santiago de Compostela, 17–20 July, 2005.
2 As I focus on the diachrony of 煞 , the form *sha4* 'evil spirit' (4th or falling tone in Mandarin) will be used throughout this paper to represent (Mandarin) Chinese 煞 , and *sha1* (1st tone or

en and Jucker 2010: 3). By using empirical data and investigating the communicative functions of language, functional linguists have shown that grammar emerges from recurrent patterns of language in use (Hopper 1987; Du Bois 1987; Thompson and Hopper 2001). These research findings led to a growing interest in historical pragmatics in the 1990s and inspired historical linguists to focus on contextualized language and the "joint negotiation of meaning" in their researches on language change (Taavitsainen and Jucker 2010: 4). The diachronic development of pragmatic markers, in particular, has been a focus of research in recent studies in historical pragmatics. It has been shown that pragmatic markers reflect the speaker's attitude, belief, and stance toward the discourse and propositional content (e.g., König 1991; Brinton 1996; Traugott and Dasher 2002; Xing 2004; Hansen and Rossari 2005). This paper investigates the emergence and diachronic development of two markers of counter-expectation (CE) in Chinese – *sha4* 'to stop; evil spirit' and *jieguo* 'to yield fruit; to have ... as a result'. The markers' semantic-pragmatic functions are then compared with those of their counterparts in Taiwanese Southern Min (TSM), *soah* and *kiatko*.³ Through an investigation of their uses in classical and contemporary Chinese, I aim to explore the mechanisms that account for the historical changes of these two markers. I will show that although *sha4* and *jieguo* originated from different semantic sources, they are highly related semantically and are both pragmatically enriched to codify an (undesirable) result.

2 Metaphor and metonymy in language change

In studies in historical pragmatics, metaphor and metonymy have been believed to be important pragmatic strategies that lead to semantic change

---

level tone) will be used to represent its homonym 殺 'to kill'. Although it is shown in the following discussion that 煞 originated as an alternate form of 殺 and took both the first and the fourth tones, it later developed meanings of its own with the evil spirit sense that takes a fourth tone. Therefore, the form *sha4* will be used to avoid confusion with 殺.

3 Taiwanese Southern Min, or Taiwanese for short, is a Chinese dialect which originated in the Southern Min region in China. It does not have standard orthography and is mainly used as a spoken dialect in Taiwan and its outlying islets. TSM has two phonological strata: the literary stratum and the colloquial stratum. Sounds which belong to the literary stratum mainly occur in compound words and used in text reading or very formal contexts. Sounds in the colloquial stratum are used mainly in daily conversation. The literary and colloquial registers for 煞 are *sat* and *soah*, respectively. As we mainly examine spoken discourse, for convenience of reference, the form *soah* will be used for 煞 throughout this paper.

"based on social and linguistic interaction in context" (Nerlich 2010: 193). Metaphor is a cognitive mechanism that involves the interaction of concepts in two domains: a source (or vehicle) domain and a target domain (Croft and Cruse 2004: 193; Barcelona 2000: 3). A concept in the source domain is mapped onto a concept in the target domain so that the former concept is understood in terms of the latter through a correspondence in meaning. A well-known metaphorical concept is ARGUMENT IS WAR, which is reflected in our everyday language (Lakoff and Johnson 1980: 3–4, examples by Lakoff and Johnson 1980: 4):

(1) a. He attacked *every weak point* in my argument.
 b. I've never *won* the argument.
 c. His criticisms were *right on target*.

(1a–c) show that arguments are conceptualized in terms of war. We can attack arguments, we win arguments, and arguments have targets. The underlying cognitive relation between the ideas in the source and the target domains is one of similarity (Geerarerts 1997: 97; Koch 2001). The conceptualization of meaning, as shown in (1), abounds in our everyday lives (Lakoff and Johnson 1980). Over time, through meaning creation with the processes of metaphor, some meanings fade and others emerge, which contributes to language change (Nerlich 2010: 198–199).

In the case of metonymy, meaning is conceptualized in terms of the contiguity relation between a trigger and its target entity (Kövecses and Radden 1998: 39; Nerlich 2010: 202). Unlike metaphor, however, the contiguity relation operates within concepts in the *same* domain. Some examples of typical metonymic relations are PART FOR WHOLE (*We don't hire* long hairs), PRODUCER FOR PRODUCT (*He's got a* Picasso *in his den*), INSTITUTION FOR PEOPLE RESPONSIBLE (*I don't approve of the* government's *actions*), THE PLACE FOR THE EVENT (*Let's not let Thailand become another Vietnam*; Lakoff and Johnson 1980: 38–39), CAUSE FOR RESULT (Fr. *chasser*: 'hunt' > 'chase', from TRYING TO CATCH to MAKING RUN), and CAUSE FOR EFFECT (Fr. tremble > fear; Koch 2001: 203, 205). In addition to metonymic relations between words, Lakoff and Johnson (1980) have shown that metonymic relations also hold between concepts (see also Kövecses and Radden 1998: 38). For example, *good heads* can be used to stand for *intelligent people*. The metonymic process here involves focusing on a person's characteristic "intelligence", which is related to the "head" (Lakoff and Johnson 1980: 36). In fact, metonymic linking is so pervasive in language that it accounts for connections of concepts in the linguistic subsystems of lexicon, speech act, discourse semantics, and grammar (Koch 2001: 209).

A special type of metonymy that mediates langauge change on the semantic-pragmatic level is the Invited Inferencing Theory of Semantic Change (IITSC; Traugott and Dasher 2002). IITSC is developed to account for the semanticization of pragmatic meanings. Essentially, utterance-token meanings develop from coded meanings to "utterance-type, pragmatically polysemous meanings ... to new semantically polysemous (coded) meanings" (Traugott and Dasher 2002: 35). The changes are motivated by invited inferences through pragmatic strengthening in communication. The governing principle that underlies IITSC is Levinson's (1995) Generalized Conversational Implicature, which includes three heuristics (Q-, R-, and M-heuristics) for preferred interpretations in conversation (Levinson 1995; Traugott and Dasher 2002: 18–19). The Q-heuristic requires that one make the contribution as informative as required and imply no more thereby (e.g., *Some of the boys came* Q implicates > 'not all'). The R-heuristic requires that one say/write no more than s/he must, and mean more thereby (e.g., *drink* implicates > 'alcoholic drink'), and the M-heuristic states that marked expressions invite marked interpretations (e.g., *He ate and ate* M implicates > 'He ate more than the normal meal;' Levinson 1995: 98–106). Among them, the main heuristics that propel language change are the R- and the M-heuristic (Traugott and Dasher 2002: 19). The R-heuristic invites inferences of utterance meanings that are richer than what is said, that is, the "pragmatic strengthening" of an utterance meaning is invited given a proper interactional context. The M-heuristic is mainly responsible for new uses of old forms, i.e., marked forms invite marked interpretations.

While the definitions of metaphor and metonymy seem to suggest that they are distinct mechanisms, Geeraerts (2010: 215) argues that the above distinctions are not as clear as they appear to be. First, one can easily find examples of metonymy involving domain crossing. In *Proust is tough to read*, *Proust* is used to replace the creative work of the person *Proust*. However, *Proust* belongs to the concrete domain of human beings, whereas his creative work belongs to the abstract domain. This contradicts Lakoff and Johnson's proposal that metonymy involves intra-domain semantic extension. Second, we can find instances of intra-domain metaphor, as in *Maggie Thatcher is the Ronald Reagan of the UK*, where *Thatcher* and *Reagan* belong to the same domain (Geeraerts 2010: 215–6). Third, it is not uncommon for one to find examples of an interaction between metaphor and metonymy (Goosens 1990: 323). Goosens introduces a term referring to a phenomenon called "metaphtonymy", which includes "metaphor from metonymy" (Goosens 1990: 328; see also Geeraerts 2010: 220) and "metonymy within metaphor/metaphor within metonymy". Metaphor from metonymy involves the successive application of two mechanisms for the semantic change of a word. For example, the word *giggle* 'laugh in a nervous way' is metonymically changed to 'say while giggling', and is later metaphorically extended to 'to say as if giggling'. The second type "metonymy within metaphor/metaphor within metonymy" involves the simultaneous operation of two mechanisms, for example, *dirty fingers on the window*. The derived reading is motivated metonymically due to a cause-effect relation and metaphorically due to similarity.

In Nerlich's (2010) terms, the understanding of metaphors is grounded on the ability to "[make] imaginary leaps", whereas metonymy "seems to depend on a discursive co-construction" of referents and referential relations (p. 207). Metaphor and metonymy interact in complex ways, and conceptualization and co-construction of meaning go hand in hand with each other in the making of meaning. In this study, I follow the assumption that metaphor and metonymy are pragmatic strategies that interact with each other to contribute to language change. Understanding of the evolution of meaning requires one to consider the two mechanisms simultaneously in addition to other accompanying factors. Before the discussion of the evolution of the counter-expectation markers, I describe the data used for the present study.

3 Data

The data in this study include contemporary (Mandarin) Chinese and TSM spoken data, and historical texts. The data of contemporary Chinese comprise fully transcribed conversation in Chinese and in TSM collected from 1997–2005, including 5 hours of conversation in Chinese and 10 hours of conversation in Taiwanese. For classical Chinese, I selected Chinese texts whose language approximates the oral tradition or vernacular literature so that the pragmatic functions are more comparable to their features in real use.

The romanization of Mandarin Chinese follows the system of Hanyu Pinyin. As TSM is phonologically distinct from Mandarin Chinese, the romanization of the TSM data generally follows the Church Romanization developed by Cheng and Cheng (1994).

For TSM *soah* and *kiatko*, the focus will be on their contemporary use in conversation instead of on their diachronic development since I find almost no instances of *soah* and *kiatko* in the earliest historical texts of Southern Min script of play – Romance of the *Lychee* Mirror.[4] The contemporary uses will

---

4 Only one case of *soah* was noted in the script of play *Romance of the Lychee* Mirror published in Qing Dyansty, meaning 'to stop' (*soah chia* [stop here]), and only one use of *kiatko* (*bi ti*

also be compared with their Chinese counterparts since they demonstrate interesting results that shed light on the general development of the counter-expectation markers.

4. Diachronic development of *sha4* 'evil spirit'

Sha4 'evil spirit' (煞) originated from the grapheme *sha1* (殺) 'to kill' in Chinese (*Shuowen Jiezi*, or *Analytical Dictionary of Characters*). The two morphemes overlap in both their verbal and non-verbal senses in classical Chinese (*Hanyu Dazidian*, a Chinese dictionary created by the National Science Council Digital Library and Museum).[5] While the focus of the current study is on the diachrony of 煞, before I discuss the diachronic development of 煞, it is first necessary to examine the uses of 殺 before the emergence of 煞.

4.1 Diachronic development of *sha1* 'to kill'

In Early Old Chinese (11th–6th c. BC), *sha1* 'to kill' was used as a verb denoting the action of killing (Zhou 2005: 138):

> V 'to kill'
(2) *Peng   jiu   si   xiang, yue **sha** gaoyang.*
    friend wine here feast   say **kill** lamb
    'My friends will eat here, and (we) said that we could kill lambs (for food).'
    (*Book of Odes*)

In Late Old Chinese (5th–3rd c. BC), 殺 *sha1* acquired the status of a noun 'killing' (3). A metaphorical sense of destroying or suppressing was also seen in the nominal (4a) or verbal use (4b):

> N 'killing'
(3) *Shan ren wei bang   bai   nian, ji   ke   sheng can*
    good man rule country one.hundred year then can win cruelty
    *qu   **sha**.*
    remove killing

---

buesiao saⁿ kiatko [not knowing what the result would be]) was found in the 1651 version of *Romance of the Lychee* Mirror.
5 Website: http://words.sinica.edu.tw/sou/sou.html.

'If there is a good man to rule a country for one hundred years, then all oppression and **killing** will disappear.'
(*Analects of Confucius*)

N 'destroyer'
(4) a. *Zhou zhi **sha** ye bi daji.*
PN of **destroyer** PAR favorite PN
'The one who destroyed Emperor Zhou was his favorite (concubine) Daji.'
(*Shiji*)

V 'to destroy; suppress'
b. *Long li yi er **sha** shi shu.*
value ceremony justice and **destroy** poetry book
'(The emperor) valued ceremonies and justice but destroyed poetry and books.'
(*Xunzi*)

In addition, *sha1* 'to kill' occurred as an adjectival compound denoting 'chilly' (*sha1 qi* 'chilly air'), as in (5). In Chinese, which is generally lacking in morphological marking, the first noun in a sequence of two nouns readily serves as an adjective. Over time, *sha1* stabilized as an attributive adjective and acquired the sense of 'chilly' through the CAUSE FOR EFFECT metonymic link because chilly air has the power/effect of destruction. In other words, *sha1* that encodes an effect sense is used to refer to the idea of chilliness (i.e. extreme cold weather), which can be a cause of destruction.

Attributive adjective 'chilly'
(5) *Xiungnu chu bei di, han, **sha** qi zao jiang.*
Hun located north place cold **chilly** air early fall
'The Huns lived in the north. When winter came, the **cold** air arrived early.'
(*Shiji*)

Around A.D. 38–220 (East Han Dynasty), *sha1*, in a few cases, functioned as a postverbal degree adverb denoting an extreme state (Zhou 2005: 139), as in (6a–b).

Degree adverb 'to an excessive degree'
(6) a. *Qiu feng xiaoxiao chou **sha** ren.*
Autumn winter whistle sadden **extremely** people

'The wind is whistling (so mournfully that) it makes me **extremely sad.**'
(*Yuefu Songs of the Han Dynasty*)

b. *Tongnan qu guafu, Zhuang nü xiao **sha** ren.*
young.boy marry widow strong woman laugh **greatly** people
'Young boys are marrying widows. This made the strong woman laugh **very hard.**'
(*Folk Songs of the Northern Dynasty*)

The killing of *sha1* in (6a–b) requires a figurative/metaphorical interpretation in that it is not related to the physical domain of killing but to the mental domain of excessiveness. In (6a), the speaker describes a saddening atmosphere felt through the blowing wind. The physical power of the wind itself is not strong enough to kill people. Rather, it is the ambience created by the wind that saddens the speaker. Therefore, the killing sense is understood figuratively as implicative of an excessive state because the killing of someone indisputably results in an extreme state most undesirable to the victim. The scenario described in (6b) also involves an unusual/extreme case – for young boys to marry widows, which was chafed by a strong woman. Since laughing would almost never result in one's death, *sha1* here is interpreted metaphorically as denoting an excessive state of laughing, hence, the rise of the excessive sense.

The metaphorical transfer observed in (6) was accompanied by a constituent reanalysis, which is a structural change of an expression revealing no "immediate or intrinsic modification of its surface manifestation" (Langacker 1977: 58). The reanalysis resulted in the loss of the full verbal status of *sha1* to make it an adverbial complement of a verbal compound meaning 'excessively; extremely', as represented in Figure 1:

(*xiao*)(*sha*)(*ren*)[(S)(V)(O) 'laugh-kill-people']

↓

(*xiaosha*) (*ren*) [(V-comp)(O) 'laugh-[EXCESSIVELY]-people']

Fig. 1: Reanalysis of the degree modifying sha1.

4.2 Emergence and diachronic development of 煞 sha4 'evil spirit'

The grapheme 煞 *sha4* 'evil spirit' emerged in the 7th–9th century (Tang Dynasty). According to *Hanyu Da Zidian*, 煞 takes two tones: *sha1* and *sha4*. *Sha1* is a homophone of 殺 and is used as a variant of 殺 with the killing sense, whereas *sha4* has nominal, adjectival and adverbial uses. The early functions of 煞 are discussed in 4.2.1. Its evolution after the Tang Dynasty is presented in 4.2.2.

4.2.1 7th–9th century (Tang Dynasty)

Among the 137 tokens of 煞, most were used as a variant of verbal 殺 'to kill' (80.3 %, 110/137), as exemplified by (7):

V 'to kill'
(7) **Sha** fu   hai   mu   jie yin   jiu.
   Kill father murder mother all due.to liquor
   'It is all because of drunkenness that one would kill one's parents.'
   (*Dunhuang Bianwen*)

Most of the remaining cases of *sha4* carried a sense of evil (spirit) (10.9 %, 15/137) or destroyal (4 tokens), or they functioned as an extreme degree modifier (4 tokens).[6] Among these uses, only the nominal use of 'evil spirit' distinguished *sha4* 煞 from *sha1* 殺:

N/Adj. 'evil spirit'
(8) a.   Wo deng gezi dai   **sha,**   bu yu   de wen nian jing zhi
       1S kind each carry **evil.spirit** not want get hear read sutra of
       sheng.
       sound
       'We each carry an **evil spirit** with us. So we do not want to hear sutra chanting.'
       (*Dunhuang Bianwen*)

   b. *Chao*   kan **sha** qi zhuang ru   xia.
       Morning see **evil** air grand   like rays.of.sun
       'In the morning, the **evil** atmosphere is as strong as the rays of the sun.'
       (*Dunhuang Bianwen*)

---

6 The meanings of the other four tokens of *sha4* are hard to determine.

V 'destroy'

(9) Wei tu   xiang   mei   **sha**   jianglai.
For seek fragrant beautiful **destroy** future
'He ruined his future by being too gluttonous.'
(*Dunhuang Bianwen*)

Adv. 'extremely'

(10) a. Yi   shixiong,   ku tai **sha**,   shique yi   zhi yan.
Recall senior.fellow cry too **much** lose   one CL eye[7]
'(I) lost one eye because I cried too **much** when I recalled the elderly man.'

b. *Ni da* **sha**   *congming.*
2S big **extremely** intelligent
'You are **extremely** intelligent.'
(*Zutangji*)

4.2.2 10th–14th century (Sung and Yuan Dynasties)

From the 10th–14th century, the functions of 煞 became gradually distinct from those of 殺 *sha1* 'to kill'. First, it ceased to be used as a killing verb, and the uses associated with 'evil spirit' or excessiveness become more frequent (23.2%, 42/181). Furthermore, there is a preponderance of *sha4* functioning as a preverbal degree adverb (65.7%, 119/181). (10b) illustrates a preverbal modifier *sha4*. (11) is a further example.[8] The preverbal modifying use has been observed to be with *sha4* since the emergence of this morpheme.

---

[7] The following abbreviations and transcribing notations are used in the gloss of the examples cited: 1S: first person singular; 2S: second person singular; 3S: third person sibgular; 2P: second person plural; 3P: third person plural; CE: counter-expectation (marker); CL: classifier; CRS: currently relevant state; DE: the morpheme *de*; DM: discourse marker; GEN: genitive marker; LE: the particle *le*; NOM: nominal; PAR: particle; PN: proper name; PRG: progressive marker; <M M>: speech delivered in Mandarin.

[8] Among the 181 tokens, three were used to indicate 'short moment', and one was used as a question word 'what'. The latter could be a phonological loan word like 啥 *sha* (rising tone) in Chinese. As it is hard to establish a semantic or syntactic link with *sha* as a question word, these two functions are not considered in the present study.

Preverbal modifier

(11) *Sui sui xiang wu qiong zhi li,* **sha** *qiang ru qianglüe de*
Year year enjoy no end of benefit **much** strong like rob GEN
goudang
unethical.business
'Year after year, (he) enjoyed endless benefit. It is **much** like robbery, no different from an unethical business.'
(*Romance of the West Chamber*)

Two new functions emerged in this period. First, *sha4* took on a counter-expectation sense in the predicate-initial position. In (12a), for example, *sha4* presents the fact that there are ten gods to worship now, which is against the general belief that there should not be too many gods to worship in a rite. As the addition of a god is a telic event where a degree reading is irrelevant, the sentence invites the interpretation related to the speaker's evaluation and attitude toward the truth of the proposition. That is, it implicates that what follows *sha4* is against the speaker's belief. The query along with the speaker's surprised mood shown in the utterance strengthens the evaluative tone. (12b) is a further example, which presents two contrasting positions taken by the commentator Zhaoziqin:

(12) a.   CE
   You wen jin zhi jiao si, hegu you xuduo di?
   Also ask now of countryside rite why exist many god
   '(He) also asked, "Why are so many gods worshipped in the rite?"'

   Yue er jin **sha** *tianchai le tian di!*
   Say and now **sha** add LE heaven god
   Gong cheng shi ge di le.
   Together become ten CL god LE
   '(Then I) replied, "And now **even** the Heavenly God is added (to the list of gods to be worshipped.) Altogether there are ten gods!'
   (*Zhuzi yulei*)

b. *Zhaoziqin shang zi xian mou shuo de shu.*
   PN even self dislike 1S say DE loose
   Bu zhi rujin **sha** *you tui xue le chu.*
   Not know now CE have retract decrease CRS place
   'Even Zhaoziqin criticized that my argument was weak. (However,) **it was unexpected** that (he should) back off now.'
   (*Zhuzi yulei*)

Second, a concessive sense was emerging. Among the 127 tokens of *sha4* in the 10–14th century, 12 instances are noted where a degree reading is no longer relevant but a concessive reading is in order. (13a–b) are from the databank, and (13c) is from the *Comprehensive Dictionary of Chinese Characters*, which defines *sha4* as a concessive adverbial:

Concession

(13) a. Xiangguo   furen **sha**   nian lao, qian   xin qi bi
prime.minister wife **although** age old devoted heart how avoid
ci   lao?
dismiss labor
'Although the Prime Minister's wife is old, she is very devoted. So how would she avoid the hardship (she would undergo in traveling far to worship Buddha)?'
(*Romance of the West Chamber*)

b. Ru   tangminghuang weiren yu fu   zi, fu   fu, jun
Like PN   behave at father son husband wife emperor
chen   fen shang, **sha**   wuzhuang,   que zhong shi
subject duty on   **although** inappropriate but end beginning
ai   xiongdi bu shuai.
love brother not decay
'Take the Emperor Ming of Tang for example. **Although** he did not have appropriate demeanor in terms of father-son, husband-wife and emperor-subject relationships, he always loved his brothers very much.'
(*Zhuzi yulei*)

In (13a–b), although *sha4* precedes a predicate that involves degree, simply attaching an intensifying sense to *sha4* would result in an odd semantic relation between the preceding and following clauses. In (13a), for example, if *sha4 nian lau* '*sha4* old' is read as '*very* old', it would be incongruous with the proposition that the mistress could endure the rigors of traveling a long distance to holy places just to worship Buddha. Instead, the *sha4* clause suggests that despite her old age, she is so devoted that she endures the long, hard trip. The rhetorical question marker *qi* 'how' in this example provides further contextual support for the contrastive reading of *sha4*. The contextual cue *que* 'but' in (13b) is also predisposed to a concessive reading. In cases like the above, the use of *sha4* is no longer associated with the meaning of 'evil spirit', but the word acquires a subjective sense signaling a subjectively oriented meaning or a meta contrast between the *sha*-clause and the main clause.

Analysis of the developmental path of *sha4* shows that the evolution of the two meanings is both metaphorically and metonymically motivated. Simultaneous operation of two mechanisms, i.e., "metaphtonymy" (Goosens 1990: 328), accounts for the rise of the discourse-pragmatic meanings of *sha4*. Regarding the counter-expectation function, the change is triggered by a transfer from a degree meaning that can be deduced from the situational context, e.g., crying too much in (10a), to a subjectified meaning that is much less observable from the context. In other words, the meaning shifts from the quality of something external to a fully internal/subjectified evaluation. The conceptualization involves a metaphorical interpretation. Meanwhile, we can establish a CAUSE FOR EFFECT metonymic relation between the intensive adverb function and the CE sense. That is, when an extreme sense is conveyed, it usually implies a very pleasant or unpleasant feeling, while an unpleasant event usually runs counter to a normative viewpoint or expectation. When the encoding of an unpleasant outcome prevailed in the use of *sha4*, the CE function emerged. Overtime, this function became conventionalized.

Regarding the rise of the concessive or meta-contrast reading, as in the change from the intensifying to the CE function, a metaphorical transfer was activated to trigger an epistemically/internally grounded interpretation. Within the metaphor, a contiguity relation is operative that is communicatively relevant. In conversation, when an extreme case marker carries a strong assertive force, it may incur challenges by the listener; to reduce the face threat and alleviate the force of the claim, a speaker may embark on a concessive repair to retract the overstatement (Pomerantz 1986; Couper-Kuhlen and Thompson 2005). For example, an affirmative statement is retracted by a subsequent negative statement as a concessive repair. In (13a–b), the intensifying function seems to be situationally irrelevant (Kövecses and Radden 1998: 70); instead, the negative overtone and the succeeding text invite a new interpretation, of concession, that, despite the existence of the fact reported in the *sha4* clause, the following proposition still holds.

Syntactically, a reanalysis took place in the rise of both the CE and the concessive use of *sha4*. In the above two uses, *sha4* is no longer a pre-modifier of the predicate but an adverbial or subordinator that conveys a CE sense while marking interclausal contrast.

4.2.3 14th–19th century (Ming and Qing Dynasties)

By the 14th century, all the functions of *sha4* had been fully developed and continued to be used through the 14th–19th century. Two further developments are noted of *sha4* used in the Ming and Qing Dynasties. First, the postverbal degree-intensifying *sha4*, which had been used only scarcely before the 14th century, came to be used significantly more frequently (12.0%, 25/209). This function is identical to that of *sha1* 殺 'to kill' exemplified in (6a–b).

Second, the destroying sense was metaphorically extended to the meaning of attracting or spell casting, as in (14):

(14) Wu   de   bu fengyun **sha**   ren.
      Nobody GEN not charm **attract** people.
      'Every part (of her) is very attractive.'
      (*Jinpingmei*)

4.2.4 Contemporary Chinese

The functions of contemporary *sha4* include the following: nominal 'evil spirit', a preverbal intensifying adverb 'very', and a homonym of *sha2* 'what' (http://dict.revised.moe.edu.tw/). However, this morpheme is rarely used, as is shown in its total frequency from the corpora used for this study. In fact, it does not appear at all in the 5-hour spoken corpus of Mandarin. A search of two other Chinese corpora, *Academia Sinica Balanced Corpus of Modern Chinese* and *Beijing Corpus of Spoken Chinese*, yields only 12 tokens of *sha4*. All of them occur in fixed or semi-fixed expressions (e.g., 煞不住 *sha4-bu-chu* 'cannot stop') and are only found in the non-spoken data. Several factors may account for the rarity of *sha4*. First, the 'evil' sense is mostly used in texts related to religious or ceremonial events, while the contemporary texts I use mainly contain casual talk. Second, the adverbial *sha4* is not a preferred degree modifier for a verb. A common construction in Chinese for the expression of manner is the *de*+complex stative construction (Li and Thompson 1981: 623), as in *qi de yao si* (angry-DE-want-die) 'extremely angry', where *de* forms a construction with the preceding verb and the following complex stative predicate to indicate an extreme state/manner. This construction has been used since the Sung and Yuan Dynasties (10–14 c.), for example, *shuo de fuqian* ('say-DE-perfunctory') in *Zhuzi yulei* till the present time. In modern Chinese, some verb-complement sequences are grammaticalized into resultative constructions such as verb-*si* (angry-die) 'very angry' to indicate an extreme state. Comparatively, the verb+*sha4* construction sounds more archaic and formal in modern Chinese. Third, after the Vernacular Movement in the early 20th century, more colloquial terms after the Movement were used. For example, *feichang*, *hen* or *hao* 'very' may have replaced the intensifying *sha4*, and *suiran* 'although' may have replaced the concessive *sha4*. The meanings and developments of these synonyms, however, await further research before we gain a better understanding of the the rare use of *sha4* in contemporary Chinese.

4.2.5 Soah in Taiwanese Southern Min

Soah in TSM is synonymous with the Mandarin *sha4* except for the counter-expectation marking use. That is, the referential meaning of *soah* is related to evil (spirit) or to the metaphorical idea of stopping, misfortunate or bad luck (Chen 1991: 1683). The non-referential uses all characterize *soah* as a bound morpheme carrying a sandhi tone. They include *soah* as a post-verbal degree modifier, a predicate-initial adverbial meaning 'immediately', and a predicate-initial counter-expectation marker, the last of which distinguishes TSM *soah* from Mandarin *sha4*.

The degree modifying use and the adverbial *soah* are less common in TSM. The post-verbal degree modifying use only appears when *soah* occurs as a reduplicated compound, e.g., *khi soahsoah* 'angry-extremely', as in (15), whereas the pre-verbal intensifier does not appear in the database but is only listed in *Dictionary of Putunghua and Southern Min Dialects* (p. 675), as in (16):

(15) I   toh   khi   **soah**   **soah**   ne.
     He then angry **extremely extremely** PAR
     'He (looked at me) angrily.'

(16) Li   tioh   **soah**   lai.
     You have.to **immediately** come
     'You have to come **immediately**.'

The CE marking *soah* is used primarily to index a speaker-oriented meaning which implies discrepancy between the speaker's understanding and the situation of talk, or it may display an addressee-oriented function of doubt that arises from the incongruity between the speaker's and the addressee's assumptions. In my contemporary TSM databank, *soah* is primarily used with such a function (62.3%, or 151/242, in the folk songs, and 83%, or 27/39, in the 10-hour TSM conversation corpus). A speaker-oriented *soah* expresses the speaker's evaluative tone about an unexpected situation that occurs as a consequence of an earlier incident (17) or state of affairs (18). The anxiety of the protagonist in (17) is depicted as the outcome of cancer and depression, whereas in (18) the fact that Liuchenghung becomes the only male adult in the family is presented as an inference made by M after M hears about Liu's family condition:

(17)   I   a   kiam   tittio <M youyucheng M>.
       3S also meanwhile get   depression
      Soah e   khilai anne ittit   kintiu^n la.
      CE   will rise thus continuously nervous PAR

'She also got depression at the same time (when she learned she had cancer). (And **she didn't expect that** these days) she would feel apprehensive easily (about things around her because of her cancer and depression).'

(18) A: *In he   siaulian   chit tai,   tioh kanna in a.*
              3P that young.age this generation then only   3P PAR
              'Only he and his young (brothers) are left in his family (because father died and their mother married another man).'

      B: *Long bo chapo, a*   **soah** *pian*   *kanna liuchenghong.*
              All   no male PAR **CE**   become only   PN
              'There is no other male adult (in his family). So Liuchenghong has become (the only male adult in his family), **which I didn't expect**.'

The addressee-oriented *soah* is used by the speaker to express his/her complaint about the addressee's lack of knowledge of an obvious fact that should have been known earlier. Such instances of *soah* also take the form of a negative rhetorical question. An example is shown in (19).

          CE
(19)   (S, F's daughter, is leaving home for work on Saturday.)
      F: *A li m si kong tu   tioh   pailak   li   mbian   khi*
          DM 2S not be say   meet touch Saturday you not.need.to go
          kongsi   a?
          company PAR
          'Didn't you say that you don't have to work on Saturdays?'

      S: *Pa, a*   **soah** *m   chaiia^n ho^n, kongsi   chuekin te   chiokho*
          Dad DM **CE**   not know PAR Company recently PRG recruit
          sine chituan   la.
          new employee PAR

Goa bo khi beh na eieng e?
1S not go will how okay PAR
'Dad, (didn't you) know that our company has been recruiting new staff members? (As the manager of the company), how can I not be present?'

The speaker and addressee-oriented function of *soah* in the CE sense arises as a result of an (inter)subjectified meaning that is contextually triggered (Traugott 2010). Compared with the CE *sha4* in classical Chinese, TSM *soah* undergoes a greater degree of metonymization and pragmatic strengthening in that *soah* is used in a wider variety of interactive contexts with a propositional content that deviates from the speaker's prior assumption. With *soah*, the speaker's assertion is strengthened and its interactive force enhanced.

4.2.6 Summary

To sum up, *sha4* 煞 emerged in the 7th century (Tang Dynasty) as a synonym of *sha1* 殺 'to kill'. Through metaphorical and metonymic changes, *sha1* evolved the senses associated with suppression, destroying, and intensification. 煞 retained all the meanings of 殺 until the 10th–11th century and was mainly used with a killing sense. After the 11th century, the killing sense was only found in sporadic cases. Second, the degree intensifying use became the predominant function of 煞 *sha4* after the 11th century. Third, through reanalysis and the metonymic change involving (inter)subjectification and pragmatic strengthening, *sha4* evolved a concessive and a CE sense in the predicate-initial position. Although it thrived from the 7th to the 19th century, its occurrence has become rather limited in modern Chinese. By contrast, TSM *soah*, the counterpart of *sha4*, still prevails in contemporary TSM. Through further pragmatic strengthening, *soah* has taken on a subjective, speaker-oriented or intersubjective, addressee-oriented meaning in several discourse-relevant ways whereby speakers express their counteractive stance toward a concurring proposition. The evolution and changes of *sha4* in the history of Chinese are indicative of the effect of metaphor and metonymy on the semanticization and adverbialization of a verbal morpheme from a simple killing verb to a highly grammaticalized pragmatic marker in Chinese. Figure 2 summarizes the pathways of *sha4*'s historical changes.

As shown by the discussion and examples presented in this section, *sha4* and TSM *soah* are largely synonymous except that *soah* is employed as a predicate initial CE marker in contemporary TSM. This suggests that the develop-

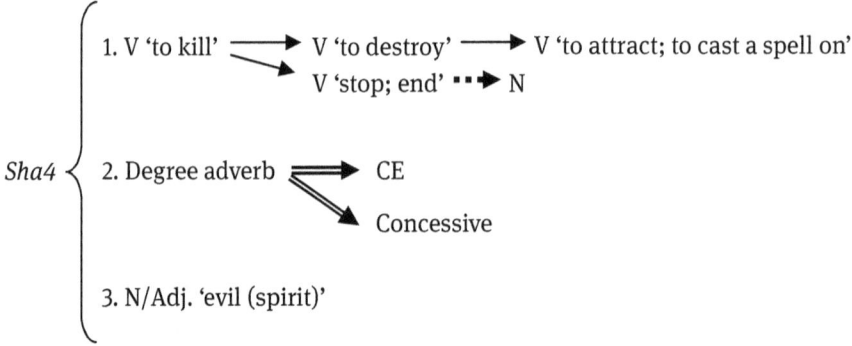

Fig. 2: Diachronic development of sha4 in Chinese.

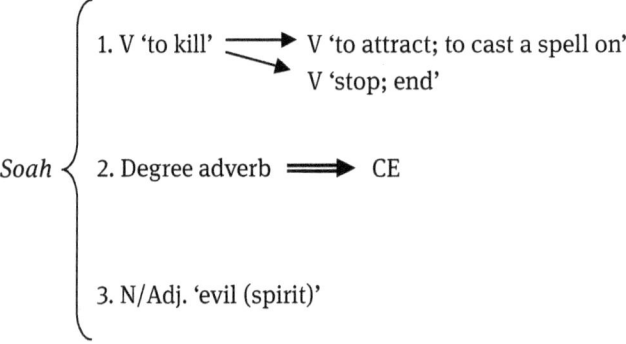

Fig. 3: Hypothetical development of soah in Southern Min.

mental path of *sha4* 煞 outlined above may be highly correlated with the evolution of *soah* despite the rarity of historical texts of TSM in the 10th–16th century and the lack of *soah* occurrences in the 16th–19th century Southern Min play script (Ming and Qing Dynasties). The correlation between Chinese *sha4* and TSM *soah* finds support in Zhang (1996), who notes that many Southern Min lexical items, including *sha4* 煞, can be found in *Zutangji* (6th–9th c., Tang Dynasty), which is one of the earliest anthologies written in vernacular Chinese. This suggests a highly plausible link between *sha4* and *soah* given their shared meanings. Accordingly, we can propose a hypothetical developmental path for TSM *soah*, as in Figure 3 (Figures 2–4, a single-line arrow stands for a metaphorical change, a thick-line arrow stands for a metonymic link, a double-line arrow represents a simultaneous operation of metaphor and metonym (and reanalysis), and a dotted line arrow stands for pure reanalysis):

5 Diachronic development of *jieguo*

Another counter-expectation marker in Chinese is *jieguo* 'to yield fruit'. Although it originated from a different semantic source, *jieguo* developed meanings that overlap with those of *sha4*. In TSM, the equivalents of *sha4* and *jieguo*, i.e., *soah* and *kiatko*, may even concur to strengthen the CE meaning.

5.1 6th–13th century (Sui, Tang and Sung Dynasties)

Jieguo originated from the compounding of *jie* 'to tie; to connect' and *guo* 'fruit', While *jie* and *guo* have been used since Early Old Chinese, the compound *jieguo* did not emerge until around the 6th century (Sui Dynasty). However, in the analyzed texts which span across eight centruies (6–13th c.), only six tokens of *jieguo* are identified. In this period of time, *jieguo* was used either as a noun or verb with a fruit yielding sense (e.g., 20, 22), or with a conclusion meaning (e.g., 21, 23), the latter of which results from a metaphorical transfer from the material domain of fruit to the abstract domain of ending or completion of an action (see also Zhou 2008):

Verb 'to yield fruit'
(20) Hua   ji   kai   fu   **jie   guo**   shi.
     Flower now.that blossom grow **yield fruit** seed
     'After the flowers blossomed, (the plant) bore fruit.'
     (*Dunhuang Bianwen*)

Verb 'to come to an end'
(21) Shuo de cheng   le,   yin jiu   ci   **jieguo**.
     Say DE success CRS   so then here   **end**
     'All the thoughts were well-developed; so (the theory) was established.'
     (*Zhuzi yulei*)

Noun 'fruit yielded'
(22) Zui   yi   zhenzhu qian   ban jieguo,   bu yi   nao   ta.
     Most different pearl   thousand form fruit.yielded not easy disturb 3S
     'Even the strangest pearl and a thousand kinds of fruit cannot disturb him.'
     (*Dunhuang Bianwen*)

Noun 'end; conclusion; completion'

(23) Gai   shi yanzi wei   dao na chu, wei   dao   na
     Because be PN   not.yet reach that place not.yet reach that
     chengjiu   **jieguo** chu.
     achievement   **ending** place
     'It is because Yanzi has not reached there that he hasn't reached his final goal (of becoming a saint).'
     (*Zhuzi yulei*)

5.2 13th–19th century (Yuan, Ming and Qing Dynasties)

In the 13–14th century, there was a significant increase in the use of *jieguo*, as shown in our databank. A total of 80 occurrences of *jieguo* are found in the database. In addition to the earlier use, a great majority (85%) of these occurrenences display a new function, i.e., *jieguo* as a transitive compound carrying the meaning 'to kill (someone's life)', as illustrated in (24).

(24) a. Gao taiwei   junzhi, jiao wo liang ge dao   zheli **jieguo** ni.
        PN commander order call me two CL come here **kill** you
        'Commander Gao ordered the two of us to end your life here.'
        (*Shuihu zhuan*)

   b. Yi   jia   yi pudao,   **jieguo** le   liang ge xingming.
      one family one horse.knife **kill**   CRS   two   CL life
      'Each family took a horse knife and killed two people.'
      (*Shuihu zhuan*)

Two grammaticalization processes are responsible for the emergence of the killing sense of *jieguo*. First, the intransitive verbal compound 'to end' was reanalyzed and transitivized to form a true compound taking an object complement. At the same time, the interpretation of the killing sense was facilitated by a metaphorical mapping from the abstract domain of the closure of an event to the closure of one's life in physical means, particularly by killing. This change is contrary to the typical process of grammaticalization, in which the target meaning is usually more abstract than the source meaning (Lakoff and Johnson 1980; Traugott 2010: 112).

After the emergence of the killing sense, *jieguo* continued to be used as a polysemous nominal or verbal expression through the 19th century. While the fruit yielding sense largely refers to a desirable result, the sense of ending found with *jieguo* in the 14th–19th century is almost always loaded with a negatively evaluated tone. The emotive attitude may be related to a negative comment (25a), may denote an adverse or undesirable result (25b with a statement and 25c with a rhetorical question), or may denote someone's future life which is a compromised result given what has happened (25d):

(25) a. Ni   zhongshen **jieguo** zi   zai beizhou.
       You   lifetime   **result** naturally at   PN
       Zheli yuan   fei ni   anshen   zhi suo.
       Here originally not you settle.down of place
       'Your **permanent residence** should be in Beizhou. This is not where you should settle down.'
       (*Pingyaozhuan*)

   b. *Xinger*   guo   shenzi zhe bian guo   le   ji   nian xin
      Fortunately spend aunt this side spend CRS several year heart
      *jing   rizi. Rujin pian   you   shi zheme ge **jieguo.**
      clear day now unexpectedly again be so   CL **result**
      'Fortunately, I had several years of peace while living at my aunt's place. But, I didn't expect I would **end up** this way now.'
      (*Hongloumeng*)

   c. *Zao   yao ruci, qingwen he   zhi   nong dao   meiyou **jieguo**?*
      Early if   so   PN   why toward play arrive not.have **result**
      'If (it had happened) earlier, how would Qingwen **end up** not (being together with the person she loved)?'
      (*Hongloumeng*)

   d. *Ta   you   meiyou   die   niang, kuang you   shi ge*
      3S   again not.have father mother besides again be CL
      linshan   xianggong, zhaoguan de ta you   ge
      government.supported intellectual care   DE 3S have CL
      *haochu,   ye   shi women liang ge de   **jieguo.***
      advantage also be 1P   twi   CL GEN **result**.
      'He has no parents, and he is a government official. Taking care of him will (benefit) us. (This) can also be considered as our (happy) **ending**.'
      (*Xingshiyinyuan*)

The negative polarity implied in the above uses either indexes an undesirable result or invites the addressee to participate in the evaluation of a result in light of a previous proposition. The conceptual mechanisms that trigger the inference of the sense of adversity or exasperation conveyed by these sentences are both metaphor and metonymy. The result denoted requires a metaphorical interpretation because *jieguo* no longer refers to a tangible fruit of a plant but an abstract ending of a process or an event, whereas metonymy serves as a 'pointer' (Barcelona 2005: 317) guiding the inferential pathway to the negatively evaluated result in the discourse context exemplified above. As speakers increasingly use *jieguo* to designate adverse endings, the implicature of its counteractive force becomes "entrenched" (Langacker 1987: 59) in the language.

5.3 Contemporary Chinese

The use of *jieguo* for contradictory results underwent further change in contemporary Chinese and TSM. In both Mandarin Chinese and TSM, *jieguo* (*kiatko* in TSM) underwent a categorical change and now acts as a prosodically independent linking adverbial (see also Zhou 2008; Yao 2008) to introduce a sentence that is a consequence or result stemming from previous statements. Forty-six tokens of *jieguo* appear in the 5-hour Mandarin corpus and 57 tokens of *kiatko* appear in the 10-hour TSM corpus. Like the nominal *jieguo* used in the 14th–19th century, contemporary *jieguo* displays an orientation toward a negative evaluation. In fact, all of the occurrences of *jieguo* (100%) and 53 tokens of Taiwanese *kiatko* (93%) indicate a counter-expectation sense. (26a–b) illustrate the use of *jieguo* as a connective with a negative prosody:

(26) a. Women wanshan de   jihua ding de hen hao. **Jieuo**   na
        2P   complete GEN plan make DE very good **as.a.result** that
        yi tian ta buneng lai. **Jieguo**   buneng lai ye jiu
        one day 3S cannot come **as.a.result** cannot come also then
        suanle. **Jieguo**   jiu konglong hai yue le lingwai yi ge
        forget.it **as.a.result** then PN   also invite CRS another one CL
        tongxue   lai, ranhou bai chi wo yi dun.
        classmate come then   free eat 1S one meal
        'We had scheduled to have dinner with her. **However, it turned out that** she couldn't come. If that had been the only **thing**, then it would've been fine. (But you know what?) **I didn't expect that** Konglong would bring one friend (to the restaurant), and I had to treat them to dinner.'

   b. **Jieguo**   mei xiang dao shang le   yanjiusuo   haishi
        as.a.result not think arrive enter   CRT graduate.school still
        yao   peng shuxue.
        have.to touch math
        '**I didn't expect that** I would still have to use math as a graduate student.'

In (26a), a young man is describing an exasperating experience about a dinner with a girl. His plan to have a nice dinner with the girl failed because she did not show up. What was worse, his friend Konglong, who had helped plan the dinner, brought a friend to be treated to a meal by the speaker. (26b) also reports an unexpected occurrence with *jieguo*. The speaker had performed poorly in math before and had hoped that she would not have to "touch" it anymore after entering graduate school; the reality, however, was contrary to her expectation.

Exactly the same syntactic, semantic and pragmatic functions of *jieguo* are found for its TSM counterpart *kiatko*. In (27), *kiatko* introduces a clause that summarizes a reported event that conflicts with a normative belief:

(27) U   chit wi lamsu pengiu ho^n, anne   lim   kah anne   siochiuchui
     Have one CL male friend   PAR this.way drink till this.way drunk
     la. **Kiatko**   ne, ka   chite <M pingjiaodao M>   tong cho si
     PAR **as. a.result** PAR give this   railroad.crossing treat as be
     thiengchhiatiu^n la!
     parking.lot   PAR
     'There was a man who was so drunk that he treated the railroad crossing as a parking lot, (parked his car, and fell asleep there).'

It is particularly worth noting tha *kiatko* may concur with the marker *soah* to strengthen an unexpected outcome toward the end of a narrative. The conversation of (28) occurred when speaker L was feeling extremely anxious about the loss of the hamster. While the sole use of *kiatko* or *soah* would convey the message that the loss is beyond L's expectation, the concurrence of *kiatko* and *soah* augments the counter-expectation sense and brings the story to a culminating end.

(28)   (L is reporting to C about a missing hamster that his friend T kept. T had asked his friend Akau's wife to look after the hamster for him. However, Akau's wife was so careless that she lost it. L exaggerates this news by first saying that the little animal is dead. He then corrects himself by saying that it is only lost. This confuses the hearer C.)

C: M he^n, a   li kong e   na   e   huan   khi huan   to?
   DM PAR DM 2S say   NOM how will reverse up reverse down

>   *Liami   li kong si   a,   liami   kong iah m chai u   si*
>   Suddenly 2S say   die PAR suddenly say still not know have die
>   *a bo. Taute   si annoua la!*
>   or no in.the.end be how   PAR
>
> 'Your words were contradictory. First you said that (the hamster) was dead; then you said that you were not sure whether (it) was dead or not. What in the world were you trying to say?'

> L: *A   li m   chai   a!   A   chite <M xiaolaoshu M> a,   toh*
>   DM 2S not know   PAR   DM   this   little.mouse   PAR then
>   *topunsoh kia   ho   akau in bo   le   chhi a.   A   **kiatko***
>   PN   send give PN   his wife PRG   feed PAR DM **as. a.result**
>   ***soah***   *phangkian la!   A   chuanpo chhuttong le   chhue*
>   **unexpectedly** missing   PAR DM all   turn.out   PRG find
>   *o.   Kau chitma koh chhuue bo.*
>   PAR till now   still find   not
>
> 'Didn't you know that the hamster belonged to Topunsoh? But he asked Akau's wife to take care of it (while he was out of town)? **It just so happened that** (Akau's wife) lost (it)! Now everybody is looking for it, but so far no one has found it.'

The development of a completive marker into an adverbial connective can also be attested in English.[9] For example, *as a result* evolved into an adverbial linker in modern English (Traugott 1982: 258). The phrase *(it) turns out (that)* also displays similar discourse-pragmatic functions (Simpson 2004) to those of *jieguo/kiatko*. These connectives occur at the end of an episode or discourse unit to bring a closure and climax to the (sequence of) events depicted in the story. Besides, the results reported contain a scenario which conflicts with the speaker's expectation but which warrants extra attention (see also Chafe 1994: 135, on the counter-expected quality of discourse topic). The surprise or disbelief figures as a "discovery" of the fact or as a summation of the events stated previously. In general, these connectives are used as a "rhetorical strategy" in a narration to enliven the talk and bring a dramatic effect to the storytelling (Simpson 2004: 56).

At this point, it is worth mentioning a specific type of mechanism that underlies the specialization of the adverse meaning of *jieguo/kiatko* – the M-

---

9 Another line of development is for a completive marker to evolve into a perfective marker, e.g., Mandarin Chinese *liao* 'finish' > *le* , perfective marker (Norman 1988: 123, 269; Heine and Kuteva 2002: 138) and Kongo *mana* 'finish' > perfective aspect marker (Laman 1912: 185–186, Heine and Reh 1984: 88, cited in Heine and Kuteva 2002: 138).

heuristic proposed by Levinson (1995; 2000), which is a special type of metonymy that governs semantic change (Traugott and Dasher 2002). According to the M-heuristic, "What is said simply, briefly, in an unmarked way picks up the stereotypical interpretation; if in contrast a marked expression is used, it is suggested that the stereotypical interpretation should be avoided" (Levinson 2000: 38). In an unmarked utterance where the connective *jieguo/kiatko* is absent, the predicate still denotes a result. However, the use of *jieguo/kiatko* adds a dramatic effect to the coextensive summarizing statement. This is nicely captured by the M-heuristic: the marked expression with *jieguo/kiatko* invites a non-stereotypical interpretation. In other words, the utterance invites a marked interpretation that what is introduced by *jieguo* or *kiatko* is a result or consequence that deserves special attention, hence an unexpected or undesirable result. As we have shown at the beginning of this section, the pragmaticization of the CE sense is so pervasive that it accounts for most of the meanings of *jieguo/kiatko* in contemporary Chinese.

The above discussion shows that *jieguo* and *kiatko* have been reanalyzed into a linking adverbial and carry the procedural function of marking a noteworthy end of a discourse topic. Similar to common linking adverbials, *jieguo* and *kiatko* contribute to the logical flow of the discourse (Biber et al. 1999: 877). Although the two compounds still retain the fruit yielding sense, the linking function predominates in conversation.

5.4 Summary

Given the preceding discussion, I summarize the diachronic development of *jieguo* with Figure 4. Although the diachronic development of TSM *kiatko* cannot be established due to a lack of evidence (cf. Section 3), the developmental path of *jieguo* brings to light the pathways of change of *kiatko*.

Jieguo emerged as a compound of *jie* and *guo* through reanalysis. Later, as a result of metaphorical change, its meaning was extended to 'end; result', and

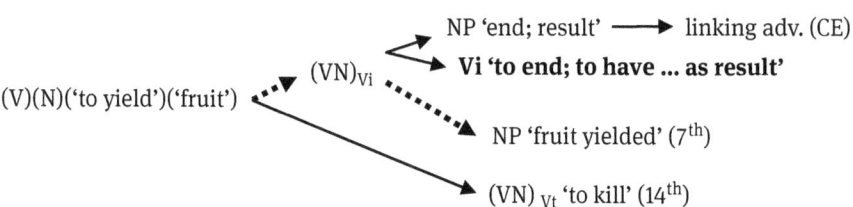

Fig. 4: Diachronic development of jieguo.

it became used as both a noun and a verb. It further underwent metonymic change motivated by the M-heuristic (Levinson 2000) and was reanalyzed as a linking adverbial indicating counter-expectation, in contemporary Chinese. Another line of development characterized the transitivization of *jieguo* into a verb of killing in the 14th century. The development of *jieguo* follows the general tendency observed of adverbials in English. Pragmatic markers commonly originate as items with content meaning. Over time, they move from clause internal adverbs to connecting adverbs (Traugott and Dasher 2002: 153).

6 Conclusion

In this paper, I have investigated the diachronic development of *sha4* 煞 and *jieguo* 結果 in Chinese and compared their contemporary uses with their TSM counterparts *soah* and *kiatko*. Although the two expressions originate from divergent semantic sources, their functions overlap considerably. A commonality of the two terms is that their meanings are closely associated with the terminal point of an event or of one's life. Eventually, both evolved toward the signaling of an unexpected outcome.

The trajectories of *sha4* and *jieguo* attest to the interaction of two major conceptual vehicles of grammaticalization, metaphor, and metonymy (Goosens 1990: 323). While the early changes of the two expressions were mainly due to metaphorical change, some of the later stages of development involved a simultaneous operation of metaphor and metonymy, that is, metaphtonymy (Goosens 1990: 328), esp. in the case of *sha4*. On the other hand, a specific type of metonymy, that is, invited pragmatic inferencing that builds on Levinson's R-heuristic and M-heuristic, plays an important role in accounting for the development of the adverbial use of *sha4* and *jieguo*. Along with the work of metonymization of metaphorization, both *soah* and *kiatko* in TSM involve subjectification as they both index the speaker's evaluation and attitude toward a negative situation.

The interplay between and division of labor of metaphor and metonymy illustrate the argument made by Nerlich (2010: 207), that metaphor involves "building conceptual systems", whereas metonymy emerges and is interpreted through the co-construction of meanings in linguistic interaction. An understanding of the evolution of meaning, therefore, can only be achieved by a close scrutiny of the situated meanings and communicative functions of the CE markers in context.

Sources

Primary sources

Early Old Chinese (11th–6th c. BC) 1. *Book of Odes*
Late Old Chinese (5th–3rd c. BC) 1. *Analects of Confucius* 2. *Mengzi* 3. *Mozi* 4. *Zhuangzi*
   5. *Xunzi* 6. *Hanfeizi* 7. *Lushichunqiu* 8. *Zuozhuan* 9. *Zhanguoce*
Pre-Middle Chinese (2nd c. BC–3rd century) 1. *Shiji* 2. *Lunheng* 3. *Shiming* 4. *Chungbenqijing*
   5. *Xiuxingbenqijing* 6. *Dabiqiusanqianweiyi* 7. *Pusabenyuanjing* 8. *Liudujijing*
   9. *Shengjing* 10. *Foshuodeguangtaizijing* 11. *Ayuwangzhuan*
Early Middle Chinese (3rd–6th century) 1. *Shishuoxinyu* 2. *Qiminyaosu* 3. *Baiyujing*
   4. *Xianyujing* 5. *Houhanshu* 6. *Fobenxingjijing* 7. *Sifenlü* 8. *Shisonglü*
Late Middle Chinese (7th–13th century) 1. *Dunhuang Bianwen* 2. *Liuzu chanjing* 3. *Shenhui yulu* 4. *Rutang qiufa xunli xingji* 5. *Zutangji* 6. *Zhuzi yulei* 7. *Yushi mingyan* 8. *Jingshi tongyan*
Pre-modern Chinese (14th–19th century) 1. *Pingyao zhuan* 2. *Shuihu zhuan* 3. *Jinpingmei*
   4. *Chuke erke paian jingqi* 5. *Xingshi yinyuan zhuan* 6. *Hongloumeng* 7. *Laocan youji*
   8. *Ernü yingxiong zhuan*
Contemporary Chinese 1. *Academia Sinica Balanced Corpus of Modern Chinese* (5,000,000 words) http://db1x.sinica.edu.tw/kiwi/mkiwi/index.html 2. *NTU Corpus of Spoken Chinese* http://homepage.ntu.edu.tw/~gilntu/english_version/intro/index.htm 3. *Beijing Corpus of Spoken Chinese* (400,000 words) http://www.blcu.edu.cn/yys/6_beijing/6_beijing_chaxun.asp
Southern Min Texts 1. *Romance of the Lychee Mirror* 2. *Kimhuelu* 3. *Solakniu* 4. Southern Min Folk songs (from Academia Sinica corpus) http://plaza16.mbn.or.jp/~sunliong/kua-a-chheh.htm

Secondary sources

Barcelona, Antonio. 2000. Introduction. In Antonio Barcelona (ed.), *Metaphor and metonymy at the crossroads*, 3–28. Berlin & New York: Mouton de Gruyter.
Barcelona, Antonio. 2005. The multilevel operation of metonymy in grammar and discourse, with particular attention to metonymic chain. In Francisco José Ruiz de Mendoza Ibáñez & M. Sandra Peña Cerbel (eds.), *Cognitive linguistics: Internal dynamics and interdisciplinary interaction*, 313–352. Berlin & New York: Mouton de Gruyter.
Brinton, Laurel J. 1996. *Pragmatic markers in English: Grammaticalization and discourse functions*. Berlin & New York: Mouton de Gruyter.
Chafe, Wallace. 1994. *Discourse, consciousness and time*. Chicago: The University of Chicago Press.
Chen, Xiu. 1991. *Taiwanhua da cidian* [A dictionary of Taiwanese]. Taipei: Yuan-Liou Publishing Co. (in Chinese)
Cheng, Robert L. & Susie S. Cheng. 1994. *Phonological structure and romanization of Taiwanese Hokkian*, 2nd edn. Taipei: Student Book Co.

Couper-Kuhlen, Elizabeth & Sandra A. Thompson. 2005. A linguistic practice for retracting overstatements. In Auli Hakulinen & Margret Selting (eds.), *Syntax and lexis in conversation: Studies on the use of linguistic resources in talk-in-Interaction*, 257–288. Amsterdam & Philadelphia: John Benjamins.

Croft, William & D. Alan Cruse. 2004. *Cognitive linguistics*. Cambridge: Cambridge University Press.

Du Bois, John. 1987. The discourse basis of ergativity. *Language* 63. 805–55.

Geeraerts, Dirk. 1997. *Diachronic prototype semantics: A contribution to historical lexicology*. Oxford: Clarendon Press.

Geerarerts, Dirk. 2010a. *Theories of lexical semantics*. New York: Oxford University Press.

Geerarerts, Dirk. 2010b. Prospects for the past: Perspectives for cognitive diachronic semantics. In Kathryn Allan, Heli Tisari & Margaret E. Winters (eds.), *Historical cognitive linguistics*, 333–356. Cognitive Linguistics Research 47. Berlin & New York: Walter de Gruyter.

Goosens, Louis. 1990. Metaphtonymy: The interaction of metaphor and metonymy in expressions for linguistic action. *Cognitive Linguistics* 1. 323–340.

Hansen, Maj-Britt Mosegaard & Corinne Rossari. 2002. The evolution of pragmatic markers. *Journal of Historical Pragmatics* 6. 177–187.

Heine, Bernd & Mechthild Reh. 1982. *Patterns of grammaticalization in African languages*. Cologne: Institut für Sprachwissenschaft, Universität zu Köln.

Heine, Bernd & Tania Kuteva. 2002. *World lexicon of grammaticalization*. Cambridge: Cambridge University Press.

Hopper, Paul J. 1987. Emergent grammar. *Proceedings of the Annual Meeting of the Berkeley Linguistics Society* 13. 139–157.

Koch, Peter. 2001. Metonymy: Unity in diversity. *Journal of Historical Pragmatics* 2. 201–244.

König, Ekkehard. 1991. *The meaning of focus particles: A comparative perspective*. London: Routledge.

Kövecses, Zoltán & Günter Radden. 1998. Metonymy: Developing a cognitive linguistic view. *Cognitive Linguistics* 9. 37–77.

Lakoff, George & Mark Johnson. 1980. *Metaphors we live by*. Chicago: Chicago University Press.

Langacker, Ronald W. 1977. Syntactic reanalysis. In Charles N. Li (ed.), *Mechanisms of syntactic change*, 57–139. Austin: University of Texas Press.

Levinson, Stephen C. 1995. Three levels of meaning. In F. R. Palmer (ed.), *Grammar and meaning: Essays in honor of Sir John Lyons*, 90–115. Cambridge: Cambridge University Press.

Levinson, Stephen C. 2000. *Presumptive meanings: The theory of generalized conversational implicature*. Cambridge, Mass.: Massachusetts Institute of Technology Press.

Nerlich, Brigitte. 2010. Metaphor and metonymy. In Andreas H. Jucker & Irma Taavitsainen (eds.), *Historical pragmatics*, 193–215. Berlin & New York: Mouton de Gruyter.

Norman, Jerry. 1988. *Chinese*. Cambridge: Cambridge University Press.

Pomerantz, Anita. 1986. Extreme case formulation: A way of legitimizing claims. *Human Studies* 9. 219–229.

Schiffrin, Deborah. 1987. *Discourse markers*. Cambridge: Cambridge University Press.

Simpson, Rita C. 2004. Stylistic features of academic speech: The role of formulaic expressions. In Ulla Connor & Thomas A. Upton (eds.), *Discourse in the professions: Perspectives from corpus linguistics*, 37–64. Amsterdam & Philadelphia: John Benjamins.

Taavitsainen, Irma & Anderas Jucker. 2010. Trends and developments in historical pragmatics. In Andreas H. Jucker & Irma Taavitsainen (eds.), *Historical pragmatics*, 1–30. Berlin & New York: Mouton de Gruyter.

Thompson, Sandra A. & Paul J. Hopper. 2001. Transitivity, clause structure, and argument structure: Evidence from conversation. In Joan Bybee & Paul Hopper (eds.), *Frequency and the emergence of linguistics structure*, 27–60. Amsterdam & Philadelphia: John Benjamins.

Tomlin, Russell S. (ed.). 1987. *Coherence and grounding in discourse*. Amsterdam & Philadelphia: John Benjamins.

Traugott, Elizabeth Closs. 1982. From propositional to textual and expressive meanings: Some semantic-pragmatic aspects of grammaticalization. In Winfred P. Lehman & Yakov Malkiel (eds.), *Perspectives on historical linguistics*, 245–273. Amsterdam & Philadelphia: John Benjamins.

Traugott, Elizabeth Closs & Richard B. Dasher. 2002. *Regularity in semantic change*. Cambridge: Cambridge University Press.

Xing, Janet Zhiqun. 2004. Grammaticalization of the scalar focus particle *lian* in Mandarin Chinese. *Journal of Historical Pragmatics* 5(1). 81–106.

Yao, Shuangyun. 2008. Fuju guanxi biaoji de dapei yanjiu [Collocational patterns of complex clause markers]. Wuhan: Huazhong Shifan Daxue Chubanshe. (in Chinese)

Zhang, Shuang-qing. 1996. Zutangji suo jian de quanzhou fangyan cihui [Quanzhou lexical items found in *Zutangji*]. *Proceedings of the Fourth International Conference on Min Dialects*, 162–168. Shantou: Shantou University Press. (in Chinese)

Zhou, Xiaolin. 2005. Chengdu buyu ju "V/A sha" shi de laiyuan ji qi yanbian [Origin and change of the degree complement "V/A sha"]. *Academic Exchange* 136. 138–142. (in Chinese)

Zhou, Biji. 2008. "Jieguo de yufahua licheng ji yuyong tedian [On the grammaticalization of "Jieguo" and its pragmatic characteristics]. *Chinese Language Learning* 6. 64–72. (in Chinese)

Wolfgang Schulze
The emergence of diathesis markers from MOTION concepts

Abstract: The syntax of most of the thirty autochthonous East Caucasian languages is characterized by a rather rigid association of grammatical relations to the foreground/background domains. In this sense, their syntax can be related to the feature of role dominance (Foley and Van Valin 1984). It follows that the ECL syntax normally lacks procedures of diathesis. Nevertheless, some of the ECL show a deviation from this rigid patterning: Basically, these show up in three types: (a) morphosyntactically marked antipassives; (b) morphosyntactically marked passives; (c) unaccusative/unergative strategies. Antipassives are quite in accordance with ergative patterns prevailing in ECL, whereas passives in ECL are more recent techniques related to the gradual accusativization of the system of grammatical relations. Both techniques are based on diathetic markers that occur as heavily grammaticalized elements within the verb. In my paper, I want to explain the grammaticalization background of some of the morphological elements present in the above-mentioned diathetic processes. Most of the relevant data are taken from two East Caucasian languages (Udi and Caucasian Albanian) that speak in favor of deriving diathetic morphological units from concepts of MOTION. In order to approach this problem, I first describe in more details a model that explains which cognitive processes underlie the choice of MOTION concepts used in these derivational processes. MOTION is viewed as an event image that results (among others) from the experience-based agglutination of a sequence of perceived figure/ground structures. The resulting shift within these structures conditions that MOTION is strongly associated with the concept of CHANGE-OF-STATE. This shift that accounts for various expression types that ground BECOME concepts in MOTION concepts is illustrated with the help of selective typological data mainly from Indo-European data. This includes a closer inspection of the distribution of GO- and COME-concepts within this shift. BECOME concepts thus highly qualify for further grammaticalization processes that result in diathetic expressions. The paper places the shift MOTION > CHANGE-OF-STATE in a broader context that also includes other MOTION types, such as TURN (AROUND), BRING (> GET). Nevertheless, data stemming from Udi and Caucasian Albanian suggest that the intermediate stage BECOME is not a necessary condition for deriving dia-

Wolfgang Schulze: Ludwig-Maximilians-Universität München thetic markers from MOTION concepts. In fact, these languages speak in favor of the assumption that the concept of diathesis may be directly grounded in MOTION concepts. Accordingly, such processes reveal a more immediate reflex of embodiment features present at least in some diathetic concepts.

1 Introduction

1.1 Purpose of the paper

In this paper, I want to take up the long-standing discussion of whether, and if yes, to which extent and how verbal forms expressing MOTION-concepts may turn into diathetic auxiliaries (or derivational elements). The relevant literature is remarkably silent with respect to the concrete processes that have to be described for this grammaticalization path. The basic question is, which properties of the conceptual domain MOTION are responsible for this process and why they qualify (among others) for the encoding of diathetic functions. Accordingly, section 2 presents a very brief model of MOTION concepts and their experiential foundation. The fact that for many languages that derive passive auxiliaries from MOTION concepts we have to assume an intermediate stage in this grammaticalization path involving the domain of CHANGE-OF-STATE/ BECOME necessitates a closer consideration of this domain, too (section 3). In section 4, I will discuss the processes that results in diathetic constructions. Section 5 of this paper analyzes in more details the MOTION > DIATHESIS path that does not include the intermediate stage just mentioned. Data are taken from two East Caucasian languages (Udi and Albanian Caucasian). Many East Caucasian languages are typical role-dominated languages (Foley and VanValin 1984) and show diathetic processes to a limited extent, only. After briefly illustrating such diathetic constructions in some East Caucasian languages (section 5.1), I will elaborate in more details the historical processes and structural properties of (innovative) passives in Udi and Caucasian Albanian (CA).

1.2 Some basic observations

In her study on passives, Anna Siewierska has argued that "[passive] auxiliary verbs do not carry a lexical meaning. They do, nevertheless, contribute to the semantics of the clause" (Siewierska 1984: 128). The second part of this assumption is based on the observation that in languages with a system of multiple passive auxiliaries (such as English *be*, *become*, *get*), the selection of the individual passive auxiliaries may be controlled by categorial features of the verbal patterns – or, turning the causal chain around, may give rise to different semantic patterns of these constructions. In addition, Haspelmath (1990: 40) notes that

> [f]or many of the periphrastic passives with intransitive inactive auxiliaries, it seems misleading to attribute the passive function to the auxiliary, because the verb form with which it is combined is already passive, a "passive participle".

Both statements refer to the fact that periphrastic passives are a rather common technique among those languages that employ a passive strategy. In addition it is often claimed that periphrastic passives have served as the starting point of grammaticalization processes resulting in morphological passive markers. In this sense, Shibatani (2004: 1161) states that

> the distinction of periphrastic versus morphological manifestations of the voice morpheme is not as interesting as the etymological origins and the semantic scope that typical periphrastic voice constructions share with certain affixal forms.

This does not imply that *all* verbal markers of diathesis (or: voice) have resulted from auxiliary verbs (or: light verbs), see Siewierska (1984), Haspelmath (1990), Shibatani (2004) and many others for source domains differing from this pattern. In the present paper, however, I want to concentrate on strategies of diathetic constructions related to light verbs, only. Given the fact that diathesis is just a functional procedure, we can hardly expect to find lexical verbs denoting something like 'passive' or so. Still, Haspelmath's claim quoted above, according to which many periphrastic passives owe their passive function to the passive-marked verb itself and not to the auxiliary, seems to be too strong or at least too strongly related to the Indo-European model of passivization, cf. Early Medieval Chinese (Peyraube 1996: 176, also compare Heine and Kuteva 2002: 146, 284):

(1) *Liangzi bei   Su Jun hai*
    Liangzi PASS Su Jun kill
    'Liangzi was killed by Su(n) Jun.'

Here, the light verb *bei* < *bei* 'to receive, suffer' is linked to the simple verb *hai* 'kill', which does not carry any sign of a passive morphology.[1] Accordingly, it

---

1 Peyraube (1996: 177) notes that the interpretation of *bei* is ambiguous. The direction of the grammaticalization path probably depends from its position: When inserted before a nominal in agentive function, it developed into a preposition-like marker indicating the back-grounded agent (English *by*). Hence, the example in (1) can also be glossed 'Liangzi by Su Jun kill'.

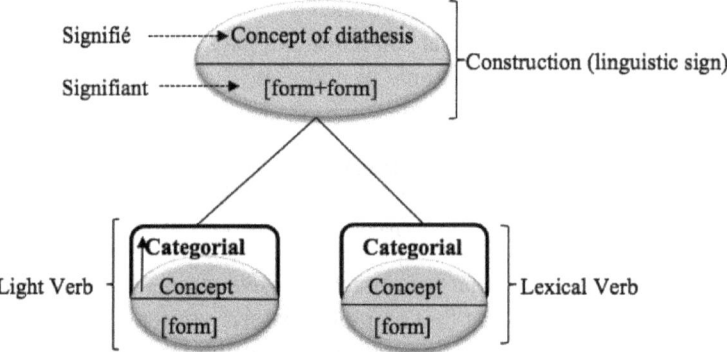

Fig. 1: Diathetic constructions as emergent concepts.

seems appropriate to refer to the construction Light Verb + Verb (LV+V) itself in order to locate the origins of its diathetic function, not to one of its parts. Obviously, we have to deal with some kind of formal *and* conceptual blending that is marked for the interaction of the signifié-domains of both types of linguistic signs.

Accordingly, certain conceptual properties of the linguistic sign 'light verb' (LV) interact with the conceptual domain of a given lexical verb in a way that results in the conceptual fixation of the construction. Figure 1 also reflects the fact that within the grammaticalization process related to the light verb, the original conceptual unit of the verb at issue is gradually expended towards a categorial domain, e.g. <MAKE > → <CAUSATION>. Likewise, it may refer to subcategories into which a lexical verb is embedded, e.g. {LV_1 + DYNAMIC}, {LV_2 + STATIVE} and so on.[2]

In order to explain the grammaticalization process present with diathetic strategies, it is hence crucial to describe (a) the categorial scope of the light verbs underlying a diathetic construction, (b) subcategorizing effects with respect to the lexical verbs (if given), and (c) the syntax of the construction itself. In the present paper, I will neglect point (b) because it is not relevant for the languages discussed in section 5 of this paper: There is no evidence that in these languages, the choice of light verbs depends on the semantics of the lexical verb.

Haspelmath (1990: 59) suggests that most light verbs embedded into a passive construction are related to the categorial domain of 'inactiveness': "Most sources of verbal passive morphology initially express [the] (...) inactivization

---

[2] See Rosenbaum Schulze (2011) for a more detailed description of this model.

of the situation". And: "This is most obvious in the case of inactive auxiliaries, probably the most important source of passive morphology". He parallels "inactive" to "non-agentive" (p.39), claiming that most light verbs involved are intransitive.³ Keenan and Dryer (2007: 336–339) refer to the same idea and suggest the following subdomains:

(2) a. being or becoming
    b. reception
    c. motion
    d. experiencing

This classification is, however, marked for a mixture of synchronic and diachronic observations: The assessment of the first subdomain for instance (*being* or *becoming*) is based mainly on the ascription of synchronic semantics. From a diachronic point of view, it can be often related to the subdomain of *motion*, cf. English *be-come*, French *de-venir* etc. (see below). The same holds for some languages with respect to the subdomain *reception*, cf. German *bekommen* 'to get' (English probably is a loan from Old Norse going back to Indo-European *g^hend-* 'seize, take'), Spanish *con-sequir* 'to receive' (ultimately related to Indo-European *sek^w-* 'to follow' → 'to accompany'). If we consider the concept of STATE as being the non-dynamic version of MOTION (← BODILY ACTION, see footnote 7), we may even consider such verbs as Russian *stat'* 'to stand, stay' → 'to become', Slovak *dostat'* 'to get', Spanish *estar* 'to lie, be (temporarily)' and many others. It follows that the assumption of Keenan and Dryer (2007: 338) according to which the MOTION type "seems less well attested" perhaps is too restrictive. In this sense, I suggest to reduce the domains listed in (2) to the two basic categorial units:

(3) a. Body
        (i) Action
        (ii) State
    b. Perception/Experience

I add the term 'perception' to that of 'experiencing' (Keenan and Dryer 2077: 338) in order to account for the fact that passive light verbs like Thai *thùuk* ('touch', cf. Filbeck 1973), Vietnamese *bị* ('suffer', cf. Siewierska 1984: 158), and Old Chinese *jian* ('see', cf. Heine and Kuteva 2002: 270) are obviously

---

3 However, he adds some transitive verbal concepts such as UNDERGO, SUFFER, RECEIVE.

grounded in the concept of perceiving (and thus being confronted with) a process.

One of the questions emerging from these preliminary observations is the following: What are the conceptual commonalities between concepts related to these domains so that they qualify for grammaticalization processes related to diathesis? I will argue that the concepts based on MOTION (that is on concepts of bodily action) are directly related to a conceptual world that is marked for some kind of CHANGE OF STATE. It is this concept that furnishes the basis for the development of some diathetic auxiliaries and morphemes, not the MOTION concept as such. Before illustrating this approach with the help of selected data stemming from some of the autochthonous East Caucasian languages, I will briefly elaborate some central aspects related to the hypothesis just mentioned.

2 Motion

If we disregard conceptualizations of motion based on proprioceptive factors, perceived acts of motion can be described as resulting from a chain of figure-ground constructions: An object image is construed in terms of a *figure* (or: trajector, Tr) that is perceived as being in a changing relationship to its *ground* (or: landmark, Lm).[4] In a very simplified model, this relationship is construed as *motion* due to the flipbook principle: In case the time span related to the perception of subsequent relations of the type Tr → Lm is below 15 msec (60 Hz), the sequence shows up as motion[5], compare Figure 2.

Figure 2 illustrates the two key features of the construction of motion perception in terms of an event image (IE): First, the trajector (TR) (in fact a refer-

---

[4] In essence, the model presented here conforms to standard hypotheses about the conceptualization of motion events as uttered (among many others) by Langacker (1986, 1980, 1999), Lakoff (1987), Sinha et al. (1994), Sinha (1999), Talmy (1991, 1996), Kreitzer (1997). It elaborates these hypotheses especially with respect to the application of the flipbook principle.
[5] According to the present model, verbs (or verb phrases) do not represent conceptual units 'by themselves'. Quite in accordance with the flipbook principle, verbs are regarded as the linguistic expression of generalized (and schematized) inferential processes emerging from the 'compilation' (sequencing) of individual event images (IE). Verbally symbolized concepts cannot be processed as such, but only in terms of scenes including more or less subcategorized/ specialized referents. This conforms to the fact that human beings cannot perceive outer world processes or states as such, but only objects in terms of referents (see Schulze 1998, 2010, 2011).

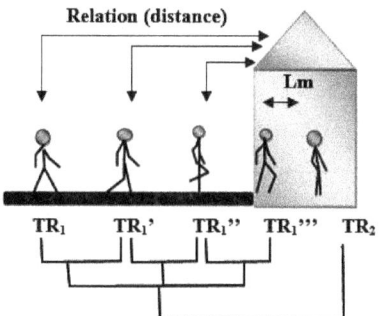

IE: [PERSON [[MOTION MOTION MOTION] IN] HOUSE]

Fig. 2: A simplified model of motion conceptualization.

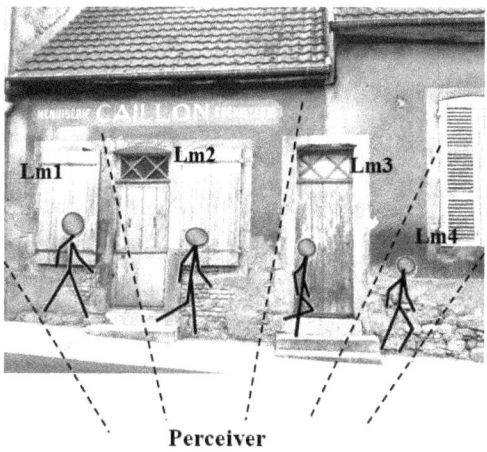

Fig. 3: Changing landmarks.

ential unit associated with *figure*) is defined as being 'in change' (TR, TR', TR'' etc.). The result is a sequence of motion constructions that are again clustered in terms of a single motion construction. Second, the trajector is related to a landmark (Lm), be it the starting point of reference or the end point of reference. Most importantly, the notion of change is linked to the landmark feature.

With standard motion verbs, the intermediate changes with respect to the Tr → Lm relation are normally construed as a 'whole'. These constructions usually are profiled with respect to the fixation of the starting point of reference or to that of the end point of reference. In a prototypical sense, one of these points of reference is highlightened (and lexically expressed), whereas the other one is inferred from the speaker's point of view or knowledge, cf. (a) and (b) in Table 1:

Tab. 1: Motion and the expression of points of reference.

	Trajector	Verb	Starting point of reference		End point of reference	
			Inferred	Given	Inferred	Given
a.	I	went to	√			the library
b.	I	came		from the library	√	
c.	I	went to		from the library		the cinema
d.	I	Ran	[√]		[√]	

We can paraphrase examples (a) as $[I_{TR} \to \text{not-library}_{LM}] \to [I_{TR} \to \text{library}_{LM}]$ and (b) as $[I_{TR} \to \text{library}_{LM}] \to [I_{TR} \to \text{not-library}_{LM}]$. A more general formal would be:

(4) $[TR \to LM_X] \to [TR \to LM_Y] \mid X \neq Y$

This formula can be read as follows: A trajector related to a landmark X is subsequently related to a landmark Y that is different from landmark X. In other words: Prototypically, the conceptual domain of MOTION is marked for the 'displacement' or 'translocation' of a referent.[6] If we refer to the initial and the final locational relation in terms of a *state*, the notion CHANGE-OF-STATE can thus be paraphrased as 'moving from one state to another'. Pending on the conceptual category to which both the trajector and the landmark belong, this type of displacement can end up in schematic models of fictive motion (Talmy 1996).

3 From MOTION via CHANGE-OF-STATE to BECOME

Langacker (1986: 462) suggests that "we (...) must (...) attribute to go a conventionally-established range of values that indicate change in non-spatial do-

---

[6] Here, I do not want to elaborate the question to which extent the two resulting motion types GO and COME are marked for the incorporation of manner concepts (by foot, by vehicle etc.). It is nevertheless interesting to see that the lexical expression of COME-concepts is often restricted to a very general verb of 'coming', whereas the world of GO-concepts may be expressed

mains" (emphasis by Langacker). The CHANGE-OF-STATE schema that is present not only in GO concepts, but in all types of MOTION concepts, however, is only one option to expend the semantic value of the corresponding linguistic sign. In their collection of grammaticalization paths, Heine and Kuteva (2002: 68–78 and 155–165) have described a set of target domains that can be typologically associated with MOTION concepts. The resulting list (see Table 2) illustrates that the two basic MOTION concepts COME and GO serve to derive a variety of conceptual target domains:

Tab. 2: The target domains of MOTION concepts (based on Heine and Kuteva 2002).

COME	CONSECUTIVE
	CONTINUOUS
	HORTATIVE
COME FROM	VENTIVE
	ABLATIVE
	NEAR PAST
COME TO	BENEFACTIVE
	CHANGE OF STATE
	FUTURE
	PROXIMAL
	PURPOSE
GO	ITIVE
	CHANGE OF STATE
	CONTINUOUS
	DISTAL
	HABITUAL
	HORTATIVE
GO TO	ALLATIVE
	FUTURE
	PURPOSE

Accordingly, the bulk of target domains is located in the sphere of SPACE and TIME. Figure 4 summarizes the metaphorization patterns with respect to these primary target domains.

The three additional domains BENEFACTIVE, CONSECUTIVE, and PURPOSE suggest that the primary target domains SPACE and TIME represent just

---

in terms of a very broad lexical field (in path framed expressions), such as English *drive*, *fly*, *march* etc., compare German ... *weil ich ja morgen früh nach Wien* fahre *und am Mittwoch direkt von dort* komme ('because I'll *drive* to Vienna early tomorrow and will *come* directly from there on Wednesday'). This suggests that COME and GO are exact conversions of each other only with respect to the feature of orientation.

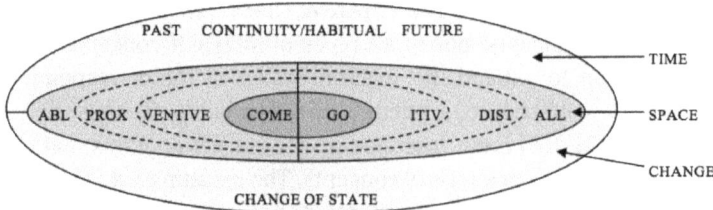

Fig. 4: The expansion of MOTION concepts.

the initial segments of a longer metaphorization chain. In addition, the distribution of COME and GO derivations is not complementary: Five of these domains (CHANGE OF STATE, CONTINUOUS, FUTURE, HORTATIVE, PURPOSE) are derived from both source domains. We may hence assume that COME and GO are embedded into a more general conceptual domain that can be best termed MOTION 'as such'.

3.1 Itive/Ventive

The most obvious metaphorization path related to non-locational target domains is MOTION → CHANGE-OF-STATE. As has been said above, this pattern is present with quite a number of languages such as English (1a, 1b), French (2), Italian (3), or Romanian (4), confer:

(1) a. *I went crazy.*
 b. *She became old.*

(2) *et moi par malheur je suis venu*
 And I.EMPH due to misfortune I.NOM COP.PRES.1SG come.PART.PAST.M.SG
 malade depuis six année
 ill since six years
 'And by misfortune, I have been ill for six years.'

(3) *Dobbiamo forse divenire più consapevoli*
 must.PRES.1PL perhaps become.INF more self-conscious.PL.M
 'Perhaps we must become more self-conscious.'

(4) *Visele devin realitate*
 dream.PL become.PRES.3PL truth
 'Dreams become true.'

English *become* has resulted from OE *becuman* 'to happen, come about', also 'to meet with, arrive' from Proto-Germanic **bi-kweman* (cf. Dutch *bekomen*, Old High German *biqueman* 'to obtain', Gothic *biquiman*). The original meaning was 'to come towards (**bi-*) someone/something'. This compound replaced OE *weorðan* 'to become' (German *werden*, see below). The COME-concept is also present in the *devenir*-type (ex. 2,3,4) < Latin *de-venire* 'to come from someone/ something, to arrive at someone/something'. The same pattern is visible in other languages such as Arabic (*ṣāra* 'to arrive (at), come to' > 'to become'), to'aba'ita (*mai* 'to come' > 'to become') or Sango (*gä* 'to come to' > 'to become'), cf. Heine and Kuteva (2002) for the last two examples.

From a prototypical point of view, the source domain of BECOME indicates motion towards another 'state', e.g.

(5) *The woman became rich*
 [TR → LM$_X$] → [TR → LM$_Y$]
 Woman in=state not-rich MOVE woman in=state rich

Most likely, the original ventive semantics of the COME-concept became less relevant in the given context. Rather, the direction 'towards a new landmark' has been highlighted (expressed e.g. in Germanic by the preverb **bī-* 'at, around something'). Nevertheless, the strong non-agentive semantics of BECOME-concepts has probably resulted from the underlying COME-dimension. This is visible for instance in German, where *bekommen* has developed into a 'verb of reception', cf.:

(6) *Sie be-kam ein Buch*
 She BE-come.PAST INDEF.N.SG book
 'She got a book'
 ← *'She came to(wards) a book'

Note that the RECEIVE concepts being derived from COME-TO (→ REACH) can also develop into a BECOME-concept, as is English *I got crazy*: The verb *get* has been borrowed from Old Norse *geta* 'to reach, obtain etc.' (Baetke 1965–1968: 195). It has replaced OEngl. *becuman* 'to come, arrive, happen, befall etc.' (Clark Hall 1916: 39) in the sense of a RECEIVE concept and added the semantics of 'to become'. The transition from RECEIVE to CHANGE-OF-STATE can easily be paraphrased in terms of an expression like 'to acquire a different state'. In sum, the metaphorization path can be described as follows:[7]

---

[7] Note that with Welsh *dyfod* 'to come' (< **to-bod-*), the metaphorization path seems to go the other way round: The verb is based on the Indo-European stem **bhu-* 'to be', augmented by a directional preverb.

(7) Source Domain   Target Domain

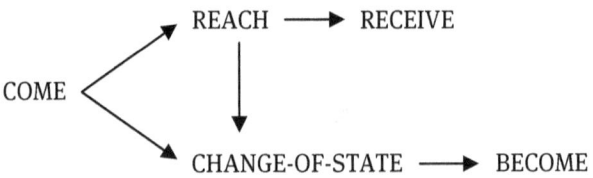

Conceptually, the degree to which a trajector 'penetrates' the region of a landmark (or the landmark itself) can affect the elaboration of CHANGE-OF-STATE-types. The above-given data reflect type (b) illustrated in Figure 5: Accordingly, the trajector moves towards the landmark in a way that is marked for close contact or even merger. This schema results in models of association and transformation (TR acquires properties of LM or merges with LM to the effect that TR *becomes* LM), confer figure 5:

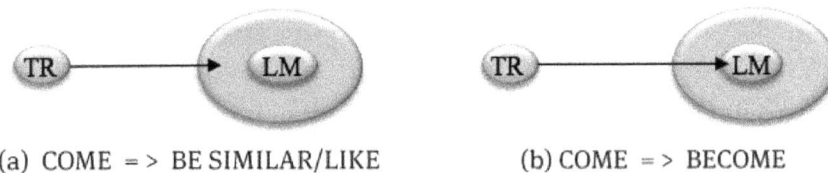

(a) COME => BE SIMILAR/LIKE   (b) COME => BECOME

Fig. 5: From MOTION to LIKE and BECOME.

Type (a) reflects one of the many schemas of similarity or likeness. It is present for instance in Udi (East Caucasian) *lari* 'like' < *la-ar-i*, past participle of *la-eğsun* 'to move up/toward', in Russian *po-xodit'* 'be similar' < *'to move to', or in the German *kommen nach* 'be similar to (a relative)'. Such LIKE-concepts may also stem from the concept of BECOME itself, such as Lezgi (East Caucasian) *xiz* 'like' that probably is an alternative infinitive of *xun* 'to become' (else *žez*) and *xtin* (adjectival 'like'), probably a participle-like form of *xun*, also present in *hi-xtin* 'which', lit. 'what being', cf.:

(8) am   bilbi   xiz   rax-az-wa
    DIST nightingale LIKE speak-INF-PRES
    'He speaks like a nightingale (sings).' (Lit.: 'He sings being a nightingale')

3.2 'TURN'

Another model of deriving BECOME-concepts from MOTION-concepts can be illustrated with the help of German *werden* or Lithuanian *vìrsti* 'to become'. The original meaning of these verbs still is preserved in Latin *vertere* 'to turn around/to', Old Slavonic *vrutěti* 'to turn', Sanskrit *vṛt-* 'to turn'. As illustrated by Latin *con-vertere* 'to turn somebody/something into', this concept is immediately related to concepts of transformation or transfiguration. Accordingly, a phrase like German *sie wird Lehrerin* ('she becomes a teacher') can be archetypically described as 'she mutates into (the role of) a teacher'. The concept of 'teacher' thus serves as a landmark, into which the trajector referent ('she') becomes integrated and by which the trajectory (temporally) acquires properties of the landmark referent. In English, OE *weorðen* 'to become' was replaced by the borrowing *turnian* (> *to turn*) from Old French *torner* 'to turn'. Contrary to the *vertere*-type, the Latin source term *tornare* is not a motion verb, but a technical term denoting 'to turn on a lathe' (Greek τόρνος 'lathe, tool for drawing circles'). Later, the metonymic extension *to turn* (in the sense of Latin *vertere*) in parts underwent the same metaphorical shift as the *vertere*-type in German or Lithuanian, cf. *she turned crazy*, including the *con-vertere*-type (*she turned us into trees*).

The metaphorization path relevant to the TURN-concept can be thus summarized as follows:

(9) Source Domain   Target Domain

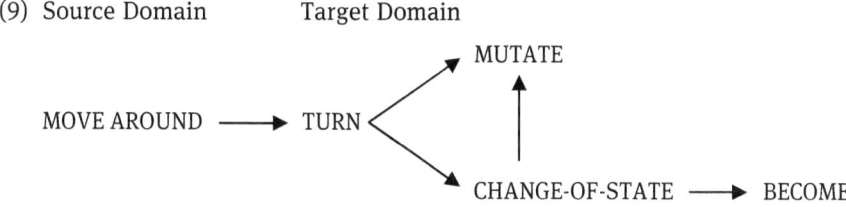

In summary, the metaphorization path MOVE → BECOME can start from at least three variant of the MOTION concept: Itive (→ GO), Ventive (→ COME (→ RECEIVE)), and TURN-AROUND (→ TURN). The overall schema is summarized in (10):[8]

---

[8] It should be stressed again that I do not consider BECOME concepts that are derived from STATE concepts, such as Russian *on stanel vračom* 'he becomes a doctor' (*stat'* 'to stand'). Normally, the STAND/STAY concept is typical with BE concepts (e.g. Italian *stato* (PPP), French *été* (PPP), Spanish *estar*, Irish *tāim*). With BECOME concepts, the Slavic model is normally marked for a dynamic derivational pattern, such as Russian *stanovit'sja*, Polish *(zo)stać się*, Czech *státi se* 'to place oneself, stay' etc.

(10)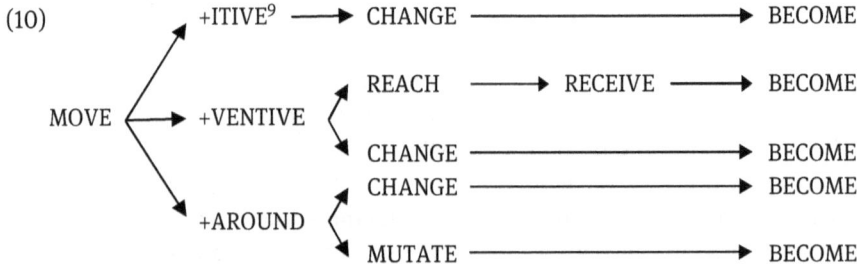

4. From CHANGE-OF-STATE/BECOME to diathesis

4.1 Some general observations

From a semantic point of view, most auxiliary passive constructions are based on the use of BECOME concepts linked to a verbal element. The verb itself does not necessarily include a passive morphology, although this pattern is very frequent especially in Indo-European languages. As BECOME concepts are rarely expressed with the help of 'primary' (semantically underived) verbs, we can expect that the MOTION concepts mentioned in section 3 play an important role in the grammaticalization of passive auxiliaries. Examples are:[10]

(11) GO → BECOME → PASSIVE
Murgi   mari   gayee
Chicken kill.PPP go > PASS.PAST
'The chicken was killed.'
[Hindi, Keenan and Dryer 2007: 338]

COME → BECOME → PASSIVE
Si   isch   grad verchaufti   cho.
ANPH.F.SG be.PRES.3SG just sell.PPP.F.SG come > PASS.PPP
'It (a villa) has just been sold.'
[Walser German (Alemannic), Bucheli 2005][11]

---

9 I have not elaborated in the details the application of the GO-concept, as it is marked for the most basic andmost obvious metaphorization path. Another example is Tamil *poo* 'verb of motion' > 'to change (with respectto state)' (Heine and Kuteva 2002), also compare German *das Motorrad geht sonst kaputt* ('otherwise the bikewill get broken').
10 See Nübling (2006) for a discussion of the grammaticalization of GIVE, BECOME, COME, and STAY concepts as passive markers in selected Germanic languages.
11 Note that this is only one of several options in Swiss German dialects, see Bucherli (2005) for a more detailed discussion.

COME-TO → REACH → RECEIVE → PASSIVE
Die   Frau   bekam   die   Haare   geschnitten.
DEF.F.SG woman get > PASS.PAST DEF.PL hair.PL cut.PPP
'The woman got her hair cut.'
[German][12]

TURN → BECOME → PASSIVE
Das   Buch wurde   vom   Mädchen gekauft.
DEF.N.SG book become > PASS.PAST by.DEF.N.SG.DAT girl   buy.PPP
'The book was bought by the girl.'
[German]

A question emerging from these patterns is, to which extent the underlying MOTION concepts contribute to the semantics of the passive construction. It may be argued that the grammaticalization process does not start from these concepts, but from the intermediate BECOME- or RECEIVE-concept. However, as has been said above, the auxiliary passive construction cannot be understood in terms of a simple segmental analysis. This analysis has to take into account the constructional pattern into which an auxiliary is embedded. With participle-based constructions (as it is true for most Indo-European constructional models), it can easily be shown that the construction is based on patterns that come close to the CHANGE pattern described above, cf. German:

(12) a. *Die   Frau   wurde   Doktor*
        DEF.F.SG woman become.PAST.3SG doctor
        'The woman became a doctor'

   b. *Die   Frau   wurde   rot*
        DEF.F.SG woman become.PAST.3SG read
        'The woman blushed.'

   c. *Die   Frau   wurde   auf der   Straße gesehen*
        DEF.F.SG woman become.PAST on DEF.F.SG.DAT street see.PPP
        'The woman was seen on the street.'

Accordingly, (12.c) can be interpreted as

(13) **Die Frau wurde (zu einer) auf der Straße gesehen(en)*
     Lit.: 'The woman became someone who was seen on the street'

---

[12] Note that in Colloquial German, *bekommen* is frequently substituted by the verb *kriegen* 'to get' < MHG *krîgen* 'to strive for, acquire, get', based on *krîc* 'exertion, conflict, enmity'.

In this sense, a dynamic passive construction based on a CHANGE-concept (← MOTION-concept) is grounded in the metaphorization of locational strategies:[13]

(14)

Trajector	LM_x		→	LM_y	
	Starting point of reference			End point of reference	
	Inferred	Given		Inferred	Given
woman	not-seen		MOVE		seen
die Frau			wird		gesehen

The fact that the 'motion' of the trajectory towards a 'new' landmark is expressed overtly (whereas the association with the original landmark is inferred) suggests that verbal concepts based on the itive direction are one of the favored source domains for passive auxiliaries. Accordingly, the GO-concept should be more prominent than the COME-concept in this respect. However, it has been argued above that COME-concepts used to derive BECOME-concepts (or concepts of CHANGE-of-STATE) often shift towards the notion of REACH, cf. Latin *de-venire*, lit. 'to come from' → 'to arrive at'. In addition, it should be noted that active transitive structures often involve a directional component (see Schulze 2010). This notion becomes apparent especially if the referent in objective function (goal) of an action is marked for a locative case (grammaticalized in terms of an accusative), e.g. (Spanish/Latin/Arabic):

(15) a. *voy   a la   casa*
       go.PRES.1SG to DEF.F.SG house
       'I go to the house.'

   b. *veo   a   la   mujer*
       see.PRES.1SG to > ACC.HUM DEF.F.SG woman
       'I see the woman.'

(16) a. *cum   autem ven-iss-et   domu-m*
       When thus   come-PLU-3SG house-ACC
       'When he had thus come into the house'
       [Matthew 9:28]

---

kriegen can be used both as a verb of reception (*er kriegte das Geld* 'he got the money') and a light verb in passive constructions (*sie kriegte die Haare geschnitten*).
13 The coreferential properties of LMY with TR in TR (LMX → LMY) can still be seen from the Swiss German example given in (10): *verchaufti* agrees in gender and number with the subject *si*. In fact, the morpheme *-i* encodes TR in LMY.

b. *Salomon   autem aedifica-v-it   (...) domu-m*
    Salomon.NOM but   build-PERF-3SG   house-ACC.N.SG
    'But Salomon built (...) a house.'
    [Acts 7:47]

(17) a. *ḏahaba   s-sūq-a*
    go:PERF:3SG:M DEF-market-ALL > ACC
    'He went to the market.'
    [Haywood and Nahmad 1965: 392]

  b. *fataḥa   l-walad-u   l-bāb-a*
    open:PERF:3SG:M DEF-boy-NOM DEF-door-ACC
    'The boy opened the door.'
    [Haywood and Nahmad 1965: 99]

The transitive action schema is thus frequently linked to (or: derived from) a motion schema that interprets the objective domain (O) as the landmark of the process, whereas the agentive domain (A) is seen as the trajector. This relational type is quite in analogy with the intransitive motion schema that includes a subjective domain (S) 'moving with respect to' a locative landmark (LOC):

(18) Intransitive: S_{TR} MOTION LOC_{LM}
     Transitive: A_{TR} MOTION > ACTION O_{LM}

4.2 GO > PASSIVE

Prototypically, the dynamic motion schema shows up in terms of a GO-schema, because it is marked for an overt expression of the landmark ('goal'). Polinsky (2005:439) has argued that "[t]he use of a prototypical transitive verb entails that the event denoted by that verb causes a change of state in the object participant". This pronounced semantic view of transitivity can be generalized, if we refer to the notion of *centrality*. It is generally assumed that the basic syntax of linguistic utterances is marked for an asymmetric alignment of actants (see Schulze 1998, 2010). Accordingly, one of the actants is placed in the center of attention, whereas the other one (if present) is placed in the periphery. 'Center' and 'periphery' automatically result from processing a perceived or mentally construed element in terms of its parts. The most basic cognitive hypothesis related to this procedure is that something that follows (i.e., that is processed second) elaborates what has been processed first, or vice versa.

Usually, the center of attention is associated with some kind of (visual → cognitive) foreground, whereas the periphery constitutes the 'background' domain (Schulze 2010a). On the language-based expressive level, the resulting asymmetry corresponds to the functional highlighting of one of the actants in transitive constructions matching the central actant in intransitive structures:

(19)

	Central	Peripheral
Accusative	S=A	O
Ergative	S=O	A

'Centrality' thus refers to the necessary condition for utterances to be processed: A central actant functions as the point of reference (or: foreground) for construing an event image whereby the semantic properties of the verbal relation are primarily attributed to this actant. If we relate the patterns in (19) to the motion > action schema given in (18), we can conclude that an accusative alignment typically centralizes the trajector (A) whereas an ergative alignment is marked for the centralization of the landmark (O).

From a protoytpical point of view, *diathesis* means that the core actants of a transitive clause change their place in this Centrality-Periphery pattern (in fact a continuum, see Schulze 2011):[14]

(20)

	Center		Periphery
Active:	A_{TR}	↔	O_{LM}
Passive:	O_{LM}	↔/DIA	A_{TR}
Ergative:	O_{LM}	↔	A_{TR}
Antipassive:	A_{TR}	↔/DIA	O_{TR}

Here, I do not want to discuss the functional values of this shift many of which are related to processes of foregrounding/backgrounding, focusing, and clausal pivoting. What is more crucial to the topics of this paper is the following: Above, I have argued that the active pattern of a dynamic transitive schema is grounded in the GO-version of the motion schema (→ ACTION-TOWARD). The overt lexical symbolization of this MOTION schema may have various semantic effects, such as the construction of a continuous aspect, a near future tense etc., confer:

---

[14] ↔ symbolizes the verbal relator. DIA indicates that the verbal relator entails a diathetic marker. With so-called labile verbs, this marker is zero.

(21) a. [The man]ₜᵣ is=going   to [hit the dog]ₗₘ

   b. [je]ₜᵣ vais   [manger]ₗₘ
      I.NOM go.PRES.1SG eat.INF
      'I'm going to/will eat.' [French]

   c. [e:n puši]ₜᵣ (...) lo[15] [was ši   gesé:]ₗₘ
      INDEF cat   GO wash POSS face
      'A cat was cleaning its face'[15]
      [Negerhollands, Heine and Kuteva 2002: 158 (Stolz 1986: 179)]

In a secondary grammaticalization step, the motion light verb may fuse with the verb(al stem), as in (22):

(22) ev-i   görü-yor-um < *görü-yor-(ir-)um[16]
     house-ACC see-PRES-1SG   see-GO-(AOR-)1SG
     'I see the house.'
     [Turkish]

In order to interpret the underlying schema, it is imporant to recall that such constructions are based on two verbal relators. Obviously, they are based on the symbolization of two event images (EI): Whereas the MOTION relator functions as a matrix verb, the second (lexical) relator shows up in a nominalized (referential) form, encoding the second event image as such (together with its internal target referent). The underlying schemas can be illustrated as follows:

(23) a. [man]ₜᵣ   hit   [dog]ₗₘ
        'The man hits a dog.'

   b. [man]ᵢ/ₜᵣ   go=to   [eᵢ hit dog]ₗₘ
        'The man is going to hit a dog.'

Accordingly, the constructions read: '[The man]ₜᵣ goes to [a hitting event that is directed towards a dog [and controlled by the man]]ₗₘ'. Note that in this construction, the agent of the motion event (grammatical relation: subjective) is coreferential with the unexpressed agent of the hitting event (agentive), sym-

---

15 *lo* < *loop* < Dutch *lopen* 'to go, run'.
16 Old Turkish *yorımaq* 'to go, walk' > Turkish *yürümek* 'to go'.

bolized by e_i in (23b). The following figure illustrates the constructional pattern:[17]

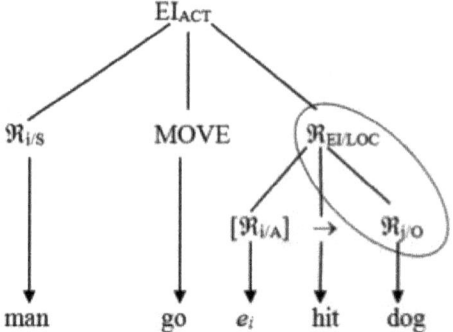

Fig. 6: The motion schema in active verbal constructions.

In passive constructions based on motions schemas, the same mechanism applies: A trajector is related (in terms of MOTION) to a landmark that represents an event image. However, the feature of coreferentiality shifts from a subjective/agentive pivot to that of a subjective/objective pivot:

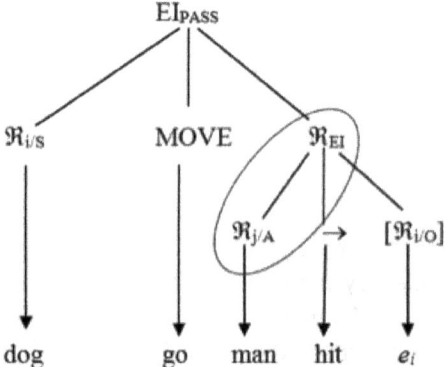

Fig. 7: The motion schema in passive verbal constructions.

---

[17] The circled units indicate those segments of the subordinated event image that may be expressed linguistically.

A simplified version of this pattern is (in analogy with (23)):

(24) [dog]$_{i/TR}$ go=to   [man hit e_i]$_{LM}$
'The dog is hit by the man.'

This constructional pattern can be read as follows: '[The dog]$_{TR}$ moves to [a hitting event controlled/possessed by the man]$_{LM}$'.[18] In a prototypical sense, it is quite expectable that the motion schema illustrated in figure (7) is preferably expressed by the COME schema. Just as it is true with the GO schema, the COME schema does not necessarily result in passive constructions, cf. Heine and Kuteva 2002: 72–73) and the following examples from French and Spanish:

(25) a. *Je   viens   de   manger*
I.NOM come.PRES.1SG from eat.INF
'I have eaten.'
[French]

b. *Vienen   dic-iendo-me   que no soy   normal*
come.PRES.3PL say-GER-1SG.DAT SUB NEG be.PRES.1SG normal
'They have been telling me I'm not normal.'
[Spanish][19]

4.2 COME > PASSIVE

In passive constructions based on the COME schema, the trajector is even more centralized than in passive GO schemas. This is due to the fact that COME includes an orientation towards the center (see above), whereas GO is orientated towards the periphery. Hence we can paraphrase a structure like

---

18 This analysis also accounts for the fact that in many languages, the background agent of passive constructions is encoded in terms of an ablative > genitive pattern, e.g. German *er kommt von der Schule* (he comes from school) vs. *er wird von der Frau gesehen* ('he is seen by the woman').
19 http://spanish.about.com/od/verbs/a/verb_gerund.htm. The authors describe the function of the *venir*+gerund construction as follows: "This construction often refers to something that has been occurring for a long time and is still continuing. It sometimes conveys frustration that the action isn't complete. (...) it is often used to indicate how long something has been occurring". The corresponding *ir*+gerund construction "usually suggests that the action in progress is proceeding gradually or steadily", cf. *vamos estudiando mejor la situación real del pueblo* 'we are coming (lit. go) to study better the real situation of the people'.

(26) [dog]$_{i/TR}$ come=from   [man hit e_i]$_{LM}$
'The dog is hit by the man.'

as follows: '[The dog]$_{TR}$ comes from [a hitting event controlled/possessed by the man]$_{LM}$'. An example from Udi is:[20]

(27) vaˤ eğ-al-le   ği evaxt'e aq'-eğ-al-le
     And come.FUT-FUT-3SG day when   take-COME>PASS.FUT-FUT-3SG
     šo-t'ğ-oxo   bäg
     DIST-PL.OBL-ABL bridegroom
     '... but the day will come, when the bridegroom shall be taken from them'
     [Mt 9:15]

Passive constructions in Udi are usually marked for the total backgrounding of the agentive referent (see 5.2). Nevertheless, the form *aq'-eğ-al-le* 'he will be taken' sufficiently illustrates that the lexical verb itself is not necessarily marked for a passive diathesis (such as a passive participle). With languages that allow the mentioning of the peripheral agent disambiguation would be sufficiently achieved by encoding this function as opposed to the peripheral objective function in active clauses, cf. the patterns in (28):

(28) man go/come   [see   dog$_O$]   = 'The man sees the dog.'
     Man go/come   [see   dog$_{A > LOC}$] = 'The man is seen by the dog.'

In languages, however, that do not license a peripheral agent in passive constructions, but allow the omission of the objective in transitive clauses (in terms of unergative verbs), ambiguity would arise:

(29)
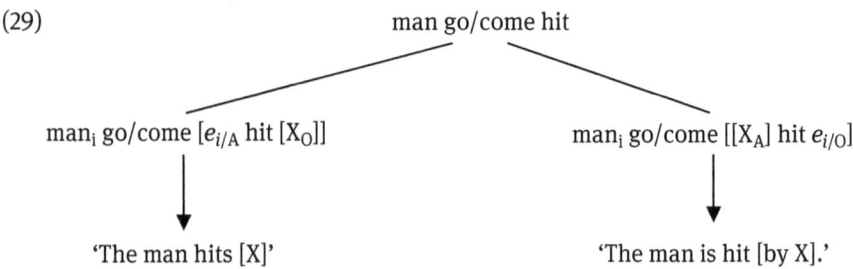

man go/come hit

man$_i$ go/come [$e_{i/A}$ hit [X$_O$]]   man$_i$ go/come [[X$_A$] hit $e_{i/O}$]

'The man hits [X]'   'The man is hit [by X].'

---

20 Throughout this text, quotes of the Udi Gospels are taken from the translation of the Gospels by Bežanov and Bežanov (1902), see Schulze (2001) for a re-edition of this text.

However, such ambiguities rarely occur. In Udi, for instance, active constructions including the auxiliary *e(y)sun* 'to come' (in its past form) differ from passive COME-constructions involving the same auxiliary with respect to position (serialization in active structures) and degree of fusion, cf. the active construction in (30a) as opposed to the passive construction in (30b):

(30) a. *ar-i* [21]   *nağl-q'un-b-i*   *ič-ğ-o*   *pasč'ağ-a ek'k'a*
come-PAST.PAST report-3PL-DO-PAST REFL-PL-GEN king-DAT what
ba-ne-k-e
become-3SG-$-PERF[22]
'Having come (> finally) they told their kind what had happened.'
[Mt 18:31]

b. *bart-a ba-q'a-n-k-I*   *ef*   *bač'an*   *tox-q'-in-en*
let   be-HORT-3SG-$-PAST your.PL stomach belt-SA-ERG
ğać-ec-i   *vaˤ* *čirağ-ux-al*
bind-COME > PASS.PAST-PAST and candle-PL-FOC
bačuk'-ec-i
lighten-COME > PASS.PAST-PAST
'Let your loins be girded about and (your) candles be lightened.'
[Lk 12:35]

We can assume that the immediate derivation of diathetic auxiliaries from motion concepts is given especially if the verb itself lacks a passive derivation. Else, passive auxiliaries seem just to support the passive semantics (given with the corresponding verb form): We are left with the impression that this use has started from the extension of motion concepts towards BECOME-concepts. For instance, the well-known case of the Italian passive pattern *venire*+PPP has been characterized as follows:[23]

> The semantic development leading to the contemporary Italian passive with *venire* therefore represents an instance of a resultative-to-passive development (...) and there is no direct connection between the semantics of motion and passivization: the path venire >

---

[21] Udi *ar-* is the past stem of the lexical verb *e(y)sun* 'to come', whereas *-(e)c-* is the corresponding stem when used as a light verb, see section 5.2 for details.
[22] The symbol $ marks the second segment of a discontinuous lexeme.
[23] Within Europe, the Italian pattern is also found in many Alpine varieties of Germanic and Romance, e.g. Surselvan and other Rhaeto-Romance varieties, Cimbrian, Bavarian, Swiss German, Walser dialects in Switzerland and Italy, Gurinerdeutsch, Pomattertitsch, Gressoney Walser, see Giacalone Ramat and Sansò (2011). In addition, parallel constructions occur among others in Spanish, Romanian, and Maltese.

passive auxiliary seems to presuppose an intermediate stage in which the verb venire has acquired a 'become' meaning. [Giacalone Ramat and Sansò 2011 (abstr.), p. 122].

In (11), I have already given an example for a COME-passive. Further examples are:

(31) a. *di   tokkn   khemmen   getoalt*
DEF piece.PL come.PRES.3PL divide.PPP
'The pieces are divided.'
[Cymbrian, Tyroller 2003: 122]

b. *it-tabib   ġie   afdat   b-il-każ*
DEF-doctor come.SG.M trust.PPP.SG.M with-DEF-case
'The doctor was entrusted with the case.'
[Maltese, Borg and Azzopardi-Alexander 1997: 214][24]

c. *in quel momento veniva   chiuso   il   portone*
in that moment   come.IMPV.3SG close.PPP DEF main=door
'At that moment the main door was being closed.'
[Italian, Giacalone Ramat and Sansò 2011]

d. *el vien   netà*
he come.PRES.3SG.M clean.PPP
'It is cleaned.'
[Venetian, Brunelli 2005: 27][25]

The main clue for distinguishing a COME > DIATHESIS path from a COME > BECOME > DIATHESIS path hence seems to be the presence of a lexical verb marked for diathesis (usually a passive participle). In this case, the participle functions as an adjectival (or, in some cases, adverbial) element. Nevertheless, it is difficult to show that original *come*+PPP constructions correspond to *come=become*+adjective constructions. An example stems from a Venetian text of the 14th century by Paolono Minorta (*Liber de regimine rectoris*), a local bishop, politician, and writer:[26]

---

[24] The pattern *ġie*+PPP produces a dynamic passive. Static passives are formed with *kien* 'was', e.g. *it-tabib kien afdat minn kulħadd* 'The doctor was (*kien*) trusted by everybody (*minn kulħadd*). Note that the verb *ġie* also serves to construe IO passives, such as *it-tfal ġew murija l-film* 'The children were shown the film', cf. Borg and Azzopardi-Alexander (1997: 214, 215).
[25] The case of Venetian is especially interesting, because the COME-passive is restricted to simple tense forms. Analytic tense forms use the auxiliary *èser* 'to be', cf. *el xe stà netà* (he be.PRES.3SG be.PPP clean.PPP) 'it has been cleaned'.
[26] Examples are taken from Giacalone Ramat and Sansò (2011: 4).

(32) *per queste doe cose   elli   vengnirave   pigri et   enviciadi*
    for these two things they come.COND.3PL lazy and spoil.PPP
    'Because of these two things they (i.e. the servants) would become lazy
    and spoiled.'
    [Old Venetian, Paolino Minorita 1313/15, ch. 64, p. 92, r. 23]

Here, the verb *venir* 'to come' refers to both an adjective (*pigri*) and a participle (*enviciadi*). As for (33) we might argue that *enviciadi* practically is an adjective. However, (34) – stemming from the same source – illustrates a full passive construction:

(33) *un çovene fazando mal no   vegniva   corecto   dal   pare*
    a young do.GER bad NEG come IMPV.3SG correct.PPP by-DEF father
    'A youngster who acted badly wasn't corrected by the father.'
    [Old Venetian, Paolino Minorita 1313/15; ch. 55, p. 79, r. 8]

As far as my data go, this type is extremely rare, however. Rather, languages seem to use the *come*-auxiliary either in the sense of a CHANGE-OF-STATE-concept or as a diathetic marker. In the some of the above-mentioned Romance languages, for instance, the BECOME-concept is lexically expressed with the help of a derivation from the COME-concept (*de-venire* etc.) and not with the help of the original lexical form (*venire* etc.). This fact suggests that the two grammaticalization paths operate somehow independently.

4.3 COME-TO > REACH > PASSIVE

A further development is the shift COME-TO > REACH > GET/RECEIVE. This model is best reflected by Germanic **bī-queman* (see above).[27] The fact that lexical expressions of GET-concepts may derive BECOME-concepts and diathetic auxiliaries seem to be more common than their derivation from COME-concepts suggests that it is the secondary BECOME-concept emerging from GET that furnishes the basis for diathetic auxiliaries, as in the following Vietnamese examples:[28]

---

[27] In other IE languages, a MOTION-based conceptualization of GET/RECEIVE is rare, if given at all. Other source domains are for instance OWN, POSSESS (Greek κτάομαι), FASTEN, JOIN (Latin *ad-ip-iscī* < *apere*, Sanskrit *āp-*), HOLD (French *ob-tenir* etc.), FOLLOW UP (Spanish *con-seguir*), and BE/STAND UP TO (Russian *do-byt'*, *do-stat'*). In addition, GET is often derived from TAKE-concepts.

[28] See Nguyen Hong Con 2008 for a discussion of Vietnamese passive constructions. Note that the *được*-passive has a strong positive connotation, whereas the alternative construction,

(34) a. *tôi được tặng một cuốn   từ điển*
      I   GET give one CLASS$_{VOLUME}$ dictionary
      'I was given a dictionary.'

   b. *Mary được mẹ   dẫn   đi sở thú*
      Mary GET   mother escort go zoo
      'Mary is taken to the zoo by her mother.'
      [Vietnamese]

Semantically, GET-passives can be regarded as the conversion of GIVE-constructions that are typical for instance for a number of East Asian languages,[29] cf. the Chinese and Manchu examples:

(35) *fángzi gěi   tǔfěi   shāo le*[30]
     House give > PASS/AG? hooligan burn ASP
     'The house was burned down by the hooligans.'
     [Chinese, Yap and Iwasaki 2003: 421 f.]

(36) *tere inenggi mi-ni   jakûn morin hûlha-bu-fi*
     That day   1SG-GEN eight horse steal-give > PASS-CV.PERF
     'On that day my eight horses were stolen (by bandits).'
     [Manchu, Di Cosmo 2006: 47, 88, 120][31]

Both GET/TAKE and GIVE can be related to the motion domain if we refer to the basic opposition of *self-propelled* vs. *externally propelled*.[32] In this sense,

---

namely the *bị* -passive (< 'to suffer'), refers to a negative effect on the patient, cf. *thành phố Vinh bị máy bay giặc tàn phá* (city Vinh SUFFER airplanes enemy destroy) 'Vinh city is destroyed by enemies' airplanes'.

29 See Gaeta 2005 for illuminating examples concerning the BECOME-orientation of German *geben* 'to give'. The author hypothesizes that the GIVE > BECOME extension is mainly based on the reinterpretation of causal relations between two entities (X → Y), including a process of internalizing properties of Y by X (Gaeta 2005: 202).

30 Cf. fn.1. Again, it is a matter of discussion whether *gěi* 'give' has grammaticalized into a passive marker or into the marker of the backgrounded agent (> dative marker).

31 In this context, I do not want to touch upon the question of whether the passive function of such GIVE-concepts is secondarily derived from a causative function, see (among others) Nedjalokv 1993, Yap and Iwasaki 2003. The corresponding path would have been: Permissive causative > unwilling permission > reflexive permission > reflexive passive > passive.

32 See Newmann (1996, 1997), Gaeta (2005), Margetts and Austin (2007) for an extensive discussion of GIVE and related typological issues. My remarks only concern some very basic motion aspects entailed in GIVE (and GET/TAKE). Hence, I do not aim at reflecting the whole semantic dimension of GIVE- and GET/TAKE-concepts.

both GET/TAKE and GIVE are instances of motion caused by *the other*, blended with a concept of contact:

(37) A_{TR} CAUSE O_{LM1} GO=TO BE=AT LOC > IO_{LM2}
      Woman cause book move   be at   boy
      'Mother gives the book to the boy'

(38) A_{TR} CAUSE O_{LM1} COME=FROM LOC_{LM2} [BE=AT A > LOC_{TR}]
      Woman cause book come from   boy   [be at   woman]
      'Mother takes/gets the book from the boy'

Just as it is true for COME-concepts (see above), GET/TAKE-concepts usually evoke an inferential process related to the construction of the goal of motion (cf. COME=TO). In individual languages, GET/TAKE-concepts may be profiled differently, leading to varying degrees of conceptual amalgamation, cf. Syrian Arabic *žīb* 'to get' < *jā'a bi-* 'to come with':

(39) *rūḥ*   *žīb*   *kam 'annīnet bīra*
      go.IMPERF.1SG   get < come-with   few bottle   beer
      'Shall I go get a few bottles of beer?'
      [Syrian Arabic, Cowell 2005: 334]

Here, the external propulsion of the 'few bottles of beer' is interpreted as some kind of piggy-backing procedure (the bottles move because they are loaded onto a person moving in terms of self-propulsion). Hence both GET/TAKE and GIVE entail the notion of motion, although the motion dimension is rarely lexi-

Tab. 3: From MOTION to passive auxiliaries.

		MOTION				
		Self-propelled		Externally propelled		
		BECOME	DIATHESIS	BECOME	DIATHESIS
ITIVE	GO	He **went** crazy	murgi mari **gayee** (12)	MAKE.MOVE (> CARRY) + HAVE > **GIVE**	No data	tere inenggi mi-ni jakûn morin hûlha-**bu**-fi (37)
VENTIVE	COME	pen an rete nan imidi-te, li **vini** mwezi (5)	si isch grad verchaufti **cho** (12)	MAKE.MOVE (> BRING) + HAVE > **GET/TAKE**	He **got** crazy	Mary **được** mẹ dẫn đi sở thú (35)

calized as such. Hence, it is difficult to show that it is just this motional component that accounts for the use of GET/TAKE and GIVE as passive auxiliaries. Nevertheless, we can set up the following table that illustrates the four relevant conceptual types (GO, COME, GIVE, GET) and examples for their use as BECOME-concepts and passive auxiliaries (numbers refer to the numbering of the examples given in Table 3).

The use of a motion-based GET-concept to encode a passive diathesis is perhaps best illustrated by German *bekommen* 'to get' (see above). In Standard German, it is normally used with so-called 'free dative adjuncts' (IO-passive), cf.:

(40) a. Active:
   Die   Mutter brachte   dem   Kind das   Essen.
   DEF.F.SG mother bring.PAST.3SG DEF.N.SG.DAT child DEF.N.SG food
   'The mother brought the child the food.'

   b. O-Passive:
   Das   Essen wurde   dem   Kind von
   DEF.N.SG food become.PAST.3SG DEF.N.SG.DAT child ABL
   der   Mutter gebracht.
   DEF.F.SG.DAT mother bring.PPP
   'The food was brought (to) the child by the mother.'

   c. IO-Passive:
   Das   Kind bekam   das   Essen von der
   DEF.N.SG child get.PAST.3SG DEF.N.SG food   ABL DEF.F.SG.DAT
   Mutter gebracht.
   mother bring.PPP
   'The child received the food from the mother.'

Nevertheless, it is difficult to reconstruct the motion schema underlying (41c). Rather, we should assume that the meaning von *bekommen* had already been extended to cover a RECEIVE-concept, before this construction came into use. This assumption is supported by the fact that the alternative construction with *kriegen* 'to get' (see fn. 13) is older than the *bekommen*-construction: The *kriegen*-construction came into use in the 16th century, whereas the earliest documentation of the *bekommen*-construction stems from 1823 (see Eroms 1978: 366).

In summary, we have to assume that quite a number of motion-based passive auxiliaries do not directly reflect the motion schema present in the corresponding lexical forms, but semantic extensions towards BECOME-concepts. Accordingly, we get two models of deriving diathetic auxiliaries (and their grammaticalization output) from motion verbs:

(41)

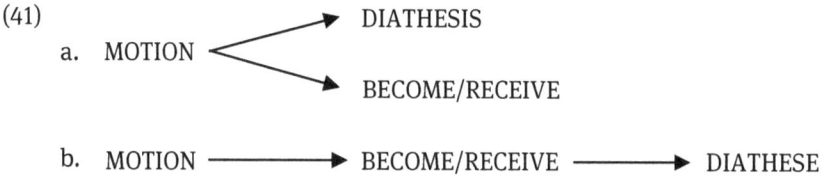

(41a) illustrates a parallel development that mirrors features of the motion concept onto both the diathetic auxiliary and the BECOME/RECEIVE concepts. (42b) first derives the BECOME/RECIVE-concept from the motion domain, before the BECOME/RECEIVE-concept is extended to passive constructions.

5 Udi and Caucasian Albanian

In this final section, I want to relate the observations and hypotheses mentioned so far to two East Caucasian languages, namely Udi and Caucasian Albanian. Udi is currently spoken by some 3.000 people mainly in one village (Nij) in Northern Azerbaijan. In addition, Udi speakers settle in a small village in Eastern Georgia (Oktomberi/Zinobiani) as well as in scattered places in Armenian, Russia, and Kazakhstan. Udi originates from a dialect of an early medieval language, another dialect of which had become the official religious and state language of the so-called Caucasian Albanian kingdom (roughly 300–700 AD). Just as it is true for actual Udi speakers, the peoples of Caucasian Albania were Christians by belief. The Caucasian Albanian language (CA), written in a proper alphabet, is documented mainly in texts written on the lower layer of two medieval palimpsests (ca. 600 AD) that have been found by Zaza Aleksidze in 2000 and have been deciphered mainly by Jost Gippert and Wolfgang Schulze (see Gippert et al. 2009 for the edition of these texts). Both Caucasian Albanian and Udi are highly divergent East Caucasian languages. This is due to the fact that both languages are marked for strong impact from (Old) Armenian[33] and local Iranian languages. In addition, Udi was later on heavily influenced by Azeri Turkic. The following diagram illustrates the position of Caucasian Albanian and Udi in the East Caucasian language family:[34]

---

33 See Schulze (2011b) for the history of Udi-Armenian language contact.
34 The diagram elaborates the structure of the Lezgian family only.

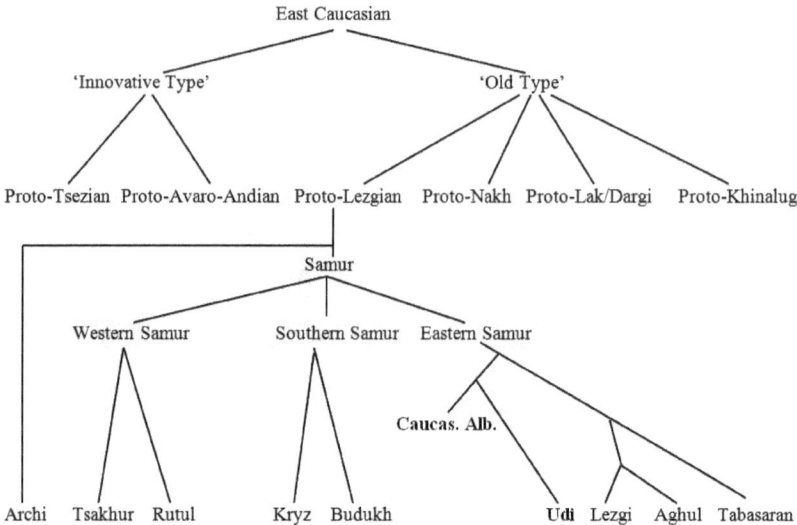

Fig. 8: The Lezgian language family.

5.1 Types of diathesis in East Caucasian

The syntax of most of the autochthonous East Caucasian languages is characterized by a rather rigid association of grammatical relations to the foreground/background domains. In this sense, their syntax can be related to the feature of role dominance (Foley and Van Valin 1984). In fact, the parameter of semantic roles is crucial to the description of grammatical relations in these languages, whereas the syntactic parameter (subject/object etc.) is less relevant, if not irrelevant (Schulze 2000). An example is the following sentence from Lezgi:

(42) *pulat-a   k'el-el   muld-cük laha-na   t^w'ar ecig-na*
  Pulat-ERG sheep-SUPERESS violet   say-PAST.PART name give-AOR
  'Pulat called the sheep 'violet' (lit.: 'Pulat gave the name that said violet onto the sheep')
  [Lezgi, Bilalov and Tagirov 1987: 24]

Here, the speaker does not have any options to change the foreground/background position of *t^w'ar* 'name', *muld-cük* 'violet', or *k'el* 'sheep' in terms of diathesis. It follows that the syntax of East Caucasian languages normally lacks procedures of diathesis. Nevertheless, some of these languages depart from this rigid pattern. Basically, diathetic processes show up in four types: (a) morphosyntactically marked antipassives, (b) labile verb constructions, (c) anticausatives, (d) 'bi-absolutive constructions', and (e) morphosyntactically marked passives. Before turning to the rare case of passive constructions, I will briefly illustrate the other diathetic processes.

5.1.1 Antipassives and labile verbs

It is rather probable that the syntax of Proto-East Caucasian (PEC) once knew a more or less elaborated strategy of antipassivization, that is the diathetic variant of ergative patterns.[35] The major function of antipassives in East Caucasian is to background the referent in objective function. In those languages that still know an antipassive, this strategy is based on semantic and pragmatic features rather than on syntactic patterns of foreground pivoting. For the time being, it is difficult to relate this strategy to specific techniques of encoding this diathesis in the verb. However, we may assume that the allomorphic variants {*-l-/-r-} had been one of the relevant devices. It has survived in some East Caucasian languages, having grammaticalized (among others) into a detransitivizing morpheme or into a marker of imperfective aspect (see Schulze 1994). An example for the diathetic function is (44):

(43) a. öž-di   qarandi   y-ö^{n}t'ö-yö
       boy.ERG hole(III).ABS III-dig-PAST
       'The boy dug the hole.'

   b. öžö   qarandi-ya-d   ö^{n}t'ö-lä:-yö
      boy(I).ABS hole-SA-INSTR I.dig-AP-PAST
      'The boy was digging at the hole.'
      [Bezhta, van den Berg 2005: 178]

Quite often, however, the verbal antipassive marker is lacking, resulting in labile verb paradigms (see below), such as Dargi (literal language):

(44) a. nu-ni   q'ac'   b-ukule-ra
       I(I)-ERG bread(III).ABS III.O-eat.PRES-1SG
       'I (a man) eat bread.'

---

[35] Antipassives are described (from different perspectives) e.g. by Heath (1976), Hewitt (1982), Cooreman (1994), Dixon (1994), van den Berg (1998), and Polinsky (2005). See Schulze (2011a) for a cognitive approach to antipassives.

b. nu   q'ac'-li   '-ukule-ra
    I(I).ABS bread-ERG > INSTR I.S-eat.PRES-1SG
    'I (a man) am eating (parts of the) bread.'
    [Dargi, Abdullaev 1986: 228]

Labile verbs can be characterized as verbal lexical stems that show up in transitive (and unergative) constructions as well as in unaccusative constructions, cf.:

(45) a. Transitive:
        čač:amaš-ca   tuop   y-üz-ira   tallarxuo-č-uo
        gunshot-INSTR rifle(III).ABS III-fill-PAST hunter-SA-ERG
        'The hunter loaded the rifle with shot.'
        [Chechen, Nichols 1992: 58]

     b. Unaccusative:
        čerma   xix   d-üz-na
        cask(IV).ABS water.LOC   IV-fill-INFER
        'The cask is filled with water.'
        [Chechen, Nichols 1992: 58]

Data from Kryz (Lezgian) seem to suggest that – pending on the semantics of the verb – the antipassive morpheme can develop into a passive marker, cf.:

(46) har   žumʕa-ž-a   lu   kel   kura-r-yu-ni
     every friday-SA-INESS PROX lamb(II).ABS slay-DIA-PRES.II-PAST
     'This lamb was sacrificed every Friday.'
     [Kryz, Authier 2012]

Functionally, such a shift from an antipassive towards a passive construction is difficult to explain. Antipassives profile transitive structures for the agentive referent, whereas passives profile them for the objective referent. Hence, contrary to the assumptions of Authier (2012), it more likely that the antipassives marker had first developed into a marker of imperfective or durative/habitual aspect that could be added to both versions of labile verbs.

(47)

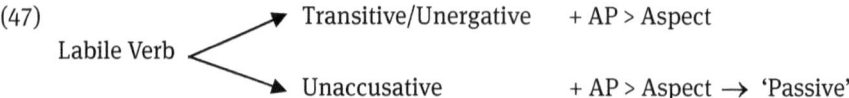

Example (49b) from Bezhta illustrates the use of an antipassive marker with an unergative construction (as opposed to (49a) which is a standard transitive clause):

(48) a. kib-ba   häk'ä: tɬ'eq'e-yo
       girl-ERG boots   sew-PAST
       'The girl sewed boots.'

   b. kid   tɬ'eq'e-la:-yo
       girl.ABS sew-AP-PAST
       'The girl was sewing.'
       [Bezhta, van den Berg 2005: 179]

The Kryz example in (50b) shows the same constructional type. In this case, however, it is based on an unaccusative reading of the verb stem *yat'-* 'to cut off':

(49) a. a-n-ir   ẋad   ya-t'-iž
       ANAPH-SA.I-ERG water(III) PV-cut-AOR.III
       'He has cut off the water.'

   b. ẋad   yiğ-in-a   sa-d   saʕat ya-r-t'-ar-e
       water day-SA-INESS one-III hour PV-DUR-cut-AP > DUR-PRES
       'The water is cut off / stops for one hour a day.'
       [Kryz, Authier 2012]

Hence, there is no need to describe a full passive paradigm for Kryz. Rather, it is an emergent pattern resulting from the additional marking (and perhaps grammaticalization) of the unaccusative version of some labile verbs. The origin of the antipassive marker *-r-/-l-/-n-* is rather obscure. Nevertheless, Authier (2012) suggests that we have to deal with a marker of verbal plurality that would be related to a nominal plural morpheme reconstructed as *-r* by Authier. It is out of the topic of this paper to discuss in details this hypothesis. However, note that the reconstruction of a Proto-East Caucasian plural morpheme *-r* is far from being ascertained.[36] Unfortunately, we do not have con-

---

[36] Also note that residues of the antipassive morpheme often show up as an infix, cf. Caucasian Albanian perfective *bicʼe-* vs. imperfective *bilʲecʼa* 'to dissolve, get rotten', *ige-* vs. *ilʲega-* 'to beat', *zetʼe-* vs. *zeltʼa-* 'to bind', *ʒexe-* vs. *ʒelexa-* 'to fix', *bå(h)e-* vs. *båla-* < *bål(h)a-* 'to go'. This would be an additional argument against the interpretation of the corresponding morpheme as a plural marker, because derivational processes related to number are generally suffixal in East Caucasian.

vincing templates derived from other languages with antipassives strategies that would help to relate the morpheme at issue to a possible source. By looking at the antipassives morphology in general, Shibatani (2004: 1162) remarks that "the available data on the affinity or the etymological relationship of the antipassive morpheme to other forms than reflexives (...) are meager". In fact, neither reflexives nor other sources observed so far (e.g. first person singular objective marker) help to interpret the East Caucasian morpheme *-r-/-l-/-n-. We cannot exclude the possibility that the antipassives morpheme originated from a verbal stem based on a motion concept. Most likely, the antipassive function of the *-r-/-l-/-n- morpheme has developed out of a marker for a continuous aspect (in its broadest sense). Heine and Kuteva 2002: 157–159 have given several examples for the grammaticalization of GO-concepts into such a function. Nevertheless, the fact that the morpheme shows up as a monoconsonantal unit renders it difficult to relate it convincingly to a verb stem denoting 'to go' in East Caucasian.

5.1.2 Anticausatives

The most prominent diathesis-like process is related to so-called anticausatives.[37] Anticausatives are semantic passives and hence are strongly derivational in nature. Usually, they are not motivated by syntactic processes such as pivoting or foregrounding/backgrounding. Contrary to unaccusative verbs, however, they are characterized by some kind of morphological marking or by compounding strategies that oppose the resulting verbs to transitive verbs, cf. Udi:

(50) a. *gärgür-besun*   'to mix'
        gärgür-baksun   'to be mixed'

    b. *biˤ-bes-t'esun*   'to make heavy'
       biˤ-baksun   'to be heavy'

The transitive verbs are marked for the light verb *b-esun* 'to do, make' (*-esun* = infinitive+masdar) that has fused with the lexical stem. Note that in *biˤbest'esun*, the light verb is again reinforced by another segment (*-t'-*) that

---

[37] Haspelmath (1987) gives a first survey on anticausatives. Here, I do not want to monitor the extended debate on the nature of anticausatives. Rather, I restrict myself to observations relevant for East Caucasian languages.

has resulted from the grammaticalization of a light verb, namely *-desun 'to give' (-d- > -t'- before -s-). The compounding nature of Udi anticausatives becomes immediately apparent, if we look at the given lexical stems. Normally, they do not represent verbal stems, but non-verbal units, ranging from nouns to adverbs, cf. the following examples:

(51)
žok'-baksun	'to get separated'	Armenian jok 'separate'
č'ap'-baksun	'to fade, be hidden'	Azeri çap(kın) 'secret'
čalxal-baksun	'to be acquainted'	čalx-al 'knowing' (PART:nPAST)
šere-baksun	'to get dry'	šere 'dry'
alaxo-baksun	'to feel sick'	alaxo 'from above'
ap'ax-baksun	'to sweat'	ap'ax 'sweat-DAT2'
bağriar-baksun	'to get a fright'	Azeri bağrı(ş) 'yelling'
havala-baksun	'to attack' (intr.)	havala 'attack'
i-baksun	'to hear' < *'be heard'	*i 'ear' (> i-mux (PL) 'ear')
k'oc'-baksun	'to bend'	Persian koǰ 'bent, curved'
kar-baksun	'to become deaf'	Persian kar 'deaf'
lal-baksun	'to become silent'	Persian lāl 'dumb'
moğor-baksun	'to wake up'	moğor 'awake'
muća-baksun	'to refresh oneself'	muća 'sweet'
muq'eit-baksun	'to be worried'	Persian/Arabic moqayyed 'attentive'
neğen-baksun	'to start weeping'	neğ-en 'Tear-ERG > INSTR'
qai-baksun	'to come back, repent'	qai 'back'
sus-baksun	'to become dumb, silent'	Azeri süst (< Persian sost) 'weak, frail'
var-baksun	'to become mad'	var 'mad'
xe-baksun	'to thaw, melt'	xe 'water'
źeˤ-baksun	'to petrify'	źeˤ 'stone'

The same holds for many other East Caucasian languages that apply the technique of combining a lexical stem with a light verb in order to produce both transitive and anticausative verbs. In some languages such as Lezgi, the original lexical stem is no longer transparent, resulting in a so-called periphrastic stem (Haspelmath 1993: 166) that shows up with the anticausative light verb ẋun 'to become', whereas the transitive form lacks an overt light verb, confer:

(52) xkaž-un 'to raise, lift' → xkaž ẋun 'to rise'
     aq'al-un 'to close (tr.)' → aq'al ẋun 'to close (intr.)'

In many East Caucasian languages, the light verb used to derive anticausatives is embedded into the world of BECOME-concepts. Even though we may assume that these light verbs are derived from motional concepts, it is difficult to relate such BECOME-concepts to verbs of motion. Nevertheless, Caucasian Albanian and Udi nicely illustrate just this process: In Udi, the BECOME-concept is expressed with the help of *baksun* 'to become'[38] that is also used to derive anticausatives (see (51)). A residue of Udi *baksun* in the sense of a motion verb 'to go' is given in the preverbally marked verb *č'e-baksun* 'to go out, pass by' that corresponds to Caucasian Albanian *č'e-båhesown* 'to come/go out, pass by, happen'. Udi *baksun* is related to the Caucasian Albanian verb *båhesown* 'to go', itself derived from the imperfective aspectual stem of *ihesown* → *aha* and preceded by the preverb *ba-* 'into'.[39] In Caucasian Albanian, *båhesown* is never used as a light verb. Instead, it is the perfective stem without the preverb (*ihesown*) that takes up this function (also forming anticausatives), cf.:

(53)   *ak'a-ihesown*   'to be(come) visible'
       ak'owk'-ihesown   'to appear, be revealed'
       axay-ihesown   'to be open(ed)'
       amec'-ihesown   'to be astonished, marvel'
       aq'atʲ'i-ihesown   'to become naked'
       arak'aˤ-ihesown   'to be involved, share'
       asam-ihesown   'to be quiet'
       ba-ihesown   'to darken'
       bai-(i)h/yesown   'to be fulfilled'
       balʲ-ihesown   'to be ill'
       bånʲi-ihesown   'to be(come) strong, be raised, grow up'
       båxnʲi-ihesown   'to be worthy'
       bowq̇ ana-ihesown   'to be loved'
       za(h)own-ihesown   'to learn, be taught'
       č'o-ihesown   'to be patient, endure'
       lamen-ihesown   'to be (made) alike, equal'

---

38 I quote Udi and Caucasian Albanian verbs in their masdar form (Udi *-sun*, Caucasian Albanian *-sown* (orthographical *-ow-* represents phonetic [u]). All Caucasian Albanian examples stem from the edition of the Caucasian Albanian texts by Gippert et al. (2009).

39 The Caucasian Albanian figure sign <å>, the exact phonetic value of which still is uncertain, often occurs when we have to assume the merger of two [a]'s. The replacement of Caucasian Albanian *-h-* by Udi *-k-* is not regular. Most likely, the two phonemes represent different reflexes of an older lateral (*-ł-/-ɬ-?).

xaš-ihesown	'to brighten, light up, dawn'
k'or-ihesown	'to return'
heč'-ihesown	'to be helpful, help'
håya-ihesown	'to believe'

Contrary to Udi, the Caucasian Albanian light verb *ihesown* can also combine with present stems (particples) of native verbs, cf. *ak'a-ihesown* 'to become visible' ← *ak'sown* 'to see' or *iha-ihesown* 'to become audible' ← *ihesown* 'to hear' (← **i(b)–(i)hesown* 'to come to ear' (cf. Udi *i-baksan* 'to hear'). In Udi, participles are only present with borrowings from Azeri (*-mIš*-particple), cf. *bağišlamiš-baksun* 'to be forgiven', *sinamiš-baksun* 'to be searched' etc.

Caucasian Albanian and Udi thus give us another clear example of deriving BECOME-concepts of motion concepts. Whether the underlying verb once had the semantics of 'to go' or 'to come' is, however, difficult to tell. In addition to *ihesown* '*to move > become' Caucasian Albanian occasionally uses the motion verb *iġesown* 'to come/go' with anticausatives. However, verbal compounds based on *iġesown* have a stronger passive meaning, see below.

5.1.3 Bi-absolutives

The pattern of bi-absolutive constructions is mentioned for sake of completeness only. It is not present in Caucasian Albanian and Udi, but frequent in other east Caucasian languages. This diathesis-like pattern does not dwell upon motion verbs, but is marked for a copula construction that splits up a transitive structure into two intransitive ones, one which being embedded in terms of subordination. An example is:

(54) a. *buwa-mu x:ʷalli b-ar-ši b-i*
   mother-ERG bread(III).ABS make-PART.PRES III-COP.PRES
   'Mother is baking (lit. making) the bread.'
   [Archi, Kibrik 1992: 349]

  b. *buwa x:ʷalli b-ar-mat d-i*
   mother(II).ABS bread(III).ABS III-make-GER.CONT II-COP.PRES
   'Mother continues making bread.'
   [Archi, Kibrik 1992: 349]

Some of the effects of this construction are similar to those of antipassives (e.g. continuous aspect). However, it differs from antipassives because it does not background the objective referent. The processual character of the bi-absolutive construction is achieved by placing the copula into the matrix clause and by linking the lexical verb to this clause in terms of subordination.

5.2 From MOTION to diathesis in Caucasian Albanian and Udi

Passives represent the fourth diathetic type that is, however, documented for few East Caucasian languages, only. They mainly occur in Caucasian Albanian and Udi. The fact that the texts contained in the Caucasian Albanian palimpsest[40] are translations based mainly on Old Armenian sources conditions that the morphosyntax of Caucasian Albanian has been strongly adapted to the patterns of the corresponding source language. Unfortunately, there are no relevant sources for Caucasian Albanian that would include native texts.[41] Hence, it is difficult to tell whether the observable passive patterns represent mere loan translations or are the expression of given linguistic practice. Nevertheless, parallel (and expended) patterns in Udi suggest that the rudimentary passive patterns of Caucasian Albanian have later on become a more regular device in Udi. In both languages, passives are usually marked for the total backgrounding of the agent. Incidentally only, the agent is expressed, usually in an ablative case form (in Caucasian Albanian also in the ergative). Examples are:

(55) a. *bütün tad-ec-i-ne   za   bez baba-xo*
       all   give-PASS-PAST3SG I.DAT my father-ABL
       'Everything is given me by my father.'
       [Udi, Mt 11:27]

   b. *eśin sel-ah-al-ank'e   e   bic'esown-own*
       then free-become > PASS-FUT-CV.TEL DEF.PL corruption-GEN
       naiʕowown-aqo   sel-ih-es-en   gåqown-˜n   ġar-i
       boundage-ABL   liberate-BECOME-INF-ERG   glory-GEN   son-GEN
       b˜ē[42]
       god.GEN

---

[40] The palimpsests contain fragments about one third of the Gospel of John and parts of a Christian lectionary.
[41] The few Caucasian Albanian inscriptions that have been found in the regions of Azerbaijan do not entail passive constructions (see Gippert et. al. 2009 for a full documentation of these inscriptions).
[42] The tilde indicates that the corresponding word has been written in an abbreviated form.

'For [they] will then be freed from the bondage of corruption by the liberation of the glory of the son of God.'
[CA, Rom 8:21]

c. q'oq'ay-he-y-ne   owp' k'ibok'esown-en
swallow-PAST-become > PASS-PAST-3SG death victory-ERG
vey
your.PL
'Death was swallowed by your victory.'
[CA, 1 Cor 15: 54]

The Caucasian Albanian passive morphology is based mainly on the two light verbs *ihesown* 'to become' and *iġesown* 'to come/go'. As has been argued above, the BECOME-concept represented by *ihe-sown* (imperfective stem *aha-*) has developed out of a motion concept the exact meaning of which, however, is difficult to reconstruct ('come' or 'go'). Most likely, the stem is related (among others) to Aghul (Koshan dialect) *xi-s*, Lezgi *fi-n*, Rutul (Ikhrek) *hə-x̌i-n*, Tsakhur *aˤlpä-has* 'to go' < Proto-Lezgian *-(ə)x̌i-* (imperfective). The fact that in many, if not most instances, the agent is totally backgrounded, conditioned that the *ihesown*-passives has merged with anticausatives.

The second light verb *iġesown* 'to go (thither), to walk' is derived from a stem *ġe-* that simply meant 'to exert a self-propelled motion'. *ġe-* was neutral with respect to the dimensions of itive and ventive. The ventive ('to go hither') was derived by using the preverb *he-* (→ *heġesown*), as opposed to *i-* in the itive. In the perfective aspect, the two domains are clearly distinguished (*-c-* 'having gone thither > 'go' vs. *-r-* 'having go hither' > 'come'). In this aspect, the preverb was freed from its discriminating function: It was replaced by the general orienteering preverb *a-*. The imperative shows another stem (*-k-*) that is again neutral with respect to the itive/ventive distinction. Quite expectably, this function is taken over by preverbs. Table (4) summarizes the relevant data:

Tab. 4: The structure of basic motion verbs in Caucasian Albanian.

	Itive		Ventive	
	Preverb	Stem	Preverb	Stem
Infinitive	i-	ġe-	he-	ġe-
Imperfective	i-	ġa-	he-	ġa-
Perfective	a-	ce-	a-	r-
Imperative	ow-	kal-	he-	kal-

The COME-version is rarely used in terms of a compound light verb. One example is *owqa-heġesown* 'to abound, overflow, redound', lit. 'to come opulent' (?). Else, *heġesown* is also present in the compound perfectives *hay-z-ari* 'having risen' (infinitive *hay-ze-sown* 'to rise') and *a-c-ari* 'being seated, having sit down' (infinitive (imperfective) *a-r-ce-sown* 'to sit'), as well as in *hay-heġesown* 'to groan' (perfective *hay-ari*), cf. *hay-iġesown* 'to be elevated, exalted').

In Caucasian Albanian, it is the GO-version of the motion concept that furnishes one of the bases to form passives. Although examples are not very frequent in the Caucasian Albanian corpus, we can nevertheless ascertain the corresponding use of *iġesown* with the help of the following examples: *aqay-iġesown* 'to come to an end', *źiź-iġesown* 'to be shaken, tossed', *pas-iġesown* 'to be scattered'. The fact that passive *iġesown*-compounds show the same type of stem suppletion as the full verb proves that the passive auxiliary stems from the motion verb 'to go', cf.

(56) a. Y˜s   ace-y-ne   å˜axoš
        Jesus   go.PAST-PAST-3SG   they.COM
        'Jesus went with them.'
        [CA, Lk 7:6]

  b. *mil^janown-ow[x]-al ćowdown*
      power-PL-FOC   heaven.GEN
      źiź-q'a-n-ace-y
      shake-HORT-3SG-GO.PAST > PASS-PAST
      'The powers of heaven will be shaken'
      [CA, Mt 24:29]

In Udi, the motion verb has developed into a full-fledged passive marker, at least in the dialect of Vartashen. The grammaticalized auxiliary immediately follows the verbal stem. The general pattern is:

(57) Passive: Verb Stem FAC[43] COME > PASS TAM
  a.   *aq'-*   *n-*   *-e-*   *sa*
       take   3.SG   PASS   PRES
       '(s)he is taken.'

---

[43] FAC = floating agreement clitic. In Udi, subject agreement clitics can take different positions inside and outside the verb, see Harris (2002) for details.

b. aq'-   n-   -ec-   i
   take 3.SG PASS.PAST PAST
   '(s)he was taken.'

The position of the floating agreement marker clearly indicates that the segment following the agreement clitic had once the status of a light verb. In Udi, the favored position of such clitics in light verb based compounds is the position following the lexical head, cf.

(58)

Base	FAC	LV	TAM	
xabar-	-re-	-aq'-	-i	'(s)he took news' > 'asked'
bes-	-ne-	-b-	-i	'(s)he made die' > 'killed'
kala-	-ne-	-bak-	-i	'(s)he became big' > 'grew'
ta-	-ne-	-d-	-i	'(s)he gave thither' > 'gave'
aq'-	-n-	-ec-	-i	'(s)he went take' > 'was taken'

Likewise, passives do not allow stem-internal endoclitization that is typical with some tense/mood forms of active stem verbs, cf. table (5) that summarizes the primary tense/mood forms (3SG, -n(e-)) for both the active and the passive version of *aq'* 'to take':⁴⁴

Tab. 5: Position of agreement clitics in Udi active and passive verbs.

	Active	Passive
PRES	a-ne-q'-sa	aq'-n-e-sa
PAST	a-ne-q'i	aq'-n-ec-i
FUT1	aq'-al-le	aq'-eğ-al-le
FUT2	a-ne-q'-o	aq'-n-eğ-o
MOD	aq'-a-n	aq'-eğ-a-n
CONJ	aq'-ay-n	aq'-eğ-ay-n
IMP (2SG)	aq'-a	aq'-eke

The position of *-n-* (3sg) in *aq'-n-ec-i* thus safely identifies the following segment as a former light verb. The following examples illustrate the formulas in (58):

---

44 The use of the stem internal endoclitization strategy depends from various factors. Alternatives are e.g. enclitization (e.g. *aq'-sa-ne* '(s)he takes') or the clitization to verb external constituents, e.g. *šum-ne aq'sa* '(s)he takes bread', see Harris (2002) for a fuller account (also see Schulze (2004)).

(59) pasč'aǧ č'e-ne-Ø-sa   beˤ-ne-ǧ-sa   aq'-n-e-sa
     King   out-3SG-go-PRES see-3G-$-PRES take-3SG-PASS-PRES
     'The king goes out, looks and is amazed (lit.: is taken).'
     [Udi, Vartashen, Bezhanov 1888: 7]

(60) ava-t'un-i-i   loroc-i   boš nišan tad-ec-e-ne
     knowing-3PL-PAST-PAST cradle-GEN in sign give-PASS-PERF-3G
     'They knew that a sign was given in the cradle.'
     [Udi (Nij), Kečaari 2001: 144]

The underlying verb in (58a) is *e(y)-sun* < **eǧ-sun* which means 'to come' in Udi. Accordingly, it is related to Caucasian Albanian *he-ġesown* 'to come'. In syllable-final position, *-ǧ-* has developed into *-y-* > *-Ø-*, compare *e-ne-sa* '(s)he comes' < **e-ne-y-sa* < **e-ne-ǧ-sa* (HITHER-3SG-move-PRES). *-ǧ-* is preserved in the modal-future stem (*e-ǧ-a(l)-*) because now the phoneme is in syllable-initial position. The extension of the use of the COME-concept to derive a diathesis marker is an innovation of Udi. Nevertheless, the corresponding perfective stem (*-ac-* ~ *-ec-*) illustrates that the use of the GO-concept typical for Caucasian Albanian has survived in Udi (see ex. (58b)) and has merged with the innovation imperfective. Table (5) summarizes the data from Caucasian Albanian and Udi (HV = heavy verb, COMP = compound light verb):

Tab. 6: The basic motion verbs in Caucasian Albanian and Udi.

	GO/ITIVE				COME/VENTIVE			
	CA		UDI		CA		UDI	
	HV	COMP	HV	COMP	HV	COMP	HV	COMP
Infinitive	i-ġe-	i-ġe-	ta-(y)-	–	he-ġe-	he-ġe-	e-(y)-	-e-
Imperfective	i-ġa-	i-ġa-	ta-(y)-	–	he-ġa-	he-ġa-	e-(y)-	-e-
Perfective	a-ce-	a-ce-	ta-c-	–	a-r-	a-r-	a-r-	[-e-c-]
Modal	–	–	ta-ǧ-	–	–	–	e-ǧ-	-e-ǧ-
Imperative	ow-kal-	ow-kal-	ta-ke-	–	he-kal-	he-kal-	e-ke-	-e-ke-

The example in (57b) shows that with past tense forms, Udi has generalized the reflex of Caucasian Albanian *ace-* 'having gone', not of *ar-* 'having come', cf. the stem patterns for Udi passives, summarized in (62) (*aq'-* 'to take'):

(61) Infinitive   aq'-e-   <   aq'-eǧ-   COME   (CA *he-ġesown*)
     Present   aq'-e-   <   aq'-eǧ-   COME   (CA *he-ġesown*)
     Past   aq'-ec-   <   aq'-ac-   GO   (CA *i-ġesown*)

Modal-Future	aq'-eǧ-	<	aq'-eǧ-	COME	(CA he-ġesown)
Imperative	aq'-eke-	<	aq'-eke	COME	(CA he-ġesown)

Most importantly, it is not the actual Udi COME-verb that has grammaticalized into the passive marker for past tense forms/perfective aspect. Udi 'to go (thither)' is *taysun* that corresponds to Caucasian Albanian *ta-iġesown*, cf.

(62) e   ašark'et'-owqoya ta-ace-y-å˜r-he-y
     DEF.PLpupil-PL his thither-go.PAST-PAST-3PL-be.PAST-PAST
     kalak-a
     town-DAT
     'His pupils had gone to the town.'
     [CA, Jo 4:8]

In Caucasian Albanian, *ta-iġesown* represents a marked version of the GO-concept expressed by *iġesown*. The preverb *ta-* denotes 'thither' and is present with many motion verbs in both Caucasian Albanian and Udi. In Udi, the reflex *taysun* < *ta-ǧsun* < *ta-iġe-sun* has become the only lexical form to express the GO-concept.[45] Nevertheless, the preverb-less form *iġe-* has been preserved in the passive auxiliary (past tenses etc.), which illustrates that the Udi passive must have been grammaticalized before the lexical replacement of *iġe- by *ta-iġe- took place. Given the fact that the COME-version *he-ġesown* is rarely used as a light verb in Caucasian Albanian, we can thus assume that the whole grammaticalization process started from the GO-concept (*iġesown*).

As for the topic of this paper, it is relevant to note that neither Caucasian Albanian *iġesown/heġesown* nor Udi *ta(y)sun/e(y)sun* can be used as lexical expressions of the BECOME concept. Instead, Caucasian Albanian *ihesown* resp. Udi *baksun* 'to become' occur in this context:

(63) a. ba-he-y-hamočk'e
         dark-become.PAST-PAST-when
         te-ne-soma-ar-i-he-y[46]   å˜axow Y˜s
         NEG-3SG-yet-come.PAST-PAST-be.PAST-PAST they.ALL Jesus
         'When it became dark, Jesus had not yet come to them.'
         [CA. Jo 6:17]

---

[45] In Udi, the itive preverb *ta-* has a strong tendency towards generalization. An example is Udi *tast'un* 'to give' literally means 'to give thither' (< *ta-d-sun < *ta-dəy-sun < *ta-dağ-sun*, cf. Caucasian Albanian *(ta)daġesown* 'to give').

[46] The perfective stem of Caucasian Albanian *ihesown* 'to become' (*ihe-*) is usually shortened to *he-*. The form *tenesomaari-hey* illustrates that *ihesown* has also grammaticalized as a tense/aspect marker.

b. *ba-ne-k-sa-y*   *beʕəʕnq' Isus gena te-ne*
become-3SG-$-PRES-PAST dark   Jesus however NEG-3SG
e-sa-y   *šo-t'ǧ-o*   *t'oʕǧoʕl.*
come.PRES-PAST DIST-PL-OBL-GEN at
'It became dark. Jesus, however, did not come to them.'
[Udi, Jo 6:17]

Above, I have argued that both Caucasian Albanian *ihesown* < **ɨ̵e-* and Udi *baksun* < **ba-ɨ̵e-* have emerged from the lexical expression of a motion concept. However, contrary to the stem *-ġe* present in Caucasian Albanian *iġesown/heġesown* and Udi *taysun/e(y)sun* (as well as in other motion verbs such as *laysun* (< **la-eǧ-sun*) 'to go up', *baysun* (< **ba-eǧ-sun*) 'to go into, enter' etc.), reflexes of the stem **ɨ̵e-* 'to move' no longer entail the notion of motion. An exception is the preverbally marked form Udi *č'e-baksun* 'to go out, pass by' already mentioned above. Another residue of the motion semantics of *baksun* is its use in terms of 'to happen', cf.:

(64) *mo-no*   *ba-ne-k-e*   *Vifavara Iordan-un t'oʕǧoʕl*
PROX-ABS.SG become-3SG-$-PERF Bethabara Jordan-GEN at
ma-te   *xaš-ne-st'a-y*   *Ioann-en*
where-SUB baptize-3SG-LV.PRES-PAST John-ERG
'This happened in Bethabara at the Jordan river, where John was baptizing.'
[Udi, Jo 1:28]

Quite expectably, the expression of the HAPPEN-concept is based on *ihesown* in Caucasian Albanian, compare:

(65) *he-y-ne*   *e*   *ič*   *ġi-rġ-ol*   *ta-båhe-y-ne*
become-PAST-3SG DEF.PL REFL day-PL-SUPERESS THITHER-go-PAST-3SG
gobicxesown Awgowst'os k'eysar-aqoc
order   Augustus   Caesar-ABL
'It happened in those days (that) an order went out from Augustus, the caesar.'
[CA, Lk 2:1]

The derivation of HAPPEN-concepts from motion concepts is a well-known pattern in many languages, compare Latin *evenire* (COME), Italian *avvenire* (COME), Greek συμβαίνω (GO), Old French *occurrir* (RUN), Irish *imthighim* (GO), or Sanskrit *udpad-* (GO/FALL). Accordingly, we can safely assume that the stem **ɨ̵e-* represented another motion concept in the proto-language of both Caucasian Albanian and Udi. For the time being, it is difficult to describe the exact semantic of both *iɬe- and *ǧe-. Nevertheless, it can safely be stated that *iɬe- must have undergone the shift from MOTION to BECOME quite early. Maybe that a once specialized semantics of *ǧe- became generalized towards a global MOTION-concept after the motion semantics of *iɬe- had bleached out. At this later stage, it was the lexical form ǧe- that furnished the base for the grammaticalization of a diathesis marker, cf. the two tables below:

Tab. 7: The grammaticalization of the two motion verbs *iɬe- and *ǧe- in Caucasian Albanian.

CA	*iɬe-	*ǧe-	
		*i- (GO)	*he- (COME)
MOTION	*ihesown	iġesown	heġesown
BECOME	ihesown	–	–
HAPPEN	ihesown	–	–
ANTICAUSATIVE	ihesown	–	–
PASSIVE	–	iġesown	rare

Tab. 8.: The grammaticalization of the two motion verbs *ba-iɬe- and *ǧe- in Udi.

Udi	*ba-iɬe-	*ǧe-	
		(ta- +) *i- (GO)	*he- (COME)
MOTION	*baksun	taysun	e(y)sun
BECOME	baksun	–	–
HAPPEN	baksun	–	–
ANTICAUSATIVE	baksun	–	–
PASSIVE	–	ec-	e(y)sun

Hence, both Caucasian Albanian and Udi give clear evidence for the development of a diathesis marker directly from motion concepts. There are no obvious traces for the intermediate stages as described in the first section of this paper. This holds especially for the domain of BECOME-concepts and for anticausatives. The fact that, at least in Udi, anticausatives are conceptualized differently from passives is illustrated by the light verb baksun that can be passivized when used as an anticausative marker, cf.:

(66) a. šu-te   bağišlamiš-b-ay-nan günäh-ğ-o šo-no
         who-SUB forgive-do-COND-2PL sin-PL-DAT DIST-ABS.SG
         bağišlamiš-bak-eğ-al-le
         forgive-ANTICAUS-PASS.FUT-FUT-3SG
         'Who of you forgives the sins will be forgiven.'
         [Udi, Jo 20:23]

b. *t'etär-al ğar adamar-i čärčäräz-bak-eğ-al-le*
   thus-FOC son man-GEN torture-ANTICAUS-PASS.FUT-FUT-3SG
   šo-t'ğ-oxo
   dist-pl.obl-abl
   'And thus the Son of Man will be tortured by them.'
   [Udi, Mt 17:12]

Both the forms *bağišlamišbakeğalle* 'will be forgiven' and *čärčäräzbakeğalle* 'will be tortured' have non-passive alternatives (*bağišlamišbakalle* and *čärčäräzbakalle*) that are nevertheless intransitive denoting something like 'forgiving will happen' and 'torturing will happen'.

6 Conclusions

In the first section of this paper, I have referred to the assumption by Keenan and Dryer (2007: 338) according to which the grammaticalization path MOTION > DIATHESIS "seems less well attested". However, data for instance from (Near)-Alpine Germanic and Romance languages suggest that this pattern is more widespread than assumed. The fact that the grammaticalization of passive auxiliaries may result in very short units makes it sometimes difficult to identify such derivational morphemes as former motion verbs. For instance, the Udi passive masdar can be distinguished from the active masdar only because it adds a vowel *-e-* to the verbal stem (*aq'sun* 'the taking' vs. *aq'-e-sun* 'the being taken' < **akq'-eğ-sun*). With infinitives (*-es*), there is no difference at all (*aq'-es* 'to take' vs. *aq'-e-s* < **aq'-eğ-es* 'to be taken'). It can be thus assumed that other languages that know a passive derivational morphology belong to the 'motion-type', too, even though the corresponding lexical source of the morpheme at issue has not been detected yet. The MOTION > DIATHESIS pattern becomes even more apparent, if we include intermediate stages such as CHANGE-OF-STATE:

(67) MOTION → ↓ CHANGE-of-STATE
                CHANGE-of-STATE → PASSIVE

By themselves, both segments of the grammaticalization path are nicely documented by typological data (see sections 3 and 4). As has been argued in this paper, both shifts are easy to model. The question, however, is whether the resulting categorial dimension of PASSIVE still entails invariant components of the primary source domain (MOTION), cf. the following figure:

Fig. 9: Invariance in the MOTION > DIATHESIS path.

At least some of the data presented in the paper argue in favor of the fact that some structural and conceptual features of passives constructions reflect properties of the original source domain, even if the corresponding derivational device (or auxiliary) is grounded mainly in the intermediate stage (CHANGE-OF-STATE). In this case, we have to deal with some kind of family resemblance that describes the transmission of features from a source domain to the ultimate target domain. Quite typically, the relevance of these features gradually fades away and bleaches out, resulting in conceptual units that seem to be fully independent from the semantics of the given source domain (see Schulze (2009) for a fuller account of this process). The second stage (CHANGE-OF-STATE > DIATHESIS) lacks features of MOTION especially in auxiliary constructions if the verb itself contains a marker of diathesis. An example is (68):

(68) a. rota   hua   bəcca   mã   ko dek^h kər cup
       cry.IMPERF.M.SG be.PART child.M.SG mother.OBJ OBJ see   SUB quiet
       ho gəya
       be go > BECOME.PERF.M.SG
       'The child who was crying became quiet when he saw his mother.'
       [Hindi, Kachru 2006: 137]

   b. b^{h}arət mẽ divalī   mənaī   jatī
      India   in Diwali.F celebrate.PART.PERF.F GO > PASS.IMPERF.F.
      hɛ
      be.PRES.SG
      'Diwali is celebrated in India.'
      [Hindi, Kachru 2006: 204]

The two variants of the motion verb 'to go' (gəya and jatī) encode both the BECOME-concept and the passive category. However, the past particple mənaī in (68b) structurally behaves as the adjective cup in (68a). From this we can conclude that (68b) is actually read as 'Diwali becomes/is celebrated in India', not as 'Diwali goes celebrated in India'. In case the lexical verb itself lacks a marker of passive morphology (for instance in terms of a passive participle), the invariant semantic component of a motion-based auxiliary seems to be better preserved (see section 4).

We may thus assume that the degree of invariance preserved in the target domain (PASSIVE) depends from the given constructional pattern. Hence, we cannot ignore the possibility that it is the intermediate stage (BECOME/ CHANGE-OF-STAGE) that serves as the starting point for the grammaticalization of passive auxiliaries. But we must likewise be open to the possibility that the original reason for this process lies in the primary source domain, namely in a MOTION-concept. If we include types of MOTION-concepts other than the standard concept of itive/ventive and self-propelled motion (GO/COME), it comes clear that the grammaticalization path MOTION > DIATHESIS is much more frequent than assumed by Keenan and Dryer (2007), confer section 3.

In section 5, I have given data from Udi and Caucasian Albanian, showing that the grammaticalization process may avoid the intermediate stage BECOME/CHANGE-OF-STATE and thus may immediately result from the grammaticalization of motion verbs. In this case, we have to refer directly to models of MOTION (as illustrated in section 2) in order to explain this path.

References

Abdullaev, Zapir G. 1986. *Problemy èrgativnosti darginskogo jazyka* [Problems of ergativity in the Dargi language]. Moskva: Nauka.
Authier, Gilles. 2012. The detransitive voice in Kryz. In Gilles Authier & Katharina Haude (eds.), *Ergativity, valency and voice*, 133–164. Berlin & New York: Mouton de Gruyter.
Baetke, Walter. 1965–1968. *Wörterbuch zur altnordischen Prosaliteratur*. Berlin: Akademie Verlag.
Bežanov, Mixail (ed.). 1888. Rustam. *SMOMPK* IV (annex).
Bežanov, Semjion & Bežanov, Mixail. 1902. *Gospoda Našego Iisusa Xrista Svjatoe evangelie ot Matfeja, Marka, Luki i Ioanna na russkom i udinskom jazykax* [The Holy Gospels of our Lord Jesus Christ according to Mathew, Mark, Luke, and John in the Russian and Udi language]. Tiflis: Izdanie Kavkazskago Učebnago Okruga (SMOMPK XXX).
Bilalov, A. B. & A. A. Tagirov. 1987. *Lezgi č'al* [The Lezgian language]. Maxačkala: Dagučpediz.
Borg, Albert J. & Marie Azzopardi-Alexander. 1997. *Maltese*. London: Routledge.
Brunelli, Michele. 2005. *Manual Gramaticałe Xenerałe de ła Łéngua Vèneta e łe só variant. Secónda publicazsion co zxónte nóve*. Basan/Bassano del Grappa.
Bucheli Berger, Claudia. 2005. Passiv im Schweizerdeutschen. *Linguistik online* 24(3/05).
Clark Hall, John R. 1916. *A concise Anglo-Saxon dictionary for the use of students*. New York: Macmillan.
Cooreman, Ann. 1994. A functional typology of antipassives. In Barbara Fox & Paul J. Hopper (eds.), *Voice: Form and function*, 49–88. Amsterdam & Philadelphia: John Benjamins.
Cowell Mark W. 2005. *A reference grammar of Syrian Arabic with audio CD*. Washington, DC: Georgetown University Press.

Di Cosmo, Nicola. 2006. *The diary of a Manchu soldier in seventeenth-century China. „My service in the army", by Dzengšeo.* London, New York: Routledge.
Dixon, Robert M.W. 1994. *Ergativity.* Cambridge: Cambridge University Press.
Eroms, Hans-Werner. 1978. Zur Konversion der Dativphrasen. *Sprachwissenschaft* 3. 357–405.
Filbeck, David. 1974. The passive in Thai. *Anthropological Linguistics* 15(1). 33–41.
Fleisher, Nicholas. 2006. The origin of passive get. *English Language and Linguistics* 10(2). 225–252.
Foley, William A. & Robert D. Van Valin, Jr. 1984. *Functional syntax and universal grammar.* Cambridge, England: Cambridge University Press.
Gaeta, Livio. 2005. Hilfsverben und Grammatikalisierung. Die fatale Attraktion von *geben*. In Torsten Leuschner, Tanja Mortelmans und Sarah DeGroodt (Hrsgg.), *Grammatikalisierung im Deutschen*, 193–210. Berlin & New York: Mouton de Gruyter.
Giacalone Ramat, Anna & Andrea Sansò. 2011. Venire ('come') as a passive auxiliary in Italian. In Javier Martín Arista (ed.), Societas Linguistica Europaea, 44th annual meeting., (book of abstracts). Universidad de la Rioja: Centro de Investigación en Lenguas Aplicadas.
Gippert, Jost, Wolfgang Schulze, Zaza Aleksidze & Jean-Pierre Mahé. 2009. *The Caucasian Albanian palimpsests of Mt. Sinai.* Turnhout: Brépols.
Harris, Alice. 2002. *Endoclitics and the origins of Udi morphosyntax.* Oxford: Oxford University Press.
Haspelmath, Martin. 1987. Transitivity alternations of the anticausative type. *Arbeitspapier des Instituts für Sprachwissenschaft*, Universität Köln, 5 (Neue Folge).
Haspelmath, Martin. 1990. The grammaticization of passive morphology. *Studies in Language* 14(1): 25–72.
Haspelmath, Martin. 1993. More on the typology of inchoative/causative verb alternations. In Comrie, Bernard & Maria Polinsky (eds.), *Causatives and transitivity*, 87–120. Amsterdam & Philadelphia: John Benjamins.
Haywood, John A. & H. M. Nahmad. 1965. *A new Arabic grammar of the written language.* London: Lund Humphries.
Heath, Jeffrey. 1976. Antipassivization: A Functional Typology. *Berkeley Linguistics Society* 2. 202–211.
Heine, Bernd & Tania Kuteva. 2002. *Word lexicon of grammaticalization.* Cambridge: Cambridge University Press.
Hewitt, B. George. 1982. Anti-passive and labile constructions in North Caucasian. *General Linguistics* 22(3). 158–171.
Kachru, Yamuna. 2006. *Hindi.* Amsterdam & Philadelphia: John Benjamins.
Kečaari, Georgi. 2001. *Orayin.* Azəbaycan Dövlət Nəşriyyatı.
Keenan, Edward L. & Matthew S. Dryer. 2007. Passive in the World's Languages. In Timothy Shopen (ed.), *Clause structure, language typology and syntactic description*, Vol. 1: 325–361. Cambridge: Cambridge University Press.
Kreitzer, Anatol. 1997. Multiple levels of schematization: A study in the conceptualization of space. *Cognitive Linguistics* 8. 291–325.
Langacker, Ronald W. 1986. Abstract Motion. *Proceedings of the Twelfth Annual Meeting of the Berkeley Linguistics Society*: 445–471.
Langacker, Ronald. 1990. *Concept, image and symbol.* Berlin & New York: Mouton de Gruyter.

Langacker, Ronald W. 1999. *Grammar and conceptualization*. Berlin & New York: Mouton de Gruyter.
Margetts, Anna & Peter K. Austin. 2007. Three participant events in the languages of the world: towards a cross-linguistic typology. *Linguistics* 45. 393–451.
Nedjalokv, Igor V. 1993. Causative-passive polysemy of the Manchu-Tungusic -bu/-v(u). *Linguistica Antverpiensa* 27. 193–202.
Newman, John. 1996. *Give: A cognitive linguistic study*. Cognitive linguistics research 7. Berlin, New York: Mouton.
Newman, John (ed.). 1997. *The linguistics of giving*. Amsterdam & Philadelphia: John Benjamins.
Nguyen Hong Con. 2008. Vietnamese Passive Sentences from a Typological Perspective. *The 18th Annual Meeting of the Southeast Asian Linguistics Society*, 21–22 May 2008, Universiti Kebangsaan Malaysia, Bangi.
Nübling, Damaris. 2006. Auf Umwegen zum Passivauxiliar – Die Grammatikalisierungspfade von GEBEN, WERDEN, KOMMEN und BLEIBEN im Luxemburgischen, Deutschen und Schwedischen. In Claudine Moulin und Damaris Nübling (eds.), *Perspektiven einer linguistischen Luxemburgistik. Studien zu Synchronie und Diachronie*, 171–202. Heidelberg: Winter.
Peyraube, Alain. 1996. Recent issues in Chinese Historical Syntax. In C.-T. James Huang & Y.-H. Audrey Li (eds.), *New horizon in Chinese linguistics*, 161–214. Dordrecht: Kluwer Academic Publishers.
Polinsky, Maria. 2005. Antipassive constructions. In Martin Haspelmath, Matthew S. Dryer, Davil Gil, Bernard Comrie (eds.), *The world atlas of language structures. With the collaboration of Hans-Jörg Bibiko, Hagen Jung, and Claudia Schmidt*, 438–441. Oxford 2005: Oxford University Press.
Rosenbaum, Christoph & Wolfgang Schulze. 2011. Cognitive morphology and the architecture of case in Modern Slovak. In Marcin Grygiel (ed.), *Slavic linguistics in a cognitive framework*, 87–119. Frankfurt a.M. usw.: Peter Lang.
Schulze, Wolfgang. 1994. Tracing aspect coding techniques in the Lezgian languages. Howard Aronson & Bill Darden (eds.), *Festschrift A. Šanidze: Papers of the IV. International Conference on the Non Slavic Languages of the USSR / Chicago 1985*, 193–208. Columbus, Ohio: Slavica.
Schulze, Wolfgang. 1998. *Person Klasse, Kongruenz*. 2 vols. Munich: Lincom Europa.
Schulze, Wolfgang. 2000. Towards to a typology of the accusative ergative continuum: The case of East Caucasian. *General Linguistics* 37. 77–155.
Schulze, Wolfgang. 2001. *The Udi Gospels. Annotated text, etymological index, lemmatized concordance*. Munich: Lincom.
Schulze, Wolfgang. 2004. Review of Harris (2002). *Studies in Language* 28(2). 419–441.
Schulze, Wolfgang. 2009. A new model of metaphorization: Case systems in East Caucasian. In Antonio Barcelona, Klaus-Uwe Panther, Günter Radden & Linda L. Thorburg (eds.), *Metonymy and metaphor in grammar*, 147–175. Amsterdam & Philadelphia: John Benjamins.
Schulze, Wolfgang. 2010. Cognitive transitivity. Manuscript.
Schulze, Wolfgang. 2011a. *The grammaticalization of antipassives*. Banská Bystrica: FHV UMB. [http:// http://schulzewolfgang.de/material/antipas2.pdf]
Schulze, Wolfgang. 2011b. A brief note on Udi-Armenian relations. J. Dum-Tragut, U. Bläsing (eds.), *Cultural, linguistic and ethnological interrelations in and around Armenia*, 151–170. Newcastle upon Tyne: Cambridge Scholars Publishing.

Shibatani, Masayoshi. 2004. Voice. In Lehmann, Christian, G. E. Booij, Joachim Mugdan (eds.), *Morphology. An international handbook on inflection and word formation*, vol 2.2, 1145–1164. Berlin & New York: Mouton de Gruyter.
Sinha, Chris. 1999. Grounding, mapping and acts of meaning. In Theo Janssen & Gisela Redeker, (eds.), *Cognitive linguistics: Foundations, scope and methodology*, 223–255. Berlin & New York: Mouton de Gruyter.
Sinha, Chris, Lis Thorseng, Mariko Hayashi & Kim Plunkett. 1994. Comparative spatial semantics and language acquisition: Evidence from Danish, English and Japanese. *Journal of Semantics* 11. 253–287.
Siewierska, Anna. 1984. *The passive. A comparative linguistic analysis*. London, Sidney etc.: Croom Helm.
Talmy, Leonard. 1991. Path to realization: A typology of event conflation. *Berkeley Linguistics Society* 17. 480–519.
Talmy, Leonard. 1996. Fictive motion in language and "ception". In Bloom, Paul, Mary A. Peterson, Lynn Nadel & Merrill Garret (eds.), *Language and space*, 211–276. Cambridge, MA: The MIT Press.
Targète, Jean & Raphael G. Urciolo. 1993. *Haitian Creole – English dictionary*. Kensington: Dunwoody Press.
Tyroller, Hans. 2003. Grammatische Beschreibung des Zimbrischen in Lusern. *Zeitschrift für Dialektologie und Linguistik, Beiheft* 111. Stuttgart: Steiner.
van den Berg, Helma. 1998. Antipassivnaja konstrukcija v darginskom i drugix dagestanskix jazykax [The antipassive construction in Dargi and other Dagestanian languages]. *Tezisydokladov IIX kollokviuma Evropejskogo Obshchestva Kavkazovedov*, 77–79. Maxačkala: DagUčPedIzd.
van den Berg, Helma. 2005. The East Caucasian language family. *Lingua* 115. 147–190.
Yap, Foong Ha & Shoichi Iwasaki. 2003. From causative to passive: A passage in some East and Southeast Asian languages. In Eugene Casad & Gary Palmer (eds.), *Cognitive linguistics and non-Indo-European languages* [Cognitive Linguistics Research 18], 419–446. Berlin & New York: Mouton de Gruyter.
Yap, Foong Ha & Shoichi Iwasaki. 2007. The emergence of 'GIVE' passives in East and Southeast Asian languages. In Mark Alves, Paul Sidwell & David Gil (eds.), *SEALS VIII: Papers from the Eighth Annual Meeting of the Southeast Asian Linguistics Society*. Canberra: Pacific Linguistics, 193–208. [http://pacling.anu.edu.au/catalogue/SEALSVIII_final.pdf].

Figurative language in culture variation

Javier E. Díaz-Vera and Teodoro Manrique-Antón
'Better shamed before one than shamed before all': Shaping shame in Old English and Old Norse texts

Abstract: In this chapter we will analyze some aspects of the literal and figurative conceptualizations of shame in two different languages: Old English and Old Norse. Our main aim consists in describing the earliest stages in the slow but firm transition from a typically Germanic shame society, where shame acts as an instrument of social control through which the deviant individual is publicly exposed and humiliated, towards a guilt culture, based on the individual's recognition of and repentance from his/her own wrongdoings and on fear of divine punishment. This change implies a progressive individualization of this emotional experience, which obviously had important consequences on its linguistic expression. Through the reconstruction and fine-grained analysis of the whole set of literal, metonymic and metaphoric expressions of shame recorded in our corpora of Old English and Old Norse texts, we try to show that this process of individualization implied the introduction of new linguistic expressions in both languages, normally through the adaptation (glosses and translations) of patristic texts into the vernacular. Broadly speaking, our texts point towards a growing conflict between honour-based and guilt-based conceptualizations of shame, represented respectively by CAUSE FOR EFFECT metonymies on the one side and metaphors and EFFECT FOR CAUSE metonymies on the other side. In fact, whereas the concept of shame characteristic of the ancient Germanic society clearly prevails in both corpora, religious texts tend to favour the introduction and early spread of the new shame-related values through the use of a brand-new set of expressions motivated by some of the physiological and behavioural effects of this emotion on the individual, most of which have become common figurative expressions of shame in the contemporary varieties of both languages.

Javier E. Díaz-Vera: Universidad de Castilla-La Mancha
Teodoro Manrique Antón: Universidad de Castilla-La Mancha

1 Introduction

The study of how language mediates our conceptualization of emotional states has been extensively approached by Conceptual Metaphor Theory (henceforth CMT; Fesmire 1994; Kövecses 1986, 1988, 1990; Lakoff 1987; Lakoff and Johnson 1980; Lakoff and Kövecses 1987). A central claim of CMT is that human emotions are largely understood and expressed in figurative terms. Research into the linguistic expression of emotions and their metaphors has, for the most part, fallen into two different positions: metaphorical universality and cultural relativity (cf. Kövecses 2005; Núñez and Sweetser 2006; Geeraerts and Gevaert 2008). Generally speaking, whereas universalist approaches to metaphorical conceptualizations of emotions tend to focus on purely biological and physiological factors (such as changes in body temperature or rate of heartbeat), the relativist perspective maintains that variation in the metaphorical conceptualization of emotions is sensitive to social, cultural and historical influences and, consequently, metaphor is not universal.

Within the second approach, Geeraerts and Gevaert (2008) and Díaz-Vera (2011, 2014), among others, have recently used historical data in order to question the universalistic view, suggesting that emotion metaphors are not necessarily universal, and that variation in the metaphorical conceptualization of emotions may be subject to socio-historical influences. Taking this claim as our starting point, in this paper we propose a comparative study of the lexical and conceptual field[1] of SHAME in Old English and in Old Norse. A detailed analysis of variation in the historical expression of shame is of major importance for our relativist approach to metaphorical conceptualization.

As shall be seen later, the expression of shame in these two languages reflects in a clear and straightforward way the progressive individualization of emotional processes and its close connection with the process of Christianization, which brought with it a new shaping of this emotional experience. In fact, we will argue here that both Old English and Old Norse written texts show a strong preference for literal expressions and for CAUSE FOR EFFECT metonymies (such as SHAME IS SCORN and SHAME IS DISHONOUR), all of which are motivated by the social fear of being punished, humiliated or ridiculed by others. Furthermore, we will show here that the adoption and progressive generalization of new figurative expressions of shame, such as EFFECT FOR CAUSE metonymies (e.g. SHAME IS REDNESS IN THE FACE) and metaphors (e.g. SHAME IS A PIECE OF

---

1 Following Lyons (1977: 253) we will use the term *conceptual field* to refer to a structured conceptual area, whereas *lexical field* will be used to refer to the set of lexical items that covers a specific conceptual field.

CLOTH), which point towards an internalization of the new moral standards brought by Christianization (where shame involves a negative evaluation of oneself), is directly related to the growing influence of Latin texts in both speech communities.

This evolution from public shame to private shame reflects some of the differences in the conceptualization of shame between collectivist and individualist cultures. As described by Hofstede (1991: 60),

> [...] individualist societies have been described as *guilt* cultures: persons who infringe on the rules of society will often feel guilty, ridden by an individually developed conscience which functions as a private inner pilot. Collectivist societies, on the contrary, are *shame* cultures: persons belonging to a group from which a member has infringed upon the rules of society will feel ashamed, based upon a sense of collective obligation.

In fact, as shall be seen later, whereas most of the expressions analyzed here consist in CAUSE FOR EFFECT metonymies where shame is shaped as an instrument of social control through which the deviant individual is publicly exposed and humiliated, there is a growing set of shame expressions (consisting in historically later lexemes whose use is especially frequent in patristic texts) that point towards a less visual, more private experience. Within this new concept of shame, fear of social condemnation is substituted by fear of divine punishment at Judgement Day. These linguistic developments are highly illustrative of the transition from a pagan society governed by the implicit threat of public shame to a Christian society that relies upon self-induced feelings of personal guilt and an intrinsic sense of subjective morality as the primary mechanisms of social control.

Together with shedding further light on our knowledge of shame words and concepts, this paper forms part of a more general project concerning the conceptualization of emotions in the earliest recorded stages of two different Germanic languages. Through a combination of historical onomasiology and cognitive linguistics, our research will propose an analysis and description both of Old English and Old Norse expressions literally meaning SHAME and expressions that do not literally refer to this concept (that is, metonyms and metaphors, both living and dead). Corpus linguistic methods (Stefanowitsch 2004; Deignan 2005) will be applied in order to measure the relative weight of each concept.

2 Methodology and data

Studies of the conceptualization of emotions in present-day varieties of languages normally rely on data produced by native speakers. Linguists can easily reconstruct the conceptualizations that lie behind the expressions used by their informants. However, historical approaches to emotion terms and concepts are severely conditioned by the lack of native speakers and by the absence of reliable lexicographic tools, such as historical dictionaries and thesauruses.² Consequently, a study of SHAME in past states of language will necessarily have to start from the analysis of the words and phrases that people actually produced and used when referring to shame in surviving, written texts, i.e. from a reconstruction of the lexical field of SHAME in the corresponding historical period.

We have used two different sets of data for our study. In the case of Old English, we have used the Old English section in the *Cognitively Annotated Corpus of Emotional Language* (hence CACELOE, 2014). Based on the *Dictionary of Old English Corpus* (hence DOEC, 2000), the CACELOE gives full semantic and grammatical information on each shame-related lexeme recorded in the bulk of Old English texts, including degrees of literalness and source domains for each figurative expression, as well as a list of the causes, experiencers and physiological consequences of each emotion as indicated in each texts.

In the case of Old Norse, and in the absence of a comprehensive textual corpus, we have used primarily the electronic version of the *Ordbog over det norrøne prosasprog – A Dictionary of Old Norse Prose* (hence ONP, 1989), which records the vocabulary of prose writings of the period subject to our analysis and is by far the largest of the dictionaries available for Old Norse-Icelandic. However, we have also checked the attestations of each individual shame-word in the printed versions of both Fritzner (1867) and Cleasby and Vigfússon (1967).³

Special attention has been paid to the definition and weighing of shame-terms in both languages, which we have classified into different groups depending on their degree of literalness. We are especially interested in exploring how shame was construed by speakers of these two languages and the role of metaphor and metonymy in that construal, as suggested by the fine-grained analysis of the set of 'shame'-related words and expressions used in the textual

---

2 In the case of Old English shame-words, we have decided to neglect the information offered by the *Thesaurus of Old English* (TOE; Roberts and Kay 1995) for two main reasons: (i) quite strikingly, the authors of the TOE consider shame an opinion (TOE 7. Opinion) rather than an emotion (TOE 8. Emotion); (ii) besides, many words defined as 'shame' in Old English dictionaries have not been included in the corresponding TOE section (where only 12 different lexical roots are listed).

3 The Old Norse examples used in this research come directly from the ONP, which records sentences from a wide variety of editorial sources illustrating very different editorial practices. Consequently, our examples do not represent a standardized variety of Old Norse.

corpus. Furthermore, following Sweetser (1990: 45–48), we will try to explore the system of interconnections between semantic fields and see to what extent the conceptual innovations in the field of shame depend on the mental and physical effects caused by this emotion.

In the same line as Geeraerts and Gevaert's discussion on the expression of OE 'anger' (2008: 327), we will assume here that whenever the 'shame' reading is the dominant sense of the word, it can considered to be literal, whereas polysemic words with secondary meanings related to this emotion are considered figurative expressions. Thereafter, we will try to show that, as in the case of anger (Geeraerts and Gevaert 2008: 340–1) and fear (Díaz-Vera 2011), although figurative imagery occupies a minor role in the Old English and Old Norse conceptualizations of shame, an increasing use of metaphoric and, much more frequently, metonymic expressions can be ascertained, that is especially clear in the case of translations, glosses and versions of patristic texts into these two languages.

3 The lexical field of SHAME in Old English and in Old Norse: A comparison

Using the historical corpora, dictionaries and wordlists referred to above, we have made a list of lexical units within the field of SHAME in the two languages under scrutiny here. These lists include all the nouns, strong verbs, weak verbs, adjectives and adverbs used in order to refer to this emotion. Thereafter, the resulting lexical units have been grouped into 'expressions', a term we will use here in order to refer to a word cluster composed of a lexical root plus all its morphological derivations (such as prefixed verbs or suffixed adverbs), as well as their orthographical, declensional and inflectional variants. For example, the OE expression *sceamu* 'shame' will be used in this paper in order to refer to the word cluster that includes the nouns *sceamu* and *woruldsceamu*, the adjective *sceamlic*, the adverb *sceamlice* and the verbs *sceamian*, *āsceamian* and *forsceamian*, among others.

A total of 26 different expressions have been identified for Old English, whereas the number of Old Norse expressions for *shame* amounts to 31. In a second stage, these expressions have been grouped into 'etymological themes' (which we will indicate using small caps) and then grouped into literal and figurative (i.e. metaphoric, metonymic and synaesthetic) expressions.[4] Our set

---

[4] The terms *expression* and *etymological theme* are taken from Gevaert (2002) and Geeraerts and Gevaert (2008: 327). In the case of polysemic words, our use of etymological information

of literal expressions includes both (i) lexemes directly derived from the Proto-Germanic semantic field of shame and (ii) monosemic lexemes meaning 'shame' in Old English or in Old Norse. In the case of figurative expressions, we have included here those lexemes derived from other semantic fields (either through metaphorization or through metonymyzation processes) that have come to express shame as their historically later meaning in Old English or in Old Norse. This estimate of literalness is undoubtedly conservative, as some of the expressions included in this group have completely lost their original, historically earlier meanings and become literal shame-words in Old English and in Old Norse.

What follows is a brief account of the findings of this analysis.

4 The literal and metaphoric expression of *shame*

According to the etymological dictionaries used here, early Proto-Germanic developed its own shame-vocabulary based on the lexeme *skamō- 'shame' and its cognate *skando- 'shame, disgrace, infamy'. Both lexemes have been speculatively related by historical lexicographers to the Indo-European root *(s)kem- 'to cover, to wrap, to veil, to hide' (Pokorny 525; Lehmann 309). Within the context of a shame culture, the act of covering is of special significance, as it refers to the act of concealing a wrongdoing with the aim of avoiding public shaming. Descriptions of shame found in the literature often describe this emotion as an intense, enduring experience of the self, a failure of being, a global sense of deficiency, or a failure to achieve one's ideas (Lewis 1998: 127).

Even if we assume that the origins of this cluster of words are to be related to the actuation of a semantic change from 'to cover oneself' to 'to feel shame', it is obvious that the original meaning 'to cover' proposed by historical lexicographers has been completely lost not only in OE *sceamu* and ON *skǫmm*, but also in the other Germanic languages, where they regularly occupy hyperonymic position within the lexical field of *shame*. Since the historically later *shame*-meaning is the only one accessible to speakers of both languages, these two lexemes will be treated here as literal expressions for shame.

The Oxford English Dictionary (hence OED) gives at least six different meanings recorded in Anglo-Saxon texts, which we present here in chronological order (with indication of the first data of occurrence in written texts):

---

is aimed at determining the historically earlier meaning of each expression and the eventual processes of semantic extension it has undergone in later historical stages.

1. The painful emotion arising from the consciousness of something dishonouring, ridiculous, or indecorous in one's own conduct or circumstances (or in those of others whose honour or disgrace one regards as one's own), or of being in a situation which offends one's sense of modesty or decency (c725).
2. To be ashamed, to feel ashamed (c888).
3. Infliction of disgrace, injurious language or conduct (c975).
4. Disgrace, ignominy, loss of esteem or reputation (a990).
5. A fact or circumstance which brings disgrace or discredit (to a person, etc.); matter for severe reproach or reprobation (a1000).
6. The privy members or 'parts of shame' (a1000).

In fact, OE *sceamu* is used in our corpus not only to refer to the emotional experience (as in example [1] below), but also to some of the factors that cause it (as in [2]) and to its different psychosomatic effects on the individual (as in [3]).

(1) *ða eode se man in beforan to ðam cynge and cwæð: Se forlidena man is cumen þe ðu æfter sændest, ac he ne mæg for **scame** in gan buton scrude.*
Then the man went forward to the king and said: The shipwrecked man after whom you sent has arrived, but he cannot, for shame, come in without clothes.
(ApT: 161)

(2) *þonne is him oþer earfeþu swa some scyldgum to sconde, þæt hi þær **scoma** mæste dreogað fordone.*
Then there will be a second misfortune likewise, to the ignominy of those found culpable, that there, brought to ruin, they will endure the utmost shame.
(ChristA,B,C: 380)

(3) *We witon þæt monige habbað ælces woruldwelan genog, ac hi habbað **sceame** þæs welan gif hi ne beoð swa æþele on gebyrdum swa hi woldon.*
We know that many are rich in worldly possessions, but they feel shame of their wealth if they are not of such noble lineage as they would have liked.
(Bo 258)

Following Kövecses (2000: 49), we will assume here that "emotions can be, and are, comprehended via both their assumed typical causes and their assumed typical effects. When this happens, we can get emotion-specific metaphorical source domains." The two patterns indicated above, EMOTION IS A CAUSE OF THAT EMOTION and EMOTION IS AN EFFECT OF THAT EMOTION, are essentially metonymic in nature. Whereas this section will focus on the literal expression of shame, in the next two sections we will analyze in detail the scope of these two metonymic conceptualizations as reflected by the surviving bulk of Anglo-Saxon and Old Norse texts.

With 615 attestations, the Old English expression *sceamu* is by far the most frequently used shame-word in the CACELOE corpus. Within this cluster of lexical roots, the verb *sceamian* (and its inflectional and orthographical variants) is found in a total of 242 attestations, distributed over a very wide variety of texts of different genres and, consequently, is the most neutral and most frequently used lexeme to indicate 'shame' in OE texts.

Directly connected to OE *sceamu* is the expression *sceand* (530 attestations in the CACELOE corpus), derived from the Proto-Germanic past participle **skandō-* 'ashamed'. The OED records four different meanings for the verb *scendan* in Anglo-Saxon texts, which we present here in chronological order (with indication of the first date of attestation):
1. To put to shame or confusion; to confound, disgrace (c825).
2. To discomfit (in battle or dispute; c893).
3. To blame, reproach, reprove (c897).
4. To destroy, ruin, bring to destruction (c900).

As can be seen here, besides the literal emotional expression indicated in (1), the three historically later meanings focus on some of the possible causes of shame, such as being defeated, reproved or spoiled. However, differently to OE *sceamu*, the concrete effects of shame on the experiencer are not focused on by any of the semantic specifications of OE *sceand*.

Besides OE *sceamu* and its cognate *sceand*, our list of expressions of shame in Old English includes several lexical clusters developed by Anglo-Saxon scribes as glosses to Latin shame-words. The fact that the lexemes included in these expressions were apparently created for the *ad-hoc* translation of Latin words and that their use is restricted to a very limited number of patristic texts, are indicative of the fact that the existing Old English vocabulary was not able to convey in a more or less faithful way the corresponding Latin meaning expressed in the original texts. Some of these Old English expressions can be considered literal *shame* denominations, in so far as the 'shame' reading is the dominant sense of the words developed by the scribes. This is the case of OE *āswārnian*, used on 22 occasions by the glossator of the Royal Psalter in order to translate four different Latin lexemes used by Cassiodorus in his *Expositio Salmorum* (see Table 1).

As indicated by this data, the verb OE *āswārnian* was developed in order to cover a wide emotional range, incorporating not only some of the causes of

Tab. 1: Uses of OE *āswārnian* in the Royal Psalter.

LATIN LEXEME	ENGLISH TRANSLATION	Nº OF ATTESTATIONS
confundere	to be confounded, ashamed	9
erubescere	to redden with shame	5
revereri	to fear, to stand in awe, to reverence	5
verecundia	shame, humility	3
TOTAL		22

shame (such as fear), but also many of the behavioural reactions which follow from the force of this emotional experience, such as awe, reverence, humility and reddening in the face.

According to Birnbaum (2014) the type of shame described by Cassiodorus, which can be interpreted as a marker of the progressive individualization of this emotion as a consequence of the Christianization of Anglo-Saxon England, was vital in the process of conversion; in fact, rather than with the social causes of shame stressed by OE *sceamu* and *sceand* (such as, for example, scorn, dishonour and disgrace), OE *āswārnian* is concerned both with the private process of recognition, confession and repentance for one's sins (as in Hofstede's 'private inner pilot'; 1990: 60) and with the individual's feeling of guilt, fear and love of the Lord that springs from confession. Within this context, the 'small shame' expressed by OE *āswārnian*, consisting in admitting your sins in private to your confessor, is contrasted with the 'big shame' conveyed by OE *sceamu*, which implies having your wrongdoings revealed before all mankind at Judgement Day, an alternative with obvious parallels in some of the Anglo-Saxon public shaming practices that we will describe later on in this chapter.

With 167 attestations, the Old Norse substantive *skǫmm* 'shame' is the most frequently used shame-word in the texts contained in the ONP. Within this cluster of lexical roots, the verb *skamma* 'To be ashamed', together with its inflectional variants, amounts to a total of 162 attestations distributed over a wide variety of prose texts of different genres.

Our analysis of the examples of ON *skǫmm* 'shame' contained in the ONP indicates that at least five of the six meanings of OE *sceamu* described above are also extant in their cognate Old Norse expressions:

(4) *þui at þat er oss ælilf* **scom** *oc brigzli ef ver fam æigi sott æitt skip með oflyianda her.*
because it will bring shame and dishonour on us, if we do not pursue a ship with such an overwhelming host.
(Óláfs saga Tryggvasonar 252[6])

(5) *Oc **scamisc** maþr illra verca.*
And one should feel ashamed for the bad deeds.
(Homilíur 67[18])

(6) *Deyjum heldr við sæmd en lifum við **skömm**.*
We would rather die with honour than live with shame.
(Hrólfs saga Gautrekssonar 52[19])

(7) *Engi maðr skal þat við annan mæla at hann have þegit **skom** a ser.*
Nobody will talk to anybody in a way that the other person will receive shame from it.
(Járnsíða 272[17])

(8) *Ef þér rekið eigi þessa réttar, þá munuð þér engra **skamma** reka.*
If you do not take vengeance for this wrong, you will avenge no shame at all.
(Njáls saga 100[24])

However, differently to OE *sceamian/sceamu*, our data indicates that the use of the substantive ON *skǫmm* is much more frequent in our corpus than that of its cognate verb *skamma* (90 attestations). Shame is in fact conceptualized in Old Norse texts as something that is either given or received by individuals within a social context, as shown by the fact that ON *skǫmm* is frequently used in combinations with transitive verbs denoting that something is being either received or bestowed by a subject (see Table 2):

Tab. 2: Combinations *skǫmm* + verb.

MEANING	ON VERBS	Nº of attestations
skǫmm as something received from others or generally considered dishonoring	þola, verða, bera, hljóta, taka/taka ímot, þiggja, sitja, fá, bíða, hafa, fanga, vera, lifa við, henda	84
skǫmm as something bestowed upon others	mæla, valda, kvæða, gera, ráða, veita, færa, festa, gefa	30

The fact that most of the occurrences of the verb ON *skamma* 'To be ashamed' are in the reflexive (ON *skammask*, 84 occurrences out of 90) and come from religious texts of different periods and proveniences (65 attestations out of 90) is probably indicative of the progress of the new concept of shame developed after the Christianization of Iceland, according to which elements of guilt and repent began to substitute the ancient honour-based view of this emotion. Here are some examples of the reflexive uses of ON *skamma*:

(9) *þá* **skammadiz** *Steinn utru sinar oc orða.*
 Steinn felt shame for his lack of faith and for his words.
 (Sturlunga saga 254[7])

(10) *en vit* **scamomsc** *nu synþar ockarar.*
 and we feel shame for our sins.
 (Jóns saga postula 19[31])

5 Metonymy (1): Cause for effect

The most frequent pattern found in the two corpora under scrutiny corresponds to the metonymic extension EMOTION IS A CAUSE FOR THAT EMOTION. The expressions included in this group focus on the circumstances of the event resulting in shame (for example, being publicly accused, exposed or humiliated). In fact, both in Old English and in Old Norse we find that shame is recurrently presented not as a feeling or an emotion on the side of an experiencer, but rather as the expected result of a previous action, wrongdoing or omission. Instead of an internal emotional experience (as in *being ashamed* or *feeling shame*), shame is conceptualized in these cases as an imposed deprivation (as in *to be put to shame*) of such things as personal honour and reputation, clothes, or even a body-part and, consequently, caused or accorded by others, indicating the loss experienced by the person affected by shame.

The set of expressions included in this large category can be further classified into four different metonymical extensions, depending on the exact nature of the loss experienced by the person put to shame: deprivation of worth (SHAME IS DISHONOUR), deprivation of reputation (SHAME IS SCORN), deprivation of a body-part (SHAME IS MUTILATION/PHYSICAL DAMAGE) and deprivation of clothes (SHAME IS NAKEDNESS).

5.1 SHAME IS DISHONOUR

Honour defines "the value of a person in his own eyes, but also in the eyes of his society" (Pitt-Rivers 1966: 21). It is now generally accepted that honour and shame were pivotal values in antiquity (Malina 2001; Peristiany 1966). Loss of honour is a frequent cause of shame in shame-oriented cultures: whereas honour denotes an ascent in esteem by society, shame denotes a descent. Within an 'honour and shame' system, loss of honour happens whenever an individual fails to comply with the collective expectations and obligations assigned to him or to her by their social group. Furthermore, since people share the point of view of the whole group, this represents a failure in their own eyes as well. According to Hiebert (1985: 212), public shaming practices (such as scorn and vexation, which we shall analyze later) in shame cultures are to be seen as a therapeutic mechanism to remove shame and to restore the honour lost:

> Shame is a reaction to other people's criticism, an acute personal chagrin at our failure to live up to our obligations and the expectations others have of us. In true shame oriented cultures, every person has a place and a duty in the society. One maintains self-respect, not by choosing what is good rather than what is evil, but by choosing what is expected of one.

Similarly to shame, honour is a relational concept in so far as it depends on the evaluation by others rather than on our own judgement. However, it is to be expected that the introduction of Christianity, with its new value system, involved the development of a new relation between shame and honour. In his analysis of the importance of honour and shame in patristic texts, Stander (2003) shows that, for example, whereas wealth was a source of honour in the pre-Christian world, Christians showed a strong preference for modesty and reject of worldly possessions. Furthermore, rather than the general social acclaim, believers preferred the honour assigned directly by God.

Within this group we have the expression OE *ārleas* (derived from the noun OE *ār(e)* 'honour, reverence, respect' plus the privative suffix *–leas* 'less'), which is recorded in 703 attestations. Within this lexical cluster, the adjective OE *ārleas* is found on 583 occasions (284 of which are glosses to L *impius* 'impious'). The DOE lists three different senses for this adjective, all of which fall within the general meaning 'without honour or grace':
1. Dishonourable, shameful.
2. Wicked, impious.
3. Showing no mercy, merciless, cruel.

As can be seen here, the first sense recorded in the DOE implies a causal relationship between shame and loss of respect.

(11) *ond se burhgerefa hraþe æfter þam swealt mid **arlease** deaðe.*
and soon after that the prefect died a shameful death.
(Mart 5 Au 22, B.7: 942)

A second expression within this group is OE *orwirþu* 'ignominy, shame, dishonour', a lexeme composed of the noun OE *wirþu* 'value' preceded by the privative prefix OE *or-* 'without'. This expression shows 8 different attestations in our corpus, four of which correspond to glosses of L *ignominia* 'ignominy, disgrace, loss of name'. According to this expression, shame is conceptualized as loss of value, and the shameful person is metaphorically seen as a worthless object:

(12) *ða reordode rices hyrde wið þære fæmnan fæder frecne mode, daraðhæb-bende: Me þin dohtor hafað geywed **orwyrðu**.*
then spoke the guardian of the kingdom, the spear-bearer, with fierce heart unto the sire of the maid: Your daughter has shown me shame.
(Jul: 54)

Combinations of nouns meaning 'honour, reverence' (such as ON *virða, vegr, sæmd, æru* and *heiðr*) plus the privative affixes are also very frequent in the Old Norse domain of shame. Within this category, we find the suffix *-lauss* 'less' in the lexemes ON *virðingarlauss* (3 attestations in the ONP), ON *sæmðarlauss* (9 attestations), and ON *ærulauss* (11 attestations), as well as the privative prefixes ON *af-, van-,* and *ú-/ó-* 'dis-' , which are used to derive a wide variety of shame-words (see Table 3).

Two different aspects are worth mentioning here. To start with, Tables 2 and 3 clearly show that the role played by domain of LOSS OF HONOUR in the conceptualization of shame is much more important in Old Norse (with 10 different expressions) than in Old English (with 2 single expressions). The relevance of this metonymical extension is highly illustrative of the pivotal role of honour and pride in Old Norse society, where "honour is the dominant ethical principle" (Meulengracht Sørensen 2000: 23). As Pakis (2005) has demonstrated, far from implying a collapse of the Old Norse ethos of honour and revenge, the introduction of Christianity in Iceland contributed to a legitimization of certain aspects of the ancient honour system. Secondly, an analysis of the textual distribution of Old Norse shame words derived from ON *virða* 'value' indicates a strong preference for the preffix *af-* (as in ON *afvirða* 'shame, dishon-

Tab. 3: Old Norse shame-words with privative preffixes.

OLD NORSE LEXEME	ENGLISH TRANSLATION	Nº OF ATTESTATIONS
afvirða, afvirðing	to despise/disrepute, fault	42
óvirða, óvirðing	to disregard disgrace	53
vanvirða, vanvirðing	to dishonour/shame	63
úvegr	dishonour	5
úsæmd	disgrace, dishonour	51
vanheiðr	dishonour	8
svívirða, svívirðing	to dishonour/shame	273

our, disdain'; 31 attestations) in versions and translations of Christian texts (such as the *Heilagra feðra æfi* and the *Barlaams saga ok Jósafat*) to render L *abominabilis* 'deserving imprecation', *deiectus* 'cast down', or *damnari* 'to damage, condemn', whereas authors of non religious texts (such as kings' sagas, sagas of Icelanders, laws, etc) were more prone to using the lexemes ON *svívirðing* 'dishonour, shame', *óvirðing* 'dishonour, shame' and *vanvirðing* 'disgrace, shame'.

5.2 Shame is scorn

Contrary to what happens with guilt, which can be relieved by confession and atonement, shame requires punishment, which is normally infringed publicly and normally implies both humiliation and physical damage. As described above, public shaming (either psychological or physical) is a recurrent practice in shame cultures. In fact, a large amount of the Old English and Old Norse expressions analyzed for this research indicate a strong connection between shame and verbal humiliation. Scorn has been associated with practices of social control, discrimination and oppression (Hartling and Luchetta 1999).

Public shaming was a frequent practice in most judicial punishments in Anglo-Saxon England. Shaming the guilt party would serve to reaffirm the norms and values of the community. In the case of smaller crimes, permanent bodily harm would normally be substituted by temporary psychological pain. As Westerhof (2008: 121) puts it, "relatively minor crimes would typically involve the humiliation of offenders in a public location, such as urban markets, by putting them in the stocks or pillory exposed to the taunts and insults of the community." Public scorn was also a frequent penance practice by the Anglo-Saxon church, and concrete punishments are profusely described in a variety of liturgical texts. According to Beningfield (2002: 233) public penance rituals include "The consultation with the bishop (...), the expulsion from the church, the expression of that at services by standing outside of the church threshold (after, interestingly, being stepped over by the others), the hairshirt, and the time-frame of Ash Wednesday to Lent."

Similar practices are described in the earliest Norwegians laws: the so called *Gulathingslög*, for example, offers a wide series of examples of the enforcement of law by resorting to corporal punishment (especially in cases of theft carried out by thralls), such as flogging (section 259) or even mutilation, as we shall see later. If proven guilty, free men accused of breaking the law were normally brought to court and sentenced to paying an economic compensation, which involved a moral sense of social responsibility, or to outlawry, which usually brought contempt both to the offender and his family and, in more than one case, meant the death of the person accused (Kanerva 2012).

The protection of one's honour (either by personal vengeance or by bringing your defamer to the local assembly or *Þing*) was a very popular motif in Old Norse literature. The amount of expressions related to verbally provoked shame/violence in Old Norse gives us a very clear idea of the importance of redressing the abuse in the appropriate way. That Icelanders and Norwegians were particularly aware of the loss of social prestige through slander is easily proven not only on the basis of the existence of laws that condemned it, but also by the regulations against other type of abject insults containing sexual accusations, known as *níð*, and against certain hostile verbal matches known as *senna* and *mannjafnaðr* which, unfortunately, fall outside the scope of our analysis. In this respect, an important aspect of the role of scorn as public shame in Scandinavian society is illustrated by the use of lampooning verses (known as ON *níðvísa*), considered a specially harsh type of insult in ON and penalized with outlawry. The use of certain words as gross terms of abuse received in Old Scandinavian laws (e.g. the Icelandic *Grágas*) the same punishment. This was the case when a man called another ON *ragan* 'effeminate' or ON *stroðinn* 'homosexual', or said that he has been sexually abused by another man (as in ON *sorðinn*). Furthermore, there also existed a minor type of lampooning, represented by expressions such as ON *flim* 'mockery' or ON *flimska* 'lampoon' (originally derived from PrIde *plī-* 'naked, bare').

ON *ámæli*, *brigzli*, *háðung*, *hróp* and *gabba* are some of the most common expressions used in Norse texts to refer to the type of shame produced as a result of public reproach, slander or defamation. Within this group, *ámæli* has the clearest oral origin, because the verb *mæla* meant literally 'to speak' (probably derived from Indo-European *mād-* 'to meet', OE *mæl* 'discourse'). This expression is especially frequent in non religious contexts (110 out of 120 examples), which points toward an association with a pre-Christian code of honour, where society and family, and not the Church, had the ascendancy over the assignation of meaning to human actions, as we can see in the following examples:

(13) *Þeir lǫgðu Þóroddi til ámælis, at hann þolði Birni slíka* **skǫmm**.
      They laid reproach on Thorod in that he suffer from Bjorn such shame.
      (Eyrbyggja saga 77[28])

(14) *ok myndi hann þá hefna frænda síns eða sitja fyrir hvers manns* **ámæli**.
      and he would have to avenge his kinsman, or have to bear every man's blame.
      (Njáls saga 117[24])

The expressions ON *háðung* (derived from Indo-European **kau-* 'to put down, discourage'), with a total of 256 attestations, and ON *brigzli* (of disputed origin; Magnússon 1989), with 141 attestations, are found both in religious and non religious contexts, especially in translated writings of both types. These two words were used alone or in combination with other near-synonymic expressions (such as ON *svívirðing* or *vanvirðing*) in order to refer to shame as the result of an action or of defamation, as in the examples:

(15) Ef maðR skeR hár af höfðe manne. eða úlar honom nokor til **haðungar** eða rífr hann klæði honum.
If someone cuts hair from someone's head, or puts something in disorder to shame him or rips off his clothes.
(Grágás & Kristinna laga þáttr 380[23])

(16) *Væri þér þat engi **brigzli** né vanvirðing, at þú ynnir henni sem eiginkonu þinni.*
And that would not mean any slander or discredit to you, if you love her as your wife.
(Tristrams saga ok Ísǫndar 170[31])

Other very common expressions are ON *spotta* (from Indo-European **(s)pīw-* 'to spit') and ON *gabba* (PrIde **ghabh-* 'to gape'), with 141 and 129 attestations respectively. Both words meant 'to fool, mock' and could be classified together with other less favoured, but synonymous expressions, such as *athlægi* or *hróp*, when alluding to the loss of honour derived from what people thought or might think about one's own behaviour, as in the following examples:

(17) *Asbiornn undi storilla ferð sinni, oc enn ver er hann heyrði slict haft at hlatri oc **spotti**.*
Asbiorn was very discontented with his trip, and even more when he heard that he was ridiculed and laughed at.
(Óláfs saga helga 297[12])

(18) *En se ek at ecki fæz af málinu nema **hróp** ok haðung.*
And I see that I will not get anything from this affair but mockery and shame.
(Bandamanna saga 54[18])

As for our Old English corpus, we have found the expression OE *bysmor* (from PrIde **smei-* 'to laugh'), with a total of 589 attestations, of which 279 correspond to the verb OE *bysmorian*. According to the DOE, the meaning 'to put to shame' is found in at least two different contexts: a military context, where the winning army humiliates the losers (as in example [19]), and a sexual context, where a man harasses sexually a woman (as in example [20]):

(19) *æfter þæm Philippus gelædde fird on Læcedemonie 7 on Thebane, 7 hi miclum tintrade 7 **bismrade**, oþ hie mid ealle wæron fordon 7 forhiened.*
Thereafter Philippus led an army against the Lacaedemonians and against the Thebans, and he tormented them and put them to shame until they all were killed and destroyed.
(Or 3: 173)

(20) *ðæs burhgerefan sunu wolde ræsan on hi on ðæm scandhuse ond hi **bysmrian**, ac fram deoflum forbroden he aslat.*
The son of the prefect wanted to attack them in the brothel and put them to shame, but he died dragged by the devils.
(Mart 5: 154)

Similarly, the expression OE *edwīt* (207 attestations in the corpus) is derived from Proto-Germanic **eduwītan* 'to reproach, rebuke', from where the two Old English meanings 'to scorn' and 'to put to shame' derive. Within this expression, the noun OE *edwīt* is especially frequent in psalter glosses (118 attestations in glosses, out of 191), where it is used to render the following Latin lexemes:

Tab. 4: Uses of OE *edwīt* in psalter glosses.

LATIN LEXEME	ENGLISH TRANSLATION	Nº OF ATTESTATIONS
opprobrium	a reproach, scandal, disgrace	70
improperium	a reproach, taunt	37
exprobratio	reproaching, upbraiding	7
probrum	a shameful act	2
apostrapha	a mark of elision	1
imputatio	an account, charge	1
TOTAL		118

Finally, the expression OE *hux* 'ignominious, involving shame, scorn, insult' (41 attestations in the corpus) is derived from the Indo-European root **keued-* 'to shout'.

(21) *ða þuhte him to **huxlic**, þæt he hiran sceolde ænigum hlaforde.*
Then he thought it too shameful that he should be subject to any lord.
(ÆLet 4: 43)

5.3 Shame is amputation/physical damage

Anglo-Saxon law codes show that mutilation was a standard punishment for a wide range of felonies: amputation of body parts was in fact frequently preferred over the death penalty in order to give the offender time to repent. According to O'Keeffe (1998), mutilation was a social indicator of shame aimed at inscribing the crime upon the body of the convict, in a way that would make others read the guilty body as a deterrent.

Even if judicial mutilation was a relatively frequent practice in Anglo-Saxon England (Swanton 1976), the Old English vocabulary of shame does not include any lexemes expressing amputation of body limbs, sexual organs, nose, tongue or ears. However, we have a couple of expression that refer to physical damage as a source of shame. To start with, the expression OE *getawian mid sceame* 'to inflict shame' yields 3 attestations in the corpus. The verb OE *tawian*, which is originally used to refer to the act of beating an animal hide in order to soften it, is used here metonymically in order to express physical torment and humiliation. This sense is especially clear in the following example, where some of the different tortures infringed on the Britons with the main aim of producing shame are listed:

(22) *Se kyngc wæs þa þone midwinter on Westmynstre, þær mon fordemde ealle þa Bryttas þe wæron æt þam brydlope æt Norðwic, sume hi wurdon geblende, and sume wrecen of lande, and sume **getawod to scande**.*
The king was then at Westminster at midwinter, where all the Britons were condemned who were at the bride-ale at Norwich, some of them punished with blindness, some expelled from the land, and some were tormented with shame.
(ChronD: 1014)

Similarly, the expression OE *þurhwadan sceame* 'to pierce with shame', with one single attestation in the corpus, illustrates the conceptualization of shame as a sharp-pointed weapon in Old English:

(23) *Beoð þa syngan flæsc **scandium þurhwaden** swa þæt scire glæs, þæt mon yþæst mæg eall þurhwlitan.*
The sinful bodies shall be penetrated with shame as the clear glass you can look through.
(ChristA, B, C: 382)

Mutilation was also considered a form of punishment in earlier mediaeval Scandinavia. The Norwegian legal text *Gulaþingslög* describes the special treatment reserved for thralls who were caught stealing. The double nature (physical and emotional) of the shaming in the following example is worth stressing:

(24) *ef hon stelr hit þriðja sinn, þa skal skera af henne nef, þa heiter hon stuva oc nuva oc stele ae ef hon vil.*
and if she steals a third time, then her nose shall be cut off, and then she will be called 'blunted nose' and 'cut-off nose' and let her keep stealing if she feels like it.
(Gulathingslov 85[11])

ON *hneykja* 'to put to shame' (probably derived from Indo-European *gneig-* 'to bend') and perhaps *hneisa* (of doubtful etymology; Magnússon 1989) clearly illustrate the link with the type of shame originated in mutilation or physical damage, especially in non religious contexts (8 out of 26 occurrences). With the arrival of Christianity, though, its meaning became gradually confined to spiritual shame, as shown in the second example:

(25) *Hafi suma látit drepa, suma hafi hún látit **kneykia** á einhvörn hátt, suma blinda, gelda handhöggva eðr fóthöggva.*
She had some of them killed, some of them humiliated in different ways, some blinded, castrated, some had their hands or their feet hacked off.
(Hrólfs saga Gautrekssonar 75[26])

(26) **hneyktir** *erum við í synd okkari.*
We are all ashamed of our sins.
(Jóns saga Postola 426[40])

The expressions ON *hýða* 'to flog' (28 occurences) or ON *afhæra* 'to shear' (3 attestations) also refer to this type of punishment, although not always can they be connected to social shaming. The humiliating element becomes especially clear in those cases where free men or ecclesiastics were the ones on the receiving end, as in the examples:

(27) *at leiða Johannem fyrir þat borgarport, er Latina kallaz, afklæddan, **hyddan** ok afhærdan með fullri háðung.*
that they are to bring Saint John to that harbour named Latina, and there strip him and flog him and cut his hair off in the most humiliating way.
(Jóns saga Postola 476[7])

(28) *at Hakon kongr ætladi at fara austr ... en presta skyllde leggia aa stiga ok* **hyda.**

King Hákon had planned to go to the East … and that he would lay the priests on to the path and flog them.
(Hákonar saga Hákonarsonar 398[28])

ON *skemma* 'to shorten' derives from Indo-European *(s)kem2*, originally meaning 'to mutilate' (not to be confused with the Indo-European root *(s)kemm* 'to cover, warp' described above). Similarly, ON *sneypa* 'to dishonour' derives from the Indo-European root *(s)neit* 'to cut, to castrate', from which the Old Norse meaning 'to put to shame by amputation'.

(29) *þeir þottozt* **skemder** *oc svívirðr er þeir skyllu missa at hava hann konong.*
they considered themselves humiliated and shamed if they failed to have him as their king.
(Barlaams saga ok Jósafats 189[5])

(30) *hefi ek aldri farit jafnmikla* **sneypu** *fyrir þeim sem nú fór þorkell fyrir Skarpheðni.*
I have never suffered such humiliation at their hands as has Thorkel from Skarphedinn.
(Njáls saga 306[7])

Given that physical torture was a frequent source of public shaming, one can confidently argue that this conceptualization of SHAME AS PHYSICAL DAMAGE has got a metonymic grounding in both languages.[5]

5.4 Shame is nakedness

Sexuality in general, and nudity in particular, are major sources of shame in Western cultures (Kaufman 1989: 63). In allegorical terms, the book of Genesis describes how humans experienced shame for the first time. Originally, Adam and Eve felt no shame for their nakedness, but their eyes were opened as soon as they ate the fruit of knowledge, realizing they were naked. They sewed fig leaves together in order to cover their sexual organs and hid their nakedness from God's eyes behind the trees. Therefore, a frequent conceptualization for shame is HAVING NO CLOTHES ON (Holland and Kipnis 1995; Stanghellini and Rosfort 2013: 162).

---

[5] This can be compared to the metaphoric expression SHAME IS PHYSICAL DAMAGE found in Present-Day English "I was shattered" (Kövecses 2000: 32).

Nudity does not seem to be a frequent topic in Anglo-Saxon literature and art (Owen-Crocker 1986: 316), whereas just a few cases of nakedness are recorded in Old Norse sagas.[6] In the case of Old English texts, most references to the naked body are to be found in the context of death and the final judgement. According to Thompson (2002: 155), the cumulative evidence in Anglo-Saxon texts shows that "nudity carried an aura of profound shame and vulnerability." Our Old English corpus shows just a couple of instances where shame is a direct consequence of nudity. However, these examples do not illustrate metaphorical uses of nakedness as a source of shame but, rather, refer to nudity in literal terms.

(31) *Ic eom wífhádes mann and eallunga lichamlicum wæfelsum bereafod, swa swa þu sylf gesihst, and þa **sceame** mines lichaman hæbbende unoferwrigen.*
I am a woman and bereft of all the bodily wraps, as you can see, and the shame of my body I have not covered.
(LS 23: 106)

Furthermore, the connection between shame and nudity is evident in the noun OE *sceamu* and its derivates *sceamlim* and *sceamigendlic*, all of which are in fact used in order to refer to the sexual member, presumably on the model of L *pudenda* 'sexual member, lit. something to be ashamed of' (neuter gerundive of L *pudere* 'to be ashamed, to feel shame'):

(32) *Syn ða butan are ealle gegyrede þe me tælnysse teonan ætfæstan, and him si abrogden swa of brechrægle hiora sylfra **sceamu** swyþust ealra.*
Let them all be dressed without respect who afflicted me with malice and their insult; and, most of all, let their shame be revealed as if pulled out of breeches.
(PPs: 1035)

Directly related to the idea of nakedness is the idea of inappropriate sexual conduct as a source of shame. According to Buck's (1948: 1141) list of Indo-European synonyms, the Old English expression *æwisc* 'shame, disgrace, foulness' (and its cognates Gothic *aiwiski* 'shame, disgrace' and Middle High German *eisch* 'ugly, repulsive'; there exist no Old Norse cognates for this root) can be related to an ancient root within the same semantic area, i.e. Indo-European

---

[6] According to Jochens (1995: 76) only two cases of female nakedness are recorded in the whole corpus, both of which inspire horror.

aig^wh- 'shame' (Pokorny 14)). Apparently, the very few uses of this Old English expression in Anglo-Saxon texts (30 attestations in all) point towards a very close connection between OE *æwisc* and the Christian notions of purity and chastity, as applied to female sexuality. In fact, our Anglo-Saxon corpus includes 19 attestations of the expression *æwisc* in Old English glosses to L *scandalum* 'scandal', *obscenitas* 'obscenity' and *inhonesta* 'shameful', most of which are recorded in Aldhelm's prose version of *De Laude Virginitatis*, a treaty on the merits of female virginity addressed at the nuns in the monastery of Barking. Similarly, the derived noun OE *æwiscnes* (nine attestations in the corpus) is used in Old English in order to gloss L *impudentia* 'shamelessness' and *opprobrium* 'reproach, scandal', whereas OE *æwiscberend* ('shame bringer'; one single attestation in the corpus) translates L *digitus impudicus* 'shameless finger', a reference to the obscene gesture of raising one's middle finger to express disrespect and insult originated in Classical Greece and then adopted by the Romans (Corbeill 2003: 6; Robbins 2008: 1042). Things being so, we can confidently argue that the type of shame expressed by the glossator through the use of OE *æwisc* has got strong connections with the expression of inappropriate sexual behaviour. Furthermore, the textual distribution of this expression, along with the fact that this link between shame and (female) sexuality is not found in any of the Old Norse words for shame studied here, are strong indicators of the non-Germanic origins of this semantic connection, whose most immediate origins are to be found in Classical Rome.

Very similarly, OE *æpsen* (5 attestations in the corpus), which can be used either substantively or adjectively, was also developed by the glossator of Aldhelm's prose version of *De Laude Virginitatis* in order to refer to impudent conduct, rendering L *obscenitas* 'obscenity' (3 hits) and L *frontosus* 'shameless' (1 hit).

As for the Norse corpus, most references to the naked body have a purely descriptive nature. Before the arrival of Christianity, nudity was not considered a source of shame, as is apparent from an analysis of the scarce attestation of naked-related words in the Icelandic family sagas. Such adjectives as ON *nökkviðr* and *berr*, 'naked', were mostly used in their literal sense in fiction, as well as in lawbooks, historical writings etc, as in the following example:

(33) *Hon uar **naukkit** suo at hon hafði onguan hlut a ser.*
She was naked because she had no clothes on.
(Eyrbyggja saga 247[3])

However, there exist a few examples where nudity could be associated with shame, especially in 13th century translations of the popular genre *chanson de geste*. Humiliation and nakedness has also been found in religious sagas, represented by the verb ON *fletta* 'to strip', which is used figuratively to express "the violent removal of clothing prior to torture or physical abuse" (Gade 1988: 231), but also in other contexts. In *Laurentius saga*, a 14th century Saga about the Icelandic bishop Laurentius, we find a clear example of the reflexive form of the verb *skamma* together with the above mentioned adjective *berr* 'naked'.

(34) *þu scallt ganga **nockviðr** i brott fra oss a foeti ... sem furumaðr.*
You will go away from us, naked and on foot as a vagrant man.
(Elíss saga ok Rósamundar 62[15])

(35) *[...] eptir bardagan þa com þorpkarl einn i valin oc villdi **fletta** mennina ... oc þat sa einn maðr oc avitaði hann um þæt hit illa verk oc hit svivirðlega.*
after the battle a man from the village came to the field and wanted to strip the corpses ... and a man saw it and admonished him against that shameful and wrongful act.
(Óláfs saga Tryggvasonar 245[16])

(36) *Heimskr madr ertu ordinn, er þu **skammazt** eigi, at þu ert **berr**.*
You have turned into a fool, if you are not ashamed of being naked.
(Laurentius saga 430[25])

The topic of sexuality is only very sparsely represented in the family sagas and other texts of native origin which have come down to us. The words used to refer to the sexual act or to the sexual organs were in most cases of a purely descriptive nature and do not take the 'nakedness/shame' conceptual complex into consideration. Or at least not until a very late date when Christianity was firmly established in the Nordic Countries, as shown in example 36, and penitentials, sermons and exempla "offered the impression that sex, women, and the devil were merely different forms of the same thing" (Cormack 1991: 103).

The expression *blygð* 'shame' (Indo-European *bhlēu-* 'bad') is the only one for which an etymological connection between sexuality and shame is more or less clear. From its original (debatable) meaning 'the genitals, the naked body', the expression might have developed into the above mentioned sense of 'shame originated in nudity' and then just into any sort of shame. The word was not widely used, it seems there are only 26 attestations, and mostly in translations and late romances of a chivalric nature. Four out of the twelve attestations of the verb *blygða* correspond to the obscene related type of shame under analysis, as the one in the example below:

(37) *hann hafdi **blýgdat** allar meýiar ... en giort oletta kongs dottur.*
he had put to shame all maidens ... and got the king's daughter pregnant.
(Vilmundar saga viðutan 154[6])

6 Metonymy (2): Effect for cause

This second group of metonymic expressions includes conceptualizations of shame of the type EMOTION IS A RESULT OF THAT EMOTION. EFFECT FOR CAUSE metonymies are often related to both physiological changes and culture-specific ideas. As indicated by Kövecses and Radden (1998), many of these expressions are related to bodily changes or feelings which coincide with or are parallel to emotional changes. The list of behaviours traditionally associated with shame (Darwin 1972/2005; Tomkins 1963; Lewis 1995) includes blushing, lowering of the head and upper part of the body, mental confusion, turning away and hiding. However, as shall be seen later, most of these effects are not restricted to shame but, rather, shared with other emotions (especially anger and fear). Consequently, the same source domains can apply to different emotion concepts and, at times, defining which emotion exactly is causing a given effect is not an easy task, especially in those cases where the corresponding shame expression does not co-occur in the same sentence as another shame-word.

Broadly speaking, the metonymic expressions analysed here are by far less frequent than literal and causal metonymic expressions in our corpus. Besides, their use is clearly restricted to Old English versions of patristic texts and, most frequently, to psalter glosses, which is probably pointing towards a foreign origin of these conceptualizations.

We have classified these metonymic expressions into three large groups, corresponding to three of the physiological reactions to shame referred to above: REDNESS IN THE FACE, TURNING AWAY and MENTAL DISTRESS.

6.1 SHAME IS REDNESS IN THE FACE/RISE IN BODILY TEMPERATURE

Blushing is a common effect of a wide variety of emotions that are accompanied by dilatation of blood vessels, such as anger, rage and shame. Consequently, the linguistic expression of these emotions relies frequently on this EFFECT FOR CAUSE relation. However, although the metonymy SHAME IS REDNESS IN THE FACE is not completely foreign to Old English texts, its incidence in our corpus is extraordinarily limited. In fact, the use of the three expressions in this category, namely OE *ārēodian* (6 attestations in the corpus) *aryderan* (3 attestations in the corpus) and *āblysian* (16 attestations in the corpus), all of which mean 'to turn red, to blush', is very reduced and normally limited to Latin glosses.

OE *ārēodian* is used on 4 occasions to translate L *erubescere* 'to redden with shame' in psalter glosses. As for the other two cases, whereas in (38) the subject is OE *andwlita* 'face', in (39) we have an impersonal construction with OE *him*:

(38) *ða nam Apollonius þæt gewrit and rædde and sona swa he ongeat þæt he gelufod wæs fram ðam mædene, his andwlita eal **areodode**.*
Then Apollonius took the letter and read, and as soon as he discovered that he was beloved by the maiden, his face all reddened with embarrassment.
(ApT: 249)

(39) *þa se ylca broðor halwendlice geþread him gesceamode 7 **areodode**.*
The brother was ashamed at this wholesome rebuke and reddened.
(GD 2: 532)

As for OE *aryderan*, this verb is restricted to psalter glosses, where it is used to translate L *erubescere* 'to redden with shame'. Finally, OE *āblysian* is predominantly used in glosses (14 attestations glossing L *erubescere* 'to redden with shame' and 1 gloss to L *revereri* 'to stand in awe'). Outside Latin glosses, OE *āblysian* is found only in the English version of the *Leviticus* (1 single attestation; see example [40]):

(40) *7 ic ga ongean eow, 7 læde eow on feonda land, oþ eower lyðre mod **ablysige**; ðonne gebidde ge for eowrum arleasnyssum.*
Then I turned against you and brought you to the land of your enemies, until your wicked spirit reddened with shame; then you paid for your sins.
(Lev: 199)

In the case of Old Norse, the expression ON *roðna* 'to redden' appears either in a literal sense or associated with anger in works of a non-religious nature, where an angry king or the warlike Icelander are said to redden and get angry (i.e. '*roðnar oc ræiðiz við*') in quick succession. As education and literacy became more common, the spread of Christian-related values and writings changed the appraisal of some emotions and thus we read that Saint John the Apostle was a virtuous man because:

(41) *Alldri sa þeir hann **roðna** ne blikna eða annan veg bregdaz í sinu yfirbragði.*
they never saw him redden or go pale or perceived any changes in his demeanour.
(Jóns saga postula 432[4])

We have a different attitude to the expression of sentiments in the more emotionally charged literature from the continent. Accordingly, it is not unusual to read that the new chivalric heroes, the likes of Percival and Erex, *roðna af skǫmm* 'redden with shame', or that innocent maidens blushed when they were first introduced into society:

(42) *Hón hafði **roðnat** nökkut, er hón var inn leidd í höllina, því at hón var eigi vön dagliga þvílíku fjölmenni.*
She blushed a little when she was brought to the hall, because she was not used to such crowds.
(Erex saga 13[15])

The expression ON *kinnroði* 'a blush of shame' (29 attestations) appears almost exclusively in religious contexts and associated with the type of shame generated through sin or immoral behaviour, as in the following example:

(43) *En því at synd hennar var opinber, bætti hun með miklum ok merkiligum **kinnroða**.*
And because her sin was known, she repented with great and remarkable shame.
(Marthe saga og Marie Magdalene 518[16])

Closely related to SHAME IS REDNESS IN THE FACE, our Old Norse corpus has yielded one single attestation of the metonymy SHAME IS BODY-HEAT, where shame is conceptualized in terms of bodyheat. This occurrence comes from a religious text from the beginning of the 13th century, the *Saga of the Virgin Mary* (ON *Maríu saga*: see example [44] below), where the verb *hitna* 'to be hot, to burn', normally linked to other emotions with similar physiological effects, such as love and anger, this time appears associated with shame:

(44) *Munkrinn **hitnar** hardla miok i sinu hiarta af sinni skomm.*
The monk's heart was burning intensely because of his shame.
(Maríu saga 823[1])

According to the data yielded by the two historical corpora used here, we can confidently argue that the use of the metonymy SHAME IS REDNESS IN THE FACE is a clear example of conceptual borrowing from Latin into Old English and Old Norse. As for its derivation shame is body-heat, its recurrence is very irrelevant (one single attestation in Old Norse) and its use is apparently limited to a religious context.

6.2 Shame is moving backwards

A second reaction to shame consists in turning away one's face in order to hide one's emotion from others. The expression OE *forwandian* (derived from OE *wandian* 'to turn aside from something) and its derivates (57 attestations in the whole corpus) refer to the instinctive reaction of moving away from the source of shame, turning the face in another direction in order not to be seen. Within this lexical cluster, the verb OE *forwandian* (35 attestations in the corpus) is used in order to refer both to the physical action of turning back (not only with shame, but also with fear, awe and respect) and to the mental action of hesitating about something, which can be considered an indicator of mental confusion produced by shame. According to our corpus, whereas fear and respect are frequently associated to these two reactions in Anglo-Saxon texts, the association between shame and backwards movement is restricted to Old English glosses of Latin texts. In fact, all the occurrences of the verb OE *forwandian* in the same sentence as a shame word (17 attestations in all) correspond to psalter glosses,[7] where it is used to translate L *confundere* 'to be confounded, ashamed' and L *revereri* 'to stand in awe, reverence'.

(45) *Sien gescende 7 hy* **forwandian** *somod þe þe secað sawle mine syn gecyrred underbecling ablysien l forscamien þa ðe þohton me yfelu.*
Both ashamed and confounded are those who seek after my soul, turned back and reddened with embarrassment those who desired evils to me.
(PsGlD: 629)

As in the previous case, the metonymy SHAME IS TURNING BACK can be considered a Latin borrowing, whose adaptation into Old English was favoured by the previous existence of the conceptualization FEAR IS TURNING BACK (Díaz-Vera 2011: 93–94). This expression contributed to stress the connection between shame, fear and awe described in our discussion of OE *āswārnian*, where fear of shame in Judgement Day is presented as a major tool to restrain from shameful sins.

As for our Old Norse textual corpus, no instances of the extension SHAME IS TURNING BACK have been found here, which is highly illustrative of the non-Germanic character of this conceptualization.

---

7 PsGlE (3 hits), PsGlH (3 hits), PsGlG (2 hits), PsGlD (4 hits), PsGlF (2 hits) and PsGlK (3 hits).

6.3 Shame is moving downwards

Directly related to turning back, the action of lowering the head and upper part of the body as a reaction to shame refers to the need to become smaller in order to try to conceal our emotion from others so as to keep it as a completely subjective experience. At the same time, as expressed by some of the verbs analyzed here, downwards motion and shrinking are closely connected to our representation of submission to a social superior in the visual mode, connecting shame to other negative emotions.

OE *hienþo* 'abasement, humiliation, shame' is derived from the Indo-European root **kau-* 'base, low' (hence 'to put down, abase'). With 67 attestations in the CACELOE corpus, this Old English noun illustrates the link between shame and grief. In fact, in most of the examples recorded in our corpus it refers to the condition produced as a consequence of physical harm, scorn or loss (example [46]). Furthermore, it is also used to refer to condemnation to eternal punishment and to the disgrace of being doomed to hell as an opposite of heaven (example [47]).

(46) *Sorh is me to secganne on sefan minum gumena ængum hwæt me Grendel hafað* **hynðo** *on Heorote mid his heteþancum, færniða gefremed.*
Sore is in my soul to say to any man what disgrace Grendel brought to me in Heorot.
(Beo: 155)

(47) *Geceosan mot swa helle* **hienþu** *swa heofones mærþu, swa þæt leohte leoht swa ða laþan niht.*
(he) may choose either the shame of hell or the glory of heaven, either the resplendent light or the loathsome night.
(ChristA,B,C: 190)

ON *niðra* 'to lower' and ON *minnka* 'to decrease' referred originally to physical debilitation, a decrease in size or strength, and thus were mostly used in a literal sense (as in ON *oc minnkaðu þesse orð hans gleði* 'and these words diminished his joy'). At a later stage, both expressions developed the new sense 'to put someone to shame' and were used as synonyms of some of the expressions analysed above, as in these examples:

(48) *þessir lutir allir sneruz sem maclict var honum til suiviðingar oc* **niðranar**.
All these things turned, as he deserved, to his shame and discredit.
(Óláfs saga Tryggvasonar 136[19])

(49) *ef hann sialfr villdi sva* **minka** *sik ad þola usæmd af brodur sinum.*
 if he wants to lower himself to tolerate his brother being put to shame.
 (Breta saga AM 573 4tº 35v²)

In the same way, ON *smán* 'disgrace, shame' (derived from PrIde *smēik-* 'a little') shows a relatively low number of attestations in our Old Norse corpus (72 attestations in all), but its distribution across different genres and sub-periods is highly regular, often as a member of alliterative pairs such as ON *smán ok svívirðing* (i.e. 'disgrace and shame').

(50) *hann þóttiz hafa bæði* **smán** *ok svívirðing af ferðum Bjarnar.*
 It seemed to him that he had only received disgrace and shame from Björn's trip.
 (Eyrbyggja saga 220⁴)

6.4 Shame is mental distress

Confusion and mental distress are frequent effects of shame. As has been seen above, OE *forwandian* is frequently used in order to refer to the hesitation that accompanies not only shame, but also fear and awe experiences. Other expressions that link shame to mental distress are OE *āswǣman* and OE *āfǣran*, both of which have the general meaning 'to trouble'.

We have found 16 attestations of OE *āswǣman* in our corpus. In two of these cases, this verb is used to gloss L *erubescere* 'to redden with shame'. In two other cases, use of the preposition *æt* and *fram* can be taken as an indicator of a situation where a subject experiences shame and reverence in front a social superior (see example [51]). In all the other cases, no exact connection between shame and trouble has been found.

(51) *þa earman fyrenfullan sculon sarige* **aswæman** *fram ansyne ures drihtnes 7 fram his haligra 7 fram þam wuldre heofona rices.*
 The poor sinners should be sorrowfully ashamed by the vision of our Lord and of his saints and of the glorious kingdom of heavens.
 (HomU 8: 39)

As for OE *āfǣran*, an expression normally used in Old English to refer to fear, this verb is used with reference to shame in one single case in our corpus, the Old English version of St Gregory's *Dialogues*, where it translates L *magnoque pudore consternati sunt*:

(52) *þa hi þas hrægl gesawon, hi gecneowon, þæt hi hi ær gehyddon, 7 wurdon **afærede mid mycelre scame**, 7 scamiende hi onfengon heora agenu hrægl, þa þe hi mid facne fræmde sohton.*
When they saw those garments, they were wonderfully confounded for thinking by cunning to have gotten other men's apparel, with shame they received only their own.
(GDPref and 3 (C): 299)

As in the case of the other EFFECT FOR CAUSE metonymies described in this section, the connection between shame and mental distress in Old English texts is secondary both in terms of number of expressions and of textual distribution of these lexemes. Also, this extension is not recorded in our corpus of Old Norse texts, which reinforces the view of this metonymy as a Latin borrowing.

7 SHAME IS ROTTENNESS: Shame as a synaesthetic experience

The expression of shame also finds a source of expressions in the domain of physical perception, where shame is experienced as an offensive smell. Shame is identified here with the odour of decay of the poor, with sickness and with the putrescence of the dead body (Woolgar 2006: 130). This synaesthetic conceptualization of shame is expressed in our Anglo-Saxon texts through OE *fūllic* 'foul, offensive to the senses' (46 attestations) and OE *lysu* 'corrupt, depraved' (5 attestations). These lexemes can be traced back to the Indo-European roots **pu-* 'to stink' and **leus-* 'to lose' (hence 'to perish' and, thereafter 'to stink') respectively.

(53) *Gif hwa **fulice** on ungecyndelicum ðingum ongean godes gesceafte ðurh ænig ðinc hine sylfne besmite, bereowsige þæt æfre þa hwile ðe he libbe be ðam þe seo dæd sy.*
Anyone who shamefully defiles himself through anything in not natural things against God's creation, he should do penance all the time that he may live for that which the deed may be.
(Conf 3.1.2 (Raith X): 29)

In the case of Old Norse, both ON *klækja* 'to disgrace, shame' and ON *klæma* 'to abuse, use shameful language' are derived from Indo-European **gelg-* and **glēm-* respectively, which originally meant 'uncleanness'. Although the original meaning is not recorded in Old Norse dictionaries, these two expressions illustrate the diachronic connection from 'dirtiness' to 'shame'.

8 SHAME IS SOMETHING THAT COVERS A PERSON

Our last group of figurative expressions includes metaphoric conceptualizations of shame. One single conceptualization has been included within this group: SHAME IS SOMETHING THAT COVERS A PERSON, which has got two different specifications: SHAME IS A PIECE OF CLOTH and SHAME IS A LIQUID SUBSTANCE. In both cases, shame is conceived of metaphorically either as a textile or as a liquid. Very obviously, both expressions are metonymically grounded, as hiding behind one of these two covers is a frequent reaction in individuals affected by shame. Furthermore, as in the case of the EFFECT FOR CAUSE metonymies described above, this conceptualization expresses a subjective experience of shame. In fact, rather than hiding a wrongdoing so that others will not be able to discover it, it is the experiencer's body (and specially his/her face) that is covered in order to conceal the emotion.

8.1 SHAME IS A PIECE OF CLOTH

The metaphor SHAME IS A PIECE OF CLOTH that covers one shame or anxiety is illustrated in a wide variety of languages. This is the case of Hebrew חסכ 'to cover with shame' (Basson 2006: 182) and Latin *induo confusione* 'to clothe with shame', the origin of which can be related to the ancient Roman *toga sordida* 'dirty toga' worn by prisoners at their trial (MacGushin 1992: 212). Example (54) below illustrates the Old English literal translation of this Latin expression (as recorded in the early 10th century interlinear translation of the *Paris Psalter*; O'Neill 1981), as well the relatively late Old Norse rather version *hyljast skǫmm*:

(54) *Ic his feondas eac facne **gegyrwe mid scame** swiðust; ofer hine scir cymeð minra segnunga soðfæst blostma.*
I covered his enemies with shame quickly; brightly came over him the pious flower of my consecration.
(PPs 131.19)

(55) *skammist ok upp gefist baktalandi menn salu mínne, **hyliest** skemd og **skǫmm** huerier leita jlla hluti mjer.*

May the enemies of my soul perish in shame; may those who want to harm me be covered with scorn and disgrace.
(Ps. 70, 10–33)

In a similar fashion, OE *oferwrigen mid sceame* (6 attestations in the Old English corpus) is used to gloss L *operio pudore* 'to cover with shame'. Also, OE *sceamu* is used once to gloss L *pallor* 'paleness', a probable reference to the colour of the piece of cloth that figuratively represents shame.

8.2 SHAME IS A LIQUID SUBSTANCE

OE *geotan* 'to pour' appears in the expressions OE *þurhgeotan on gescyndnesse* (11 attestations) and *ofergeotan med sceame* (1 single attestation), both of which mean 'to pour shame over someone', where shame is conceptualized as a liquid covering (part of) the body.[8] Both expressions can certainly be connected to the action of weeping as a direct physiological effect of shame. Whereas the use of the first expression is limited to glosses of L *perfundo confusione*, the latter appears in the Anglo-Saxon *Letter to Sigeweard*, a work of biblical teaching composed by Ælfric of Eynsham around the year 1005-06 (Hall 2003: 67). Finally, the expression OE *sceame onmētan* 'to paint with shame' (1 single attestation in the corpus) is used to translate L *perfundo confusione* 'to besprinkle with shame'.

Consequently, in the view of this data we can confidently assume that Anglo-Saxon translations of Latin texts allowed the progressive introduction of the SHAME IS A COVER metaphor and its two specifications, SHAME IS A PIECE OF CLOTH and SHAME IS A LIQUID SUBSTANCE, in spite of which the use of these metaphors outside Latin translations is not illustrated in our corpus.

No instances of this conceptualization have been found in the Old Norse corpus used here, which further confirms the non-Germanic origin of the corresponding metaphoric expressions.

9 Discussion and conclusions

The overall result of this onomasiological analysis of shame-expressions is represented in Table 5 (Old English data) and Table 6 (Old Norse data). Based on the model used by Geeraerts and Gevaert (2008: 339), these two tables mention

---

[8] According to the MED, the two expressions 'to clothe with shame' and 'to cover with shame' continued to coexist in Middle English, with a growing preference for the latter (a probable

Tab. 5: Literal and figurative shame-expressions in Old English.

theme	OE expression	semantics	Nº	
EMOTION: SHAME	sceamu, sceand	literal	1145	
EMOTION: SHAME/ GUILT	āswārnian	literal	22	1167
DISHONOUR	ārleas, orwirþu	CAUSE FOR EFFECT METONYMY	711	
SCORN	bysmor, edwīt, hux	CAUSE FOR EFFECT METONYMY	837	
AMPUTATION	getawian, þurhwadan	CAUSE FOR EFFECT METONYMY	4	
NAKEDNESS	sceamu, æwisc, æpsen	CAUSE FOR EFFECT METONYMY	30	1582
REDNESS IN THE FACE	ārēodian, aryderan, āblysian	EFFECT FOR CAUSE METONYMY	25	
MOVING BACKWARDS	forwandian	EFFECT FOR CAUSE METONYMY	57	
MOVING DOWNWARDS	hienþo	EFFECT FOR CAUSE METONYMY	67	
MENTAL DISTRESS	āswǣman, āfǣran	EFFECT FOR CAUSE METONYMY	17	266
ROTTENNESS	fūllic, lysu	synaesthesia	51	51
A PIECE OF CLOTH	oferwrigan, gegirwan	metaphor	7	
A LIQUID SUBSTANCE	geotan, onmētan	metaphor	13	20
total				2986

all the etymological themes yielded by the two corpora, the actual Old English and Old Norse expressions corresponding to each etymological theme, the semantic mechanisms they illustrate and their total number of attestations in the two corpora used for this research.

Following Radden (2003), who argues that the distinction literal-metonymy-metaphor is scalar, three different degrees of literalness will be distinguished here. Each table is divided into two parts: one for literal meanings (upper half of the table) and one for figurative meanings (lower half of the table), which is further divided into four subparts: (i) CAUSE FOR EFFECT metonymies (upper row), (ii) EFFECT FOR CAUSE metonymies (upper central row) (iii) metonymic synaesthesias (lower central row), and (iv) conceptual metaphors (lower row).

As can be seen form Table 5, with 1145 attestations (38.5% of the total number of occurrences of shame-words in Old English), the literal denomination OE *sceamu* clearly dominates in the corpus. Furthermore, the conceptual connection between shame and scorn (837 attestations, 28.0%) and between shame and dishonour (711 attestations, 24.0%), as represented by the metony-

---

influence of French *couvrir d'honte*). For later uses of the metaphor SHAME IS SOMETHING THAT COVERS A PERSON in English, see Tissari (2006: 148).

Tab. 6: Literal and figurative shame-expressions in Old Norse.

theme	ON expression	semantics	Nº	
EMOTION: SHAME	skǫmm	literal	329	329
DISHONOUR	virða, vegr, sæmd, æru, heiðr (+ privative prefixes af-, van-, ú/ó- or the suffix –lauss)	CAUSE FOR EFFECT METONYMY	495	
SCORN	athlægi, ámælis, brigzli, gabba, háðung, hróp, flim, flimska, spotta	CAUSE FOR EFFECT METONYMY	772	
AMPUTATION	hneykja, hneisa, skemma, sneypa	CAUSE FOR EFFECT METONYMY	390	
NAKEDNESS	blygð, fletta	CAUSE FOR EFFECT METONYMY	50	1707
REDNESS IN THE FACE/ RISE IN BODILY TEMPERATURE	roðna, kinnroði, hitna	EFFECT FOR CAUSE METONYMY	56	
MOVING DOWNWARDS	niðra, minnka, smán	EFFECT FOR CAUSE METONYMY	96	152
ROTTENNESS	klæma, klækja	synaesthesia	65	65
A PIECE OF CLOTH	hylja	metaphor	1	1
total				2254

mies SHAME IS DISHONOUR and SHAME IS SCORN, are indicative of the importance of the CAUSE FOR EFFECT conceptualization of shame in Old English. EFFECT FOR CAUSE metonymies and metonymic synaesthesias for the expression of shame show 217 attestations in the corpus, whereas the two metaphorical extensions analysed here are found on only 20 occasions in the whole corpus.

As described above, many of these EFFECT FOR CAUSE metonymies and metaphors appear exclusively in Old English glosses to patristic texts, which is indicative of their foreign character. Such conceptualizations as SHAME IS REDNESS IN THE FACE and SHAME IS SOMETHING THAT COVERS A PERSON, traditionally described as frequent shame-metaphors in Present-Day English (Kövecses 2000: 32), are in fact directly connected to the Christianization of England and to the progressive change in the local system of values, which involved a slow substitution of the old, honour-based model by a new conceptualization of shame, based on the subjective recognition of one's guilt. Very similarly, the metonymy SHAME IS NAKEDNESS is apparently another borrowing from Mediterranean cultures, from where it expanded to the North as the new faith was embraced by the different Germanic societies.

Based on this linguistic data, we can confidently argue that the Old English represents the early beginnings of the transition from the ancient shame culture to the later guilt culture, a process that was not completed until the end of the medieval period.[9] Furthermore, our study reveals the importance to this process of Old English translations of Latin religious texts.

Very similarly, the Old Norse corpus indicates an overwhelming preference for CAUSE FOR EFFECT metonymies (1707 occurrences out of 2254). Not surprisingly, the four etymological themes yielded by the Old Norse corpus within this category are identical to the Anglo-Saxon motifs, and the distribution of occurrences is practically identical (with a clear preference for the conceptualization of shame as SCORN, followed by DISHONOUR and AMPUTATION and, finally, NAKEDNESS). The CAUSE FOR EFFECT metonymy SHAME IS AMPUTATION is however much more frequent in Old Norse (390 occurrences out of 2254) than in Old English (4 single occurrences out of 2986), which is illustrative of the survival of mutilation as a shame practice in Norwegian-Icelandic laws and legal practice (as illustrated by the *Gulaþingslög* and other medieval legal texts).

The Old Norse corpus has also yielded two different EFFECT FOR CAUSE metonymies for shame, namely SHAME IS REDNESS IN THE FACE and shame is MOVING DOWNWARDS. As in the case of Old English, the connection between shame and changes in body temperature and skin colour is almost entirely limited to religious writing and, less frequently, to the chivalric literature that flourished in Iceland by the end of the 13th century and the subsequent translation of a high number of texts from French, German and Anglo-Norman (Eiríksson 1991: 151). However, the two corpora used here point towards a Germanic origin for the mapping SHAME IS MOVING DOWNWARDS, a metonymy based on the psychological need to escape or hide as a response to shame.

Finally, the corpus has yielded one single occurrence of the conceptual metaphor SHAME IS A PIECE OF CLOTH, which is used to translate the Latin expression *induo confusione*. This confirms the close link between the Christianization of Northern Europe and the progressive introduction of new conceptualizations of shame, which focus not on the causes provoking this emotional experience but on the physiological reactions on the side of the experiencer.

---

9 Cook (2008) analyzes the tensions between these two cultural types as reflected in *Sir Gawain and the Green Knight* (composed by the end of the 15th century), concluding that the external symbols and pressures of Germanic shame culture were clearly embedded in late medieval English society.

From this analysis, it is clear that the concept of shame inherited from the ancient Germanic society is still prevalent in Anglo-Saxon England and in medieval Scandinavia. The Christianization of these two societies did not imply the immediate individualization and subjectification of shame-related experiences, and public shame continued to be a powerful instrument of social control throughout the medieval period. The texts included in these two corpora illustrate, indeed, the very first steps towards the generalization of the new system of values brought by Christianity. In sum, the conceptualization of shame in these two cultures is heavily influenced by the prevailing social and cultural norms that regulate social behaviour, and conceptualizations based on the physiological (and, consequently, universal) responses to shame occupy a completely peripheral position, both in terms of number of mappings and number of occurrences. It goes without saying that speakers of Old English and Old Norse felt these physiological reactions in more or less the same way as modern speakers of these two languages do (a combined study of verbal and visual data, as the one proposed for Old English fear by Díaz-Vera 2013, would probably corroborate this), in spite of which their onomasiological choices unmistakably point towards a preference for shame expressions based on the social causes of shame and its role as a source of law and order. Physiological responses to shame occupy a completely peripheral position in the verbalization of this emotion, and only with the arrival and progressive spread of the new Christian moral standards biological embodiment will start to develop a significant salience in the verbal conceptualization of shame-related experiences.

As an overall conclusion, our analysis of shame expression in two ancient Germanic languages shows that universal biological responses to emotion experiences can be entirely ignored by speakers in the conceptualization of those emotions. As has been shown here, very concrete social and cultural aspects of shame (related to the set of social practices used in both Germanic societies in order to inflict public shame on the deviant individual and as an instrument of social control) are a major conceptual source in Old English and Old Norse texts. Our study clearly confirms previous studies on the non-universality of conceptual metaphors for such emotions as anger (Geerarts and Gevaert 2008) and fear (Díaz-Vera 2011); furthermore we have demonstrated the importance of specific sociocultural features in the conceptualization of an emotion with a very strong social value.

Social and cultural changes (such as, for example, the Christianization of Northern Europe) can eventually produce the progressive development, borrowing and spread of new conceptual mappings within a given social group. Not surprisingly, the new conceptualizations will be based either on universal embodiment (as in the case of SHAME IS REDNESS IN THE FACE) or on culture-specific factors (as in the case of SHAME IS A PIECE OF CLOTH). In either of the two cases, the successful acceptance of a new expression by the whole community of speakers will depend on the onomasiological choices made by the individual language users and on the concrete aspect or aspects of the emotional experience that they prefer to stress through their selection of one concrete emotion expression, be it literal or figurative.

References

Corpora and dictionaries

Buck. 1948. Buck, Carl D. *A dictionary of selected synonyms in the principal Indo-European languages*. Chicago: The University of Chicago Press.
CACELOE. 2014. *Cognitively annotated corpus of emotional language: Old English section*.
Cleasby & Vigfússon = 1967. Cleasby, R. & Vigfússon, G. *An Icelandic-English dictionary*. Oxford: Clarendon Press.
DOE. 2008. *Dictionary of Old English: A–G on CD-ROM*. Toronto: DOE Project.
DOEC. 2000. *The dictionary of Old English corpus in electronic form*. Toronto: DOE Project.
Fritzner. 1867. Fritzner, J. *Ordbog over det gamle norske sprog*. Copenhagen: Karl & Werner.
Lehmann. 1986. Lehmann, Winfred P. *A Gothic etymological dictionary*. Leiden: Brill.
Lewis & Short. 1956. *A Latin dictionary founded on Andrews' edition of Freund's Latin dictionary*. Oxford: Oxford University Press.
Magnússon. 1989. Magnússon, Á. B. *Íslensk orðsifjabók*. Reykjavík: Orðabók Háskólans.
OED. 2000: *Oxford English dictionary* (2nd edn. on CD-ROM). John Simpson, ed. Oxford: Oxford UP.
ONP. 1989. *Ordbog over det norrøne prosasprog – A Dictionary of Old Norse Prose*. Copenhagen: The Arnamagnæan Institute.
Pokorny. 1959. Pokorny, Julius. *Indogermanisches Etymologisches Wörterbuch*. Bern: Francke.
TOE. 1995. Roberts, Jane & Christian Kay. *A thesaurus of Old English*. 1995. London: King's College, CLAMS.

Secondary references

Basson, Alec. 2006. *Divine metaphors in selected Hebrew psalms of lamentation*. Tübingen: Mohr Siebeck.
Beningfield, M. Bradford. 2002. Public penance in Anglo-Saxon England. *Anglo-Saxon England 31*: 223–255.
Birnbaum, Tahlia. 2014. Naming shame: Translating emotion in the Old English psalter glosses. In Alice Jorgensen, Jonathan Wilcox & Frances McCormack (eds.), *Anglo-Saxon emotions: Reading the heart in Old English literature, language and culture*. Farnham: Ashgate.

Cook, April E. 2008. Honor and transgression: The poetics of shame and guilt in 'Sir Gawain and the Green Knight'. *Universitas* 4(1). 1–7.
Corbeill, Anthony. 2003. *Nature embodied: Gesture in ancient Rome*. Princeton, NJ: Princeton University Press.
Cormack, Margaret. 1991. Fiolkunnigri kono scalattu i fadmi sofa. In *The audience of the sagas: The eighth International Saga Conference, Volume 1*, 103–108. Gothemburg: Gothenburg University.
Darwin, Charles. 1972/2005. *The expression of the emotions in man and animals*. New York, NY: Appelton.
Deignan, Alice. 2005. *Metaphor and corpus linguistics*. Amsterdam & Philadelphia: John Benjamins.
Díaz-Vera, Javier E. 2011. Reconstructing the Old English cultural model for 'fear'. *Atlantis: Journal of the Spanish Association of Anglo-American Studies* 33(1). 85–103.
Díaz-Vera, Javier E. 2013. Embodied emotions in medieval English language and visual arts. In Rosario Caballero & Javier E. Díaz-Vera (eds.), *Sensuous cognition – Explorations into human sentience: Imagination, (e)motion and perception*, 195–220. Berlin & New York: Mouton de Gruyter.
Díaz-Vera, Javier E. 2014. From cognitive linguistics to historical linguistics: The evolution of Old English expressions of 'shame' and 'guilt'. *Cognitive Linguistic Studies* 1(1). 55–83.
Eiríksson, Eyvindur. 1991. Some remarks on Middle English influence on Icelandic. In Vladimir Ivir & Damir Kalogjera (eds.), *Languages in contact and contrast: Essays in contact linguistics*, 147–154. Berlin & New York: Mouton de Gruyter.
Gade, Kari Ellen. 1988. The naked and the dead in Old Norse society. *Scandinavian Studies* 60. 219–245.
Geeraerts, Dirk & Caroline Gevaert. 2008. Hearts and (angry) minds in Old English. In Farzad Sharifian, René Dirven, Ning Yu & Susanne Niemeier (eds.), *Culture and language: Looking for the mind inside the body*, 319–347. Berlin & New York: Mouton de Gruyter.
Gevaert, Caroline. 2002. The evolution of the lexical and conceptual field of 'anger' in Old and Middle English. In Javier E. Díaz-Vera (ed.), *A changing world of words: Studies in English historical lexicology, lexicography and semantics*, 275–299. Amsterdam: Rodopi.
Hall, Thomas N. 2003. Ælfric and the Epistle to the Laodiceans. In Kathryn Powell & Donald Scragg (eds.), *Apocryphal texts and traditions*, 65–83. Cambridge: Brewer.
Hartling, Linda M. & Tracy Luchetta. 1999. Humiliation: Assessing the impact of derision, degradation, and debasement. *Journal of Primary Prevention* 19(4). 259–278.
Hiebert, Paul G. 1985. *Anthropological insights for missionaries*. Grand Rapids: Baker Book House.
Hofstede, Gert. 1991. *Cultures and organizations: Software of the mind*. Maidenhead: McGraw-Hill.
Holland, Dorothy & Andrew Kipnis. 1995. American cultural models of embarrassment: The not-so egocentric self laid bare. In James A. Russell, José-Miguel Fernández-Dols, Antony Manstead & J. C. Wellenkamp (eds.) *Everyday conceptions of emotions: An introduction to the psychology, anthropology and linguistics of emotion*, 181–202. Dordrecht: Kluwer Academic Press.
Jochens, Jenny. 1995. *Women in Old Norse society*. Ithaca, NY: Cornell University Press.
Kanerva, Kristiina. 2012. Ógæfa (misfortune) as an emotion in thirteenth-century Iceland. *Scandinavian Studies* 84. 1–26.
Kaufman, Gershen. 1989. *The psychology of shame: Theory and treatment of shame-based syndromes*. New York: Springer.

Kövecses, Zoltan. 1986. A figure of thought. *Metaphor and Symbolic Activity* 6. 29–46.
Kövecses, Zoltan. 1988. *The language of love: The semantics of passion in conversational English*. Lewisburg: Bucknell University Press.
Kövecses, Zoltan. 1990. *Emotion concepts*. New York: Springer-Verlag.
Kövecses, Zoltan. 2000. *Metaphor and emotion: Language, culture and body in human feeling*. Cambridge: Cambridge University Press.
Kövecses, Zoltan. 2005. *Metaphor in culture: Universality and variation*. Cambridge: Cambridge University Press.
Kövecses, Zoltan & Günter Radden. 1998. Metonymy: Developing a cognitive linguistic view. *Cognitive Linguistics* 9(1). 37–77.
Lakoff, George. 1987. *Women, fire, and dangerous things: What categories reveal about the mind*. Chicago: The University of Chicago Press.
Lakoff, George & Mark Johnson. 1980. *Metaphors we live by*. Chicago: University of Chicago Press.
Lakoff, George & Zoltan Kövecses. 1987. The cognitive model of anger inherent in American English. In Dorothy Holland & Naomi Quinn (eds.), *Cultural models in language and thought*, 195–221. Cambridge: Cambridge University Press.
Lewis, Michael. 1995. *Shame: The exposed self*. New York, NY: The Free Press.
Lewis, Michael. 1998. Shame and stigma. In Paul Gilbert & Bernice Andrews (eds.), *Shame: Interpersonal behavior, psychopathology, and culture*, 126–140. Oxford: Oxford University Press.
Lyons, John. 1977. *Semantics, Volume 1*. Cambridge: Cambridge University Press.
MacGushin, Patrick. 1992. *Sallust, the Histories, volume 1*. Oxford: Oxford University Press.
Malina, Bruice J. 2001. *The New Testament world: Insights from cultural anthropology*. Louisville, KY: Westminster John Knox Press.
Meulengracht Sørensen, Preben. 2000. Social institutions and belief systems of Medieval Iceland (c. 870–1400) and their relations to literary production. In Margaret Clunies Ross (ed.), *Old Icelandic literature and society*, 8–29. Cambridge: Cambridge University Press.
Núñez, Rafael E. & Eve Sweetser. 2006. With the future behind them: Convergent evidence from Aymara language and gesture in the crosslinguistic comparison of spatial construals of time. *Cognitive Science* 6. 401–450.
O'Keeffe, Katherine O'Brien. 1998. Body and law in late Anglo-Saxon England. *Anglo-Saxon England* 27: 209–232.
O'Neill, Patrick P. 1981. *The Old-English prose psalms of the Paris Psalter*. Philadelphia: University of Pennsylvania dissertation.
Owen-Crocker, Gale R. 1986. *Dress in Anglo-Saxon England*. Manchester: Manchester University Press.
Pakis, Valentine A. 2005. Honor, verbal duels, and the New Testament in medieval Iceland. *Tijdschrift voor Skandinavistiek* 26(2). 163–185.
Peristiany, Jean G. 1966. Introduction. In Jean G. Peristiany (ed.), *Honour and shame: The values of Mediterranean societies*, 1–18. Chicago: University of Chocago Press.
Pitt-Rivers, Julian. 1966. Honour and social status. In Jean G. Peristiany (ed.), *Honour and shame: The values of Mediterranean societies*, 19–77. Chicago: University of Chocago Press.
Radden, Günter. 2003. How metonymic are metaphors? In René Dirven & Ralf Pörings (eds.), *Metaphor and metonymy in comparison and contrast*, 407–434. Berlin & New York: Mouton de Gruyter.

Robbins, Ira P. 2008. Digitus impudicus: The middle finger and the law. *UC Davis Law Review* 41: 1403–1485.

Stander, Hennie. 2003. Honour and shame as key concepts in Chrysostom's exegesis of the Gospel of John. *HTS Teologiese Studies/ Theological Studies* 59(3). 899–913.

Stanghellini, Giovanni & Rene Rosfort. 2013. *Emotions and personhood: Exploring fragility – Making sense of vulnerability*. Oxford: Oxford University Press.

Stefanowitsch, Anatol. 2004. 'Happiness' in English and German: A metaphorical-pattern analysis. In Michael Achard & Suzanne Kemmer (eds.), *Language, culture, and mind*, 137–149. Stanford: CSLI.

Swanton, Michael J. 1976. 'Dane-Skins': Excoriation in early England. *Folklore* 87(1) : 71–78.

Sweetser, Eve. 1990. *From etymology to pragmatics: Metaphorical and cultural aspects of semantic structure*. Cambridge: Cambridge University Press.

Thompson, Victoria. 2002. *Dying and death in later Anglo-Saxon England*. Woodbridge: Boydell Press.

Tissari, Heli. 2006. Conceptualizing shame: Investigating uses of the English word 'shame', 1418–1991. In Roderick W. McConchie, Olga Timofeeva, Heli Tissari & Tanja Säily (eds.), *Selected Proceedings of the 2005 Symposium on New Approaches in English Historical Lexis (HEL-LEX)*, 143–154. Somerville, MA: Cascadilla Proceedings Project.

Tomkins, Silvan S. 1963. *Affect imagery consciousness: Volume II, The negative affect*. New York, NY: Springer.

Westerhof, Danielle. 2008. *Death and the noble body in Medieval England*. Woodbridge: Boydell Press.

Woolgar, Christopher M. 2006. *The senses in late Medieval England*. New Haven, CT: Yale University Press.

Dylan Glynn
The conceptual profile of the lexeme *home*: A multifactorial diachronic analysis

Abstract: Despite the descriptive power of the Idealised Cognitive Model (Lakoff 1987), the analytical framework faces two inherent problems. First, Idealised Cognitive Models treat language-culture to be a homogenous object study, producing 'idealised' results that do not readily account for social variation or change. Second, they produce results that are not systematically falsifiable, an essential tenet of scientific method. In a diachronic study of the American concept of HOME, this study seeks to develop analytical tools for the empirical description of conceptualisation that produces results sensitive to social variation and that can be falsified. Employing the profile-based usage-feature method (Geeraerts *et al.* 1994, Gries 2003), the study examines samples taken from texts by three 19C American writers (James Cooper, David Thoreau and Fredrick Turner) and two 20C lyricists (Woody Guthrie and Bruce Springsteen). The aim is to determine whether usage-feature analysis is capable of capturing the kind of conceptual structure typical of studies on Idealised Cognitive Models. The analysis focuses on a set of metaphoric source concepts and a range of usage-features chosen as indices of conceptual structure. Using multivariate statistics, it investigates the relationship between the different metaphors relative to their usage over the course of two centuries. The study demonstrates the proof-of-principle that socially sensitive and falsifiable descriptive studies of culturally determined conceptual structure are possible.

1 Introduction

The Idealised Cognitive Model, proposed by Lakoff (1987), represents a powerful descriptive tool for making generalisations about language, society and cultural worldview. However, the analytical framework it employs and the methodological premises it assumes face two fundamental limitations. Firstly, the 'idealised' nature of the proposed language-culture structures is at odds with the theory's usage-based assumptions (Langacker 1987) and does not produce descriptions that are sensitive to social variation. Secondly, the analytical

---

Dylan Glynn: University of Paris VIII

method of lexical semantic co-occurrence lacks a means for the falsification of the findings it produces, a limitation that runs contrary to the broader methodological assumptions of empirical science. Despite this, the study does not argue that the analytical method of Idealised Cognitive Models is inherently flawed. Indeed, its role is essential in developing hypotheses about socio-cultural-linguistic structure. Instead, it is argued that we need to develop an empirical methodology designed to test hypotheses proposed with the Idealised Cognitive Model framework.

The goal of this study is to demonstrate the feasibility of using multivariate usage-feature analysis for the description of conceptual structures in language and culture. This method was developed by Dirven *et al.* (1982), Rudzka-Ostyn (1989), and Geeraerts (1990). However, the application of multivariate statistics to the results of the analysis is the step that gives the method its descriptive power. Drawing on established quantitative methods in sociolinguistics, Geeraerts *et al.* (1994, 1999) and Gries (1999, 2003) developed the use of such categorical multivariate techniques. In recent years, the method has gained popularity and is termed the profile-based approach by Gries and Divjak (2009), Divjak (2010a, 2010b) and Deshors and Gries (2014) and multivariate usage-feature analysis by Glynn (2009, 2010a, 2010b, 2014c, 2014d, submitted), Krawczak and Kokorniak (2012), Krawczak (2014a, 2014b), Fabiszak *et al.* (2014) and Klavan (2014).

The concept of HOME is a fundamental one in Germanic languages and culture. This study draws on both qualitative and quantitative methods in an attempt at describing the concept and its diachronic variation in 19th and 20th century Anglo-Saxon American culture. It bases its analysis on two specific genres and a single lexeme, but is part of a larger project that examines a range of lexemes and genres (Glynn to appear). The results presented here include occurrences of the lexeme *home* in J. Cooper (1789–1851), H. Thoreau (1817–1862), and F. Turner (1861–1932), for the 19th and from the ballads of W. Guthrie (1912–1967) and B. Springsteen (1949–) for the 20th century. Although these sources and the text types are distinct, their place in two diachronically distinct contexts is arguably comparable.

Limiting the study in such a way makes it possible to better control for stylistic effects, but limits the representativeness of the findings. It is argued that by selecting the sources in this manner, we can be precisely sure of what our results represent, even if this is at the cost of being able to make broad generalisations. In order to establish how general the results are, future studies, taking divergent sources, would need to be undertaken.

Section 2 presents the data and the analysis. The results of the analysis and their interpretation are found in section 3. The discussion ends with a summary in section 4.

2 Data and Analysis

2.1 Lexeme and concept

Both the concept HOME and lexeme *home* (*hjam* Northumbrian; *hjem* Cumbrian; *haim* Scots, *Heim* German, *heim* Icelandic, *hem* Swedish, Danish) hold a special place in Anglo-Saxon culture and, indeed, Germanic culture and languages more generally. The Proto Germanic origin **haimaz*, like its contemporary counter part, appears to be an abstract concept, not restricted to a building and ultimately derives from the Proto Indo-European root **tkei-* 'To lie, settle down'. The abstract nature of the meaning of the lexeme is evident synchronically in how it is extended to include a country, a street, a village or, in fact, any place where one holds an emotional attachment, perhaps related to one's origins or a feeling of personal security. The same is true diachronically and this is evident in the wide range of uses and variants, across the Germanic languages, which are not restricted to a specific lodging or building.

In this, the lexeme is distinct from that of *house* (*Haus* German, *huis* Dutch, *hus* Swedish and Danish, *hús* Frisian and Icelandic, *house/hoose* Scots, **husan* Proto Germanic), whose ultimate origin is uncertain, but which profiles the function of a building, its role in sheltering and protecting. This understanding of the word is in line with a proposal expressed by various dictionaries that the word derives from a proto Indo-European root **keudh-* 'hide'. (Cf. West Germanic **hudjan*). Importantly, the lexical semantic distinction between *house* and *home* is present in all but one Germanic language, while it is effectively absent in other European language families.[1] The *casa* and *dom* roots in the Romance and Slavic languages typically mean 'house' or even 'building', but not specifically 'home'.[2]

---

[1] Modern Dutch and Frisian have no cognate, but have modified a form of the cognate for *house* to indicate 'home'. The lexemes *huis* and *hûs* 'house' have produced *thuis* and *thús* respectively and mean something closer to the abstract concept of HOME than 'house' *per se*. The existence of the variant is, perhaps, testimony to the importance of the concept. However, of course, that the original cognates for *home*, *heem* (Middle Dutch) and *hem* (Old Frisian), were lost could be offered as a counter argument. Note also, that the South Slavic languages, Bulgarian, Macedonian, Serbo-Croatian and Slovenian, have the distinction between 'home' and 'house', drawing on the Germanic root in the alternation. For example, in Slovenian, the lexeme *doma* refers to the English equivalent *home*, while the lexeme *hiša* indicates 'house'. It is important to note that these observations should not be taken to suggest that other European languages lack a means for expressing the concept of HOME. Often, a partially lexicalised phrase fills the role, such as *u sebja* in Russian or *chez soi* in French, both of which express a concept of being at one's own place, wherever that may be.

[2] Cf. *casa* Spanish, Italian and Catalan, *casă* Romanian, *chambre* French, *domo* Sardinian, *dom* Polish and Russian, *dim* Ukrainian, and *dům* in Czech.

However, the aim of this study is to go beyond lexical semantics. It seeks to operationalise the Idealised Cognitive Model in order to render falsifiable the broad cultural generalisations typical of the work of Wierzbicka and Lakoff. A cloudless flight across Europe will reveal the transition from the sparsely placed 'hams' of northwest Europe to the village clusters of southwest Europe. In the north, large houses surrounded by fields, fenced off from their neighbours by a close row of trees are in direct contrast to the tightly knit clusters of the idyllic Mediterranean villages. Although such cultural generalisations are possible, when based on *ad hoc* observations of lexical semantics or even town planning, regardless of how true or informative, such generalisations do not make social science. Instead of examining lexical semantics *per se*, we examine, systematically, the *contextualised use* of the lexemes, in the hope that generalisations about culture can be made in way that is not only falsifiable, but also sensitive to diachronic social variation.

2.2 Choice of data

This study seeks to develop methods for the description of cognitive models. The diachronic dimension that this paper focuses upon is an example of the kind of descriptive challenge an empirical method for conceptual analysis must be able to meet. In total, 300 occurrences, 150 from both the 19th and 20th centuries, were taken with substantial context.[3] The relatively small number is due to the fact that examples must be manually analysed. Moreover, the choice of sources for the data is somewhat unusual and warrants justification.

Rather than examine a diachronic corpus, such as Davies (2010), five specific writers were chosen. There are two justifications for this. Firstly, the inherent limitation of corpus-driven research is that every occurrence is treated equally. In other words, each use of a form is assumed to have the same value or degree of contribution to the language-culture system. Although a valid operationalisation, such an assumption cannot completely explain language', cultural knowledge or conceptual structure. Certain occurrences, due to differences in perceptual salience or cultural relevance, carry more or less weight. By biasing the data in favour of certain types of examples of language use, the study is an experiment that seeks to respond to this methodological limitation.

---

[3] The data were extracted and cleaned by Joakim Sten. An entirely distinct analysis of the data is presented in Sten and Glynn (2011).

Secondly, having explained the use of specific authors, we need to consider why we chose authors from different genres. When performing diachronic studies, one normally seeks to obtain data from a single text type or genre. Despite the sound reasoning of this line of methodology, it entails an inherent circularity. Firstly, a genre is a part of the time it comes from. Although some genres do persist over long periods, they all eventually die or become something entirely different. The novel, in the contemporary understanding of the term, is a relatively new genre, just as news press. Already, many would consider, rightly or wrongly, the novel to be on track to be replaced by other media. News press is also changing and in such a dramatic way that it is becoming difficult to speak of a single genre diachronically. The broadsheet is already dead in the English speaking world and the six o'clock news, online news sites and editorial blogs are in line to end Fleet Street, even within the current generation. Those few genres that have persisted over longer periods of time, such as poetry and theatre, are arguably archaic if one is seeking linguistic evidence for a contemporary conceptualisation of the world. That is not to say that they are uninformative, but there is an argument to be made for taking a genre that is typical of its time, rather than a genre that exits in two different times. In other words, by keeping genre a constant in a diachronic study on culture or conceptual structure, one may actually weaken the representativeness of the data. For this reason, texts that are representative of the distinct periods are chosen rather than selecting texts that maintain genre consistency. Due to this choice, care must be taken not to interpret stylistic variation in terms of any underlying cultural or conceptual structure.

For the 19th century, the works of two writers are taken: James Fenimore Cooper, a popular writer of historical romances about the nation building era of the United States of America and Henry David Thoreau, a popular philosopher who was also concerned with the topic. A single text, *The Frontier in American History* (1893), by Frederick Jackson Turner, written somewhat later, though still within the culture and times of the 19th century, is also included. It is felt that this text is in keeping with the style and era concerned and addresses especially the concept of HOME in the nation building of North America.

Turning to the 20th century, the idea is to work with texts that have a comparable socio-cultural role to the texts of the 19th century. To these ends, we draw upon the popular ballads of two writers who are held to be spokespeople of their generation and nation. Like their 19th century compatriots, the popular songwriters Woodrow Wilson Guthrie and Bruce Frederick Springsteen are concerned with their nation, its wellbeing and identity (Shelton 1986; Marsh 1987; Cray 2004). Moreover, the concept of HOME, both in the personal sense and in the society sense of homeland, is an important theme in their work (Partridge 2002; Guterman 2005; Cowie and Lauren 2006; Jackson 2007; and Lifshey 2009). Songs such as "This land is your land" (Guthrie 1940), *"Pastures of plenty"* (Guthrie 1941*)*, *"Bound for Glory"* (Guthrie 1942), *"Hard travelin'"* (Guthrie 1944*)*, *or* "Born to run" (Springsteen 1974), "Backstreets" (Springsteen 1975), "The river" (1979) and "Born in the USA" (Springsteen 1982) would be known, as least passively, to most contemporary English speakers. Like so much of their work, these exampels treat the notion of home, to varying degrees, in relation to the individual, to their generation and even to the nation.[4]

2.3 Usage-Feature Analysis

The aim of the feature analysis is to operationalise semantic profiling in such a way that the use of the lexeme (as opposed the the lexeme itself) can be treated as an index of conceptual structure. Before we exemply the actual usage-feature analysis, we begin with some examples of the texts in question. Examples (1) to (5) are chosen to represent the diverse styles, yet similarity in theme across the authors and periods. It should be noted how the examples include instances of use that go beyond the strict lexical semantics of *home*. It is an essential part of the proposed methodology that the emerging picture is one of the cognitive model in the broad cultural sense and not of the concept associated with the lexeme in any strict sense. The italics are added.

(1) Others left the country; seeking in that place they emphatically called *home*, an asylum, as they fondly hoped, for a season only, against the confusion and dangers of war.
(Cooper, *The Spy: A tale of the neutral ground*)

(2) But the place which you have selected for your camp, though never so rough and grim, begins at once to have its attractions, and becomes a very center of civilization to you: *Home* is home, be it never so homely.
(Thoreau, *Canoeing in the Wilderness*)

(3) The Mississippi Valley has been the especial *home* of democracy. But the democracy born of free land, strong in selfishness and individualism.
(Turner, *Frontier in American History*)

---

4 For sake of consistency, Guthrie's novel *House of Earth* is not included in the sample.

(4) Yes, we ramble and we roam. And the highway that's our *home*. It's a never-ending highway. For a dust bowl refugee.
(Guthrie, *Dust Bowl Refugee*)

(5) Sent me off to a foreign land. To go and kill the yellow man. I come back *home* to the refinery. Hiring man says "Son, if it was up to me".
(Springsteen, *Born in the USA*)

The challenge for a quantitative analysis is to operationalise the kind of meaning carried by this lexeme in such a way that falsifiable generalisations can be made. In order to approach this question, we need to think about how *home* is being used to profile different dimensions of the concept HOME. In example (1), the referent of *home* is a 'country', that is a political entity associated with a physical place. Whether this should be treated as a metaphor, a metonym, or a literal usage depends on how one defines the lexeme *home* in the first place. If the literal understanding of *home* is a 'house' where you feel safe or where you grew up, then the reading is metaphoric. If the literal definition of *home* is a place where you feel safe or from where you originate, then the reading is metonymic. If *home* is defined as any association of belongingness or safety, then the reading is literal. We will leave this question aside for the moment (q.v. section 2.3.1).

Thoreau's example of *home* (2), typical of the complex relationship between 'land' and 'home', speaks of taking untamed land, which is not a home and making it one by taming it. This example not only highlights important characteristics of what HOME is (and is not), it appears to speak of one's natural desire to make any place safe and homely, regardless of where it is or how unfriendly the context. The third example is from Turner who is later than Thoreau or Cooper and stylistically quite distinct. As a historian, his discourse is much more concerned with politics and law, but his examples are narrative descriptions of the trials and tribulations of home and land. In example (3), LAND is the source concept for HOME, regardless of what kind of conceptual relations that entails, but it not the home of a human, instead of an abstract idea.

The songwriters of the 20th century are, of course, markedly different in style, but they share the same concern for the concept at hand. In contrast to the role of 'land' in the 19th century, the relationship between *streets* and *home* is especially important in the 20th century texts. At a denotation level, it is far from obvious why streets would be chosen as a counter part to the 19th century land. However, in the urban 20th century, when we are discussing a social space, that can be your home by heritage, or can be made your home, a place you belong, the concept of STREET, in its metaphoric or metonymic usage, is a comparable concept.

Example (4) serves as a good example of how the concept of STREET, here profiled as highway, is a source domain for HOME. Such questions are not treated in this study, but are important in the broader research project (cf. Glynn to appear). In Springsteen's example (5), *home* is used in an abstract sense, but not linked to LAND, NATION or HOUSE, but an ABSTRACT PLACE, here metonymically represented by an oil refinery. The individual comes home from war, to find he has no home because his job has gone. The lexeme *home* is understood here in a complex metaphoric and metonymic sense. The refinery is, in fact, not the home, but it represents security and origins, standing for HOME metonymically.

2.3.1 Conceptual structures of similarity and contiguity

The feature analysis of the conceptual structure faces several challenges. Instead of identifying metaphors and metonymies, the analysis simply identifies what are termed 'source concepts'. This is in order to avoid the issue of distinguishing conceptual structures of similarity and contiguity, which proved impossible to adequately operationalise. Let us briefly consider why.

Firstly, the concept of HOME was often found to have a complex relationship with the concept of LAND. Consider examples (6a) and (6b).

(6) a. America was not simply a new *home*; it was a land of opportunity.
(Turner, *The Frontier in American History*)
b. ... rapid conquest of the wilderness. We have so far won our national *home*.
(Turner, *The Frontier In American History*)

The complexity arises from the fact that the notion of 'home' itself is so abstract that almost anything can be used to indicate home, or at least a feeling of home. Example (7) demonstrates why this is important.

(7) Now honey, I don't wanna clip your wings. But a time comes when two people should think of these things. Having a *home* and a family. Facing up to their responsibilities.
(Springsteen, *I Wanna Marry You*)

Are these examples figurative? At first, we might assume them to be literal. However, in the context of the genres in question, it is a reasonable argument that the author is expecting the audience to extrapolate from this literal reference in a metonymic, and perhaps even, metaphoric manner. In example (7) the meaning of *home* is the physical place where one feels safe and experiences a sense of belonging. At some level, of course, the relationship between these two facets of the meaning is figurative. In a given example, if one is foregrounding the actual place and backgrounding the abstract associations that determine the place, then the reading is metonymic – the place stands for the association. A quotidian expression such as *I'm going home* would be an example of this kind. In such a situation, the place one feels safe is foregrounded and the state of feeling safe is backgrounded, the place metonymically standing for the abstract concept. However, if one is foregrounding the abstract concept and the concrete place is not the referent, then we can interpret this as a metaphor. For example, the idiom *wherever I leave my hat is home* is clearly metaphoric, even if the source domain could be interpreted as metonymic; the place that you 'leave your hat' standing for the place you 'feel at home'. The complexity arises in natural examples, such as (7). Springsteen is speaking in abstract terms, with no specific physical shelter in mind. This is made clear by the reference to 'clipping of wings', where freedom is set up as the opposite of the staid concept of HOME and reiterated by the collocation – *having a home*, which, like *having a family*, is often associated with metaphoric uses. This example, which is both relatively straightforward and typical of the usages of the lexemes in the sample, poses a serious analytical question. Are such examples literal, metaphoric or metonymic? If they are figurative, what then are the source domains or broader concepts that are activated?

The metaphoric structuring in examples (8a) and (8b) should be clearer.

(8) a. Tonight I got dirt on my hands but I'm building me a new *home*.
   (Springsteen, *Lucky Town*)
   b. It meant to them, as to the American pioneer that preceded them, the opportunity to destroy the bonds of social caste that bound them in their older *home*, to hew out for themselves in a new country a destiny proportioned to the powers that God had given them, a chance to place their families under better conditions and to win a larger life than the life that they had left behind.
   (Turner, *The Frontier in American History*)

In example (8a), the metaphor is that of hard work being the foundation for a HOME. Such examples of the Protestant work ethic abound in the sample but it is not always clear whether this is metonymic or metaphoric. Example (8a) is of the same kind as that identified by Goossens (1990), which he terms metaphtonymy. Since it is not always clear whether the source concept is a part of the target concept or distinct from the target concept; whether the conceptual relation is one of contiguity or similarity is difficult to determine. In natural dialogue, unless the speaker intends a pun or blend, such ambiguity is probably quite rare. However, in literary texts, such as those we are considering here, such ambiguity is commonplace. In (8a), the agent is literally working and literally getting his or her hands dirty doing so, but we cannot know whether this is literally part of building a shelter that will serve as a home or whether the physical labour is distinct from the abstract nature of home building, but metaphorically designates it, by, for example, going out to work every day to earn money to buy a home. Indeed, in (8a), it is likely that dirt is used metaphorically for criminal activity, adding further to the complexity of the interpretation. Knowing that this is literary text and thus necessarily decontextualised, such examples are inherently both metaphoric and metonymic and are probably intended as such by their authors.

It is not the point of this study to delve into the intricacies of metaphor analysis. Despite the importance of such a discussion, our concern here is a simple operationalisation of these subjective notions that will enable repeatable and falsifiable results. For these reasons, no effort is made to distinguish metaphor and metonymy in the analysis. For each example, the target concept, be that an independent concept (metaphor) or a dependent 'part' of the source concept (metonymy), is annotated. The same principle is applied to the source concept. When the lexeme *home* refers to a 'house', the source concept is treated as HOUSE, when it refers to 'land', it is treated as LAND and when it refers to an abstract place, it is annotated as PLACE. By pairing the two at the end of the analysis, we know what two concepts are involved in each example, but not whether their relation is one of similarity of contiguity. Further details on exactly what concepts are identified are offered below in section 3.1.

Example (8b) represents yet another problem in the conceptual analysis. Here we have two conceptual profilings of HOME. The first, similar to that of (7), is of a constrained existence: the experiencer is 'bound' to their 'home' by 'social caste'. However, in the example, a second conceptualisation of HOME,

Tab. 1: Frequency of source concepts relative to period.

	place	house	land	nation	Total
19C	42	57	29	11	139
20C	61	61	14	12	148
Total	103	118	43	23	287

contrasted with the previous, is also presented. The Protestant belief that hard work is the basis of a good life is overtly indicated with the reference to God and the metaphor of hewing out a nation, which we can read as 'building a home'. So, which metaphor is relevant here, the WORK-BUILD metaphor or the CONSTRAINT-LIMIT metaphor? In such situations, the metaphor directly associated with the lexeme in question in analysed and not any others. This leads to situations where the more conceptually rich metaphor is omitted from the study, but following this principle systematically is the only way of operationalising the analysis.

The systematic analysis of all the examples revealed the following source concepts: HOUSE, LAND, NATION, PERSON, STREET and ABSTRACT PLACE. The concepts PERSON and STREET were only found in the 20th century and were infrequent. These examples are not included in the study. The frequencies of the remaining examples, distributed across the different source concepts, are presented in Table 1.

2.3.2 Semantic usage-features

The theory of Idealised Cognitive Models is not exclusively about metaphoric and metonymic structuring. Indeed, on the contrary, it is an abstraction across representations of the world, indexed by language structure, and, from a usage-based approach, across the usage of language. Usage-based cognitive models, based on re-occurring instances of actual language use, permit the addition of formal and semantic characteristics to the description of metaphors: just as each utterance is analysed for its source and target concept, a range of other usage features are annotated.

For example, two formal and objectifiable identifiable categories, the main verb and the preposition of the *home* noun phrase, can be used as clues to the semantic nature of the source domain. In the above examples, the prepositional and verbal collocates, 'have a home", "in the land", "build a home", "in their home", when identified across all the occurrences can be found to be associated with or indicative of certain metaphors and or metonyms. This approach is not employed here, but is used in Glynn (to appear). In the current study, we focus on a range of purely semantic features.

The semantic analysis is based on determining the *designatum* for each occurrence and then through a semantic analysis of the context, a set of semantic features are ascribed to the utterance. The semantic features are what the Russian tradition would term conceptual analysis (Stepanov 1997 and Vorkachev 2007 *inter alia*). In the Cognitive Linguistics tradition, they are simply encyclopaedic semantic usage-features. Systematically identifying such features is the basis of the methodology and was established by Dirven *et al.* (1982), Rudzka-Ostyn (1989) and Geeraerts (1990).

Each of these semantic usage-features is operationalised with a simple question. There are three possible values in response: (i) the attribute in question is profiled in the example; (ii) the absence of the attribute is profiled in the example, (iii) the attribute is not profiled (its absence or presence) in the example. This third category is important since, in many examples, not all the features are applicable. The semantic features include:

Lodging: Is the designatum serving as a place to 'live'?
Shelter: Is the designatum designed to protect from nature?
Comfort: Is the designatum felt to provide comfort?
Security: Is the designatum expected to provide security?
Origins: Is the designatum understood as a place of origin?
Belonging: Is the designatum held to be a place of belonging?
Possession: Is the designatum profiled as being owned?
Struggle: Is the designatum perceived as a goal in a struggle?
Building: Is the designatum described as something to build?

The analysis of such features is inherently subjective and therefore of questionable reliability. There are four responses to this important and valid criticism. First, all semantic analysis is inherently subjective. Obviously introspection and elicitation methods are subjective, but the usage-based observation of formal and objectifiable phenomena also possesses an inherently subjective dimension. Collocation studies and other corpus techniques that restrict the data to formal occurrences and co-occurrences may be objective in the actual data analysis, but the interpretation of the results of formal analysis remains entirely subjective. What it means that a given form (co)occurs more often than another form is far from obvious, especially when the exact uses of the forms in question are unknown. In contrast to such studies, the repeated and close manual nature of usage-feature analysis means that the details of the use are taken into consideration.

Second, the overt, systematic and repeated analysis of contextualised examples maximises the reliability of the analysis. The overt nature of this method means the analysis can be checked and/or repeated and multiple 'coders' can analyse the same data and their results compared. If this is done, a Kappa score can be used to determine the reliability of the analysis. Zeschel (2010) and Glynn (2010a) are examples of the use of such a technique.

Third, for the most part, the subjective analysis is straightforward, in that it is clear which conceptual or functional category applies to a given example.

Therefore, for the majority of examples, the analysis, although subjective, is reliable.

Fourth, the results are modelled using statistical analysis. This arguably lends a degree of objectivity to the interpretation of the results. Not only does statistical analysis tolerate a certain amount of 'noise' in the data, the reliability of the results can be ascertained using predictive modelling (cf. Glynn 2014a) Although this does not actually add objectivity to the analysis, it does allow a means for testing accuracy. There is a strong argument that, in semantic analysis, accuracy is more important than objectivity, which is ultimately impossible. If a subjective analysis is found to be able to predict natural language use, then this adds to the argument that the original analysis, though subjective, was accurate. Let us now consider each of the features.

The first feature is that of 'lodging'. This category is quite straightforward and distinguishes *designata* that are houses or lean-tos and cabins from homelands and hometowns and streets of one's childhood. It is exemplified in (9).

(9) Some guys they just give up living. And start dying little by little, piece by piece. Some guys come *home* from work and wash up. And go racin' in the street.
(Springsteen, *Racing in the Street*)

'Shelter' is equally straightforward and is used to identify examples where protection from the elements or nature is important. Although one would expect it to be distinctly associated with frontier literature, where the dangers of nature were real and ever-present, it is interesting, that this feature of the concept is also important in the 20th century examples. Perhaps this is because of the homelessness caused by the Great Depression about which Guthrie wrote and the hardships of urban youth culture, which Springsteen treats metaphorically as life on the streets.

(10) I was trying to make it *home* through the forest before the darkness falls.
(Springsteen, *My Father's House*)

The semantic feature of 'comfort' is slightly more subjective since it is largely determined through speculation based on context. In examples where it was not reasonably clear that this dimension of the concept of HOME was profiled, the feature was not annotated. Example (11) is representative of this feature.

(11) Still, there was a smiling expression of good-humor in his happy countenance, that was created by the thoughts of *home* and a Christmas fireside,

with its Christmas frolics.
(Cooper, *The Pioneers*)

In example (12), *home* is used in contrast to the tent in a battlefield encampment. Although *home* here surely entails comfort, we can also infer that it represents a place of 'security' away from the war. In both the 19th and 20th century data, there is a substantial number of examples that concern coming home or being away from home because of war but also of examples the world is depicted as a dangerous place, in contrast to HOME, which is safe.

(12) Lord, squatter, when I was a man in the pride and strength of my days, I have looked in at the tent door of the enemy, and they sleeping, ay, and dreaming too, of being at *home* and in peace!
(Cooper, *The Prairie*)

The next semantic feature is that of 'origins'. An important, though quite marked conceptual profile is where the principle *designatum* is one's national origin (in terms of migration) or one's hometown / streets. This feature is surprisingly common with over 100 occurrences and is reasonably simple to identify. Examples (13a)–(13b) are representative

(13) a. At sixteen she quit high school to make her fortune in the promised land. She got a job behind the counter in an all night hamburger stand. She wrote faithfully *home* to mama.
(Springsteen, *Big Things One Day Come*)
b. ... as this lady, a younger sister of their deceased mother, had left her paternal *home*, in the colony of Virginia ...
(Cooper, *The Spy: A Tale of the Neutral Ground*)

The most difficult feature to identify is 'belonging'. This is designed to capture the very abstract emotional attachment between an experiencer and the *designatum* conceptualised as home. Great care was taken to restrict the annotation to instances where this feature was clearly profiled. However, the subjective nature of the category warrants caution in interpreting results based upon it, especially since it is imaginably quite a 'central' element to the conceptualisation of HOME. Examples (14a) and (14b) are typical.

(14) a. Wherever you may roam. You'll never find what you left behind. Your loved ones and your *home*.
(Guthrie, *Ramblin' Reckless Hobo Letra*)

b. ... but the truth is, their houses are floating ones, and their *home* is on the ocean.
(Thoreau, *Cape Cod*)

Although not rare, the semantic feature of 'possession' was not particularly common, only 56 occurrences being identified for the target concept of HOME. Typically, it is associated with the themes of land squatting and repossession / mortgage foreclosure. Its identification was straightforward as can be seen in example (15). Typically, it was the absence of possession that was profiled.

(15) a. Rich man took my *home* and drove me from my door.
(Guthrie, *I Ain't Got No Home*)

The feature of 'struggle' is also a highly subjective feature to identify yet surprisingly important with 104 occurrences. The notion of struggle included the concepts of fighting and winning and should not be understood as necessarily linked to hardship. Whether this is merely a result of the genres that make up the data set or a characteristic of the American concept of HOME cannot be determined, but it is surely a result that warrants further investigation. Consider examples (16a) and (16b).

(16) a. Now I was young and pretty on the mean streets of the city. And I fought to make 'em my *home*.
(Springsteen, *When Your Alone*)
b. ... the cry of rapid conquest of the wilderness. We have so far won our national *home*, wrested from it its first rich treasures ...
(Turner, *The Frontier in American History*)

The final semantic feature of the actual conceptual profiling of HOME is termed 'building', exemplified in (17a)–(17c). This feature is straightforward and identifies instances where the building of the home, whether literal or figurative, plays a role in the conceptualisation.

(17) a. Lincoln represents rather the pioneer folk who entered the forest of the great Northwest to chop out a *home*, to build up their fortunes in the midst of a continually ascending industrial movement.
(Turner, *The Frontier in American History*)
b. We can spend our lives in love. You're a hesitating beauty Nora Lee. We can build a house and *home*.
(Guthrie, *Hesitating Beauty*)

c. Wish me luck my lovely, I'll send for you when I can. And we'll make our *home* in the American land.
(Springsteen, *American Land*)

3 Results and Interpretation

In order to understand the relative associations between the different semantic features and the conceptual structures, we employ two exploratory multivariate techniques. Firstly, we cluster the examples, using hierarchical cluster analysis. This allows us to check whether the semantic features profile the source concepts identified and not the stylistic variation between the two genres. Secondly, the data are submitted to a binary correspondence analysis. This reveals what associations are causing the clustering in the previous analysis. The systematicity of the data behaviour is explained, and any differences and similarities between the two periods identified. A third step, submits the same data to a multiple correspondence analysis in order to look for relations between the semantic features themselves. The results of this analysis are, in turn, clustered in order to determine the underlying structure of the results.

3.1 Clustering of concepts relative to semantic features

The first step is to determine how the different source concepts in question cluster, relative to the semantic features and the two periods. In other words, how do the semantic features group the concepts across the 19th and 20th century datasets? If we were to find that the concepts are clustered into two groups, 19th and 20th century, then it would be likely that the semantic features are interacting with the stylistic differences and cannot be used to describe the conceptual variation. Figure 1, below, is a dendrogram of a hierarchical agglomerative cluster analysis with multiscale bootstrap resampling.[5] The distance matrix employed is the Euclidean, which is the simplest and most neutral. The agglomerating method is Ward, which is standard for small sample (Divjak and Fieller 2014).

In Figure 1, the numbers under the branches indicate the order of clustering and the numbers above are the bootstrapped confidence scores. The number to the left (au) is an unbiased probability, calculated with multiscale boot-

---

[5] Cluster analysis performed with the R package pvclust (Suzuki and Shimodaira 2011).

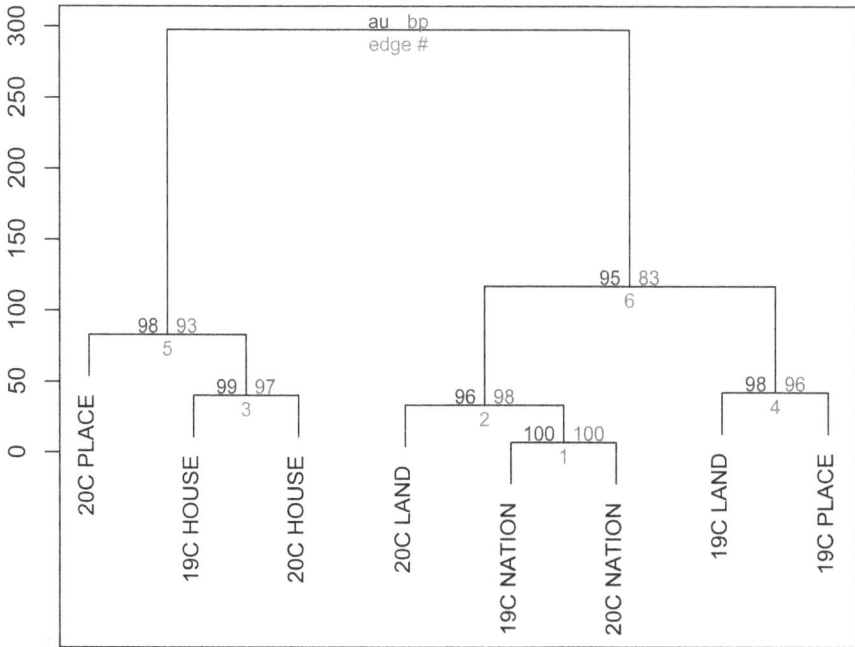

Fig. 1: Cluster analysis of century and concept relative to semantics.

strap resampling and the number to the right a standard bootstrap probability. The former is argued to be more accurate (Shimodaira 2004). The bootstrapped estimated *p*-values are all high, especially considering the number of semantic features and the small sample size.

Intuitively, two clusters, 19C and 20C HOUSE and 19C and 20C NATION appear informative. That these concepts group together across the two periods demonstrates that, at least for these concepts, the semantic features are not primarily interacting with stylistic differences between the genres. In contrast to this, the cluster of 19C LAND and 19C PLACE could be argued to be a result of stylistic similarity. However, given that the 20C LAND and 20C PLACE show no evidence of clustering along genre lines and that we expect variation between the two periods, we can conclude, with some confidence, that the possibility that the semantic features merely identify stylistic differences between the two periods is not the case.

If we accept this, we have a first result. The conceptualisation of HOME as HOUSE and as a NATION has not changed over the last 200 hundred years, yet conceptualisation of LAND and ABSTRACT PLACE as HOME may have. We can now investigate these possibilities by examining how the different semantic features cluster the concepts relative to period.

Tab. 2: Principal inertias (eigenvalues).

dim	value	%	cum%	scree plot
1	0.109238	53.3	53.3	*************************
2	0.046959	22.9	76.2	***********
3	0.027404	13.4	89.6	******
4	0.009982	4.9	94.5	**
5	0.006780	3.3	97.8	**
6	0.003215	1.6	99.3	*
7	0.001366	0.7	100.0	
Total	0.204944	100.0		

3.2 Correspondences between concepts and semantic features

Correspondence analysis is an exploratory multivariate technique that identifies associations in complex data (Glynn 2014b). We use it here in an attempt to reveal what causes the clustering revealed in Figure 1 and, in doing so, we obtain a semantic profile of each of the conceptualisations relative to period. Before we interpret the biplot presented in Figure 2, we need to determine if the analysis is stable and if the two-dimensional representation is capable of capturing the interactions in the data. Consider the scree plot of the analysis presented, above, in table 2.[6]

We see in the scree plot that the first two dimensions, those visualised, accurately represent 76 % of the complexity (inertia). The score represents a reliable result. However, note that there is no clear 'elbow' in the scree plot and that the third dimension, not included in the visualisation, would contribute another 13.4 % to the explanation of the behaviour of the data. This suggests that two-dimensions are not entirely sufficient to represent the behaviour of the data. For this reason, some care must be taken in the interpretation of the results.

This correspondence analysis is based on 21 mathematical dimensions, corresponding to all the semantic features concerned, minus one (the scree plot, above, includes only the first seven). The analysis calculates the contribution of each of the semantic feature dimensions to the first two axes – visualised dimensions. In other words, it quantifies how important a feature is in explaining the behaviour of, or the structuring of, the data. These values are also calculated for the concepts. Based on these values and the overall analy-

---

[6] Scree plot produced using R package ca (Nenadić and Greenacre 2007).

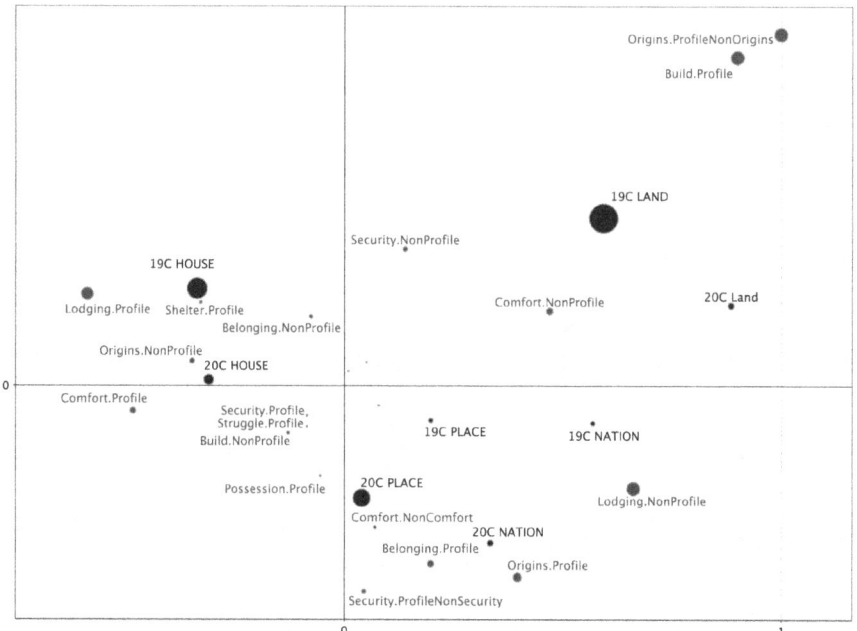

Fig. 2: Binary correspondence analysis of concept-period and semantics.

sis, it is possible to calculate the accuracy, or quality, of the representation of each data point of the plot. Using the ca package in R (Nenadic and Greenacre 2007), these quality scores were calculated, each score out of 1000. Data points with scores lower than 500 should be treated with caution (Greenacre 2007). For practical reasons, the scores are not presented, but all of the concept data points obtained quality scores over 500 save 19C PLACE and 20C LAND. For the semantic features, the 'shelter' and 'belonging' features both scored between 400 and 500 and the 'struggle' data points scored beneath 200.

Having established that the representation is reasonably stable and identified which data points could be misleading, we can interpret the results of the analysis visualised in Figure 2.[7] Three data points, 19C LAND, 19C HOUSE and 20C PLACE, dominate the structure of the plot in terms of contribution, indicated by the size of the 'bubble' identifying the data point. The contributions of 20C HOUSE, 19C HOUSE and the semantic feature of 'lodging' are also important. The position of 20C PLACE, close to the y-axis, means that it is associated with

---

[7] The correspondence analyses in Figures 2 and 3 and the various analyses in Figure 4 were performed with the R package FactoMineR (Husson *et al.* 2012).

all the features in the bottom half of the plot. However, given that the majority of the features in the left bottom quadrant contribute little to the structuring of the data (they are close to the *x*-axis, thus not strongly associated with the data space in the bottom of the plot), we should be careful interpreting any strong degree of correlation. Nevertheless, it is clear that the semantic features clustering broadly around 20C PLACE are characteristic of this concept. Perhaps most importantly, it must be noted that 19C PLACE groups clearly with the same set of semantic features as 20C PLACE, suggesting that the two concepts have not changed over the two centuries.

In the same quadrant, we have 19C and 20C NATION, sharing the association of the semantic features with the 19C and 20C PLACE data points. This appears to be a clear result showing that the semantic profiles of PLACE and NATION are extremely similar and that both have remained largely constant over the two periods. However, as we will see below, this particular pattern may be misleading.

The top right-hand quadrant is dominated by 19C and 20C HOUSE. This set of associations is surely stable. The position of 20C HOUSE on the *x*-axis means that the features in the bottom left quadrant are associated with it, in contrast to 19C HOUSE, which lies in the centre of the quadrant. Although the differences are small, they are intuitively sound: 19C HOUSE being associated with 'shelter' and 'lodging' more than the 20C, which is distinctly associated with 'security' and 'struggle'. Given the urban – rural difference between the centuries and that the feature 'shelter' concerned protection from the wilderness contrary to 'security', which was understood as abstract emotional security, this kind of difference is to be expected.

The top right quadrant is clearly dominated by 19C LAND. Note, however that 20C LAND lies in the centre of the quadrant, even if its contribution is minimal. The concept of LAND, in both centuries is associated with the semantic features of 'building' and 'lack of origins'. It is the second feature that makes it distinct from NATION. It appears that the concept of LAND is associated with uses where one's 'origins' are lost or unattainable, in contrast to ABSTRACT PLACE, which is associated with returning to one's 'origins' and with the sense of 'belonging' evoked by this.

These results paint a clear picture of the concept of HOME, based on the figurative uses of the single lexeme *home*. It seems that the four conceptualisations are reasonably stable over the 200 hundred years, though certain differences do appear. However, the cluster analysis suggested a more complex picture and one must be cautious with binary correspondence analysis for such complex data. The next section reports the results of a multiple correspondence analysis, which reveals that, although the overall findings are accurate, there is perhaps more complexity than the binary correspondence analysis would suggest.

3.3 Semantic map of the diachronic conceptual variation

Multiple correspondence analysis follows the same principle as binary correspondence analysis, save that instead of stacking, or concatenating, all the semantic features into a single factor, they are treated as separate and independent factors. The result is more complex and less reliable, but allows us to consider how different semantic features might interact between themselves and not just in relation to the concept.

The same data, submitted to a multiple correspondence analysis produces a reasonably stable result. Normally, the explained inertia scores of the first two-dimensions are not interpretable in multiple correspondence analysis. However, Greenacre (2007: 145) has proposed an algorithm that produces interpretable scores, although with some caution. Using the adjusted algorithm, 56% of the inertia is explained. The scree plot below, in table 3, gives a dimension breakdown for the explained inertia of the analysis visualised in Figure 3.[8]

Greenacre (2007) has also proposed another method for estimating explained inertia, which he terms the 'joint' method. This method deletes the uninformative bi-rows from the calculation. Using this method, 64.7% of the variation is accounted for. Although both scores are low, relative to the binary correspondence analysis, they still represent interpretable results. The quality

Tab. 3: Principal inertias (eigenvalues).

dim	value	%	cum%	scree plot
1	0.034778	43.0	43.0	*************************
2	0.010487	13.0	13.0	********
3	0.00548	9.3	65.3	*****
4	0.005985	7.4	72.7	****
5	0.000864	1.1	73.8	*
6	0.000395	0.5	74.3	
7	2.e-050	0.0	74.3	
8	3e-06000	0.0	74.3	

---

[8] Note that the correspondence analysis was performed in both the FactoMineR (Husson et al. 2012) and ca (Nenadić and Greenacre 2007) packages. The numerical summaries, quality scores and scree plot were produced using ca and Greenacre's (2007) 'adjusted' method, where the biplot was produced using a standard Burt matrix the FactoMineR package. There was no noticeable difference in the plots produced by the Burt and 'adjusted' correspondence analyses. The FactoMineR package was used for the biplot because of its superior graphics options.

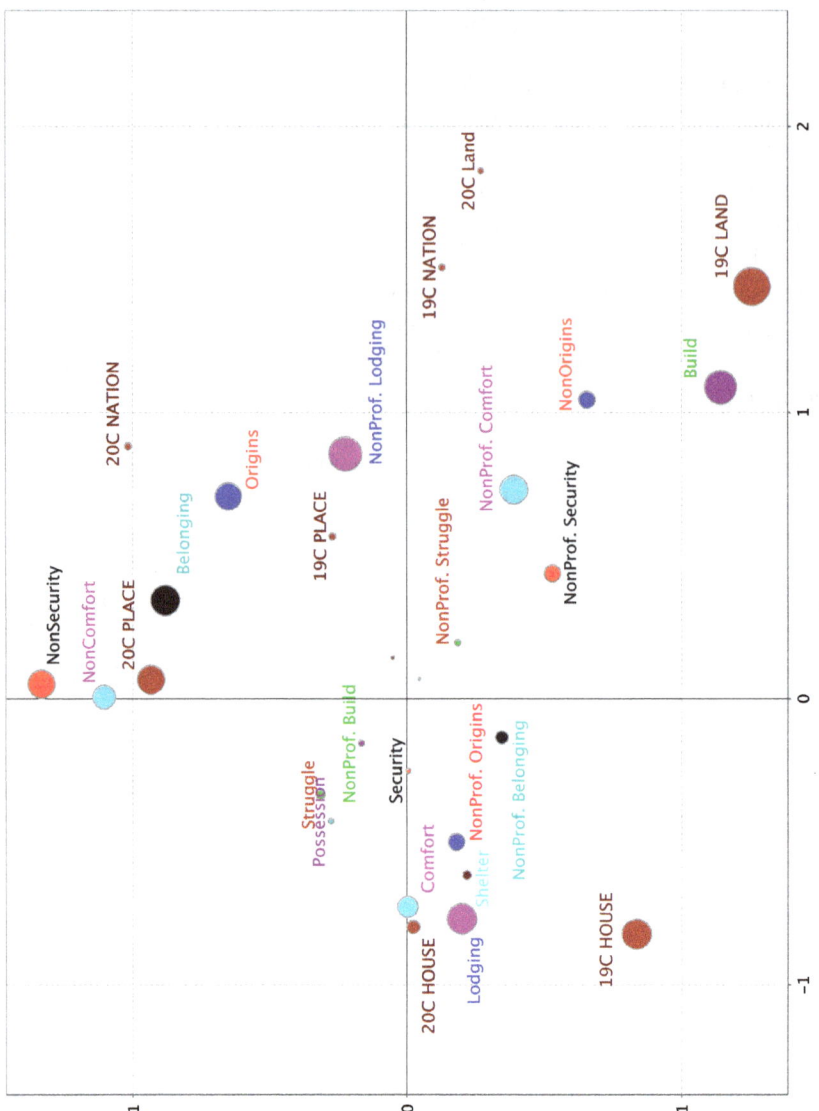

Fig. 3: Multiple correspondence analysis of concept-period and semantic features.

scores for the concepts 20C LAND and 20 NATION were still both beneath 500. Also the semantic features of 'non-comfort', 'security' and 'struggle' re-appear as questionable and should be interpreted with caution.

Figure 3 presents the results of the multiple correspondence analysis of concept-period and the full set of semantic features. Firstly note that the overall structure of the data is maintained. The source concept HOUSE is still clearly associated with 'comfort' and 'lodging' and the 19th century and 20th century data points are clearly sharing the same associations. Note that 20C HOSUE still lies on the x-axis and, therefore, is also associated with 'struggle' and 'possession'. Given that the 19C HOUSE lies in the centre of the bottom-left quadrant, 'struggle' and 'possession' are distinctively 20th century. We obtained low quality scores for 'struggle' in both correspondence analyses, but it appears quite stable in relation to 20C HOUSE.

The source concept LAND also appears consistent with the previous analysis, although it should be noted that the association of the 19th century data point and the semantic feature of 'building' is the anchor for this clustering and that the clear association of 20C LAND appears to be drifting towards the x-axis. This suggests it is not distinctly associated with any of the features on the right side of the plot.

It is this general spread of features across the left-hand side of the plot that brings us to the major difference between the two analyses. Instead of three distinct semantic conceptual clusters, we have a continuum from 20C PLACE, strongly structuring the data at the top on the y-axis, across to 19C LAND in the bottom right-hand quadrant. It seems that these two concepts are distinct and that the other concepts are 'floating' between them. The contribution of the non-profiling of 'lodging' is, obviously, common to all these concepts and it could be that this feature is causing otherwise distinct clusters to appear associated. The question is, does patterning on the right-hand side of the plot represent two or three semantico-conceptual structures? A more straightforward way of asking this question is: does 20C PLACE and, perhaps, 20C NATION represent, quantitatively, a distinct pattern and, therefore, diachronic variation in the overall conceptual profile of HOME.

The binary correspondence analysis in Figure 2 revealed what was a clear and intuitively sound result. There was no noticeable variation between the two periods and the four concepts were structured by three semantic profiles as HOUSE, LAND, and PLACE-NATION. However, the multiple correspondence analysis reveals the possibility of a more complex picture. By looking at the interaction of the semantic features, we see that 20C PLACE, in association with 'no comfort' and 'no security', is distinct from the LAND-PLACE semantic profile and the association's contribution to the overall structure of the data is important.

In order to determine whether the behaviour of data can be best explained as three or four structures, we can return to the cluster analysis, presented in section 2.1. Firstly, the data with which the binary correspondence analysis was performed are submitted to a *k*-mediod cluster analysis.[9] Unlike the hierarchical clustering in Figure 1, *k*-mediod clusters the data with a pre-determined number of clusters. In our case, we have two possibilities – three clusters or four clusters. If we run two *k*-mediod analyses and compare the results, we can use quantitative measures to determine which clustering better explains the data.

The results of the *k*-means clustering confirm the subjective interpretation of Figure 1 and Figure 2. A silhouette coefficient measure was used to compare the clusterings, and a three-way cluster better explains the data than a four-way clustering.[10] However, several important points must be made. First, these *k*-mediod clusterings are based on the stacked arrangement of the data employed in the hierarchical cluster and binary correspondence analyses. Therefore, this clustering solution tells us nothing directly about the results in Figure 3, it only confirms our interpretation of the binary analysis. Secondly, neither of the silhouette coefficient scores was high and there was not a large difference between them. The scale for the silhouette coefficient measure is: < 0.25 no substantial structure found; 0.26–0.50 structure is found but it is weak; 0.51–0.70 a reasonable structure identified; 0.71–1.0 a strong structure identified (UNESCO 2013). The three-way cluster produced a score of 0.52, just above the rule of thumb for a stable structure, but the four-way cluster produced a silhouette coefficient score of 0.50, also right on the cusp and only fractionally worse than the three-way cluster. Moreover, the four-way cluster identified 20C PLACE as outside the general clustering of the examples with a poor individual score. In fact, it is the 20C PLACE score that brings the entire silhouette coefficient score below the 0.50 threshold. In other words, although the three-way cluster is the best, the difference between the two is the behaviour of 20C PLACE making it difficult to identify structures across the entire dataset. It could be that 20C PLACE is so varied that it is semantically hyperonymic to the other concepts and, therefore, resists categorisation or it could be that there is something going on between the semantic features that the binary analysis is missing. It is precisely in such a situation that multiple correspondence analysis might offer an explanation.

---

[9] *K*-mediod analysis performed with R package cluster (Maechler *et al.* 2012).
[10] Dey *et al.* (2011) explain the silhouette coefficient measure. In line with the hierarchical cluster analysis, the *k*-means analysis was done using the Euclidean distance matrix.

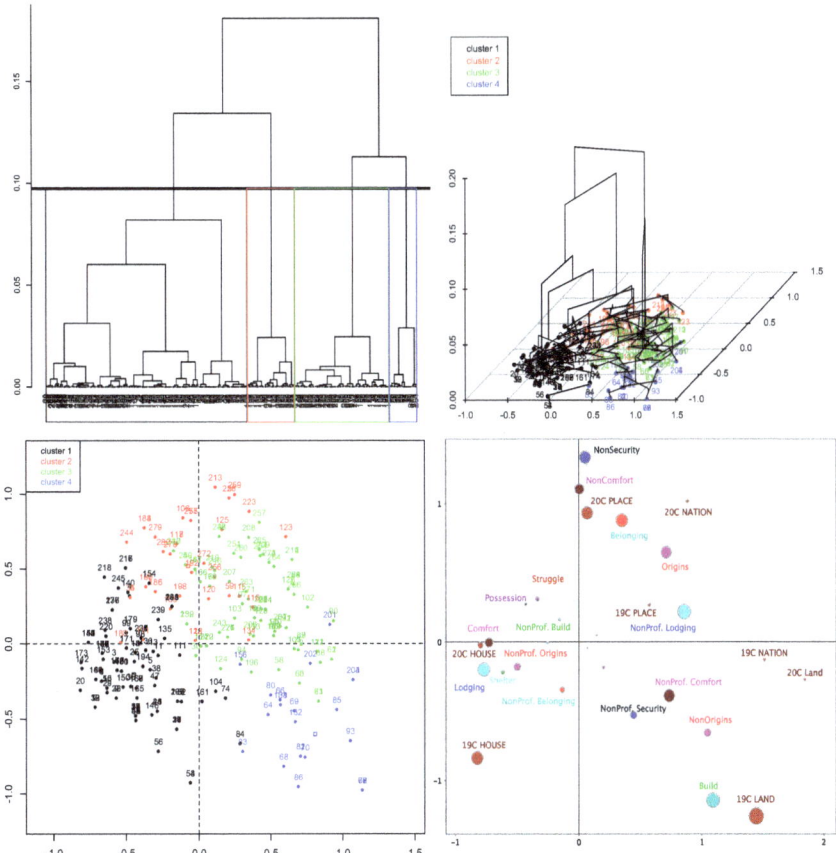

Fig. 4: Hierarchical cluster analysis of multiple correspondence results.

Figure 4 presents the results of a clustering of the output of the multiple correspondence analysis. The top left plot shows the clustering of the individual examples in the correspondence analysis. The dark line through the centre is the *k*-means suggested cut. Note that the automated suggestion of the *k*-means analysis of the output of a multiple correspondence analysis is now a four-way clustering. The plot on the top right is a three-dimensional depiction of the clustering of the data on a biplot. It allows us to see how the cluster analysis is dividing up the data points in the multiple correspondence analysis. The bottom-left plot is the factor map, a colour depiction of how the cluster analysis has identified the structuring of the data into 4 clusters (here factors). The bottom-right plot is a duplication of the plot in Figure 3. It is added to aid in the interpretation of the clustering.

From this, it would appear that our interpretation of the multiple correspondence analysis in Figure 3 is accurate. The concept of ABSTRACT PLACE in the 20th century represents a distinct pattern characterised by lack of 'security' and lack of 'comfort'. In this, it has split off from the cluster of PLACE-NATION identified in the binary correspondence analysis, leaving a cluster of 19C PLACE, 20C NATION and 20C NATION, on the one hand, and a cluster of 19C LAND and 20C LAND, on the other.

4 Summary

Four basic source concepts for HOME were found. These include HOME as a HOUSE, HOME as a LAND, HOME as a NATION, and HOME as an ABSTRACT PLACE. Three basic semantic profiles of the concept of HOME were identified grouping PLACE and NATION together. These were found to be reasonably stable across the 19th and 20th century datasets. However, there is strong evidence that HOME as an ABSTRACT PLACE appears to be emerging as a distinct semantic profile of the concept HOME in the 20th century. If future research confirms this pattern, then a reasonable interpretation would be that as society becomes more mobile, both socially and in terms of physical locations, it is reasonable that the concept of HOME would shift from concrete sources such as HOUSE, LAND, and NATION to a more abstract and emotionally constructed space. Despite this intuitively reasonable interpretation of the results, due to the narrow sample, restricted to five authors from two genres, any such interpretation remains speculative until a broader and more representative sample can be examined.

The aim of the paper was to demonstrate the feasibility of the multivariate usage-feature method for the description of conceptual structures. Although the sample was too small to permit confirmatory statistical analysis, the principle of usage-feature analysis / profile-based analysis has been demonstrated to adequately capture the abstract structures typical of conceptual analysis. Moreover, it was shown that usage-feature analysis enables a quantification of the phenomena in question, permitting the application of multivariate statistics. The ability of multivariate analysis to explore the complex nature of the data and identify language patterns, sensitive to social variation, was established. It is hoped that such methodological approaches will lead to the development of an analytical apparatus that identifies usage-based, rather than idealised, cognitive models.

References

Cowie, Jefferson & Lauren Boehm. 2006. Dead Man's Town: "Born in the U.S.A.," Social history, and working-class identity. *American Quarterly* 58. 353–378.

Davies, Mark. 2010. The Corpus of Historical American English: 400 million words, 1810–2009. Available online at http://corpus.byu.edu/coha/

Deshors, Sandra & Stefen Th. Gries. 2014. A case for the multifactorial assessment of learner language. The uses of *may* and *can* in French-English interlanguage. In Dylan Glynn & Justyna Robinson (eds.), *Corpus methods for semantics. Quantitative studies in polysemy and synonymy*, 179–204. Amsterdam & Philadelphia: John Benjamins.

Dirven, René, Louis Goossens, Yvan Putsey & Emma Vorlat. 1982. *The scene of linguistic action and its perspectivization by SPEAK, TALK, SAY, and TELL.* Amsterdam & Philadelphia: John Benjamins.

Divjak, Dagmar. 2010a. *Structuring the lexicon: A clustered model for near-synonymy.* Berlin & New York: Mouton de Gruyter.

Divjak, Dagmar. 2010b. Corpus-based evidence for an idiosyncratic aspect-modality relation in Russian. In Dylan Glynn & Kerstin Fischer (eds.), *Quantitative cognitive semantics. Corpus-driven approaches*, 305–331. Berlin & New York: Mouton de Gruyter.

Divjak, Dagmar & Nick Fieller. 2014. Cluster analysis. Finding structure in linguistic data. In Dylan Glynn & Justyna Robinson (eds.), *Corpus methods for semantics. Quantitative studies in polysemy and synonymy*, 405–441. Amsterdam & Philadelphia: John Benjamins.

Dey, Debangana, Thamar Solorio, Manuel Montes y Gomez & Hugo Jair Escalante. 2011. Instance selection in text classification using the silhouette coefficient measure. In Ildar Batyrshin & Grigori Sidorov (eds.), *Mexican International Conference on Artificial Intelligence*, 357–369. Heidelberg: Springer.

Fabiszak Małgorzata, Anna Hebda, Iwona Kokorniak & Karolina Krawczak. 2014. The interaction of prefix and patient semantics in the Polish verb *to think*. In Dylan Glynn & Justyna Robinson (eds.), *Corpus methods for semantics. Quantitative studies in polysemy and synonymy*, 223–251. Amsterdam & Philadelphia: John Benjamins.

Geeraerts, Dirk. 1990. The lexicographical treatment of prototypical polysemy. In Savas Tsohatzidis (ed.), *Meanings and prototypes. Studies in linguistic categorization*, 195–210. London: Routledge.

Geeraerts, Dirk, Stefan Grondelaers & Peter Bakema. 1994. *Structure of lexical variation. Meaning, naming and context.* Berlin & New York: Mouton de Gruyter.

Geeraerts, Dirk, Stefan Grondelaers & Dirk Speelman. 1999. *Convergentie en divergentie in de nederlandse woordenschat.* Amsterdam: Meertens Instituut.

Glynn, Dylan. 2009. Polysemy, syntax, and variation. A usage-based method for Cognitive Semantics. In Vyvyan Evans & Stéphanie Pourcel (eds.), *New directions in cognitive linguistics*, 77–106. Amsterdam & Philadelphia: John Benjamins.

Glynn, Dylan. 2010a. Testing the hypothesis. Objectivity and verification in usage-based cognitive semantics. In Dylan Glynn & Kerstin Fischer (eds.), *Quantitative cognitive semantics. Corpus-driven approaches*, 239–270. Berlin & New York: Mouton de Gruyter.

Glynn, Dylan. 2010b. Synonymy, lexical fields, and grammatical constructions. A study in usage-based cognitive semantics. In Hans-Jörg Schmid & Suzanne Handl (eds.), *Cognitive foundations of linguistic usage-patterns*, 89–118. Berlin & New York: Mouton de Gruyter.

Glynn, Dylan. 2014a. Techniques and tools. Corpus methods and statistics for semantics. In Dylan Glynn & Kerstin Fischer (eds.), *Quantitative cognitive semantics. Corpus-driven approaches*, 307–341. Berlin & New York: Mouton de Gruyter.

Glynn, Dylan. 2014b Correspondence analysis. Exploring data and identifying patterns. In Dylan Glynn & Kerstin Fischer (eds.), *Quantitative cognitive semantics. Corpus-driven approaches*, 443–485. Berlin & New York: Mouton de Gruyter.

Glynn, Dylan. 2014c. The many uses of *run*. Corpus methods and cognitive socio-semantics. In Dylan Glynn & Justyna Robinson (eds.), *Corpus methods for semantics. Quantitative studies in polysemy and synonymy*, 117–144. Amsterdam & Philadelphia: John Benjamins.

Glynn, Dylan. 2014d. The social nature of ANGER: Multivariate corpus evidence for context effects upon conceptual structure. In Iva Novakova, Peter Blumenthal & Dirk Siepmann (eds.), *Emotions in discourse*, 69–82. Frankfurt/Main: Peter Lang.

Glynn, Dylan. Submitted. *Mapping meaning. Corpus methods for cognitive semantics*. Cambridge: Cambridge University Press.

Glynn, Dylan. To appear. Conceptualisation of HOME in popular Anglo-American texts. A multifactorial diachronic analysis.

Greenacre, Michael. 2007. *Correspondence analysis in practice*. London: Chapman & Hall.

Gries, Stefan Th. 1999. Particle movement: A cognitive and functional approach. *Cognitive Linguistics* 10. 105–145.

Gries, Stefan Th. 2003. *Multifactorial analysis in corpus linguistics: A study of particle placement*. London: Continuum.

Gries, Stefan Th. & Dagmar Divjak. 2009. Behavioral profiles: A corpus-based approach towards cognitive semantic analysis. In Vyvyan Evans & Stephanie Pourcel (eds.). *New directions in cognitive linguistics*, 57–75. Amsterdam & Philadelphia: John Benjamins.

Goossens, Louis. 1990. Metaphtonymy: The interaction of metaphor and metonymy in figurative expressions for linguistic action. *Cognitive Linguistics* 1. 323–340.

Guterman, Jimmy. 2005. *Runaway American dream*. Cambridge: Da Capo Press.

Husson, Francois, Julie Josse, Sebastien Le & Jeremy Mazet. 2012. FactoMineR: Multivariate exploratory data analysis and data mining with R. R package version 1.19.

Klavan, Jane. 2014. A multifactorial analysis of grammatical synonymy. The Estonian adessive and adposition peal 'on'. In Dylan Glynn & Justyna Robinson (eds.), *Corpus methods for semantics. Quantitative studies in polysemy and synonymy*, 253–278. Amsterdam & Philadelphia: John Benjamins.

Krawczak, Karolina. 2014a. Shame and its near-synonyms in English: A multivariate corpus-driven approach to social emotions. In Iva Novakova, Peter Blumenthal & Dirk Siepmann (eds.), *Emotions in discourse*, 84–94). Frankfurt/Main: Peter Lang.

Krawczak, Karolina. 2014b. Epistemic stance predicates in English: A quantitative corpus-driven study of subjectivity. In Dylan Glynn & Mette Sjölin (eds.), *Subjectivity and epistemicity: Corpus, discourse, and literary approaches to stance*, 355–386. Lund: Lund University Press.

Krawczak, Karolina & Iwona Kokorniak. 2012. A corpus-driven quantitative approach to the construal of Polish 'Think', *Poznan Studies in Contemporary Linguistics* 48. 439–472.

Lakoff, George. 1987. *Women, fire, and dangerous things. What categories reveal about the mind*. Chicago: University of Chicago Press.

Langacker, Ronald. 1987. *Foundations of Cognitive Grammar*. Vol. 1. *Theoretical prerequisites*. Stanford: Stanford University Press.

Lifshey, Adam. 2009. The borderlands poetics of Bruce Springsteen. *Journals of the Society for American Music* 3. 221–241.
Maechler, Martin, Peter Rousseeuw, Anja Struyf, Mia Hubert & Kurt Hornik. 2012. cluster: Cluster analysis basics and extensions. R package version 1.14.2.
Nenadic, Oleg & Micahel Greenacre. 2007. Correspondence analysis in R, with two- and three-dimensional graphics: The ca package. *Journal of Statistical Software* 20. 1–13.
Shimodaira, Hidetoshi. 2005. Approximately unbiased tests of regions using multistep-multiscale bootstrap resampling. *Annals of Statistics* 32. 2616–2641.
Suzuki, Ryota & Hidetoshi Shimodaira. 2011. pvclust: Hierarchical clustering with p-values via multiscale bootstrap resampling. R package version 1.2–2.
Sten, Joakim & Dylan Glynn. 2011. The American concept of HOME. A multifactorial corpus-driven study. *Interstudia* 10. 65–79.
Stepanov, Juri. 1997. *Константы: Словарь русской культуры*. Moscow: Shkola Jazyki russkoj kultury.
Vorkachev, Sergei. 2007. *Любовь как лингвокультурный концепт*. Moscow: Gnozis.
Wierzbicka, Anna. 1985. *Lexicography and conceptual analysis*. Ann Arbor: Karoma.
UNESCO. 2013. Statistical guide for partitioning around medoids, section 7.1.1, http://www.unesco.org/webworld/idams/advguide/Chapt7_1_1.htm.
Zeschel, Arne. 2010. Exemplars and analogy: Semantic extension in constructional networks. In Dylan Glynn & Kirsten Fischer (eds.), *Quantitative cognitive semantics. Corpus-driven approaches*, 201–221. Berlin & New York: Mouton de Gruyter.

Cristóbal Pagán Cánovas
Cognitive patterns in Greek poetic metaphors of emotion: A diachronic approach

Abstract: Poetic imagery systematically integrates archetypical emotion scenes with schematic narratives grounded on spatial cognition. To model these recurrent imaginative patterns, I use generic structures of conceptual integration (Fauconnier and Turner 2002), exposing conceptual templates recurrent across different periods of Greek poetry. These patterns recruit *image schemas* (Johnson 1987), that is, condensed redescriptions of perceptual experience, to construct imaginary narratives (Turner 1996) that blend basic spatial events with emotional meaning. Image schemas lie at the basis of the human conceptual system, as shown by developmental research on cognition in the first months of life (Mandler 2004). These generic integration networks underlie a wide variety of poetic metaphors. For example, an erotic emission coming from the body or from a superior force (as in the arrows of love, or a light or scent from the beloved) has been repeatedly used to conceptualize love causation in literature, everyday language, or rituals, from Antiquity to the twentieth century (Pagán Cánovas 2009). To analyze these emotion discourses, or *emotives* (Reddy 2001), we need both a historical and a cognitive perspective (Reddy 2009). Studies of the language of emotions (e.g. Kövecses 1986, 2000) often incur in Anglocentrism (Wierzbicka 2009a–b) and neglect cultural diachrony in their search for universal patterns (Geeraerts and Grondelaers 1995, Geeraerts and Gevaert 2008). In order to avoid both flaws, this paper introduces a more complex cognitive model studying productive recipes of poetic creativity, and explores the wide diachrony of Greek poetry, with an emphasis on ancient and medieval texts. Since Greek culture has been at a geographical and historical crossroad for three millennia, the study is enriched through comparison with literary traditions from East and West. Crucially, the instantiation of these conceptual templates varies significantly across individuals, communities and contexts, thus providing significant data about the history of emotion concepts. These conceptual blends of emotional and spatial meanings have a history, which sometimes can be traced back to the conceptual materials and cultural settings from which they arose (Pagán Cánovas, forthcoming). By using Blending Theory's dynamic model for meaning construction, the history of

---

Cristóbal Pagán Cánovas: Institute for Culture and Society, University of Navarra

emotions can take an important step towards becoming a cognitive social science (Turner 2001, Eddy 2009).

1 Emotion, metaphor, conceptual integration, and diachrony

Metaphor researchers in cognitive linguistics have been interested in the conceptualization of emotions from the early stages. Mappings from bodily sensations and spatial relations to emotion concepts constituted some of the first case studies in Conceptual Metaphor Theory (Lakoff and Johnson 1980, chap. 15; Lakoff 1987: 380–415; Kövecses 1987). This research has repeatedly shown that there are stable mapping templates for emotion recurring across cultures (Kövecses 2003; Kövecses 2006), that these templates influence poetic imagery (Kövecses 2003: 23; for general metaphoric templates and poetic metaphors see Lakoff and Turner 1989), and that there is an experiential and embodied basis in the conceptualization of affective experience (see Kövecses 2003, especially for emotion causation as force).

However, these studies have not fully acknowledged how problematic it is to establish universal patterns across emotion concepts – and consequently also across emotion metaphors – and how easy it is to incur in cultural biases, especially for an approach based on target concepts (Wierzbicka 2009). Asking how cultures around the world conceptualize love, fear, or anger is a biased question. It is inescapably influenced by the cultural models underlying those English words. Many cultures have no such concepts, or have several lexical items where English has only one.

Moreover, the vastness of conceptual domains and the inflexibility of ontological mappings may make Conceptual Metaphor Theory (CMT) unsuitable for studying poetic metaphors (Tsur 2000), or any other examples of verbal creativity in the expression of affect. Paying more attention to cultural and contextual variation seems to be a pressing necessity for the study of conceptual mappings in general, and especially for CMT. This theory has so far focused on abstract patterns and de-contextualized examples of language use. Some of the recent work in CMT addresses this issue (Kövecses 2010; for metaphoric patterns of emotion across cultures, see Soriano forthcoming).

A key idea concerning this problem is the fact that we use conceptual templates not merely to conceptualize emotion, but also, and crucially, to achieve an effective representation (Crawford 2009). This is probably also true for meaning construction in general. We do not merely rely on our experiential basis for conflating, say, a feeling with a spatial event; we also do this in a way that allows us to achieve certain goals, within a certain context, and within a certain cultural diachrony. We want to conceptualize emotion, but we also want other things at the same time: to influence the behavior of others, to tell a story, to make sense of an event, to achieve aesthetic or pragmatic effects, to situate ourselves with respect to a tradition, etc.

We do not do any of this in a vacuum, but in rich cultural and communicative contexts. Identifying an embodied pattern across disparate individual cases is very useful, but only if we do not consider it as a timeless and decontextualized entity. We should rather examine how the pattern interacts with a variety of situations, and how this interaction evolves in time. The literary material, especially in the case of long diachronies like those of Greek or Chinese, can be particularly useful to understand the interplay between creativity and entrenchment under very different conditions.

In terms of Conceptual Integration Theory (Fauconnier and Turner 2002), achieving a representational objective means building the most appropriate network of mappings, in order to come up with the most effective conceptual blend. Conceptual Integration Theory (CIT) offers a more flexible model for the study of meaning construction, because the cognitive operation it describes is a dynamic process, where entrenched structures are only part of what is happening. Instead of conceptual domains, the central construct in CIT are mental spaces (Fauconnier 1985; Fauconnier 1997), small conceptual packets that we build as we think and talk. In discourse, action, or thought, we are constantly activating mental spaces, which are connected through mappings to form networks. In a conceptual integration network, selected elements from input spaces are integrated in a blended space, where new structures emerge.

Any particular conceptual blend, or any particular instantiation of a generalized conceptual blend (Fauconnier 2009), is the result of the interaction between diachronic and synchronic processes, experiential and cultural structures, and on-line and entrenched factors. Gilles Fauconnier and Mark Turner have summarized this in the terms *cobbling* and *sculpting* (Fauconnier and Turner 2008).

Thus the central CMT question, what source domains are used to project structure to a target domain, greatly differs from what would be the corresponding question in CIT: what input spaces – shaped by both entrenched structures and local, on-line factors – are put together, and how do they adjust to each other, the network of mappings, and the blended space, to produce a conceptual blend that suits our purposes in communication and action.

But there are several problems with CIT too. To start with, CIT researchers have paid almost no attention to emotion. Neither have they attempted the systematic study of conceptual templates, but have mainly concentrated on exposing the cognitive operation in individual examples, or on establishing the governing principles of conceptual blending. Also, as Fauconnier and Turner themselves acknowledge, *cobbling* and *sculpting* are very general terms (Fauconnier and Turner 2008: 53–54). CIT needs much more work on the interaction between conceptual templates, cultural diachrony, and communication (Coulson and Pagán Cánovas 2013).

In particular, adopting diachronic strategies for the study of conceptual mappings is necessary, and definitely indispensable for affective meaning, which can vary so much from one representation to another. Cognitive linguistics will thus be able to participate in the intense methodological discussion that is currently taking place in the history of emotions. This emergent field is increasingly focusing on the evolution of the cognitive-cultural habits acquired for the construction of affective meaning (Reddy 2001; Reddy 2009), as well as on the social environments in which these "recipes" are articulated and become meaningful, through the combination of individual and collective processes, within *emotional communities* (Rosenwein 2002; Rosenwein 2010). How to study habitual construals of affective meaning within a diachronic framework is perhaps the central question in the field right now (Wierzbicka 2010).

2 Evolution, instantiation, and conceptual templates across emotion imagery

There are at least two diachronic strategies that researchers in conceptual mappings should care for: the study of evolution and the study of instantiation. The present work concentrates on the second. Combining the detailed study of conceptual templates with that of their individual instances – what CMT would call "linguistic metaphors" – is not the usual methodology in CMT or in CIT, but it is indispensable to reach a full understanding of meaning construction. This full picture is especially relevant for literary studies or emotion research, which are interested in knowing not only about what connects individual cases, but also about the particularities of each individual expression.

The importance of studying the evolution of emotion metaphors has been shown by Dirk Geeraerts and his collaborators (Geeraerts and Grondelaers 1995; Geeraerts and Gevaert 2008). By tracing back the origins of anger metaphors and metonymies as far in the past as one can get for English, these researchers show that the conceptual metaphor analysis is defficient, and can be challenged by a study with an adequate diachronic perspective.

Generic templates of conceptual integration have recently been used to address the problem of the origins of the arrows of love in the Greek archaic period (Pagán Cánovas 2011). Also, the importance of studying the origins and history of conceptual blends has been highlighted in a number of case studies, such as complex numbers (Fauconnier and Turner 2002: 270–274; Fauconnier 2005), the desktop interface (Fauconnier and Turner 2002: 22–24; Terkourafi and Petrakis 2010), or the timeline (Coulson and Pagán Cánovas forthcoming; Pagán Cánovas and Jensen 2013).

Studying the origins and evolution of a conceptual template is obviously necessary, but it is not the only possible strategy for a diachronic study. Another possibility is to study independent, or largely independent, instantiations of an abstract conceptual pattern. I propose to do this with the CIT model, by treating a pattern as a *generic integration template* (Pagán Cánovas 2010), a cognitive solution based on basic frames and mappings, which can be found independently in different periods.

Evolution and instantiation are complementary processes, indispensable to one another. A particular instantiation of an abstract template can be stabilized in the culture, and transmitted diachronically. The evolution of any conceptual template is the sum of its individual instantiations. However, what I show in this study is that comparing different instantiations of the same template also gives us precious information about all the other representational objectives in these individual examples. The template also provides a powerful tool to analyze how concepts, in this case emotion concepts, are shaped by cultural factors.

Once we have identified the common template, we can use it as a tool for comparison, to separate the mental pattern from the synchronic factors, and to observe the stylistic and cultural differences. If put in relation with a repertoire of recurrent integration templates and an adequate set of cultural data, a small sample of figurative language can give us very rich information about the way author and audience think. It can also help us appreciate better how expressive innovations work, and how the way in which emotions are felt can vary with the historical development of concepts and communities.

Generic integration templates can be observed even across the most creative examples of verbal art, such as poetic imagery. The observation of a pattern across creative, seemingly unrelated examples of figurative language indeed makes the pattern more apparent. But identifying a template is not the end of the job. In fact, it is just the beginning. By studying how the template adjusts to different synchronic and diachronic factors, we can learn about the interaction of entrenched and on-line processes in meaning construction. By comparing how different moments and individuals instantiate the pattern, we can also undertake stylistic, cultural, or linguistic analyses that would not be available to us otherwise.

These observations are likely to become more relevant if we study more and more different templates, in corpora as large, cross-cultural, and cross-modal as possible. To show a little of what can be done with examples from a long diachrony, I examine instantiations of what I call the *love-emission pattern*, in three different periods of Greek literature, sampling ancient lyric, oral folksongs of medieval tradition, and avant-garde 20th century poetry. With the analytic tools provided by CIT and the notion of generic integration templates, I compare how similar affective experiences, related to erotic attraction, are conceptualized and expressed very differently in these three moments of Greek literature.

3 Comparing the instantiations of a template: love-emission blends in Greek poetry

The *love-emission integration template* (Pagán Cánovas 2009, 2010) can be observed across many different examples of poetic imagery and conventional metaphors, in a variety of languages. The pattern can be instantiated in many different ways. One of the oldest and most stable motifs, which already seems traditional in Aeschylus, in the 5th century BCE (see *Agamemnon* 742–743 or *Suppliants* 1003–1005), is that of the arrows from the eyes. Here is an example from Guido Cavalcanti, from 13th century Florence, over one and a half millennia after Aeschylus:

> Questa vertù d'amor che m'ha disfatto
> da' vostr' occhi gentil' presta si mosse:
> un dardo mi gittò dentro dal fianco
> Si giunse ritto 'l colpo al primo tratto,
> che l'anima tremando si riscosse
> veggendo morto 'l cor nel lato manco.
> (Rima XIII, 9–14)

> This power of love that has undone me
> Issued swiftly from your noble eyes:
> It cast a dart into my side.
> The blow came so straight at the first draw
> That my soul, trembling, was startled
> At seeing my heart struck dead on my left side.
> (Translation: L. Nelson)

Without leaving the scene in which the loved person glances at the lover, another possibility is light irradiation from the eyes, as in the example by Pindar that I analyze in the next section. The same pattern is in this passage by Shakespeare:

> So sweet a kiss the golden sun gives not
> To those fresh morning drops upon the rose,
> As thy eye-beams, when their fresh rays have smote
> The night of dew that on my cheeks down flows:
> Nor shines the silver moon one half so bright
> Through the transparent bosom of the deep,
> As doth thy face through tears of mine give light:
> Thou shin'st in every tear that I do weep:
> No drop but as a coach doth carry thee;
> So ridest thou triumphing in my woe.
> (*Love's Labour's Lost*, IV, 3, 1345–1355)

Another possibility: emission of sound. In these lines from a sonnet by Federico García Lorca, the voice of the beloved has liquid properties as well:

> Tu voz regó la duna de mi pecho
> en la dulce cabina de madera.
> Por el sur de mis pies fue primavera
> y al norte de mi frente flor de helecho.
> ("El poeta habla por teléfono con el amor". *Sonetos del amor oscuro*)

> Your voice watered the dune of my breast
> in the sweet wooden telephone box.
> South of my feet it was spring
> and north of my forehead fern flower.
> (The poet talks to his love on the phone. *Sonnets of the dark love*. My translation)

The conceptual template connecting these examples of poetic imagery is a recipe for building an integration network that, in its minimal version, brings together two inputs, which share a generic structure of event causation: A causes *x* in B.

One of the two inputs is a typical situation, depicted time and again by love poetry across periods and cultures: two or more people interact, and one of them makes the other, or others, fall in love, feel erotic passion, be sexually aroused, or experience an emotion of the kind. Although the concepts of what we call love or erotic passion may vary enormously, both historically and cross-culturally, this generic scene could be a good candidate for a universal frame or scenario.

In any of its many possible instantiations, this scene of interaction is the kind of mental structure that can provide the content for a mental space. Building this mental space for the particular purposes of the love-emission network already requires conceptual integration: we are interpreting causation of emotion in this situation in a particular way. We are not, for example, interpreting that those who feel this emotion are at the same time the cause of it, because of some predisposition of their own. On the contrary, in this scenario, for whatever reason, we prefer to think of the cause as external to the experiencer. Even if there is no conscious action (e.g. an attractive person who just happens to be there, and does nothing in particular), in this representation somebody is doing something to the person who feels the emotion. This interaction event is thus integrated with a generic structure of causation, which includes an agent, an action (deliberate or not), and one or more patients.

This scene is familiar in everyday life, and very easy to identify for both the lyric poet and his audience. It is, so to say, a classic of the genre. Across most – perhaps all – poetic traditions, there are innumerable texts, or moments within a text, which try to make sense of this type of scene, to embellish it, to describe it, to suggest it, etc. For any of these purposes, a poet may recruit further conceptual structures, integrate them with this first input, and produce a useful conceptual blend.

The second input in this minimal love-emission network is a mental space containing an image schema, a redescription of a spatial gestalt (Johnson 1987; Lakoff 1987: 438–460). The projection of skeletal spatial stories to provide structure for a conceptual blend is a central process in conceptual integration, studied from the early stages of the theory (Mark Turner 1996). In the phenomenon termed *parable* by Mark Turner, a simple narrative structure is imported to give coherence and manageability to a blend, and to enhance vital relations such as cause and effect. The integration of image schemas with other conceptual materials seems to be a very early cognitive habit, which could play an important role in the first conceptualizations of emotional experience (Mandler 2012).

I call this particular image schema *emission*. The emission schema describes an event in which an emitter emits something towards a receiver, and produces some kind of reaction or change. Again, this schema is a very familiar one, which we can experience many times every day: sound, irradiation, throwing, pouring, etc. In this skeletal form, *emission* does not require force or intentionality, and thus can be described as an event schema involving caused motion and at least two objects, origin and destination. This schema can be built on some of the spatial primitives that cognitive psychologist Jean Mandler has proposed as the foundations of the conceptual system during the first months of life (Mandler 2004; Mandler 2010): *thing, location, (in)to, motion* and *contact*. Thus this structure is also a good candidate for universality.

The resulting blend contains a scene of interaction where an emission event takes place. Emitter and causer, as well as receiver and experiencer, are fused. Any actions or properties of the causer that are relevant in the input of emotion causation can be imported to the blend, although this is not compulsory. If these elements end up in the blend, they can be the cause of the emission, but not of the emotion directly.

The emission and the thing emitted, specified in one of the many possible instantiations of the schema, are imported to the blend. This *is* compulsory. In the blend, it is contact, attention, or some other direct engagement with the thing emitted what causes the emotion in the receiver. The thing emitted needs no counterpart in the input of emotion causation. A usual emergent structure in this kind of blend is a person performing an impossible emission, such as light irradiation, or a possible emission with impossible properties, such as a scent that is hyperbolically powerful. The light, the scent, or whatever is emitted, directly causes the emotion. In the blend, the emotion depends entirely on the emission.

This network is a cognitive solution that can be achieved independently by different individuals or cultures, at different moments in a diachrony. To run this mental simulation, and to negotiate meaning within this conceptual template, no fixed, ontological mappings are necessary. The inputs to the network have an experiential basis (spatial cognition, causation, agency ...), but also include structure that, at least partially, needs to be acquired through exposure to culture, such as the specific realization of the interaction scene, or the culturally valid notion of the feeling aroused. The inputs and the blend happen to be simple structures that any culture or period could produce, but the network, although it includes an embodied understanding of an emotional experience, is not compulsory. It is one possibility of conceptualization among others. It is not an algorithmic rule, but rather an attractive recipe, easily found and easily shared.

Many speakers, poets or not, do find the network efficient to serve certain communicative or representational goals. Consequently, it recurs across periods and cultures more often than what could be expected from chance. The associated communicative goals also show commonalities across all examples, such as the wish to express this emotional experience as an event with immediate consequences, caused by an external agent, and thus beyond the control or responsibility of the person that feels the passion.

This blended scene could be a universal of emotion conceptualization, both in literary traditions and in conventional linguistic expressions, *but it does not have to be*. This is something the data will tell, if we gather enough data. Also, no elaborate conceptual domains of love, space, or force, and hence no direct projections between them, are necessary for the construction of this blend. This is rather a recipe for building a local, ad-hoc conceptual blend from simple, entrenched structures, recruited on the fly to serve certain discursive or representational purposes.

This type of network can be constructed locally on many different occasions, giving rise to a great variety of surface products. These products, in our case different examples of poetic imagery, show great variation, as they adapt to different pragmatic settings, rhetorical purposes, and cultural backgrounds. However, the skeletal structure of the network, its basic mappings, integrations and emergent structures, remain the same across all examples. If we break one of these constraints, either the blend does not work well, or we come up with a clearly different conceptualization.

3.1 The rays from Theoxenus' eyes

This is Pindar's encomium of Theoxenus of Tenedos, from the first half of the 5th century BCE:

> Χρῆν μὲν κατὰ καιρὸν ἐρώ-
> των δρέπεσθαι, θυμέ, σὺν ἁλικίᾳ·
> τὰς δὲ Θεοξένου ἀκτῖνας πρὸς ὄσσων
> μαρμαρυζοίσας δρακείς
> ὃς μὴ πόθῳ κυμαίνεται, ἐξ ἀδάμαντος
> ἢ σιδάρου κεχάλκευται μέλαιναν καρδίαν
> ψυχρᾷ φλογί,
> πρὸς δ' Ἀφροδί-
> τας ἀτιμασθεὶς ἑλικογ'λεφάρου
> ἢ περὶ χρήμασι μοχθίζει βιαίως
> ἢ γυναικείῳ θράσει
> ψυχρὰν† φορεῖται πᾶσαν ὁδὸν θεραπεύων.
> ἀλλ' ἐγὼ τᾶς ἕκατι κηρὸς ὣς δαχθεὶς ἕλᾳ
> ἱρᾶν μελισσᾶν τάκομαι, εὖτ' ἂν ἴδω
> παίδων νεόγυιον ἐς ἥβαν·
> ἐν δ' ἄρα καὶ Τενέδῳ
> Πειθώ τ' ἔναιεν καὶ Χάρις
> υἱὸν Ἀγησίλα.
> (Snell and Maehler 123)
>
> One must reap loves, my heart,
> in due season and at the proper age.
> But he who sees the glowing
> rays flashing from Theoxenus' eyes,
> and is not shaken by waves of desire,
> has a black heart of steel or iron

forged with a cold flame,
and, having lost the favor
of quick-glancing Aphrodite,
either is forced to toil for money,
or, a slave of female boldness,
is towed down an utterly (cold?) path.
But I, by Her will, melt like wax of the holy bees
bitten by the sun's heat, when I look upon
the fresh-limbed youth of boys.
Surely also in Tenedos
Seduction and Grace dwell
in the son of Hagesilas.

The rays from Theoxenus' eyes are an example of a love-emission blend. Here, just like in the previous text by Shakespeare, the *emission* schema is instantiated as light irradiation from the eyes. The interaction scene is one in which a young man is admired by one of his elders in the homoerotic context of the *symposium*. The metaphor prompts for all the mappings and integrations of the generic template (for a detailed analysis see Pagán Cánovas 2010). We have an interesting emergent structure: anyone who sees (δρακείς) these glowing rays (ἀκτῖνας) has to feel a strong desire, unless he is unfit for it due to some terrible, unnatural reason: having a heart of steel or iron, or being a slave of greed or of female whim. Otherwise, there is nothing you can do: if you see the light from Theoxenus' eyes, passion immediately follows.

How is the blend prompted for by linguistic forms in this particular text? How is its generic conceptual structure, which it shares with many other linguistic examples, adapted to the goals and context of this specific situation? Does a poetic image, studied in comparison with other instantiations of the same integration template, give us information about the way emotion was experienced and conceptualized in the society where it was produced?

After having identified a conceptual template, such a second battery of questions should come forth. Metaphor or blending theorists should not consider these questions less interesting. The isolation of patterns such as love-emission can help us understand embodiment or conceptual mappings, but this is only one part of the job. Meaning is never constructed at a purely generic level. A pattern is not a pattern until it is fleshed out for specific purposes.

Any answers to those questions will need the help of philological and historical data. Just a couple of examples: in this case it is crucial to know about the Homeric precedents of the light-from-the-eyes motif (Groningen 1960), or about the frequent emission motifs related to glance in Antiquity (Davies 1980). Pindar, a poet specialized in choral lyric, is here composing a symposiac poem, and, as always, he is working within long traditions. The erotic encomium is a very old subgenre in choral lyric itself, and we even find it combined with the light irradiation motif as early as Alcman ("I sing the light of Agido", First Parthenion, PMG 1, 39–40), almost two hundred years before the encomium to Theoxenus.

A first interesting thing to note here is that Theoxenus, the emitter and causer of the passion, is doing practically nothing in this poem. He is not the subject of any verb in the text. He is not overtly performing any conscious action. The instantiation of the emission schema as light makes it difficult to represent control over the emission. In the case of throwing, for example, it is much easier to direct the emission towards a specific target. However, this can be corrected in a number of ways, and one of them is precisely to make the rays come out exclusively from the eyes. Theoxenus can direct his glance at will, and this could be used to represent intentionality. But none of this happens here.

Pindar does not describe the ephebe's appearance. Neither does he tell us about what Theoxenus thinks. Instead, the poet is rather interested in conveying the emotional reactions to the emission, as well as in singing a praise of homoerotic love, an emotion of high status in the society and period in which Pindar lives. Further on, in lines 10–12, the poet even adds that he melts like wax at the sight of young boys. Again, young boys do not really need to do anything for this to happen. Seduction and Grace (Πειθώ καὶ Χάρις) simply choose to dwell in young men like Theoxenus.

The speaker's emotional response to the rays from Theoxenus' eyes is thus not only natural – his heart is not of steel or iron – but also the socially accepted one. This is the way you should feel, unless you let your life be controlled by lesser passions, and have lost the favor of Aphrodite, the goddess that plays perhaps the most central role in the happiness of mortals. In a few lines Pindar neatly presents the whole worldview of the Aristocratic class: its two biggest enemies, money and women, are set against its firm, conservative religious values.

Underlying this is a preoccupation for the changes taking place in this period. In the political sphere, the increasing power of business men is a menace for the aristocracy, now a much less wealthy class, and, in private affairs, women seem to be becoming bolder in their "natural" inclination to "interfere" in the affairs of men. The defense of aristocratic values against these two evils is a standard theme in archaic Greek lyric.

In contrast with the greed of traders and the weak character of those who are at the mercy of female passion, Pindar turns towards the traditional cult of the goddess of love. The homoerotic love of noble men for young boys is a sign of nobility, it has been sanctioned by Aphrodite, it shows that you are spending your life among the best citizens, worshipping the gods and cultivating the aristocratic values of beauty, honor, and excellence, transmitted through the institution of erotic mentoring of the young by their elders.

The poem has the love-emission blend at its center, and greatly focuses on the receiver's reaction to the emission, but in quite a particular way. In love-emission imagery the praise of the beloved is often articulated as a praise of the thing emitted, of the power or beauty of the light, the sound, the arrow ... However, little is said here about the rays from Theoxenus' eyes. The poem is rather a social reaffirmation of the speaker's feelings, and the emission of the erotic light is rather taken as the excuse to sing the praise of the emotion it produces, which should be felt by all noble men.

Even if we did not have much more information about homosexuality in the archaic and classical periods, this text, contrasted with unrelated instantiations of the love-emission blend, would give us a very rich picture of how certain emotions are conceptualized and experienced in the culture. The encomium of Theoxenus does not complain about the overwhelming effects of the emission, as many other texts do, including the ones by Cavalcanti and Shakespeare quoted above. It does not use the emission event as a narrative of the moment of passion (Cavalcanti, Lorca), not even to give us a detailed, imagistic description of the emotion (Shakespeare, Lorca).

Instead, the imagery focuses on the different counterfactual scenarios in which someone could fail to react to Theoxenus' light, providing explanations for this indifference. Pindar is inviting his *emotional community* (Rosenwein 2002; Rosenwein 2006), which does not necessarily coincide with his nation or his kin, to respond to the erotic light emitted by Theoxenus, in a way coherent with their shared values and inclinations. It is by feeling and thinking according to this common worldview that such a community can be preserved.

3.2 The beloved who competes with the sun

This is a very successful motif in Western lyric poetry. Besides Juliet, or the Princess of France in the Shakespearean passage above, many others have been compared to the sun or the moon, with brightness having a metaphoric value related to beauty or excellence (see also Sappho, fragment Voigt 96, on the beloved as the moon, from around 600 BCE). This is not the love-emission template. This type of blend uses a different schema: an object being salient among others of the same category, because of size, color, brightness, etc. In instantiations such as light irradiation, the two patterns are easy to combine. You can have the beloved excel in brightness among other shining objects *and* cause an immediate emotional response through her light:

Εδώ σε αυτή τη γειτονιά δεν πρέπει να είν' φεγγάρι,
μον' πρέπει νά ναι συννεφιά, νά ναι βαθύ σκοτάδι,
γιατ' έχω μια αγαπητικιά κ' εκείν' είν' το φεγγάρι,
π' όντες προβάλλει να τη διω σκορπιέται το σκοτάδι.
Και με τον ήλιο μάλωνε, και με τον ήλιο λέγει:
«Ήλιε μου, για έβγα, για να βγω, για λάμψε, για να λάμψω».
Έλαμψε ο ήλιος το ταχύ, μαραίνει τα χορτάρια,
πρόβαλε η κόρη π' αγαπώ, μαραίνει παλικάρια,
φλογίζει νιούς, και καίγει οχτρούς, σκλαβώνει παλληκάρια,
καίγει κ' εμένα π' αγαπώ μέσα στα φυλλοκάρδια.
(Politis 98)

Here in this neighborhood there should be no moon,
there should only be clouds, there should only be deep darkness,
because I have a loved one and she is the moon,
and when she leans out for me to see her the darkness is dispersed.
And she quarreled with the sun, and she was telling the sun:
"Dear sun, go ahead, come out, so that I come out, shine, so that I shine"
The sun quickly shone: it withers the grass,
the girl I love leaned out, she withers lads,
she sets young men into flames, and burns the enemies, enslaves lads,
also burns me, who am in love deep in my heart.

This is an oral folksong of medieval tradition, collected by folklorist Nikolaos Politis around 1900. We see here the two patterns, *beloved as a sensorially salient object* and *love-emission*, working in combination. Oral poetry is especially adept at combining traditional motifs, and conceptual integration is a dynamic and opportunistic process. Both templates have produced a number of motifs, available from the tradition. They also share part of their conceptual structure, are associated to similar emotions, and perform similar discursive functions, such as the praise of the beloved. Thus it is not surprising to find them together when their schemas are instantiated in a compatible way, just like in the previous passage from *Love's Labour's Lost*.

Many conceptual integration templates can be combined in a piece of discourse, but not anything goes. Among other factors, the particular instantiation of the image schema in one of the input spaces imposes a strong constraint on the compatibility with further patterns. Combining saliency and emission is easy when there is an instantiation as light, but much more difficult with other instantiations, such as arrow shooting, or water sprinkling:

Στάλα τη στάλα το νερό τρουπάει το λιθάρι,
κ' η κόρη με τα νάζια της σφάζει το παλληκάρι.
(Politis 121, 3–4)

Drop by drop the water drills the stone,
and the girl with her mincing slaughters the lad.

This song depicts a similar action of the beloved on the powerless lover, with an analogous outcome. In both examples, the emotional effect is magnified by a hyperbolic choice of the verbs expressing the action: σφάζω (to kill, and in a violent way), in Politis 121, μαραίνω (wither), φλογίζω (inflame), καίω (burn), σκλαβώνω (enslave), in Politis 98. Despite all these coincidences in the rhetorical goals and the formal resources, we do not easily imagine how the beloved as sensorially salient could have been incorporated to the simile of the gestures of coquetry (νάζια) as water drops drilling the stone. Comparing sources of the emission would have been problematic here, given the purposes and the instantiation choices of this particular text.

In song 98, of the beloved competing with the sun, the first half develops the pattern of the salient object. Then, when attention is turned towards the effects of the woman on her admirers, the simulation incorporates the love-emission pattern as well. The comparison is then expanded to the effects of both sun and beloved.

The stylistic and cultural comparison of these folksongs with the encomium of Theoxenus is not an easy job. Almost everything is different, and it would be hard to know where to start, if we did not have a common pattern. In the first place, the two passages would have probably never been connected. Their link is that they are instantiations of the love-emission blending template. Precisely, if we focus on their different treatment of this conceptual template, we can see how the pattern interacts with different worldviews, giving us interesting data about the conceptualizations of emotional experience in these two distant moments of Greek literature and culture.

We see that, unlike Theoxenus, the emitter here is quite active. The woman's personality, her "boldness" – to borrow the term θράσος, from Pindar – to challenge the sun, is in fact the strongest character trait depicted in the song. We know much more about her than about Theoxenus. The differences between the ephebe, the static object of desire from the classical period, and the dangerous, arrogant αγαπητικιά of the folksong show the very different erotic preferences of very different emotional communities. Besides heterosexual versus homosexual love – who do not seem to produce essentially different imagery in poetry –, these differences are reflected on the type of light they emit, how they emit it, and the consequences they cause.

As it often happens in modern Greek folksongs, the poem has a strong narrative component. The text does not reflect too much on the implications of the feeling, but rather tells the spatial story in the direct, paratactic style of oral compositions. There is no intention to "educate" an emotional community either. The effects of the emission are natural and inescapable, and are not compared to any counterfactual scenario in which they could perhaps not be felt. The traditional motif of the beloved woman as an enemy of the lover is operative here. Although this theme was not absent from ancient love poetry, it was not so readily available for Pindar.

Both texts are using the same abstract recipe for conceptual integration, performing the same mappings, and producing similar emergent meanings. They are both recruiting further structures in an analogous way, to represent the feelings resulting from the reception of the light. Pindar's waves of desire and melting wax activate the conventional mappings that relate this kind of emotion to force and heat, and the sunshine and the withering of the young men in the folksong similarly connect the feeling to heat, and to the conception of people as plants. These other patterns have been repeatedly pointed out by conceptual metaphor theorists since the beginnings of this approach.

The template is not working in isolation, but in relation with other templates (for metaphor composition, see Lakoff and Turner 1989: 67–72). It is not working exclusively at the generic level either. The skeletal structure of mappings and integrations, which strongly relies on the basics of our spatial cognition, allows us to immediately grasp what is going on, but vast amounts of cultural knowledge are necessary to flesh out the pattern. Thus the same template allows for the representation of very different emotional experiences. We see this again in our last example, formally much more complex, written by Giannis Ritsos around 1938.

3.3 The scent of freshly-washed sky

Βηματίζεις
μέσα στα σκονισμένα δώματά μου
μ' ένα πλατύ ανοιξιάτικο φόρεμα
που ευωδιάζει πράσινα φύλλα
φρεσκοπλυμένο ουρανό
και φτερά γλάρων
πάνω από θάλασσα πρωινή.

Μέσα στο βλέμμα σου ηχούν
κάτι μικρές φυσαρμόνικες
από κείνες που παίζουν
τα πολύ εύθυμα παιδιά
στις εαρινές εξοχές.
(*Εαρινή Συμφωνία* IV)

You tread
on my dusty chambers
with a wide spring dress

that has a scent of green leaves
freshly-washed sky
and wings of sea gulls
over a morning sea.

Inside your glance
some little harmonicas sound
of the kind that
very cheerful children play
in the spring countrysides.
(*Spring Symphony* IV)

Ritsos combines different sensory modalities to represent the effect of the beloved on the lover. This effect is less explicitly linked to the emission event than in other examples. The text also attains a stronger feeling of intimacy: the emotions expressed seem more personal, as they are connected to private memories and associated to scenes of positive affect.

We get the impression that the loved person is observed in a mysterious way by the lover, and that this person is bringing deep changes to the lover's life, which go beyond the mere "waves of desire" or "burning" in our previous examples. This all results in a very different emotional experience, which shows a very different conception of the emotion and the relation between lovers. Nevertheless, emotion causation is here structured through the same love-emission pattern. Let us see how it works.

One very interesting innovation here is the fusion of the properties and effects of the emission in the blend. This renders a very powerful compression. Conceptual compression is achieved when a relation between elements in different mental spaces is turned into one single element or relation within the same blended space (Fauconnier and Turner 2002, chapters 6, 7 and 16; Fauconnier 2005; Turner 2006). In the first lines of our passage, we have one input space with the emission of scent. In the other space, emotion causation, the beloved causes strong feelings in the lover, which he associates with certain pleasant memories.

We have the usual mappings emitter-beloved, receiver-lover. The emission of scent could map on specific actions of the beloved in the emotion causation input but, as we have seen, the emission and the thing emitted need no counterparts in this network. The physical effects of the emission map on the emotional effects. This mapping can also be used in the blend. We have it in the beloved who competes with the sun, and burns the lovers with her shining, thus importing a possible effect of sunlight to produce a metaphoric emotional meaning in the blend. But the mapping can also be ignored, as Pindar chooses to do: Theoxenus' rays cause the speaker to "undulate with desire" (πόθῳ κυμαίνεται), an expression that does not import a direct physical effect of light, but resorts to different metaphoric resources.

In Ritsos' text, the reception of the scent and the memories it brings are compressed into one single feeling. This results in a strong poetic effect: the beloved smells like things that do not really have a smell, or like things she could not easily smell like: green leaves (πράσινα φύλλα), freshly-washed sky (φρεσκοπλυμένο ουρανό) – which incorporates a smell-related adjective to something that cannot have a smell – and sea gull wings over a morning sea (φτερά γλάρων πάνω από θάλασσα πρωινή).

This technique relies on conventional compression patterns of smell and effects (e.g. this smells like failure/success). Its poetic use is especially rich in some texts from the 20th century. For example, Pablo Neruda uses the same pattern in his poem "Ode to her scent" (Oda a su aroma), from this 1956 book *New elemental odes* (*Nuevas odas elementales*). In this poem, the scent of the beloved can be, among many other things, smell of light upon the skin (*olor de la luz en la piel*), smell of life with dust from a road (*de vida con polvo de camino*), coolness of morning shade on the roots (*frescura de matutina sombra en las raíces*), etc.

This procedure contributes to establish a more intimate relation between emitter and receiver. There is a big difference, for example, with instantiations that are essentially narrative, such as the scene of the woman that can burn her lovers with her light just by leaning out for them to admire her. In this case, there is no point in bringing back childhood memories. On the other hand, and in order to serve Ritsos' quite different rhetorical purposes, the "scent" of personal memories and experiences is a very powerful tool to connect the beloved to the inner world of the lover.

With this same objective, the pattern continues in the next stanza. We have here yet another example of emission from the eyes. As in Theoxenus, the emitter is not really doing much, not even glancing consciously at the receiver. The big difference here comes from the change of sensory modality: it is not rays, but harmonicas resonating, what the observer perceives in the eyes of the beloved.

Surrealism and other avant-garde movements made poets discover greater conceptual possibilities. Sound from the eyes is an example of how modern poetic imagery explores novel metaphorical relations across sensory modalities. However, all the constraints of the conceptual template still need to be preserved if the image is to work well. The beloved's spring dress (ανοιξιάτικο φόρεμα) can easily emit a scent, and the source of the scent can be fused with the memories it evokes. Now we turn to a part of her body, the eyes, for another source of yet another memory-experience. This memory involves sound. Quite opportunistically, this sound, which is a memory brought by the emotional effects of the glance, is projected to the blend as the emission itself. This is another powerful cause-effect compression.

Problem: eyes do not easily resonate, and this may result in an awkward image.

The solution to the problem is to recruit another very familiar and conventional pattern. The *container* schema can be easily integrated with a wide variety of conceptual materials, both abstract and concrete. It is very common in poetry for the eyes or the glance to contain a relevant element. The combination of this pattern with love-emission is very productive, because it enables the poet to place an emitter, or a source of emission, *inside* any part of the beloved, who thus becomes an indirect cause of the emission. An almost standard procedure is to place Cupid/Eros inside the beloved's glance. For instance: "love in her eyes sits playing / and sheds delicious death" (John Gay, *Acis and Galatea*).

Ritsos does this here too. The glance of the beloved becomes a container, where the scene of the children playing the harmonicas takes place. By compressing cause and effect in this way, Ritsos avoids a direct narrative of the emission scene, such as "I have received this emission *and* it makes me feel this emotion". Instead, he first tells us "This emission feels like (the emotions I feel when I think of) this or that memory", and then "This memory (along with its related emotions) is an emission, and its source resides in the glance of the emitter".

Since, after all, it is small spatial narratives that are being compressed, we also have compression of viewpoints (Dancygier 2005; Dancygier 2012, chapter 4). The lover is watching the beloved, whom he addresses in the second person, while at the same time he is an observer in the scene of the children playing the harmonicas, which is narrated in the third person. Similarly, in the scent metaphors of the preceding lines, the speaker is evoking events that do not belong in the scene in which he is contemplating the beloved's dress, but rather in memories of other experiences.

Combined with the address in the second person, this special treatment of the love-emission template produces a strong effect of closeness between lover and beloved. This suggests a more intimate communication between them, which goes much further than the merely visual attraction we saw in our previous examples. The beloved seems to be bringing all these memories of happiness and innocence to the lover's dark chambers, and thus to be dramatically changing the place he inhabits, and hence his life and feelings. She must be admirable for something else than her beauty.

The same love-emission pattern is used here to achieve a scene at human scale, but the way this emotion is being experienced and conceptualized is very different. Rather than an appeal to an emotional community, or a narrative of a seduction scene, this is a personal expression of feelings within a much more symmetric relationship. The diachronic comparison shows to what extent this is a different way of conceiving and expressing an emotion, which belongs to a different society and period, and to a different individual. The scent of freshly-washed sky could not have easily appeared in the affective poetics of Greek literature before the 20th century.

4 An invitation to diachrony, cross-cultural comparison, and poetic metaphors

We have seen the love-emission template at work in texts from a variety of European traditions, and with more detail in three very different moments of Greek literature. They are also three moments of the history of emotions in Greek culture and language. Long diachronies give us the possibility of comparing extremely distant historical settings and emotional communities, like fifth-century BCE Greek aristocracy and modern artists in the Greece of the 1930s.

In the pattern we have been examining, two events are blended: a scene in which somebody causes an erotic response in other person(s), and the familiar schema A emits x towards B, B receives x, and B undergoes significant change. Part of the resulting emergent structure can be predicted: there will be fusion of roles (emitter-beloved, receiver-lover); contact or direct engagement with x, which needs no counterpart in the love causation scene, will be the cause of emotion in the blend; the feeling will in most cases be conceptualized as sudden and powerful, although some types of emission can produce different effects.

This blend of the interaction scene and the emission schema provides a variety of possibilities for creativity. First of all, the abstract scene and schema can be instantiated in a variety of ways, depending on context and goals. Intentionality can be introduced or not, which results in different meanings. Causes and effects can be further compressed, as in Ritsos' integration of memories with scent and sound coming from the beloved. Different viewpoints can be adopted. Different attention can be paid to the manner of the emission, to the thing emitted, to the outcome of the emission, etc. Crucially, many different – but not just *any* – patterns can be activated and integrated with love-emission. And the list of possibilities goes on and on. Locating the pattern is just the beginning of the analysis.

It is by further developing the abstract pattern within its own constraints that creativity operates. Therefore, we need to identify templates if we are to understand creativity. At the same time, the most creative examples are the best for observing a pattern: a structure that remains stable throughout so many different examples of poetic figurative language is a good candidate for a robust conceptual template.

Literary texts are a splendid material to study how a conceptual pattern is manipulated to serve different representational purposes. The comparative study allows us to make the conceptual template apparent and robust, but this is only part of the task. Research on conceptual mappings should care both about the historical evolution and the particularities of instantiation of any given template.

Comparison with other instantiations of the same conceptual template is necessary for an adequate diachronic perspective. This perspective will allow us to understand the particularities of an individual example with respect to others, as well as to establish regularities in the interaction of a blending pattern with a variety of pragmatic and cultural situations. Multiplying the number of details observed, across a big number of examples from many different periods, can also give us precious information about the evolution of emotion concepts, or of concepts and worldviews in general.

CIT has the potential to analyze how emergent meanings recur diachronically, and not just how they result from very specific online processes. But we must remember that this theory is still embryonic in many aspects. A more developed CIT model should be able to combine the study of:
a) the integration of structures and habitual construals at the generic level (long-term memory),
b) the online blending that renders specific concepts and mental simulations, along with their surface products: metaphors, metonymies, etc. (mainly relying on short-term memory), and
c) how these processes are shaped by diachrony and discourse. The study of conceptual templates at the middle level between individual cases and general principles is indispensable for this.

CMT has a long research tradition at this intermediate level of analysis, but its vast domains, its ontological mappings, and its great focus on the experiential basis of conceptual mappings pose great difficulties to carry out an analysis like the one I have proposed here. Especially, concerning emotion metaphors, this methodology can bring us too close to the universalist fallacy (see Geeraerts, this volume), by neglecting the non strictly experiential factors.

The claim that the cognitive operation of blending, along with its governing principles, its objectives, and its vital relations, is universal, seems much less problematic. However, if we want to have analytic tools at the intermediate level of conceptual templates, blending theorists should also feel invited to systematically model conceptual templates in terms of mental spaces and conceptual integration networks. Different cultures might find similar solutions for meaning construction. However, there might still be many generic mapping templates that we should expect to find across different places and times. Variation is caused by the manifold ways in which these structures are instantiated in the different contexts, as well as by the various paths along which these templates evolve, within a given tradition. The factors influencing instantiation, both synchronic and diachronic, should be studied in combination with the cross-cultural patterns.

By dealing with individual instances in more detail, the field of conceptual mappings would incorporate a great number of philological and historical data, which right now are not receiving enough attention in cognitive linguistic research on metaphor and emotion. The cognitive approach could thus be brought closer to other disciplines in the humanities, such as literary studies or the history of emotions, which are not only interested in generic patterns, but also in what these patterns can teach us about the particularities of a text, a period, or an author, and how they evolve in the cultural diachronies that all humans inhabit.

References

Cavalcanti, Guido. 1986. *The poetry of Guido Cavalcanti*. Edited and translated by Lowry Nelson, Jr. New York: Garland. First appeared in anthologies from 1310 onwards. First printed edition Florence: Eredi di Filippo di Giunta [1527]

Coulson, Seana & Cristóbal Pagán Cánovas, C. 2013. Understanding timelines: Conceptual metaphor and conceptual integration. *Cognitive Semiotics* 5(1–2). 198–219.

Crawford, L. Elizabeth L. 2009. Conceptual metaphors of affect. *Emotion Review* 1(2). 129–139. doi:10.1177/1754073908100438.

Dancygier, Barbara. 2005. Blending and narrative viewpoint: Jonathan Raban's travels through mental spaces. *Language and Literature* 14(2). 99.

Dancygier, Barbara. 2012. *The language of stories*. Cambridge: Cambridge University Press.

Fauconnier, Gilles. 2005. Compression and emergent structure. *Language and Linguistics* 6(4). 523–538.

Fauconnier, Gilles. 2009. Generalized integration networks. In Vyv Evans & Stéphanie Pourcel (eds.), *New directions in cognitive linguistics*, 147–160. Amsterdam & Philadelphia: John Benjamins

Fauconnier, Gilles. 1985. *Mental spaces: Aspects of meaning construction in natural language*. Cambridge: Cambridge University Press.

Fauconnier, Gilles. 1997. *Mappings in thought and language*. Cambridge: Cambridge University Press.

Fauconnier, Gilles & Mark Turner. 2002. *The way we think: Conceptual blending and the mind's hidden complexities*. New York: Basic Books.
Fauconnier, Gilles & Mark Turner. 2008. Rethinking metaphor. In Raymond W. Gibbs (ed.), *The Cambridge handbook of metaphor and thought*. Cambridge: Cambridge University Press.
Geeraerts, Dirk & Caroline Gevaert. 2008. Hearts and (angry) minds in Old English. In Farzad. Sharifian, René Dirven & Ning Yu (eds.), *Culture and language: Looking for the mind inside the body*, 319–347. Berlin & New York: Mouton de Gruyter.
Geeraerts, Dirk & Stefan Grondelaers. 1995. Looking back at anger: cultural traditions and metaphorical patterns. In John Taylor & Robert E. Maclaury (eds.), 153–179. *Language and the cognitive construal of the world*. Berlin & New York: Mouton de Gruyter.
Johnson, Mark. 1987. *The body in the mind: The bodily basis of meaning, imagination, and reason*. Chicago: University of Chicago Press.
Kovecses, Zoltan. 1987. *Metaphors of anger, pride, and love: A lexical approach to the structure of concepts*. Amsterdam & Philadelphia: John Benjamins.
Kövecses, Zoltán. 2003. *Metaphor and emotion: Language, culture, and body in human feeling*. Cambridge: Cambridge University Press.
Kövecses, Zoltán. 2006. *Metaphor in culture: Universality and variation*. Cambridge: Cambridge University Press.
Kövecses, Zoltán. 2010. A new look at metaphorical creativity in cognitive linguistics. *Cognitive Linguistics* 21(4). 663–697. doi:10.1515/COGL.2010.021.
Lakoff, George. 1987. *Women, fire and dangerous things. What categories reveal about the mind*. Chicago: University of Chicago Press.
Lakoff, George & Mark Johnson. 1980. *Metaphors we live by*. Chicago: University of Chicago Press.
Lakoff, George & Mark Turner. 1989. *More than cool reason: A field guide to poetic metaphor*. Chicago: University of Chicago Press.
Mandler, Jean M. 2010. The spatial foundations of the conceptual system. *Language and Cognition* 2(1). 21–44.
Mandler, Jean M. 2012. On the spatial foundations of the conceptual system and its enrichment. *Cognitive Science* 36(3). 421–451. doi:10.1111/j.1551-6709.2012.01241.x.
Mandler, Jean M. 2004. *The foundations of mind: Origins of conceptual thought*. New York: Oxford University Press.
Pagán Cánovas, Cristóbal & Max Flack Jensen. 2013. Anchoring time-space mappings and their emotions: The timeline blend in poetic metaphors. *Language and Literature* 22(1). 45–59.
Pagán Cánovas, Cristóbal. 2011. The genesis of the arrows of love: Diachronic conceptual integration in Greek mythology. *American Journal of Philology* 132(4). 553–579.
Pagán Cánovas, Cristóbal. 2010. Erotic emissions in Greek poetry: A generic integration network. *Cognitive Semiotics* 6. 7–32. A: PRv
Pagán Cánovas, C. 2009. La emisión erótica en la poesía griega: una familia de redes de integración conceptual desde la Antigüedad hasta el siglo XX. Murcia: University of Murcia dissertation.
Page, Denys L. 1962. *Poetae Melici Graeci*. Oxford: Oxford University Press.
Politis, Nikolaos G. (Νικολάος Γ. Πολίτης). 1914. *Εκλογαί από τα τραγούδια του ελληνικού λαού*. Athens: Bagionaki.
Reddy, William M. 2009. Historical research on the self and emotions. *Emotion Review* 1(4). 302–315. doi:10.1177/1754073909338306.

Reddy, William M. 2001. *The navigation of feeling: A framework for the history of emotions.* Cambridge: Cambridge University Press.

Ritsos, Giannis (Γιάννης Ρίτσος). 1986. *Εαρινή Συμφωνία.* Athens: Kedros. [1938]

Rosenwein, Barbara H. 2010. Problems and methods in the history of emotions. *Passions in Context: Journal of the History and Philosophy of the Emotions* 1. 1–32

Rosenwein, Barbara H. 2002. Worrying about emotions in history. *The American Historical Review* 107(3). 821–845. doi:10.1086/532498.

Rosenwein, Barbara. 2006. *Emotional communities in the early Middle Ages.* Ithaca, NY: Cornell University Press.

Snell, Bruno & Herwig Maehler. 1975, 1980. *Pindarus I–II.* Leipzig: Teubner.

Soriano, Cristina. Forthcoming. Conceptual metaphors and the GRID approach in the study of anger in English and Spanish. In J. Fontaine, K. R. Scherer & C. Soriano (eds.). *Components of emotional meaning: A sourcebook,* Oxford: Oxford University Press.

Terkourafi, Marina & Stefanos Petrakis. 2010. A critical look at the desktop metaphor 30 years on. In Low, Graham, Zazie Todd, Alice Deignan & Lynne Cameron (eds.), *Researching and applying metaphor in the real world,* 145–164. Amsterdam & Philadelphia: John Benjamins

Tsur, Reuven. 2000. Lakoff's roads not taken. *Pragmatics and Cognition* 2. 339–359.

Turner, Mark. 2006. Compression and representation. *Language and Literature* 15(1). 17–27. doi:10.1177/0963947006060550.

Turner, Mark. 1996. *The literary mind.* New York: Oxford University Press.

Voigt, Eva-Marie. 1971. *Saphho et Alcaeus: Fragmenta.* Amsterdam: Athenaeum-Polak & Van Gennep.

Wierzbicka, Anna. 2009. Overcoming anglocentrism in emotion research. *Emotion Review* 1(1). 21–23. doi:10.1177/1754073908097179.

Wierzbicka, Anna. 2010. The 'history of emotions' and the future of emotion research. *Emotion Review* 2(3). 269–273. doi:10.1177/1754073910361983.

Juan Gabriel Vázquez González
'Thou com'st in such a questionable shape': Embodying the cultural model for GHOST across the history of English

Abstract: This paper aims to reinforce the role of culture variation in the reconstruction of the cultural model for GHOST across the history of English. By means of corpus linguistics analysis, we will contrast the results obtained for this and related terms in the Old English and Contemporary British English periods. The type of culture variation that we envisage here is thus diachronic and within-culture in essence, but also incorporates the cross-cultural perspective via lexical borrowings. We have followed a methodology that weighs GHOST words onomasiologically and also determines their exact position in the metaphor-metonymy-literal language *continuum*. I am particularly interested in proving that the role that metaphor plays across the history of the English GHOST group is reduced and variable and that even though the two periods analyzed may share some similar patterns of conceptualization, the literal and figurative processes for each of these are highly distinct in qualitative and quantitative terms. Finally, and as part of an attempt to redirect the field of emotions research towards cultural linguistics, I will also prove that the GHOST group is diachronically motivated by FEAR.

1 Introduction

In *Metaphor in Culture* (2005: 01–02), Zoltán Kövecses profiles the relationship between metaphor and culture in the following terms:

We can think of culture as a set of shared understandings that characterize smaller or larger groups of people. [...] The shared understandings suggested by anthropologists as a large part of the definition of culture *can often* be metaphorical [...] when the focus of understanding is on some intangible entity, such as time, our inner life, [...], emotions, [...]

Culture is here conceived of as a community-based and dynamic network of conceptual constructs predominantly metaphorical in essence. This reflection, which works as an ice-breaker for the cited volume, actually reflects two of the most widely held beliefs since the publication of *Metaphors We Live By*

Juan Gabriel Vázquez González: University of Huelva

(Lakoff and Johnson 1980) in Conceptual Metaphor Theory (henceforth CMT): the universal and panchronic nature of conceptual metaphors. In what follows and in other works, Kövecses (2006: 155–180) counteracts the beliefs cited above by developing a proposal that matches the restriction of universal or quasi-universal metaphors to certain domains – emotions, event structure, time, etc. – with a full-fledged theoretical analysis of the types (within-culture and across-culture) and factors involved in metaphor variation.

More revealingly, Kövecses' reflection also portrays the centrality granted traditionally by proponents of CMT to the role of metaphor in the expression of abstract terms in general and of emotions in particular. This centrality was later on partly shared with metonymy in the construction of cultural models (Lakoff 1987; Lakoff and Kövecses 1987: 195–221) but has since then by and large persisted. As a corollary, CMT linguists have largely disregarded the existence of other processes like synesthesia until relatively recently (Grossenbacher and Lovelace 2001: 36–41) and, more significantly, they have also tended to ignore the impact of literalness on linguistic conceptualization and the need for a global quantification of figurative and non-figurative processes.

Cross-culturally, the impact of culture specifics on the creation of particular metaphorical construals is already a commonplace in the comparative (Matsuki 1995: 137–151) and anthropological fields (Palmer 1996: 170–221). Apart from checking the claim for universality in the metaphorical scope of some EMOTION metaphors (Stefanowitsch 2006: 63–105), the use of corpus linguistics methods like metaphorical pattern analysis has helped elucidate why sometimes some languages favor some conceptual metaphors in detriment to others (Stefanowitsch 2004: 137–149). What is still in need of empirical quantification is the part that metaphor plays in linguistic conceptualization. In this respect, the literature is scarce. In his comparative analysis of the figurative uses for *mouth*, *tongue* and *lip* in current English and Malay, Charteris-Black (2003: 289–310) proves a tendency of English for metonymy whereas Malay opts for (often metonymically-based) metaphorical constructions. The difference lies, he argues, in a culture-specific preference for hyperbole or euphemism respectively.

Within-culturally and diachronically, there is also a growing body of literature that not only bears out the cultural specificity of metaphor but also restricts the role of the former in the construction of some cultural models. This has been demonstrated in Old English (hence OE) for some emotions like ANGER (Gevaert 2002: 275–299; Geeraerts and Gevaert 2008: 319–47) or FEAR (Díaz-Vera 2011: 85–103) and a sound methodology based on the use of onomasiological analysis for the relative measurement of all possible patterns of conceptualization proposed.

In this paper, I will develop an onomasiological contrastive study of GHOST terms in Old and Contemporary British English (henceforward CBE). The concept of ghost may not be universal, since among the Tiv tribe in South Eastern Nigeria the former is alternatively conceptualized as an omen, a spell, or even as a zombie (Bohannan 1966: 28–33). However, the quasi-universal status of this construct cannot be contested, as the latter also forms part of the Arab, Buddhist and Chinese cultures (Finucane 1984: 01–04; Moreman 2008: 77–160). On more Western grounds, and leaving theological debates aside (Dover Wilson 1959: 51–78), when prince Hamlet meets his father's ghost he questions the late deceased king's appearance. Shape represents just one among the manifold typicality effects profiled in ghosts. Ghosts form part of popular beliefs, are straightforward cultural products, link with the world of emotions (FEAR, ANGER, etc.) and, above all, belong to the abstract domain. As the body of cognitive linguistics literature on emotions is already substantial, I firmly believe that we should verify the former's results in the cultures of the languages involved, past and present.

I will make use of the *Dictionary of Old English Corpus* (diPaolo Healey et al. 2000) and the *British National Corpus* online (2007; henceforward BNC) to quantify each GHOST lexical set (Stefanowitsch and Gries 2006), whose members I will also classify according to their degree of literalness (Radden 2002: 409). After contrasting the results thus obtained for the two periods, I will demonstrate that metaphor plays a relatively minor role when compared with metonymy and competing literal patterns of conceptualization and will also prove that the GHOST group is consistently motivated by FEAR across the history of English.

2 Corpus compilation and methodology

I started corpus compilation at section 16.01.03 *A spectre, ghost, demon, goblin* in *A Thesaurus of Old English:*

Tab. 1: The GHOST group as proposed by Roberts, Kay and Grundy (2000: 655).

16.01.03 A spectre, ghost, demon, goblin: becola[og], grīma, egesgrīma, griming[og], nihtgenga, orc[g], scīn/scinn, scucca, thyrs, wearg, yfelwiht	**.A demonic creature**: ellengǣst[op], ellorgǣst[p], helrūna, wǣlgǣst[p]
.A spectre, phantasm: scinnhīw, scinnlāc	**16.01.03.03 A doomed spirit**: gēosceaftgāst[op]
16.01.03.01 Soul of a deceased person: dēath, gāst, sāwol	**.A sad spirit**: cargēst[op]
16.01.03.02 A demonic apparition: dēofolscīn	**.Walker(s) in darkness/evil spirit(s)**: orcnēas[op], sceadugenga[op]

However, as this section seemed not to make a clear distinction between the notion of ghost and those for demon and goblin, I decided to use the *Dictionary of Old English Corpus on CD-ROM* (2000; henceforward DOEC) and searched for the most common Latin ghost synonyms: *phantasma, imago, larua* or *larba* and *umbra* (Lewis and Short 1958). After checking and cross-checking the matches thus obtained in the OE lexicography (*Dictionary of Old English A–G*, the *Digital Edition of the Bosworth-Toller Anglo-Saxon Dictionary*, Clark Hall's *A Concise Anglo-Saxon Dictionary*) and the DOEC again for a few unexpected findings, the final list was reduced to 10 terms (*becola, (ge)dwimor, yfelwiht, scin(n), hīw, scinnhīw, gāst, gliderung, grīma* and *egesgrīma*) and 108 quotations. I also made use of the *Nerthus* database (Torre Alonso et al. 2008; Martín Arista 2010 and 2012) to retrieve the derived and word-compounded related vocabulary.

In turn, the initial pilot list extracted from section 01.07.03.02 *Ghost/phantom* in the *Historical Thesaurus of the Oxford English Dictionary* (Kay et al. 2009: 902; henceforward HTOED) was significantly cut short after I checked in the online version of the *Oxford English Dictionary* if the units still formed part of current usage and then compared results with the BNC proposed list of synonyms for *ghost*. The group finally consisted of 24 units (*apparition, barrow-wight, duppy, ghost, ghoul, hantu, jumby, phantasm, phantom, poltergeist, spectre, spook, wraith, haunt, manifestation, presence, revenant, spirit, evil spirit, shade(s), shadow(s), fetch, doppelganger* and *life-in-death*) and the total number of occurrences in the BNC amounted to 1293.

The type of empirical onomasiology that I have followed (Geeraerts and Gevaert 2008; Díaz-Vera 2011) for the analysis of the OE GHOST group assumes a literal/non-literal distinction on (first) sense-arrangement grounds and proceeds to classify a given term or idiomatic construction according to their exact position in the literalness-metonymy-metaphor *continuum* (Radden 2002: 409). This methodology also distinguishes between the *theme* (or etymology) and the *expression* of a given concept, the latter covering the totality of the derived and word-compounded related lexicon. As regards the CBE period, we have chiefly sought the measurement of the GHOST group in BNC terms providing the number of matches for each unit and have filtered through the cases of irrelevant quotations rising from polysemy or other factors.

We are aware that the results obtained from a contrast between 108 and 1293 quotations require a certain degree of idealized empiricism, since the DOEC is but a computerized version for what remains of a dead language and cannot match the size, textual range and research potential of the BNC. Even if so, the relative measurements we will draw will bear out the minor role played by metaphors in the two periods and their culture-specificity and will also prove relevant in other aspects.

3 The GHOST group in Old English

After the survey of the cited OE lexicography, the GHOST group amounted to 25 lexical units containing simple nouns (prefixed and unprefixed), adjectives, adverbs and compounds (see Appendix 1). This initial lit is then reduced to eight expressions with their corresponding etymological themes: *becola* (1), *dwimor* (19), *yfelwiht* (5), *scinn* (36) *hīw* (17), *gāst* (8), *gliderung* (1) and *grīma* (19). As can be quickly deduced from their number of occurrences, none of the cited expressions may be said to work as the hyperonym or prototypical centre in the GHOST group. In this respect, the rate of variation in the degree of lexical productivity (Díaz-Vera 2002: 55–56; henceforward DLP) shown by the three most frequent expressions as shown above is relatively similar: 7/3/8 respectively. The eight expressions should rather be viewed as competing patterns of linguistic conceptualization instead.

Becola epitomizes the spirit of hapax legomena in OE lexicography, glossing *larva* "ghost, spectre" in the Latin Glossaries from MS. Cotton Cleopatra. Of uncertain etymological theme (probably resin, according to the DOE), this word shows up collocating with *egesgrīma* in a section about deception that continues with *scinn* and its Latin counterpart, *fantasma*.[1] Perhaps related to Aldhelm's use of *larva* and *masca* in his *Carmen de Virginitate*, the word may have probably referred to a nocturnal female spectre impersonated when wearing a face-mask (Welsford 1929: 94–95):

> Linquentes larvam furvum fantasma putabant". (l. 2244) [...] Ut procul effulgeret facies larvata nefandi. [...] Nam tremulos terret nocturnis larva latebris, / Quae solet in furvis Semper garrire tenebris; / Sic quoque mascarum facies cristata facessit, / Cum larbam et mascam miles non horreat audax ... (ll. 2856–2859).[2]

Whatever its real nature and for a concept that comes from the 2nd half of the 7th century, a period that was still not utterly deprived of the influence of heathenism, the presence of mask-wearing female ghosts causing panic in soldiers constitutes a physical representation of FEAR IS AN OPPONENT (Kövecses 1989: 128–129).

---

1 [197300 (1973)] *Deluditur wæged wæs.* [197400 (1974)] *Larbam becolan, egesgriman.* [197500 (1975)] *Fantasma scin, idem et nebulum.*

2 The leaving thought the larva to be a furtive phantasm [...] That the masked face of the spectre one may flee far away [...] For the larva who is wont to howl ever in furtive darkness terrifies the timid in nocturnal coverts, and so also does the crested face of witches when the bold soldier does not fear the larva and the masca (Welsford 1929: 94–95).

The interpretation of OE *dwimor* alternates between delusion – or, in the medieval period, and according to the OED, sorcery, witchcraft – and that of apparition, phantom, which is attested in 21 occurrences in the DOEC. The word is glossed by *fantasma, phantasma(ta)* four times[3] and may refer to a variety of contexts ranging from a maiden transformed into a mare, Jesus walking on water (Mathew 12: 22-33) or to nightly spirits befalling on the sinful Herod:

> ÆCHom I, 5 Hine gedrehte singal slepleast: swa þæt he þurhwacole niht buton slepe adreah. [006600 (221.139)] And gif he hwon hnappode þærrihte hine drehton nihtlice gedwimor: swa ðæt him þæs slæpes ofþuhte.
>
> [He was afflicted by a never-ending sleeplessness in such a manner that he endured wakeful vigils without sleep. And when he happened to get a short slumber, nightly ghosts immediately tormented him in such a way that he regretted falling asleep]

Apart from countless physical diseases, the cited nocturnal spirits are but a small share of the torment that is justly inflicted by God to Herod in this section of Ælfric's Catholic Homilies. According to Pokorny (1959: 261-267), OE *dwimor* comes from PG *dwemanan, to smoke, and ultimately from PIE *dhem-, *dhemə- and *dheu-, *dheu̯ə- to smoke, burn. Apparitions were thus conceptualized as the outcome of a process in which fire was somehow involved. In turn, this bears out that the unit is diachronically motivated by the FEAR IS HEAT metaphor (Stefanowitsch 2006: 24-26).

Of uncertain connections outside Germanic, OE *wiht* refers to living beings in general and, when premodified by *yfel*, it enters the supernatural domain. The *ghost* reading is acknowledged in the first quotation under 1.b. by the OED, glossing *phantasma*. More significantly, it shows up 5 times in the Lindisfarne Gospels, in Mathew, Mark, one of their glossaries and in related marginalia to refer to the Jesus walking on water motif:

> MkGl (Li) *at illi ut uiderunt eum ambulantem super mare putauerunt phantasma esse et exclamauerunt* soð hia þæt gesegon hine geongende ofer sae hia woendon yfel wiht were & ceigdon & clioppadon.
>
> [But when they saw him walking upon the sea, they supposed it had been a spirit, and cried out (King James)]

---

3 Short Title: HyGl 2 (Milfull) [004600 (11.2)] *Procul recedant somnia & noctium fantasmata hostemque nostrum comprime* [...] swefna & nihta gedwymeru & feond urne ofþrece [012800 (30.2)] *Fantasma noctis decidat,* [...] gedwimor nihte fealle [...].

The gospel goes on with Jesus confirming his disciples on the boat that he is not a spirit, but Himself. In his Catholic Homilies, Ælfric retells the same episode more freely:

> ÆCHom II, 28 Ða ða drihten ðam scipe genealæhte. ða wurdon hi afyrhte. wendon þæt hit sum *gedwimor* wære; [008100 (226.151)] Drihten cwæð him to. Habbað eow truwan. Ic hit eom. ne beo ge ofdrædde. ne eom ic na *scinnhiw*. swa swa ge wenað.

> [When the Lord approached the boat, they were then very scared. They believed it to be an apparition. The Lord said unto them: Have faith. It is me. Do not be afraid. I am no ghost, as you [now] believe]

Another native term, *gedwimor*, takes the place of *yfelwiht* this time, which, together with the later presence of *scinnhiw*, make of this episode a treasure-hoard for *ghost* terms.

The largest OE expression is *scin(n)*, with a neuter *scin(n)* showing up 8 times in the DOEC, a weak masculine noun *scinna* (7) and a suffixed neuter formation *scīn(n)lac* that outnumbers the former terms (13). The Minor Latin-Old English Glossaries from MS Cotton Cleopatra match it with *fantasma* and the meaning covers a whole spectrum of possibilities, ranging from the mythological collocation *scuccum and scinnum* in lines 936–39 from Beowulf[4] to a peculiar combination of illusion, sorcery and ghost-like apparitions that is so proper of exegetic works like the Dialogues of Gregory the Great:

> GDPref and 4 (C) Soðlice hit gelamp þæt sum wer [...] hæfde ænne sunu [...] þone he lufode [...]. & þa se ylca cniht, [...] yfelsacode þæs ælmihtigan Godes mægnþrym in wyrginge & in wanunge & in scinna ciginge. Se ylca [...] for þrym gærum wæs mid cwylde & [...] becom to his deaðe.

> [Truly it came to pass that a certain nobleman had one son whom he loved [...] but the young man worked against the glory of God Almighty through blasphemies, complaints and invocations of spirits. This young man was afflicted with pestilence during three years and died]

Preceded by a reflection on the gaining of Heaven by baptized children dying young, the text above acts as a reminder on the dangers of blasphemy and religious misconduct. *Scin(n)* is etymologically related to the verb *scīnan*, of common Germanic distribution, and to PIE *skī-* shimmer, shadow. With cog-

---

4 [...] Wea widscofen witena <gehwylcum> ðara þe ne wendon þæt hie wideferhð leoda land-geweorc laþum beweredon *scuccum ond scinnum*. [...] Woe widespread for each of the sages / those who did not hope that in the span of their lives / the nation's fortress from foes they could protect, / from shucks and shines. Taken from Benjamin Slade's *Beowulf on Steorarume*, http://www.heorot.dk/beo-intro-rede.html, (Last accessed May 01, 2013).

nates like Sanskrit *chāyā* shade or Greek σκιά shadow, this theme bears out the diachronic motivation of ghosts in FEAR IS LIGHT (Stefanowitsch 2006: 24–26).

OE *hīw* is more frequent when it appears in the form of the compound neuter *scinnhīw* (15) than on its own (2). When put together, the number of occurrences for the expressions *scinn* and *hīw* amount to nearly 50 % of the total (53/109). The meanings granted to *hīw* and *scinnhīw* in the OE lexicography are apparition and illusion or spectre respectively. The following excerpt is quite revealing about the manner in which these concepts were understood:

> Lives of Saints 23 (Mary of Egypt) Ða geseah he him on þa swiðran healfe þær he on gebedum stod, swa swa he on mennisce gelicnysse on lichaman hine æteowan, and þa wæs he ærest swiþe afyrht, forþan þe he wende þæt hit wære sumes gastes scinhwy [...]
>
> [Then he saw to the right of where he stood in prayer, just like him, in human shape, to appear something to him, and he was then very scared, as he thought it was the apparition of a soul]

In the encounter of Zosimus and Mary of Egypt at the desert, a very popular story in the Middle Ages, monk Zosimus' first impression of Mary (sun-tanned, white haired and stark-naked but chastely seen at a distance) is that he is facing the apparition of a soul or *gastes scinhwy*. This is actually in consonance with the anthropological belief in many cultures that ghosts are an exact replica of the dead and the soul a body within another body that can be set loose when dying (Beals and Hoijer 1977: 569–575). In the OE rendering of the Book of Habakkuk, this folk-model also holds for inanimate referents like sea depths:

> PsCaC (Wildhagen) tostredynde wætru on siðfatum his sealde nywulnys stefnhys fram heanysse scinnhiwys hys upahafynys *aspargens aquas in itineribus suis dedit abyssus uocem suam ab altitudine fantasie sue eleuatus est*.
>
> [The mountains saw thee, and they trembled: the overflowing of the water passed by: the deep uttered his voice, and lifted up his ghost on high]

The sea abyss is here conceptualized as a fighter who, after having been defeated by the warrior-God Yahweh, exhales his spirit into the void. In *hīw*, the sense for apparition is produced through metonymy from its primary meaning: form, shape, colour. The synaesthetic basis of this concept is also attested in Germanic cognates such as Gothic *hiwi*, shine, ONorse *hy* skin, complexion (PIE *$\hat{k}i$-u̯o-*), with clear cognates outside Germanic such as Gk κίραφος, κίρα fox and Old Indian *śi-ti-* white (PIE $\hat{k}ei$- a kind of dark colour). The existence and frequency of the compound *scinnhīw*, when compared with *hīw* (15/2), is also revealing in this respect.

Out of 3100 occurrences in the DOEC, the reading ghost, spectre is only attested in 5 occurrences for OE *gāst*. It is not difficult to guess the metonymical chaining that develops the idea of the soul from that of breath, the first sense according to the DOE. What is not so clearly perceived is the way in which a central Catholic dogma, the belief in the existence of a *spiritus*, accommodates to a cultural model that is common to many ancient cultures by which breath is just the ultimate reflection of the person within the person, as the etymologies of Latin *spiritus* or Gk πνεύμα bear out. According to the DOE, a similar metonymical process also in common West Germanic is responsible for the existence of the cited *ghost* reading. The scarcity of occurrences (5) may be somehow due to taboo on religious grounds as the OE translators preferred, on the whole, to avoid this term and use other GHOST words instead. Be it as it may, the term is predominantly used in the Old English Martyrology for apparitions of tortured Catholics seeking to gain eternal rest through proper burial or for the cited Jesus walking on water motif:

> Lk (WSCp) 24.36: se Hælend stod on hyra midlene, & sæde him ... ic hit eom ne ondræde ge eow; ða wæron hig gedrefede & afærede & hig wendon þæt hig gast gesawon (cf. Lk 24:37 existimabant se spiritum videre).
>
> [Jesus himself stood in the midst of them, and said unto them "It is Me ... Do not be afraid". But they were terrified and affrighted, and supposed that they had seen a spirit]

The context is the same as for *yfelwiht*, *scinnlāc* and *gedwimor*. West Germanic *gaisto-z relates to Pre-Germanic *ghoizdo-z, with cognates like Sanskrit *hḗḍas* anger or Avestan *zōižda-* ugly. Accordingly, ghosts are thus diachronically proved to be motivated not only by FEAR, but also by ANGER sometimes. Indeed, it is sometimes very difficult to separate the two emotions, since they combine metonymically and involve the human and the supernatural participants respectively.

OE *gliderung* is the second hapax legomenon in the *ghost* group. It shows up in the Latin-Old English Glossary, in MS. Cotton Cleopatra:

> ClGl 1 (Stryker) *Fuluis* geolwum & deorcum. [...] *Fantasmate* þære glyderinge. [...] *Fertur* is sæd. *Fuluis* pale yellow & dark [...] *Fantasmate* ghost [...] *Fertur* is filled.

Unlike other A–Z glossaries, this one does not show any synonym in the neighbourhood of the term involved. Acknowledged by Clark Hall and the TOE, this ACTION FOR AGENT metonymy is related to the adjective *glidder*, slippery, which, together with *glīdan*, spring from PIE *ĝhleid-* softness, smoothness. The ability to glide reflects a widespread belief in many folk-models concerning a ghost's lighter, more subtle essence, which is also in accordance with the above-mentioned person-within-the-person assumption.

According to the DOE, *grīma* (19) tends to appear primarily in glosses, matching *masca, mascus, musca, larba, larbo* and *larvula* and collocating with *becola* in one of these occurrences. Apart from *grīming* (1), this expression primarily consists of the weak masculine noun *grīma* itself (9) and its compound *egesgrīma* (9). Of the two quotations available, the first comes from the Old English Martyrology:

> Mart 5 (Kotzor) ond he clypte ða hweras ond cyste ða pannan, ðæt he wæs eall sweart ond behrumig. Ond þa he ut eode, þa flogon hine his agene mæn ond wendon þæt hit wære larbo, þæt is egesgrīma.
>
> [And he hugged the caldrons and kissed the pans so that he was all black and sooty. And when he went out, then his own retinue flew away from him thinking that he was a *larbo*, that is, an egesgrīma]

In the preceding lines, Dulcitius, a high-officer in the days of Dioclitian, entered the kitchen in warlike gear and with perverse intentions where Saints Agape, Chione and Irene were confined. As it was night, and through God's intercession, he ended up fondling the pans and got so blackened that he was taken for a ghost by his soldiers. Riddle 40 reinforces the warlike associations for *grīma*:

> Rid 40: ic eom to þon bleað, þæt mec bealdlice mæg gearu gongende grima abregan, ond eofore eom æghwær cenra [...]; ne mæg mec oferswiþan segnberendra ænig ofer eorþan, nymþe se ana god [...]
>
> [I am so timid that a ghost going swiftly may boldly frighten me, but I am in every respect bolder than a wild boar [...]. No banner-bearer can overpower me except for God alone]

For an enigma whose baffling answer is creation, the context makes manifest that the latter is personified as one more warrior in the battlefield, where it happens to meet a fleeting ghost. The battleground is also responsible for the metaphorical mapping from the primary sense – *(visored) helmet, visor* – to the secondary but commoner *ghost, spectre* (2/9). The basis for this mapping is metonymical in essence, as the spectral figure is certainly conceptualized as face-masked, which holds well with Aldhelm's use of *masca*. Despite appearances to the contrary, *grīma* does not show a straightforward etymological relation to the adjective *grimm* (fierce, savage) or the deadjectival noun *grimness* (ferocity, cruelty). It is cognate with ONorse *grīma* (mask, helmet; riddle) and both come from PG **grim-* and PIE **ghrēi-* to smear, the sense development having evolved through the idea of a covering. Instead, the first member in the compound *egesgrīma*, OE *ege*, with cognates like Greek ἄχος (fear, pain, grief) or OHG *agiso, egiso egisa* (fear, fright), goes back to PIE **agh-* (fear) and once again provides the diachronic motivation of ghosts with FEAR.

3.1 The OE GHOST group weighed

We have followed Geeraerts and Gevaert (2008: 339) and Díaz-Vera (2011: 99) in the design of Table 2. The table displays the etymological theme, expression, semantics and number of occurrences for a given term in the horizontal axis, dividing the perpendicular dimension scalarwise into several parts in terms of their degree of literalness (Radden 2002: 409). Accordingly, literal meanings are confined to the upper section and figurative ones to the lower. In the non-literal domain, the higher section involves metonymy and synesthesia, the lower one relates to metaphor in turn.

Tab. 2: Literal and figurative GHOST expressions.

THEME	OE EXPRESSION	SEMANTICS	total	108
RESIN?	becola	literal	1	
SMOKE, VAPOUR	dwimor	literal	21	
THING, CREATURE	yfelwiht	literal	5	
SHINE	scin(n)	literal	36	63
SHAPE, FORM, APPEARANCE, COLOUR	hīw	metonymy	2	
SHINE	scinnhīw	metonymy	15	
BREATH	gāst	metonymy	8	
GLIDE, SLIP	gliderung	metonymy	1	26
VISORED HELMET, VISOR	grīma	metaphor	10	
	egesgrīma	metaphor	9	19

As can be easily observed, literal terms are more frequent than non-literal ones in the DOEC, amounting to 58.33% of the total. Non-figurative occurrences would indeed rate higher were the compound neuter *scinnhīw* no longer considered to be metonymical in essence (72.22/27.78). Of the remaining 41.66 ascribed to figurative terms, metonymies come first (24.07) and metaphors follow last (17.58), thus showing a relatively unimportant role in the OE domain of GHOST terms.

4 The GHOST group in Contemporary British English

The list of 24 units compiled after an extensive survey of current British English lexicography and included in section 2 above increases considerably when these units are conceived of as expressions (Díaz-Vera 2011: 87–88). As can be observed in Appendix 2, and after incorporating each unit's derived and compounded lexicon into the final list, the GHOST group amounts to 235 units of diverse morphological nature in CBE.

Of these 24 expressions, *ghost* stands out over the rest. The impact on the BNC amounts to 785 occurrences (60.71%) and 74 derived and word-compounded units (35.05) according to the OED. When measured, the following five high-frequency terms show a much lesser BNC impact: spirit (118), apparition (68), presence (49), spectre (41) and phantom (39). Their number of derived and word-compounded, related vocabulary is correspondingly smaller also: spirit (31/14.68%), apparition (2/0.94), presence (1/0.5), spectre (33/15.63), phantom (28/13.26). From an onomasiological perspective, *ghost* is thus obviously the hyperonym or prototypical centre.

Nevertheless, these measurements are not the only means that prove the prototypical status of *ghost* in CBE. Indeed, more than one synonym may show up in the neighbourhood, as the use of the collocates search tool in the BNC makes manifest. The collocates list for *ghost* is by far the largest: *spirit* (24), *phantom* (15), *apparition* (8), *spectre* (7), *shadow* (4), *doppelganger* (4), *fetch* (4), *wraith* (3), *poltergeist* (3), *ghoul* (3), *shade* (3), *spook* (2), *shades* (1) and *presence* (1). The quotations are conveniently sorted out in text types and look like as follows:

> HOME, THE **GHOST** AND THE EXORCIST **Spirit** ousted to save dad PRINCESS Diana's ancestral home was exorcised in a desperate attempt to save her dying father Earl Spencer. The Spencer family feared the ghost of the Earl's father was slowly killing him following a stroke. The Sunday People. 1337 s-units.

Passages like this one, concerning the life of Princess Diana's father, when taken together, are also empirically informative as regards the centrality of each of the terms involved. In this respect, the figures shown above prove that *spirit* is also *ghost*'s most frequent collocation, which holds for a unit showing the second largest number of occurrences in the BNC.

A long and complex arrangement of senses may also point to prototypicality. Apart from rendering the concept of the soul or spirit, religious dogmas like the Holy Ghost and other values which were already present in OE, this word also refers to a trace or vestige, is diversely applied in the fields of biology, optics, spectroscopy, radars and television and may also relate to shadow writers. In turn, and in consonance with the cited Lexical Productivity Principle (Díaz-Vera 2002: 55–56), the greater the semantic coverage, the wider the range of lexical variation associated with a given unit. This is observed in the relatively high number of idioms created (*to give up the ghost, (not) the ghost of a chance, the ghost in the machine, to raise a ghost, the ghost walks*, etc.), unparalleled among the rest of GHOST terms. Finally, the etymological theme is the same as for OE *gāst*, which proves that the diachronic motivation of *ghost* alternates between FEAR and ANGER.

For a term showing the third higher frequency of occurrences (68/5.25%), *apparition* does not display a slightly lower DLP (0.94%) than *spirit* (124/14.68) or a similar one to *phantom* (39/13.26). Acknowledged by the OED as currently being the predominant sense for this word, it is distinguished from *appearance* in being unexpected and startling:

> 'Father Reynard! Please, Father Reynard, help me!' The Franciscan made the sign of the cross in the air. Was it a **ghost**? An **apparition**? An earth-bound soul? The ghost of the dead Lady Eleanor?' The prince of darkness. Doherty, P C. London: Headline Book Pub. plc, 1992, pp. 3940 s-units.

The collocates are also scarce, co-occurring with *ghost* three times and one with *ghastly* and *shade*. According to the OED, the word was borrowed from Old French *apparition, aparoison*, which comes in turn from the Latin verb *adpārēre, appārēre* to appear, and ultimately from the combination of *ad* and *pārēre* to come in sight, come forth.

Barrow-wight (1/0.07), *duppy* (7/0.54), *hantu* (1) and *jumby* (1) show the lowest BNC frequency in the literal domain. The first term is inextricably linked with The Fellowship of the Ring and J. R. R. Tolkien's revisitation of Anglo-Saxon burial mounds –and perhaps charms– on Middle-Earth grounds:

> [...] when such heroes die they go, in Tolkien's opinion, neither to Hell nor Heaven, but to Limbo:' [...] perhaps at worst to wait with the **barrow-wight**' Where gates stand for ever shut, till the world is mended'. The road to Middle-Earth. Shippey, T A. London: Allen and Unwin, 1982, pp. 103–192. 1567 s-units.

In spite of its obvious literary register and of a different 1st compound member, this unit matches OE *yfelwiht* etymologically. Co-occurring with ghost four times and of probably African etymology, *duppy* is used among black West Indians for their understanding of dead spirits:

> # **Duppy** # A type of voodoo ghost found in the West Indies who is usually summonsed by villagers to undertake some act of revenge. [...] by pouring a glass of rum on the grave of a person newly dead, then calling their name until they appear. Myths, gods and fantasy: a sourcebook. Allardice, Pamela. Bridport, Dorset: Prism Press, 1990, pp. 30–155. 2315 s-units.

In turn, *hantu* appears 7 times in the BNC and is used to refer to many types of invisible evil spirits of mysterious workings in Malay culture. The only reference found for the former in the BNC is more prosaic, though:

> With human-like mouth and hands, and enormous eyes in a head which can swivel 180 degrees, the Dyaks of Borneo refer to him as **hantu** – meaning "ancestral **spirit**". Like an apparition of our goblin beginnings, the tarsier still stalks the treetops at night. Ring of fire. Blair, Lorne. London: Bantam (Corgi), 1988, pp. 9–127. 1622 s-units.

According to the OED, *jumby* is used chiefly among West Indian black people for evil spirits and occurs only once in the BNC:

> [...] Do you know him well?" Got to, over the years. Francis had me watch over him since he was a kid and his mother couldn't cope. He got into some trouble down in **Jumby** Village. "I heard about it." The possession of Delia Sutherland. Neil, B. London: Bloomsbury Pub. Ltd, 1993, pp. 59–179. 4086 s-units.

This term is cognate with *zombie* and shows a CAUSE FOR EFFECT metonymical development from the very idea of a fetish in African Kongo.

Doppelganger enters the English language in 1851 and obtains 14 matches in the BNC. As the term is obviously of non-native ascription, it shows no DLP. The definition combines apparitional, physical likeness and ill-omened features, as this reproduction of yourself is believed to become visible only to announce your death.

> **Doppelganger** [...] the "double" or identical likeness of someone who is about to die. [...] they haunt that person alone and by so doing indicate some terrible tragedy is imminent. A **doppelganger** is invisible except to its owner ... Myths, gods and fantasy: a sourcebook. Allardice, Pamela. Bridport, Dorset: Prism Press, 1990, pp. 30–155. 2315 s-units.

The concept is original because it does not focus on either the form or the ways of the apparition, but on the former's function. The dead do not come back from the afterlife or remain in this world because they may be troubled. As with *fetch* below, this unit represents a portend of death to the seer. The etymology is that of the German *doppelgänger* or Dutch *dubbelganger* double-goer.

In a list of 24 terms, *ghoul* occupies the ninth place and shows 22 occurrences in the BNC. The term co-occurs with *ghost* (5), *spirit* (4) and *apparition* (1) and, according to the OED, portrays an evil spirit that preys on human corpses taken from their graves. If the return of the dead causing fear is almost a cultural universal, when their comeback is cannibalistic the effect caused is then sheer panic. However, the quotes found in the BNC are mostly devoid of any gore:

> # Ian gives up the ghost # DRIVER Ian Sharpe reported knocking over a girl and was told by police: 'That's a **ghoul**.' Ian, 54, was heading home [...] when the **apparition** just stepped out. Police said other motorists had reported seeing the **ghost** of Judith Lingham, who died with two friends on nearby Blue Bell Hill. Today. 7528 s-units.

The term thus seems to operate more like a synonym for *ghost*. According to the OED, it comes from Arabic *ghūl*, to seize. Together with *egesgrīma*, both units are proof for the conceptualization of ghosts as OPPONENTS IN A STRUGGLE.

Phantasm and *phantom* emerge in the history of English at about the same time, with a time gap between them of 46 years: 1430/1384. The OED foregrounds the incorporeal nature of ghosts in the definition for *phantasm*, which bears out the cited person-within-the person folk model belief in the very manifestation of these supernatural experiences.

> What counts, then, is that Frodo should go on choosing. We perceive his doubt and weariness simultaneously as a natural reaction to circumstances, and as a temptation, even a **phantasm** or illusion of the Dark Tower. The road to Middle-Earth. Shippey, T A. London: Allen and Unwin, 1982, pp. 103–192. 1567 s-units.

Phantasm collocates in the neighbourhoods of *ghost* and *apparition* 2 and 1 times respectively. This term shows a low frequency (5/0.38) that is in consonance with the archaic and rare labels assigned by the OED but that does not match a relatively rich DLP, where it occupies the fifth highest position (4.73%). Contrariwise, *phantom* shows a relatively high frequency (39/3.01) and a higher DLP, being fourth (28/13.26) after *ghost* (67/35.05), *spectre* (33/15.63) and *spirit* (31/14.68) and responsible of expressions such as *phantom limb* or *p. pregnancy* in medicine or *p. circuit* in telecommunications. The term, no longer labeled as *phantasm*, also shows a richer syntactical productivity (with the phrase *a phantom of*) and co-occurs with several GHOST members: *ghost* (17), *spectre* (2), *ghastly* (1), *apparition* (1) and *shadow* (1). The definitions consulted in the cited lexicography, whilst foregrounding the immaterial essence of ghosts, seem to relate the former to a human shape most of the times:

> Redlaw, Mr, a lecturer in chemistry who is haunted, in the shape of a **phantom** alter ego, by bitter memories of past sorrows and wrongs. Yielding to the **phantom**'s temptation to remove all power of memory from him, [...]. The Dickens index. Burgis, Nina; Slater, Michael; Bentley, Nicolas. Oxford: OUP, 1990, pp. 182–239. 3786 s-units.

The two terms come from Anglo-Norman and Old French *fantosme, fantasme*, and these from Latin *phantasma*, which means ghost but is also used in post-Classical Latin times to express the concept of illusion, delusion. The second sense is nevertheless absent from the ancient Greek noun φάντασμα (appearance, vision, dream, ghost, apparition), created from φαντάζειν to make visible, present to (or as to) the eye, bring to light, and ultimately from PIE *bhā-1*, to shine. It is curious to observe that the semantic development the PIE stem underwent via Greek already shows up in the *bhā- lexical output: Old Indian *bhā́na-m* shiners, apparition and Tocharian A *pāt* for apparition, too. On etymologically grounds, *phantasm* and *phantom* are the counterparts of OE *scin(n)* and *scinnhīw*, bearing out the diachronic motivation of ghosts by LIGHT.

Poltergeist is a relatively recent coinage, appearing in the English language in 1848 for the first time. The term was imported from German and, according to the OED, incorporates two new definitional nuances: the making of loud noises and the movement of objects. Apart from these features, the majority of the 22 matches found in the BNC display some other poltergeistic habits:

> His **ghost** became known as the Bad Lord, it being a noxious **poltergeist** who irritates the family's descendants [...] – roaring in the cellars, splintering furniture and frightening maidservants. Myths, gods and fantasy: a sourcebook. Allardice, Pamela. Bridport, Dorset: Prism Press, 1990, pp. 30–155. 2315 s-units.

The semantic prosody of *poltergeist* alternates between neutral and negative. The unit co-occurs with *ghost* (8) and *spirit* (3) only. Likewise, the DLP for the former nears zero, which contrasts with other GHOST terms of similar frequency. Finally, the etymological theme is original insofar as it introduces the (loud) noise component for the first time into the history of the English GHOST group.

Specter shows up in 41 matches in the BNC, the fifth higher-frequency term in the list (3.17). It also rates high in DLP, with the second overall position (33/11.84) after *ghost* itself. The unit shows a relatively higher semantic complexity, with the sense of apparition, phantom at the core and semantic extensions towards the world of imitations and visual reflections, commonest among the 237 matches obtained in the BNC. This time, the semantic prosody is clearly negative, profiling the terrifying nature or aspect of the supernatural being:

> A ghostly figure appeared, dressed in flowing robes of blue and white. The **spectre** carried a great staff and, [...]. In loud, sepulchral tones, this vision warned James to give up war and consorting with wanton women. 'The white rose murder'. Clynes, Michael. London: Headline Book Pub. plc, 1992, pp. 73–209. 3259 s-units.

Of literary register, the word comes from 16th century French *spectre* and ultimately from Latin *spectrum* appearance, vision, apparition and the related verb *specĕre* to look, see. The PIE *spek̂- stem, with a similar meaning – to watch – also shows a similar semantic development in Latin *speciēs* from sight to apparition.

Spook appears first in American English (1801), then in British English (1859) and is found in 10 occurrences in the BNC. As the term is practically a newcomer, its DLP is small (7/3.31). The units comprised under the cited DLP are characterized by the OED as being colloquial or nonce-formations, and the semantic prosody that this term shows is of a jocular and colloquial character:

ANNIE SPOOKED Annie [Lennox]'s plans for a restful break were shattered when she discovered the holiday hideaway has a **ghost**. But while psychic Philip Steff has offered to help, a record company spokesman said: "Annie is a strong lady and she's not about to let a **spook** ruin her summer break." *The Daily Mirror. London: Mirror Group Newspapers, 1992, pp. 5648 s-units.*

Co-occurring with *ghost* five times, the very notion of *spook* breaks away from that of *ghost* as it expresses an ineffective spirit that is motivated by HUMOUR rather than by FEAR or ANGER. This is anthropologically feasible: in the realm of supernatural sightings, some are more dangerous than others. With cognates like Middle Dutch *spooc* and Middle Low German *spok*, the word is of common Germanic ascription but of dubious connections with PIE * *sp(h)eng-* to shine, which would bear out the diachronic motivation of ghosts by LIGHT.

Wraith comes last in the list of GHOST terms placed in the literal domain. A Scotticism first appearing in 1513, the term shows up 26 times in the BNC (2.01) and displays a relatively poor DLP (5/2.36). This unit collocates with *ghost* (5), *fetch* (2) and *doppelganger* (1) and, according to the OED, may refer to the spectre of a dead person and/or to a fetch: an apparition announcing someone's death. The matches found in the BNC favour the first of these senses (22/4):

> She delighted in their charm and their attractiveness, responded without reservation to these two young men, [...] who [...] would not disappear like a **wraith** the moment she turned her back. *Strawberries and wine. Nash, E. Cheltenham: New Author Pub, 1993, pp. 181–280. 3035 s-units.*

The Scottish word is of uncertain etymology. Klein (1966: 1753) claims a Celtic origin, perhaps from Gaelic and Irish *arrach* spectre, apparition.

The first unit in the metonymical section of the figurative domain is *haunt*. The unit is first recorded in 1843 and shows a time gap with its original verb of three centuries, the latter having been popularized in Shakespeare's plays. The disparity is made more manifest when the over 600 BNC matches obtained for the verb are measured against the only one found for the noun:

> [...] the Dyaks of Borneo refer to him as **hantu** – meaning "ancestral spirit". Like an apparition of our goblin beginnings, the tarsier still stalks the treetops at night. [...] It was from the same **haunts** as the tarsier that the [...] orangutan ... *Ring of fire. Blair, Lorne. London: Bantam (Corgi), 1988, pp. 9–127. 1622 s-units.*

Despite referring to this strange mammal species, the term owes its meaning to a metonymical PLACE FOR EVENT process: the place frequented for the apparition itself. The unit comes from Old French *hanter* visit, frequent, ultimately of Germanic origin (ON *heimta* to bring home, fetch or OE *hāmettan* to shelter) and focuses on the type of comeback that is inextricably linked with a particular location.

Of the 424 matches in the BNC, only 5 correspond to *manifestation*. The term only co-occurs with *ghost* once, does not show any DLP and is only included in the list of *ghost* synonyms in the BNC. The spiritual sense is first attested in 1860 in the OED, but it refers to the effects of a spirit's presence rather than to the spirit itself. The quotations found in the BNC point otherwise:

> It seems likely that Ba [...] was released or separated from the body after death. It remained on earth as a **manifestation** of the deceased and was depicted as a bird with a human head. The home of the Ba was the body in the tomb, but it was able to go out freely and bring back life to the body [...] Egyptian gods and myths. Thomas, Angela P. UK: Shire Pub. Ltd, 1989, pp. 6–60. 525 s-units.

A prerogative of the Egyptian gods, the Ba is also found in their kings before and after death. The metonymical process implied is that of EFFECT FOR CAUSE, as fear is caused by an apparition. *Manifestation* ultimately goes back to classical Latin *manifestāre* to reveal, discover, disclose.

Presence shows 49 matches in the BNC, ranking fourth in frequency (3.78) in spite of a rather poor DLP (1/0.5). The definition once again profiles the incorporeality of the spirit, whose presence is felt or perceived rather than seen:

> Teesdale sat alone in his study. Once more he had the feeling of another **presence**, a strange **spirit**, in the room. [...]. "If the **spirit** continues to live after the death of the body, [...] is it so very surprising if it remains in this world for a time? Ghost stories: Oxford Bookworms edition. Border, Rosemary. Oxford: OUP, 1989, pp. 1–86. 2155 s-units.

The list of co-occurrences reveals a relatively central role: *ghost* (11), *spirit* (6), *shade* (3), *phantom* (2) and *poltergeist* (1). The difference between perceiving a disembodied ghost and actually seeing it is accounted by a PART FOR WHOLE metonymical process. The etymology refers to Latin *praesentia* fact of being present, from *praeesse* being before.

Revenant is another relatively recent term (first recorded OED quotation in 1827), a product of the decline of religion and the rise of spiritualism in the Romantic period. This unit shows 3 BNC quotations, no DLP and a definition that oscillates between merely expressing the return of the dead in incorporeal form and the description of reanimated corpses. The bodies of these spirits may be perhaps dead, but they nevertheless show a physical, corporeal character again:

> [...] decline of faith went hand in hand with the evolution of the Gothic story, imported from Germany; the hour of the **revenant**, the **Doppelganger**, the werewolf and the vampire had come. The masks of death. Cecil, Robert. Lewes, East Sussex: The Book Guild Ltd, 1991, pp. 1312 s-units.

The metonymical motivation is PART-PART, instantiating a RESULT FOR ACTION process. The etymology is that of the corresponding French adjective *revenant*, returning, coming back. The term profiles the unnatural and undesirable passing of the dead from the afterlife to the real world, a move feared by humans in many pre-modern folk-models.

Spirit is the second largest GHOST group unit, the prototype`s stronger competitor. This unit shows 118 BNC matches (9.12), the third higher DLP (14.68) and greater semantic complexity than *ghost* itself, as it may variously refer to the animating or vital principle in man, the immaterial sentient element of a person, the essential character or qualities of something, vigour, courage, breath, wind, the mind, the world of distilled liquids, etc. The list of compounded (*spirit-doctor*) and derived terms (*spiritism*), phrases (*Holy Spirit*) and idiomatic constructions (*that's the spirit*) is also remarkably high. The OED definition balances the disembodied nature of the ghost with its capability of becoming visible and acknowledges a frequent terrifying and/or hostile semantic prosody:

> They had lived in fear after hearing many noises and seeing objects fly across rooms. The expert used a ouija board in an attempt to contact the **spirit** that was believed to be tormenting them. The board spelled out FIRE ... Paganism and the occult. Logan, Kevin. Eastbourne: Kingsway Pub, 1988, pp. 79–178. 1740 s-units.

The unit co-occurs with *ghost* (47), *presence* (6), *poltergeist* (5), *phantom* (5), *haunt* (2) and *wraith* (2). The word may also be qualified diversely, hence the colligation *evil spirit* (6), which is the perfect match for OE *yfelwiht*. The PART FOR WHOLE mapping from breath to (evil) soul is in consonance with the above-mentioned person-within-the-person folk-model belief, where this inner person is of an ethereal essence and can be perceived when exhaling. The etymological theme bears this out, with Latin *spiritus* (*spīrāre* to breathe) and Old Indian *picchōrā* flute, both from PIE *(s)peis- to blow.

Fetch is the first GHOST term in the metaphorical section. Like *doppelganger* above, the term involves a supernatural being portending death to a human. It is first attested in 1787 and possibly the native counterpart of the previous German term. *Fetch* obtains 5 matches in the BN:

> John Aubrey, in his Miscellanies (1696) vividly describes a **fetch**'s appearance: The beautiful lady Diana Rich, [...], as she was walking in her father's garden, [...] being then very

well, met with her own **apparition**, habit and everything, as in a looking-glass. About a month after, she died of the smallpox. Myths, gods and fantasy: a sourcebook. Allardice, Pamela. Bridport, Dorset: Prism Press, 1990, pp. 30–155. 2315 s-units.

The term co-occurs with *ghost*, *apparition* and *wraith* one time each. The OED editors seem to relate the claim for an original Northern English provenance of the term to the existence of OE *fæcce* and are of the opinion that our term eventually developed from the corresponding verb. In turn, OE *feccan* seize, fetch, earlier OE *fetian*, is of common Germanic ascription and comes from PIE * pĕd-/pŏd- foot. Nevertheless, what matters here is not so much the journey and the movement involved in the event, but the violence implied in being seized by a supernatural being. *Fetch* thus confirms the conceptualization of ghosts as opponents and is thus proof for the diachronic motivation of FEAR IS AN OPPONENT IN A STRUGGLE (Kövecses 1989: 128–129).

The word *shade* is confined to literary use, may appear in the singular or plural (*the shades*) and obtains 29 matches in the BNC (2.24%). The OED describes its meaning as a form or shape that is discernible but not tangible and specifies the connections of this term with the mythological abode of the dead, the Hades, and the more than probable influence of Latin *umbra* in the unit's creation:

> [...] when Hardy in these poems confronts the **shade** of his recently deceased and estranged wife Emma, not only does Aeneas in Aeneid 6 confront the reproachfully haughty **ghost** of Dido, but Dante's pilgrim confronts for the first time the **shade** or **apparition** of his lost Beatrice. Studies in Ezra Pound. Davie, Donald. London: Carcanet Press, 1991, pp. 2098 s-units.

In turn, *shadow* is recorded a bit earlier than the former (1464/1616), seems to operate in identical manner to the former unit and, apart from exhibiting a higher DLP (11/4.72) shows an almost identical BNC rate (33/2.55). Perhaps as a means for avoiding lexicographical circularity, the OED definition for these terms backgrounds the comparative darkness that is inherent to the two units. Both *shade(s)* and *shadow(s)* come from OE *scead(u)we*, of common Germanic ascription (Old Saxon *scado*, Go. *skadus*) and a PIE *skot- shadow, darkness (Greek. σκότος darkness, Old Irish scāth shadow). In her analysis of SADNESS IS DARK, Deignan (2005: 84–86) affirms that the commonest mapping for the former source domain involves some kind of haunting. She goes on to focus on *shadow* itself, suggesting in her corpus study that the latter term invokes as much feelings of sadness as of fear apart from other negative emotions. The analysis of the 29 occurrences for *shade* in the BNC reveals a complex scenario where SADNESS prevails (14/29) and FEAR follows at a relative distance (9/29).

This points to the diachronic motivation of SADNESS IS DARK (Stefanowitsch 2006: 32–36) and FEAR IS DARK (Stefanowitsch 2006: 27–28).

Last in the literal-non-literal *continuum* we find the blended spaces section (Fauconnier and Turner 2002; Oakley and Coulson 2000: 175–196). In this, we find the expressions *life-in-death* (1) and *death-in-life* (1). The first is acknowledged by the OED and HTOED as a GHOST unit; the second is not, but we have found it operating as such in the BNC. We believe these to be blends because they combine life and death in such a way that the distinction between the natural and supernatural is blurred:

> # Death has already dressed him # His face a **ghoul**-mask, [...] # What a change! From that covenant of Polar Light # To this shroud in a gutter! # What a **death-in-life** – to be his own **spectre**! # His living body become death's puppet! Selected poems 1957–1981. Hughes, Ted. London: Faber and Faber Ltd, 1982, pp. 35–235. 4365 s-units.

The living somehow deadens and the dead, in turn, enlivens:

> # in our likeness: we have likeness, # the desire to feel us # in our bones. # And if I re-lived # my **life-in-death**, I would # change nothing, and especially # not our blossoming, our # particular fruition. For now. Godbert, Geoffrey and Ramsay, Jay. London: The Diamond Press, 1991, pp. 1–108. 2775 s-units.

As can be observed by the quotations above, the two expressions are literary. *Death-in-life* tellingly co-occurs with *spectre*.

4.1 Weighing the GHOST group in Contemporary British English

As with the OE GHOST group above, Table 3 displays the literal and non-literal domains for CBE. The figurative domain is divided into metonymy, metaphor and blending.

As can be easily perceived, literal terms (80.58) are more frequent than non-literal ones (19.42) once again. In the figurative space, metonymies are more numerous (182/14.07) than metaphorical and blending processes (69/5.33). In spite of the time span between the OE and CBE periods, the predominance of the literal over the non-literal and of metonymies over metaphorical outputs shows diachronic consistency. As for the rate differences between OE and CBE, I believe that taboo on religious grounds may have played its role in the decrease of the rate for literalness (58.33 < 80.58). In this respect, we have to acknowledge that the figurative domain rates higher in OE (41.65) than in CBE (19.40) with metaphors placed below (17.58) but slightly behind metonymies (24.07).

Tab. 3: Literal and figurative GHOST expressions in CBE.

THEME	EXPRESSION	SEMANTICS	bnc total	1293
TO COME IN SIGHT, COME FORTH,	apparition	literal	68	
MOUND-THING, CREATURE	barrow-wight	literal	1	
DOUBLE GOER	doppelganger	literal	14	
UNKNOWN	duppy	literal	7	
BREATH (OF LIFE)	ghost	literal and prototype	785	
TO SEIZE	ghoul	literal	22	
UNKNOWN	hantu	literal	1	
FETISH	jumby	literal	1	
APPEAR	phantasm	literal	5	
	phantom	literal	39	
NOISE	poltergeist	literal	22	
PERCEIVE, LOOK	spectre	literal	41	
SHINE?	spook	literal	10	
UNCERTAIN	wraith	literal	26	1042
VISIT, FREQUENT	haunt	metonymy	1	
REVEAL, DISCOVER	manifestation	metonymy	5	
BEING BEFORE	presence	metonymy	49	
RETURN	revenant	metonymy	3	
BREATH (OF LIFE)	spirit	metonymy	118	
	evil spirit		6	182
SEIZE?	fetch	metaphor	5	
DARKNESS	shade(s)	metaphor	29	
	shadow(s)	metaphor	33	
DEATH, LIFE	death-in-life	blending	1	
LIFE, DEATH	life-in-death	blending	1	69

5 Metaphors and their words: a case of diachronic-within-culture variation

The great majority of the expressions analyzed in this work contain the FEAR element in their definitions. Kövecses (1989: 128–129) postulated the existence of FEAR IS A SUPERNATURAL BEING with examples like *He was haunted by fear*. We believe that if this metaphor, later borne out by Stefanowitsch (2006: 26) by means of metaphorical pattern analysis, epitomizes the very essence of ghosts, then at least some of the source domains for FEAR should also show up in the GHOST group.

The patterns of conceptualization analyzed for both periods show varying but recurring links with verbs related to the senses that somehow express FEAR predominantly, perhaps ANGER or SADNESS in some cases. Among these verbs, "see" is the most frequent, giving rise to the notions of an apparition (*apparition, phantasm, phantom, spectre, spook*) and its consequences (*manifestation*) and to the idea of bounded shape or form (*hīw*). Instead, other verbs may not incorporate SIGHT into their semantics but blend more than one sense (*presence*). Some units denote sound (*poltergeist*), other terms point to smell through breath (*gāst, ghost, spirit*) or express movement (*gliderung, haunt, revenant*).

On the whole, the ghosts of the OE period seem to have been conceived of as more fully embodied than their current counterparts. Evil creatures (*yfelwiht*), shapes (*hīw, scinnhīw*) and battle enemies (*grīma, egesgrīma*) amount to nearly 38 % of the total. Contrariwise, the sum of the *apparition* terms cited above and the prototype yields 77.49 % in CBE. The bodily nature of OE ghosts is actually in consonance with medieval burial practices in which the dead were variously prepared – tied, beheaded and/or looking down, etc. – for their journey into the afterworld to avoid and undesired comeback. This embodiment, which is frequently depicted in terms of masked helmets and armour, was lost on the Tudor stage when suits of armour gave way to drapery (Jones and Stallybrass 2000: 248). Despite a rising current tendency in the use of terms bordering the concept of the living dead and cannibalism (*doppy, ghoul, jumby, hantu* and *revenant*), the emphasis on disembodiment that is so current in our times thus originated in the Renaissance period, continued with the cited rise of spiritualism and, in my opinion, epitomizes an era in which mankind is already in control of all the material – and some immaterial – forces and looks beyond to face their own fears.

The differences between the two periods also concern the extent of the influence of synesthesia. In the OE period, LIGHT shows up in *scin(n)* and *scinnhīw*, and the conceptual core of *hīw* inextricably links the idea of bodily shape with colour. In all, the number of occurrences amount to 49.07 % of the total (53/108). LIGHT is also one of the mappings proposed for FEAR by Stefanowitsch (2006: 27). However, there is no darker shade in OE. The CBE period shows both. LIGHT appears in the etymological themes for *phantom* (39) and *phantasm* (5) and perhaps in the etymological basis for *spook* (10). In turn, *shade* (29) and *shadow* (33) instantiate the well-known FEAR IS DARK metaphor (Stefanowitsch 2006: 28). Nevertheless, when compared with the OE period, the influence of synesthesia in CBE is reduced, reaching 8.19 % (106/1293).

HEAT shows up in OE *dwimor* (21) and, more dubiously, *becola* (1). The type of apparition that *dwimor* involves is obviously based on an increase of temperature caused by fire, since the etymology makes clear the role of smoke, vapour in the event. The rate is relatively high, with a 19.44 of the total (21/108). What is really surprising is to find no instances of FEAR IS HEAT (Stefanowitsch 2006: 27) in CBE. This may be perhaps due to the prevalence of incorporeality.

Metaphorical or pseudo-metaphorical enemies are also present in the two periods. They show up in *grīma* (10) and *egesgrīma* (9) and take us directly back to the Anglo-Saxon battlefield, whether mythological (*becola*) or not. Likewise, *ghoul* (22) and, above all, *fetch* (5) are the CBE proof for the FEAR IS AN OPPONENT metaphor (Kövecses 1989: 128–29; Stefanowitsch 2006: 24–28). Again, the corpus evidence proves that in the OE period the metaphor is more active than nowadays (17.59/2.08).

Concerning the rest of source domains mappings for FEAR as found in Stefanowitsch (2006: 24–28), some are incompatible – hot fluid/substance in a container, a superior – and the rest – cold and high/low (intensity) – are not activated. Nevertheless, the GHOST group in the OE period is highly motivated, as the sum of source domains related to FEAR amounts to 91/108 occurrences. The motivation of the CBE group is found in the very prototype and in the rest of source domain, FEAR-related members: 68.90 %. The decrease in the rate is mainly due to the impact of borrowing in the vocabulary of contemporary English.

6 Conclusions

In this work, I have presented a list of OE and CBE terms for the GHOST group and have arranged them in the semantic space according to the literal-nonliteral *continuum* (literal-metonymy-metaphor-blending). I have measured the impact of each of these terms by using corpus linguistics methods and have also provided their etymological themes in order to obtain a map of shared figurative and non-figurative patterns of conceptualization.

The results obtained reveal that the impact of figurative processes on the vocabulary of English is smaller than thought. This is particularly true for metaphorical processes, which are overruled by metonymy in the OE and CBE periods. They also show the role of diachronic variation in the GHOST group, where we find relatively similar patterns of conceptualization operating diversely in the two periods involved. In the non-figurative domain, HEAT and LIGHT, which were basic constitutive factors in OE, disappear or are replaced by DARKNESS in the contemporary period. In spite of being active in CBE, the OPPONENT IN

A STRUGGLE metaphor cannot match the weight of its OE counterpart in cultural terms. These differences are also quantitative, as the figurative domain rates higher in OE, with metaphor being close to metonymy itself.

Likewise, I have pointed towards a validation of the cognitive linguistics literature on emotions in the cultural domain in general and, more particularly, in those cultural constructs that may be conceived of as by-products of emotions. In this respect, and starting from the relevance of FEAR IS A SUPERNATURAL BEING, which is crucial for the creation of the very concept of ghost, I have proved that ghosts are primarily motivated by FEAR as the cited source domain mappings (HEAT, LIGHT, DARKNESS, OPPONENT) appear recurrently across the history of English GHOST words and their etymologies. I have also validated the cited motivation quantitatively, in terms of occurrences. Finally, I have also determined that this diachronic motivation is variable and reduced by the influx of borrowings in the contemporary period.

Acknowledgements: This research has been funded through the Project *Polos Semánticos en el Léxico del Inglés Antiguo. Construcción del Significado, Primitivos Semánticos y Formación de Palabras* (FFI2011-29532). I should like to thank Francisco Javier Martín Arista and Javier E. Díaz Vera for their insightful comments and suggestions on the Old English section of this work. All disclaimers apply.

References

Primary sources

B&T. 2007. *Digital edition of the Bosworth-Toller Anglo-Saxon Dictionary*
    http://bosworth.ff.cuni.cz/ (Last accessed 30 April, 2013).
BNC. 2007. *The British National Corpus*, version 3 (BNC XML Edition). Distributed by Oxford University Computing Services on behalf of the BNC Consortium. URL: http://www.natcorp.ox.ac.uk/
CH. 2003. *John R. Clark Hall. A concise Anglo-Saxon Dictionary*. Germanic Lexicon Project by Sean Crist. http://lexicon.ff.cuni.cz/texts/oe_clarkhall_about.html (Last accessed 24 April, 2013).
DOEC. 2000. *The dictionary of Old English Corpus in electronic form*. Antonette diPaolo Healey, Joan Holland, Ian McDougall & Peter Mielke (eds.). Toronto: DOE Project.
DOE. 2008. *The dictionary of Old English: A–G on CD-ROM*. Toronto: DOE Project.
Klein, Ernest. 1966. *A comprehensive etymological dictionary of the English language*. Amsterdam: Elsevier.

HTOED. 2009. *Historical thesaurus of the Oxford English Dictionary*. Christian Kay, Jane Roberts, Michael Samuels & Irené Wotherspoon. Oxford: Oxford University Press.
IEW. 1959. *Indogermanisches Etymologisches Wörterbuch*. Edited by Julius Pokorny. Bern: Francke.
Lewis, Charlton T. & Charles Short. 1969. *A Latin dictionary*. Oxford: Oxford University Press.
NERTHUS. 2008. Martín, Arista, Javier, Roberto Torre Alonso, Ana Ibáñez Moreno, Elisa González Torres, Luisa Caballero González & Carmen Novo Urraca. *Nerthus Project Database*. http://www.nerthusproject.com/search-database (Last accessed April 20, 2013).
OED. 2013. *Oxford English dictionary* online. Edited by John Simpson. Oxford: Oxford University Press.http://0-www.oed.com.columbus.uhu.es/ (Last accessed May 01, 2013).
TOE. 2000. Roberts, Jane, Christian Kay & Lynne Grundy. *A thesaurus of Old English*. Two Volumes. Amsterdam: Rodopi.

Secondary sources

Beals, Ralph L., Harry Hoijer & Alan R. Beals. 1977. *An introduction to anthropology*. New York: MacMillan.
Bohannan, Laura. 1966. Shakespeare in the Bush. An American anthropologist set out to study the Tiv of West Africa and was taught the true meaning of Hamlet. *Natural History* 75. 28–33.
Charteris-Black, Jonathan. 2003. Speaking with forked tongue: A comparative study of metaphor and metonymy in English and Malay phraseology. *Metaphor and Symbol* 18. 289–310.
Deignan, Alice. 2005. A corpus-linguistic perspective on the relationship between metonymy and metaphor. *Style* 39(1). 72–91.
Díaz-Vera, Javier Enrique. 2002. Lexical and non-lexical linguistic variation in the vocabulary of Old English. *Atlantis* 25(1). 29–38.
Díaz-Vera, Javier Enrique. 2011. Reconstructing the Old English cultural model for FEAR. *Atlantis* 33(1). 85–103.
Dover Wilson, John. 1959. *What happens in Hamlet*. Cambridge: Cambridge University Press.
Fauconnier, Gilles & Mark Turner. 2002. *The way we think: Conceptual blending and the mind's hidden complexities*. New York: Basic Books.
Finucane, Ronald C. 1984. *Appearances of the dead: A cultural history of ghosts*. Buffalo, New York: Prometheus Books.
Geeraerts, Dirk & Caroline Gevaert. 2008. Hearts and (angry) minds in Old English. In Farzad Sharifian, René Dirven, Ning Yu & Susanne Niemeier (eds.), *Culture, body, and language: Conceptualizations of internal body organs across cultures and languages*. 319–347. Berlin & New York: Mouton de Gruyter.
Gevaert, Caroline. 2002. The evolution of the lexical and conceptual field of ANGER in Old and Middle English. In Javier E. Díaz-Vera (ed.), *A changing world of words: Studies in English historical lexicology, lexicography and semantics*, 275–299. Amsterdam: Rodopi.
Grossenbacher, Peter G. & Christopher T. Lovelace. 2001. Mechanisms of synesthesia: Cognitive and psychological constraints. *Trends in Cognitive Sciences* 5. 36–41.
Jones, Ann Rosalind & Peter Stallybrass. 2000. *Renaissance clothing and the materials of memory*. Cambridge: Cambridge University Press.

Kövecses, Zoltan. 1989. *Speaking of emotions*. New York: Springer.
Kövecses, Zoltan. 2005. *Metaphor in culture: Universality and variation*. Cambridge: Cambridge University Press.
Kövecses, Zoltan. 2006. *Language, mind and culture: A practical introduction*. Oxford: Oxford University Press.
Lakoff, George. 1987. *Women, fire and dangerous things. What categories reveal about the mind*. Chicago: University of Chicago Press.
Lakoff, George & Mark Johnson. 1980. *Metaphors we live by*. Chicago: University of Chicago Press.
Lakoff, George & Zoltan Kövecses. 1987. The cognitive model of anger inherent in American English. In Dorothy Holland & Naomi Quinn (eds.), *Cultural models in language and thought*, 195–221. Cambridge: Cambridge University Press.
Martín Arista, Javier. 2010. Building a lexical database of Old English: Issues and landmarks. In John Considine (ed.), *Current projects in historical lexicography*, 1–33. Newcastle: Cambridge Scholars Publishing.
Martín Arista, Javier. 2012. The Old English prefix *ge-*: A panchronic reappraisal. *Australian Journal of Linguistics* 32. 411–433.
Matsuki, Keiko. 1995. Metaphors of anger in Japanese. In John Taylor & Robert MacLaury (eds.), *Language and the cognitive construal of the world*, 137–151. Berlin & New York: Mouton de Gruyter.
Moreman, Christopher M. 2008. *Beyond the threshold. Afterlife beliefs and experiences in world religions*. Plymouth: Rowman & Littlefield Publishers, Inc.
Oakley, Todd & Seana Coulson. 2000. Blending basics. *Cognitive Linguistics* 11(3/4). 175–196.
Palmer, Gary. 1996. *Toward a theory of cultural linguistics*. Texas: The University of Texas Press.
Radden, Günter. 2002. How metonymic are metaphors? In René Dirven & Ralf Pörings (eds.), *Metaphor and metonymy in comparison and contrast*, 407–434. Berlin & New York: Mouton de Gruyter.
Stefanowitsch, Anatol. 2004. Happiness in English and German: a metaphorical-pattern analysis. In Michel Achard & Suzanne Kemmer (eds.), *Language, culture and mind*, 137–149. Stanford, CA: CSLI publications.
Stefanowitsch, Anatol. 2006. Words and their metaphors: a corpus-based approach. In Anatol Stefanowitsch & Stephan Th. Gries (eds.), *Corpus-Based approaches to metaphor and metonymy*, 63–105. Berlin & New York: Mouton de Gruyter.
Torre Alonso, Roberto, Javier Martín Arista, A. Ibáñez Moreno, E. González Torres & L. Caballero González. 2008. Fundamentos empíricos y metodológicos de una base de datos léxica de la morfología derivativa del inglés antiguo. *Revista de Lingüística y Lenguas Aplicadas* 3. 129–144.
Welsford, Enid. 1929. *The court masque: A study in the relationship between poetry and the revels*. Cambridge: Cambridge University Press.

APPENDIX 1: OE expressions of "ghost".

EXPRESSIONS	ETYMOLOGICAL THEMES	SEMANTICS	LEXICAL UNITS	Nº	TOTAL
BECOLA	resin?	literal	becola n.	1 (og)	1
DWIMOR	smoke, vapour	literal	dwimor n.	2	21
			dwimer n.	1	
			gedwimor n	9	
			dwimorlīce adv.	1	
			dwymorlīce adv.	1	
			gedwimorlic adj.	4	
			gedwimorlice adv.	3	
GĀST	breath	metonymy	gāst m.	5	8
			gāstlic adj.	2	
			gæstlic adj.	1	
GLIDERUNG	glide, slip	metonymy	gliderung n.	1	1
GRĪMA	visored helmet, visor	metaphor	grīma n.	9	19
			egesgrīma n.	9	
			grīming n.	1	
HĪW	shape, form, appearance, colour	literal	hīw n.	1	17
			hīwung n.	1	
			scinnhīw n.	15	
SCIN(N)	shine	literal	scin(n) n.	8	36
			scinlic adj.	3	
			scinsēoc adj.	1	
			scingedwola m.	1	
			scīnlāc n.	13	
			scinlǣce adj.	1	
			deofolscinn n.	2	
			scinna m.	7	
WIHT	being, creature	literal	yfelwiht	5	5

APPENDIX 2: Derived and word-compounded GHOST units in Contemporary British English.

EXPRESSIONS	LEXICAL UNITS	Nº	RATE	TOTAL
apparition	apparitional adj., apparition v.	2	0.94 %	0.94
barrow-wight	barrow-wightish adj.	1	0.5	0.5
fetch	fetch-like n.	1	0.5	0.5
ghost	ghost v., ghostdom n., ghostess n., ghosthood n., ghostified adj., ghostiness n., ghostish adj., ghostism n., ghostless adj., ghostlet n., ghostlike adj., ghostliness n., ghostly adj. (28), ghostly adv. (255), ghostship n., ghosty adj, ghostily adv., ghastly adj. (49), ghastly adv., aghast adj.	20	9.47	35.05
	ghost-apparition, -appurtenance, -ballad, -candle, -dance, -demon, -dim, -family, -fear, -fearing, -filled, -form, -god, -haunt, -haunted, -hour, -house (6), -hunter, -land, -light, ghost line, -lore, -lover, -marriage, -moth, -name, -plant, -poisoned, -raiser, -ridden, -seeing, -seer, -service, -soul, -story (14), ghost town (30), ghost train (18), -trod, -white, -wise, -word, -world, -worship, -write, ghost writer, -writing, -written	47	22.27	
	the ghost walks, to lay a ghost, the loath ghost, the local ghost, (not) the ghost of a chance, to raise a ghost, the wicket ghost	7	3.31	
ghoul	ghoul-eye, -haunted, -head, -like	4	1.89	1.89
phantasm	phantasmal adj., phantasmally adv., phantasmatic adj., phantasmatical adj., phantasmally adv., phantasmic adj., phantasmical adj., phantasmically adv., phantamological adj., phantasmology n.	10	4.73	4.73
phantom	phantom n., phantom adj., phantomatic adj., phantomic adj., phantomical adj., phantomically adv., phantomish adj., phantomize v., phantomizing adj., phantom-like, adj.and adv., phantomy adj.	11	5.21	13.26
	phantom-chaser, p. circuit, p. land, p. life, p. limb, p. limb pain, p. nation, p. pain, p. pregnancy, p. shape, phantomship, p. tribe, p. tumour, -warning, -white, phantomwise, p. withdrawal	17	8.05	
poltergeist	poltergeistic adj., poltergeistism n.	2	0.94	0.94

EXPRESSIONS	LEXICAL UNITS	Nº	RATE	TOTAL
presence	Presenceless	1	0.5	0.5
shade(s)	the shades	1	0.5	0.5
shadow	shadowing adj., shadowily adv., shadow-land n., shadowly adv., shadowy adj.	5	2.36	4.72
	shadow-fight, shadow train, -wife, -word, -world	5	2.36	
	to wear (oneself or another) to a shadow	1	0.5	0.5
spectre	spectred adj., spectredom n., spectrish adj., spectrogram n., spectrograph n., spectrological adj., spectrology n., spectrous adj.	8	3.79	15.63
	spectre-bark, -candle, -chimera, -doubt, -faint, -fashion, -fighting, -haunted, -horse, spectre hound, spectre knight, spectre-lean, -like, -looking, spectre monarch, spectre-mongering, -pale, -pallid, -queller, spectre shape, spectre ship, spectre-staring, -thin, spectre train, spectre woman	25	11.84	
spirit	spirit v., spiritdom n., spirited adj., spirithood n., spiritism n., spiritist n., spiritistic adj., spiritlike adj., spirit-rapping n.	9	4.26	14.68
	spirit-body, -bride, -charmer, -hunter, -monger, -ridder, -seer, -wrestler, -doctor, -enemy, -photograh, -photography, -haunted, -lady, -medium, -mischief, -possession, -realm, -visit, -voice, -wall, -world	22	10.42	
spook	spook v., spookic adj., spookical adj., spookish adj., spookism n., spookological adj., spookology n., spooky adj.	7	3.31	3.31
wraith	wraith-land n., -like adj., -seeing n., -ship n., -spell n.	5	2.36	2.36
		211		

Index

abstraction levels 98–100, 115, 117
ancient Greek lyric 300, 306
anticausative 201, 204–207, 209, 215

Basque 9, 65–66, 71, 75–76, 78–82, 84, 86–88, 90
– *hatz* 9, 65, 76, 78–85, 88–89
– *hatzamar* 84–85
BECOME concept 181, 183–184, 186, 193, 195, 198, 206–207, 209, 213, 215, 217
blending 174, 295, 298, 305, 309, 315–316, 339–340, 342
borrowing 9, 31–35, 37, 41, 46–48, 51, 55, 58, 102, 111, 183, 207, 250–251, 254, 258, 260, 319, 342–343
bridging mechanisms 74

Caucasian Albanian 171–172, 199, 203, 206–210, 212–215, 218
Chinese 10, 101–103, 106, 109–113, 115, 118, 141–143, 145–147, 150, 152, 154–155, 157–159, 162, 164–166, 173, 175, 196–197, 321
Cognitive Linguistics 15, 24, 26, 33, 66, 132, 227, 275, 296, 298, 321, 343
colour 95, 98, 109–118, 256, 259, 326, 329, 341
COME schema 191
common ground 123–127, 137–138
conceptual system 3, 95, 97–98, 101, 104, 106, 108–109, 113–114, 116, 166, 295, 302
Contemporary British English 10, 110, 319–320, 329, 334, 339, 347
conventionalisation 123–124, 126, 128, 131, 135
conversation 142, 144–145, 153, 155, 163, 165
corpus linguistics 227, 319–320, 342
counter-expectation 10, 141–142, 145–146, 150–151, 153, 155, 159, 162–164, 166
cultural schemas 9, 65–66, 68–71, 74, 76–79, 82–83, 87–90
culture 7, 9–10, 15, 17–18, 21–22, 26, 48, 69, 88, 95, 99–101, 105–117, 225, 227, 230, 235–236, 238, 244, 248, 259–260, 265–269, 277, 295–296, 299, 301, 303, 307, 309, 314, 316, 319–322, 326, 327, 331, 340

dead metaphor 3, 31–33, 35, 38, 127, 227, 254, 269
deal (noun and verb) 9, 51–55, 60
deliteralization 15, 25–26
diachronic metonymic chain 76, 78
diathesis 10, 171–173, 176, 184, 188, 192, 194, 197–201, 204, 207–208, 212, 215–218

embodiment 8–9, 95–109, 111–117, 172, 260, 305, 341
emotions 8, 24, 38–39, 95–96, 103–106, 114–117, 226–227, 231, 248–250, 252, 260, 295–296, 298, 307–308, 311, 313–314, 316, 319–321, 327, 338, 343
– history of emotions 298, 314, 316
– anger 4–5, 8, 20–21, 23–24, 58, 101–104, 113, 115–117, 229, 248–250, 260, 296, 298, 320–321, 327, 331, 335, 341
– guilt 225, 227, 233–234, 238, 242, 258–259
– shame 10, 225–260
empirical methods 266, 268
encyclopedic knowledge 65, 67–68, 72, 82
entrenchment 24, 75, 78, 83–84, 126–128, 130, 297
etymological metaphor 34, 47

fallacy 8–9, 15–16, 19–20, 24, 26, 315
falsification/falsiable 265–266, 268, 271, 274
figurative language 3, 8–9, 115, 299, 315

gesture 85–88, 129, 246, 309
GET/TAKE concepts 196–198
ghost terms 324
GO schema 187, 191
grammaticalization 6–10, 55, 60, 123, 132–137, 141, 154, 157, 160, 166, 171–174,

176, 179, 184–186, 189, 195–196, 198, 201, 203–205, 210, 213, 215–216, 218

historical metaphor 19, 26, 31, 33, 35, 38, 44, 47
historical semantics 77
home concept 10, 265–267, 270–275, 277–280, 284

iconicity 127–128
idealised cognitive model 265–266, 268, 275, 290
image schemas 4–5, 96, 99, 117, 295, 302, 308
language as a complex adaptive system (CAS) 65–67, 69, 72, 74–75, 77–78, 89

lexical loss 51–52, 57–58
linking adverbial 141, 162, 165–166

memorisation 123, 126, 133, 135, 138
metaphor 3–10, 15–22, 24–26, 31–35, 38, 42, 44, 47, 51, 70, 83, 95–103, 106, 108–118, 123–138, 141–145, 153, 158, 162, 166, 225–228, 255–260, 265, 271–275, 296, 298, 305, 310, 313–316, 319–322, 324, 329, 339–343, 346
metaphorical extensión 128, 131, 135, 137, 258
metaphorization 8–10, 15, 19, 24, 26, 60, 103, 106, 107, 166, 179–181, 183–184, 186, 230
metaphtonymy 10, 144, 153, 166
metonymy 4, 5–7, 9, 10, 19–20, 51, 59–60, 77–78, 82, 113, 126, 141–145, 157, 162, 155, 166, 228, 230, 235, 248, 250–251, 254, 257–259, 274, 319–322, 326–327, 329, 339–340, 342–343, 346
– serial metonymy 5, 9, 65, 66, 76–77, 83–84, 89
modern Greek folksongs 309
motion verbs 177, 183, 198, 206–207, 209–210, 212–218
multivariate statistics 265–266, 280, 282, 290

Old English 5–6, 8–10, 20, 43–44, 53, 56, 60, 102–104, 110, 113, 117, 225–230, 232, 235, 237, 240–243, 245, 248, 250–260, 319–323, 325, 327–328, 343
Old Norse 10, 175, 181, 225–230, 232–235, 237–239, 244–246, 249–251, 253–260
onomasiology 19, 52, 227, 322
ostensive-inferential communication 123–124, 127–130, 135, 138

passive 10, 59, 132–133, 171–175, 184–188, 190–199, 201–204, 207–213, 215–218,
polysemy 4, 9, 22, 31–32, 51–52, 61, 76–77, 110, 322
polysemous network 76
profile-based analysis 290
prototype semantics 51–53

reanalysis 6, 80–83, 85, 135, 141, 148, 153, 157–158, 165
recursive causality 67

semantic change 3, 5, 9, 10, 18, 22, 32, 51–52, 57, 61, 66, 68, 72–74, 77, 79, 142, 144, 165, 230
semantic field 9, 45–47, 58, 69, 95, 114–117, 229–230,
semantic shrinking 59
semasiology 8, 15, 19, 26, 52
social variation 265, 268, 290
sociohistorical shift 23
Sociolinguistics 266
starve 9, 51–52, 56, 59–61
symbolism 86, 98, 109–111, 115, 117–118, 123, 127, 130

Taiwanese Southern Min 141–142, 155
theory of humours 4, 8, 21–25, 103

Udi 171–172, 182, 192–193, 199, 204–208, 210–216, 218
universal trends 95–97, 99–102, 117
usage-based cognitive model 275
usage-feature analysis 265–266, 270, 276, 290

www.ingramcontent.com/pod-product-compliance
Lightning Source LLC
Chambersburg PA
CBHW070604170426
43200CB00012B/2589